RUSSIA IN A BOX

RUSSIA
IN A BOX

Art and Identity in an Age of Revolution

Andrew L. Jenks

NORTHERN ILLINOIS UNIVERSITY PRESS

DeKalb

© 2005 by Northern Illinois University Press

Published by the Northern Illinois University Press, DeKalb, Illinois   60115

Manufactured in the United States using acid-free paper

All Rights Reserved

Design by Julia Fauci

Library of Congress Cataloging-in-Publication Data

Jenks, Andrew L.

Russia in a box : art and identity in an age of revolution / Andrew L. Jenks.— 1st ed.

p.   cm.

Includes bibliographical references and index.

ISBN-13: 978-0-87580-339-5 (clothbound : alk. paper)

ISBN-10: 0-87580-339-3 (clothbound : alk. paper)

1. Miniature painting, Russian—Russia (Federation)—Palekh. 2. Lacquer boxes—
Russia (Federation)—Palekh. 3. Communism and art—Soviet Union. 4. Soviet Union—
History—Revolution, 1917–1921—Art and the revolution. I. Title.

ND1337.R8J46 2005

751.7′7′094733—dc22   2004030006

CONTENTS

ACKNOWLEDGMENTS

I owe a debt of gratitude to numerous colleagues, mentors, institutions, and family for their support and input. Nearly all the chapters for this book were presented in one form or another to the Stanford University "kruzhok" on Russian and Soviet history, as well as to a gathering of Stanford and Berkeley graduate students and professors of history. Many thanks are due to the organizers of those gatherings, especially Amir Weiner and the late Reggie Zelnik. The comments and criticisms of my work at those get-togethers, and in watering holes and eating establishments afterward, constantly altered my thinking about this book, as did a number of other conferences and workshops inside and outside the field of Russian history. In December 1999, the Ivanovo State Archive of the Russian Federation asked me to present my research at a conference in honor of the eightieth anniversary of the archive. Local historians, amateur and professional, endured my tortured Russian and later provided numerous leads on sources and alternative interpretations. In January 2002, I presented many of the ideas regarding Old Believers to a conference on Old Belief held at Stanford University, organized by Nancy Kollmann. I first presented my notions for the early Soviet period to participants of the April 2001 University of Maryland Workshop on New Approaches to Russian and Soviet History. Later, in June 2001, I discussed the phenomenon of Soviet Palekh at the University of Giessen in Germany, a talk arranged by Jochen Hellbeck and Jan Plamper. In December 2003, I tested out ideas from the book's section on the era of Nicholas II at the International Conference on European History: From Ancient to Modern in Athens, Greece. Finally, in June 2004, I discussed issues relating to Soviet folk art, national identity, and foreign relations at the thirtieth annual conference of the Society for Historians of American Foreign Relations at the University of Texas, Austin.

Amir Weiner's constant criticisms, comments, and suggestions have been vital to the shaping and reshaping of this project from start to finish, as have those of Steve Barnes. I am also indebted to colleagues who were willing to read and comment on often very rough drafts of earlier versions of parts or all of the manuscript—from the time this project was still known as my "dissertation" and on through the constant process of revision resulting in its transformation into a "book." They include Richard Wortman, Alexander Martin, Bert Patenaude, Nancy Kollmann, Marc Raeff, Nicholas Riasanovsky, Wendy Salmond, Terence Emmons, Norman Naimark, and the anonymous readers contacted by the Northern Illinois University Press. During the summer in which I made final revisions, my colleagues in the Niagara University History Department, especially Bob Kane and Tom Chambers, cheerfully provided a sounding board for my ideas—as did Susan N. Smith at the University of Washington. Mary Lincoln at the Northern Illinois University Press has been enthusiastic and supportive of this project from the start—and she greatly eased my anxieties and doubts about the whole process of turning a manuscript into a book.

The research and writing of this book was supported by grants from the Social Science Research Council, the Research Scholar Program of the American Councils for International Education ACTR/ACCELS, and the Mazour fund of the Stanford University Department of History. Niagara University, where I have taught since 2003, provided generous grants to underwrite the costs of purchasing photographs and the use of color in this book. The Hillwood Museum and Gardens in Washington, D.C., offered much-needed assistance in finding suitable photographs for reproduction in this book, as did Maxim Stoulov of the Russian firm Black Lacquers, located in Ivanovo, and Andrew Stonebarger of Tradestone Gallery in Baltimore, Maryland. The artists Ol'ga Subbotina and Misha Larionov were gracious hosts, allowing me into their homes and personal archives in the village of Palekh. Without their help, and the willingness of so many of the citizens of Palekh to discuss their craft and village in private conversations, the information I encountered in the dusty folders of Russian archives would have made much less sense to me. Ashot Grigoryan of Ivanovo State University was incredibly helpful in finding accommodations for me in Palekh and Ivanovo. Finally, in nearly every one of the dozens of archives and museums in which I worked I encountered competent, professional, and helpful archivists, especially in the party and state archives of the Ivanovo oblast'. Back in the United States, Molly Molloy and Linda Wheeler of the Hoover Institution Library and Archives and Kristen Regina of the Hillwood Museum and Gardens were always eager to answer my questions and locate materials.

An earlier version of chapter 1 and the conclusion of chapter 3 appeared in the *Donald W. Treadgold Papers in Russian, East European, and Central Asian Studies* 2 (June 2004) under the title "Iconography, Power and Expertise in Imperial Russia." Sections of chapter 4 appeared in *Kritika: Explorations in Russian and Eurasian History* 3 (Summer 2002): 427–58, under the title "From Center to Periphery: Palekh and Indigenization in the Russian Heartland, 1917–1933." Parts of chapter 8 appeared as "Palekh and the Forging of a Russian Nation in the Brezhnev Era," in *Cahiers du Monde russe* 44 (October–December 2003): 629–56. I thank all three journals for allowing me permission to reproduce materials from these essays.

The Hillwood Museum and Gardens granted permission to publish many of the illustrations: 1, 2, 17, 19, 23, 26, 27 (bequests of Marjorie Mereiweather); 6,

7, 8, 9, 13, 15, 16, 20 (gifts of Madame Augusto Rosso). Edward Owen did many of the provided photographs. Andrew Stonebarger and Tradestone Gallery (www.lacquerbox.com) produced the photographs of illustrations 14 and 22 (courtesy of Jack Turner). Maxim Stoulov and Black Lacquers Co-operative (www.palekh.net) supplied the images for illustrations 12, 24, and 25. Illustrations 4, 5, 10, 11, 18, and 21 came with permission from the personal archive of Ol'ga Stanislavovna Subbotina.

Finally, I am forever grateful for the tremendous sacrifices made by my wife and family. My wife, Deanna, was willing to tote our two-year-old child to Russia and endure my long absences at the archives. She managed to master enough Russian to do nearly all the shopping and caretaking for the family while I slaved away for endless hours in archives in Moscow, St. Petersburg, Vladimir, Ivanovo, and Palekh. Amazingly, she even agreed to move with me into an unheated, one-room apartment in the provincial city of Ivanovo—in the dead of winter—as I culled through reams and reams of documents. She stoically endured her stay, even as we all became horribly ill for a one-week stretch—and as she witnessed two corpses being taken out of adjacent apartments and carried off to the morgue. I still marvel that she was willing to stick with me from the start to the finish of this project.

RUSSIA IN A BOX

INTRODUCTION

In Search of Russian National Identity

Aleksandr Baldenkov (1872–1928), formerly a religious icon painter from the village of Palekh, found himself out of a job after the October Revolution. An aspiring poet with revolutionary inclinations, he decided to join the Red Army to help crush a massive uprising against Soviet power in the Tambov region. As luck would have it, he contracted typhus before being deployed. After recovering in Moscow, Baldenkov returned to his native village of Palekh in 1921 and searched in vain for work; the village's religious icon-painting shops were now shuttered, their owners dispossessed and languishing in poverty and depression. Three months of wandering and drinking followed (the alcoholic Baldenkov drank anything he could get his hands on) before the party cell in the region ordered him to paint over the murals of a church in the village of Kalinin (formerly Berezniaki). As Baldenkov approached the village, he had a flash of recognition: thirty years earlier he had created the church murals he was now ordered to destroy, including an image of St. Nicholas. "How much labor I put into it," he recalled. "It was so difficult to pull myself away from it then, and now I am going to destroy it." Although suffering from a hangover, he recalled a painting based on a work by Nikolai Gogol that showed Taras Bulba before his traitorous son. The caption on the painting read: "I created you and I will kill you." In a dream the same night, St. Nicholas approached Baldenkov and turned into the drunken icon teacher of his youth, who used to beat him mercilessly. When the teacher lunged forward, Baldenkov, the icon painter-turned-iconoclast, parried with a brush handed to him by a prominent local Bolshevik. A bloody battle ensued in which Baldenkov, bathed in blood-red paint, was gravely wounded. Baldenkov rushed to the church the next morning in a cold sweat and used fiery red vermilion to paint over his icon of St. Nicholas. "The first stroke of the brush was like a bloody wound," he remembered. He finished the job with a red hammer and sickle and a five-pointed star on the ceiling. For his troubles, he received a document affirming that he was "an honest revolutionary house painter."[1]

Baldenkov's "sobering" encounter with the Bolshevik Revolution was typical for the icon painters of Palekh. Yet, through grit and determination (most were far more sober than Baldenkov), these painters carved out a new role for themselves as celebrated folk artists. Honored as People's Artists of the Soviet Union, they exhibited across the world and were praised in the art pages of the communist daily *Pravda* as well as in the newspaper of record in the capitalist world, the *New York Times*. This book tells the improbable tale of Baldenkov's storied village. It recounts the growing fame of the artists before 1917, the trauma of the revolutionary upheaval, and the surprising triumphs of the Palekh artists through much of the Soviet era. Indeed, Palekh's unique status in Russian culture, before and after 1917, makes it an ideal instrument for examining continuity and discontinuity across numerous revolutionary divides. The "classic" Palekh lacquer boxes of the Soviet era featured Russian folk motifs, fairy tales, troikas, and firebirds—all done in the various styles of Russian Orthodox religious icons. While this art form was in fact a product of the 1920s, few are aware that Palekh was a celebrated center of Russian national culture before the Bolshevik Revolution. During the nineteenth century, the peasant "masters" of Palekh, as they were known, were fêted as folk painters of Russian religious icons. Tsars Alexander III and Nicholas II made this village, located three hundred kilometers northeast of Moscow deep in the Russian rural heartland, a central part of their attempts to create a "people's autocracy." In the Soviet period, when the masters switched to secular folk themes, the regime unexpectedly honored them as national treasures and prominently displayed their art both abroad and at home. Even today, every visitor to Russia encounters Palekh's art—either in Russia's many museums or in the hands of aggressive hawkers of Russian exotica. On all sides of the revolutionary divide, Palekhians were thus at the center of state attempts to define Russian identity—from the post-Napoleonic era, through Bolshevik modernization and terror, up to World War II and its aftermath.

THE PROBLEM OF RUSSIANNESS

In relating the story of Palekh, this book chronicles a significant center of Russian cultural and economic life ignored in the English-language literature and too often dismissed as so much state-sponsored kitsch. Scholars who have examined issues of culture and identity tend to focus either on the supposedly higher forms of culture (belles-lettres and avant-garde and modernist art) or on more conventional socialist realist "tractor" literature. Peasant artists have largely been omitted from this story, an especially odd omission, given the numerical predominance of peasants through most of modern Russian history. This book thus sheds light on an unjustly ignored group of peasant artists and, through them, on the Russian state's policies toward its sizable agrarian population. In the process, readers will learn about the religious icon-painting traditions in Russia and their fate after the Bolshevik Revolution. They will gain insight into the marketing, secularization, and professionalization of Russian folk art, as well as an interpretation of the political, cultural, and economic significance of this folk art before and after 1917. Recounting the many events and forces that buffeted Palekh's craft and its avatars over two centuries, this study is ultimately a cautionary tale of an artisanal tradition in a period of revolutionary upheaval and state-directed modernization.

At the same time, this book fills a paradoxical gap in the broader field of imperial Russian and Soviet nationalities studies. What did it mean to be Russian? Since the break-up of the Soviet Union, scholars have written detailed examinations of Ukrainian, Georgian, Uzbek, Kazakh, and numerous other non-Russian nationalities within the former imperial Russian and Soviet domain. Yet the national identity of the largest ethnic group in the Russian and Soviet empires, the Great Russians, has received comparatively little attention. One of the few recent studies to discuss "Russianness" looks at artistic production as politics by other means. Soviet leaders, argues Yitzhak Brudny, used art and culture to debate the past, present, and future of the Russian nation.[2] Brudny's excellent study, which is confined to the period from 1953 to 1991, nonetheless ignores much of the social and economic context of cultural production. By contrast, the present study examines the many factors, including ideology, markets, and social conditions, that shaped modern Russian national culture from 1814 to 2001. In doing so, it provides a comprehensive exploration of Russian national identity across several historical epochs.

This book similarly serves as a case study of the neglected problem of "majority national identity." The special challenges of majority ethnic groups in multinational empires have often been ignored. Benedict Anderson describes the tension between the "universal-imperial" ethos of the Habsburg, Hohenzollern, and Romanov dynasties, and the newer "particular-national" conceptions of state and society emerging in the nineteenth century. By the end of the nineteenth century, even the old regimes began to embrace the seemingly subversive notion of representing an exclusive national community. In Russia and elsewhere, social and political tensions were exacerbated by various state programs of official nationalism, which involved "stretching the short, tight skin of the nation over the gigantic body of the empire."[3] After 1917, similar tensions arose between the particularistic Russian identity and the universal "Soviet" identity. Few scholars of Russian history have examined in any detail how these tensions played out from the perspective of the majority ethnic group, the Great Russians.[4]

The conditions of Russia's historical development made the formation of a particularistic Russian identity even more challenging. Russian Orthodoxy, a key marker of imperial Russian identity, was itself a foreign import—borrowed from a universal Christian church, open to peoples of all creeds and ethnicities. Attempts to enlist the church as a resource for building Russian national identity raised serious issues about the boundaries separating Russians from other ethnic groups. During the rise of Muscovy in the sixteenth century, the Russian state aggressively assimilated non-Russian elites into the power structure, adopting many of their traditions and belief systems. When Russia emerged as a European power, this willingness to import and adapt foreign ways was embodied by Peter the Great's wholesale westernization project. Elite culture in the eighteenth century became self-consciously cosmopolitan and European—creating a Russian identity that was inspired by broader European currents. The Russian Imperial Academy of Sciences, designed by the great German scientist Leibniz and at first staffed mostly with Germans, was a case in point.

In the eighteenth century, Russia's first academicians nonetheless developed a new sense of Russian identity. Distancing themselves from their western mentors, they began researching and gathering materials about Russian folkways and customs. The great polymath Mikhail Lomonosov symbolized the newly educated Russian academician, when he challenged both his German colleagues at the Russian Imperial Academy of Sciences and the idea that Scandinavians, rather than Slavs, had organized the early Russian state known as Kievan Rus'.[5]

In the nineteenth century, the quest for Russianness received additional impetus from romantic nationalists in Europe, who located the nation among the *Volk*. Russian Slavophiles followed the lead of these nationalists, articulating a new sense of what it meant to be Russian. They looked for values, ideals, and cultural forms among the ethnic Great Russians. They idealized peasant folk culture—an activity encouraged by sympathetic portraits of the long-suffering muzhik in literary works such as Ivan Turgenev's 1852 *Hunter's Sketches*. Seeking to co-opt a potentially dangerous shift of authority to the people, Alexander III and Nicholas II later integrated many aspects of this romantic nationalist project into their own cultural policies, grafting it to an elite culture that nonetheless retained a cosmopolitan outlook and background.[6]

The Bolshevik Revolution, at least according to the Marxist rhetoric of international proletarian solidarity, marked an end to the search for a distinctive Russian national identity, as the unfortunate Baldenkov seemed to discover. To be Russian now meant to be part of a world revolutionary community unbounded by national borders—and liberated from the constraints of the prerevolutionary order. Historical reality, however, turned out to be far more complex. The formation of Soviet Russian culture and identity was a chaotic and improvised affair, marked by constant debates about the relationship of the prerevolutionary legacy to the new society. Especially troubling was the question of the proper relationship between the supposedly benighted Russian muzhik (formerly the object of romantic idealization among Russian populists and nationalists) and the darling of the Bolsheviks, the proletariat. During the 1920s and 1930s, national and populist conceptions of community frequently clashed with class-based notions of a new proletarian culture and society.[7] In a

climate of heightened debate about the contours of the new society, late imperial visions of Russian culture and society constantly surfaced in articles, literature, and visual imagery.

Despite rhetoric about creating a workers' state, Soviet nationalities policies
in the 1920s also encouraged identities with an explicitly national rather than
class-based orientation. In line with the policy of "indigenization"—the Bolshevik policy of exploiting national sympathies to gain support for revolutionary policies—officials attempted to construct Soviet communities that would
be, as the slogan went, "national in form but socialist in content." For many
cultural activists in the Russian heartland, this policy applied to Russians as
well as to other ethnic groups. For them, Palekh was a central test of nationalities policy, as the masters attempted to fill the old religious icon-painting
forms with new secular content. It became a testament of faith that socialist
and proletarian content would ultimately prevail over national form and eventually create its own forms.[8] Yet from the very start, party leaders could not
agree on the precise nature of this synthesis, or even if such a synthesis was
possible. What distinguished socialist content from national form? What were
the telltale signs of a genuinely socialist culture? As Martin Malia points out,
the Soviets knew socialist culture would not be capitalist, but since no one had
created socialism before they were less sure what socialist culture would and
should actually look like.[9]

The absence of a clear party line created an undefined space in Soviet culture, a kind of cultural vacuum into which an astonishing array of forms and
ideas presented themselves for party inspection. Within this vacuum, many
forces outside party control began to influence Soviet Russian identity, including consumer tastes and especially the legacy of late imperial Russian culture
with its canon of romantic "Volkish" Russianness. The lack of ideological clarity on the problem of socialist identity thus allowed for the development of a
surprisingly diverse and retrospective culture, notwithstanding the regime's obsession with ideological purity and with escaping the constraints of the historical past. Equally important, the lack of ideological clarity in cultural matters
encouraged participation "from below" in the interpretation of Soviet Russian
culture. Culture producers very often had to determine their own themes and
approach, since commands from the center were either vague or nonexistent.
Consequently, creators of Soviet culture, such as the Palekh artisans, became
accomplices in the project of cultural construction rather than mere fulfillers of
party commands. They believed that Soviet Russian culture was as much their
own culture as it was the regime's. As one of Baldenkov's colleagues from
Palekh put it in 1932, he was determined to show a Russia that must never
"live in . . . gigantic stone boxes, . . . sleep in . . . identical holes, dress in . . .
identical gray clothing, eat bread with corn and corn kasha *[kukuruznaia kasha]*
and . . . turn everything with living spirit *[vse odushevlennoe]* into a geometrical
standard."[10] In a word, this producer of official iconography, a religious icon

painter–turned–Soviet propagandist, propagated a personal vision of Russia that was anything but proletarian, technocratic, or industrial. Equally important, his art helped make that personal vision one key component of Soviet Russian culture.

This chaotic process of cultural formation, and the doubts it constantly raised about the revolutionary nature of the new society, certainly troubled many Soviet ideologists. For Soviet ideologues, Palekh embodied everything Soviet culture was not—the world of the Russian muzhik, his icons, rustic ways, superstitions, and inefficiency. Driven by a fear of counter-revolutionary backsliding, cultural officials periodically attempted to purge the cultural landscape of ideologically suspect forms—especially in the early 1930s, after World War II, and again in the early Khrushchev era—but such efforts ultimately failed to resonate with the population. When it came to building a coherent sense of identity, few other forces on the cultural scene, including western popular culture, the avant-garde, and even notions of class, seemed to provide alternatives to romantic visions of the Russian nation, planted firmly in the native soil of the Russian countryside.

A growing reliance on Great Russian patriotism on the eve of and during World War II further encouraged the party's tightening embrace of romantic Russianness. The Nazi destruction of ancient Russian monuments compounded the revolution's earlier destruction of cultural values, triggering an intense feeling of cultural loss in the population—and in many party circles. As part of this nostalgic turn, many Soviet Russians after World War II looked back beyond the 1917 revolutionary divide for cultural roots and identity. Palekh, with the help of the market, provided an outlet for satisfying these nostalgic yearnings. By the last years of the Khrushchev era, a supposedly primordial peasant Russianness, rather than class affiliation or international solidarity, became a main building block of Soviet Russian identity. Socialist culture had matured, and its final form, as the present study demonstrates, drew heavily upon notions of the Russian nation first articulated long before 1917. In the aftermath of the revolution, these notions were advanced in a hypercharged ideological climate that lacked a clear and coherent cultural agenda.

THE OUTLINE OF THE BOOK

Recounting Palekh's role in this long process of cultural formation, the first section of the book traces the prerevolutionary fate of the Palekhians and the debates over Russian national identity that their fate stimulated. Although the peasant icon painters of Palekh had been painting religious icons since at least the sixteenth century, they only became recognized national artists after Russia's victory over Napoleon. The changing view of Palekh resulted from a powerful and conscious reaction to the universal rationalizing spirit of the Enlightenment, which many elites identified with the vandalism, plunder, and destructiveness of the French Revolution.[11] In a climate of reaction to the shock of the French Revolution, national traditions, as elsewhere in Europe, acquired a new and positive value.

Since European currents stimulated the quest for Russianness, it was only fitting that Europe's greatest cultural authority, the poet Goethe, first drew attention to Palekh. Goethe believed that Russian peasant icon painters preserved a sacred past threatened by the chaos and uncertainty of revolution and industrialization. His query about the peasant icon painters of Russia in 1814, communicated through his Russian friends in Weimar, prompted the tsarist state to open its first police file on Palekh. From that point on, Palekh was no longer merely a center for religious icon painting, but rather became a source of national tradition that had to be preserved, propagated, and displayed. It is therefore with Goethe's discovery of Palekh that chapter 1 of this study begins.

By the 1840s, Palekh was swept up in a broader Russian search for authentic national culture. Conservative elites began constructing Russian culture from supposedly pure and ancient sources, which were contrasted with the "false" culture of modern civilization. During the reign of Nicholas I, a new ideological scenario emerged in which the appreciation and preservation of national tradition joined the old Petrine imperative to reform and renovate Russian society.[12] Patriotic Russian elites began to enjoy the "privilege of backwardness," to use a term coined by the Russian scholar V. V. Vorontsov in 1882. One of those privileges included a spirituality supposedly lacking in the more technologically advanced West. If Russia's distinctiveness was its soul, then some believed the ancient practice of religious icon painting, like a great suture, could help heal the rift between elite and mass Russian culture opened by Peter the Great's reforms. These individuals, mostly academics, pioneered the study of the Russian icon in the 1860s, and they also generated the first proposals for controlling and deploying peasant icon painting as a national cultural resource. Palekh had become a central part of the regime's retrospective national utopia.

The effort to exercise the "privilege of backwardness" gained momentum in 1901, when Nicholas II formed the Committee for the Tutelage of Russian Icon Painting. The factors leading to the formation of this committee are the subject of chapter 2. The committee's activities were encouraged by the physical discovery of the classic works of the great medieval icon master Andrei Rublev and by the elite's infatuation with Russian folk culture, primitive art, and sacred aesthetic practices. Using the authority of archaeological science, the committee sought broad control over the teaching, production, and sale of all religious icon painting in Palekh. Treating Palekh as a kind of miniaturized template for broader social transformation, the committee attempted to construct a conservative utopia based upon agrarian craftsmanship, the eradication of market forces, and idealized visions of Russian spirituality.

Yet despite the increasingly nostalgic orientation of tsarist ideology in the reign of Nicholas II, the old Petrine imperative to reform and renovate did not disappear completely. In Palekh, the search for authentic national roots had to be combined somehow with a program of reform and modernization. The new breed of Palekh icon painter, like the new Russian citizen imagined by the committee, had to be a creative personality, a cultured and self-aware individual, yet also loyal to the ancient traditions and the native soil. He had to master the traditional ancient technique and canon of Russian Orthodox icon painting, yet command the latest techniques of post-Renaissance art, including the realistic and natural representation of human figures and landscapes. Late imperial cultural policies thus had a split personality, oriented on the one hand toward an idealized Muscovy and on the other toward the European vision of the educated modern artist.[13] Out of this synthesis, it was hoped there would emerge a new kind of Russian—one part European and one part idealized Muscovite, one part Orthodox saint and one part cosmopolitan aesthete.

In the end, Nicholas II's icon committee sowed more discord than national unity, as illustrated in chapter 3. First, the identification of imperial citizenship with Russian Orthodoxy excluded millions of non-Orthodox subjects. This was an especially problematic omission during World War I, when the military, short of recruits, desperately needed to draft non-Orthodox subjects for the armed struggle.[14] Second, the committee willfully ignored the ongoing secularization of Russian society, which reached far beyond Russian elites. In Palekh, for instance, many of the peasant masters, such as Baldenkov, began visiting the empire's urban centers, and from the cosmopolitan aesthetes encountered there, they now envisioned their future as secular rather than religious artists. In this climate, connections between religion and politics, and between religion and culture, seemed increasingly archaic. Finally, the committee's anticapitalist rhetoric sharpened tensions between state officials and Palekh's private icon producers. As the conflict grew, two alternative models of Russian culture emerged. One was driven by the state and self-proclaimed academic experts hostile to the emergence of a political nation with free and equal citizens. These "experts" asserted tutelage over the people and claimed the right to shape their lives according to a utopian image of Russian history and art. This model was pitted against a vision of Russian culture "from below" in which markets and consumer tastes predominated. Palekh, with its vibrant tradition of artistic entrepreneurship, was at the epicenter of these competing models. The upshot was a crisis of national values. The crisis was a kind of dress rehearsal for more intense state efforts after 1917 to counter market influences, when officials of the Bolshevik party-state, like the previous academic experts allied with the tsar, unsuccessfully attempted to dictate the contours of the emerging nation.

Amazingly enough, Palekh's art not only survived the revolution, albeit in a new medium (the miniature lacquer box) and with new subject matter (folk motifs instead of holy saints); it also thrived. Beginning in 1923, the Palekh masters gained a new life as producers of Soviet folk art—thus completing their own transformation into secular artists, which for many had already begun in the 1880s. Along the way, they filled the old forms of Russian Orthodox icon painting with various folk themes, most of which they borrowed from the market for Russian exotica that had emerged in the last half of the nineteenth century and during World War I. Ironically, the market so hated by the Bolsheviks played a vital role in Palekh's success: sales of Palekh lacquers to well-heeled foreign urban dwellers provided the regime with valuable foreign currency with which to buy machine tools and tractors. Thanks in large part to the entrepreneurial skills of the peasant artisans themselves, as well as to high-level patronage and foreign buyers, Palekh became a celebrated enclave of rural craftsmanship by the mid-1930s.

At the same time, Palekh continued to incite political controversy. The work it produced in the 1930s eluded the control of state cultural officials, whose intense desire to control Palekh's art, and purge it of "bourgeois" and religious influences, was matched only by their inability to agree on its precise purpose and content. (See illustration 1 for an icon typical of the art produced in Palekh in the late 1800s and illustration 2 for an example of Palekh art after 1917, which retained many of the stylistic attributes of the religious icon but with new secular content.)

Chapter 4 chronicles Palekh's tumultuous transformation from a center of religious icon production into a center of Soviet Russian arts and crafts in the 1920s and early 1930s. A rich array of sources, including economic records, official investigations, speeches, memoirs, letters, exhibits, and published accounts, reveal the surprising dynamics of Russian cultural production in this early Soviet period. The chapter shows that the relationship between Soviet state authority and Russian identity was far more complex than is often assumed. Soviet Russian culture was nurtured not by party fiat, but rather by a complex nexus of foreign market demand, domestic patronage, and romantic nationalist strivings. For Palekh's supporters, as for many of the artists themselves, the hamlet also provided a safe haven from impersonal monumental art and the features most often identified with Soviet modernization: urban blight and the glorification of the factory milieu. In the process, Palekh became a rallying point for a revival of Russian peasant culture in Soviet society.

The dictates of Leninist ideology, however, did not disappear completely in the mid-1930s, as discussed in chapter 5. Palekh's cultural synthesis faced a new round of attacks, underscored by the arrest and execution of one of its most respected artistic leaders in 1938. Moscow overseers attempted to eradicate all vestiges of the unique Palekh style, replacing it with the conventions and style of urban Soviet monumental art. The masters were viciously attacked for their dependence on market forces and religious and peasant roots. Official histories of Soviet Palekh excised the crucial role of markets in Palekh's earlier Soviet triumphs, making it clear that Soviet-Russian identity was to be built in opposition to the very market upon which Palekh depended. Subsequently,

Palekh's connection to foreign consumers became the village's "dirty little secret," ignored in official histories and carried as a badge of shame by the masters themselves. For the Palekh masters, the Great Terror signaled that there
could be no great retreat to prerevolutionary and bourgeois values.

Just as the Palekh artistic community seemed on the verge of collapse,
Hitler's blitzkrieg came to their rescue. Chapter 6 addresses the fate of the Russian nation during the Great Patriotic War, when the perceived need for national unity erased the previous doubts about Palekh's value in Soviet society.
The result was an outpouring of both state and popular support for the hamlet, which in turn reflected the emergence of a new sense of Soviet Russian
community. Palekhians were now free to pursue new market opportunities, independently of direct state supervision. The regime encouraged a growing
identification of Russian culture with the legacy of Russian Orthodox religious
art, coming perilously close to reestablishing the link between religion and national identity decisively severed in 1917. At the same time, the Leninist privileging of class over nation, and its bias against the peasantry, receded further
into the background of Soviet policies, as peasants by the millions joined the
epic battle with Nazi invaders.

Much to the chagrin of many Palekh masters, especially the older generation, this dramatic ideological shift turned out to be short-lived. The dictates
of revolutionary restructuring were reasserted following the war, casting doubt
again on the appropriateness of Palekh's art for Soviet society. From 1947 to
1958, as chapter 7 illustrates, the party redoubled efforts to Sovietize Palekh,
which meant severing ties with its supposedly reactionary religious past, ac-
quainting it with the accomplishments of urban Soviet art, and eliminating its
reliance on "vulgar" market tastes. As during the Great Terror, the campaign
very nearly resulted in the collapse of the Palekh system of artistic production.

Finally, chapter 8 examines Palekh in the period of "developed socialism,"
when Palekh's cultural synthesis (above all, its unique style and peasant folkloric content) was finally and unambiguously appropriated by the regime as the
essence of Soviet Russianness. Ironically, this development came just as Russia
itself had become, at least numerically, a predominately urban society. The
process of co-opting the Russian nation was ultimately nurtured by two com-
plementary attitudes: a nostalgic yearning for stability and consensus in Soviet
Russian society and a longing for the idealized comforts of the native soil. The
devastation of the war and the miserable quality of life for most urban Russians
meant that, when Soviets now surveyed the cultural landscape, they saw in the
countryside and native traditions more things worth preserving than transforming. The spirit of nostalgia eroded the perceived need for ideological vigilance, which had previously made life so difficult for the Palekh artists.

Palekh's embrace was also encouraged on economic grounds, for by 1980
Palekh was earning the regime one million convertible gold rubles annually.
To square Palekh's official embrace with what was left of the communist

agenda (or with more xenophobic Russians who condemned any contact with foreigners, market or otherwise), Palekh's dependence on bourgeois consumers was again ignored in official histories, and the village was celebrated as a center of Russian artistic genius. Even many Palekh artists absorbed the party line, vilifying the market relations in which they were so thoroughly enmeshed. Such was the price the Palekh masters had to pay for their privileged status as celebrated artists—a role they had sought since the late imperial era and had finally achieved. Perhaps more than anything, being Soviet (and Russian) now meant depending on the market while denying its influence, earning one's living from market exchanges yet looking toward the state as the ultimate arbiter and sanction of culture. Seen in a longer chronological perspective, it was a striking contrast to the positive association of professional identity in Palekh before 1917 with commercial savvy and entrepreneurship.

Given the Soviet Union's unexpected collapse during Gorbachev's final restructuring, this development was highly ironic. The party's embrace of Palekh's vision of Russian culture came at precisely the moment when the Soviet system, as Stephen Kotkin has suggested, unwittingly committed suicide during Gorbachev's revolutionary perestroika.[15] In one last bout of revolutionary transformation, Russian culture, along with its producers, was orphaned just as state authorities seemed willing to embrace it. The masters now stood alone against the market they had learned to condemn (and upon which they simultaneously depended). Not surprisingly, many Russians experienced a new kind of nostalgia: they looked back upon the Brezhnev era as a time of social harmony when Russian national traditions were nurtured and protected by the state. Meanwhile, and in stark contrast, many Palekh artists felt that the state since the late 1980s had abandoned Russia to the forces of urban consumer capitalism.

In the final analysis, anti-market values and a yearning for the idealized comforts of the countryside, paradoxically combined with market dependence and a relentless drive to modernize Russian society, constituted a crucial nexus around which modern Russian identity has been formed. The formation of this nexus predated the Bolshevik Revolution. It first developed against the backdrop of urbanization, the emergence of a consumer society, and a growing market for cultural symbols and icons. In response, many elites (on the right and left) developed a scathing critique of the ethos of consumerism, and the urban capitalist system that seemed to spawn it, as detrimental to the interests and integrity of Russian society. After 1917, the anti-market mentality of educated Russians, and even much of their idealization of the countryside, then merged into the Soviet order, where it was eventually absorbed by the Palekh masters themselves. Indeed, by the end of the Soviet era opposition to the supposedly vulgar impact of the market, along with the urban forces that fueled it, became fundamental to the masters' own sense of Russianness. Irony pervades this outcome, since the artists learned to condemn an urban market milieu that had always been essential to their livelihood. The epilogue explores the daunting challenge of disentangling this complex nexus in an age when consumers and markets, rather than state bureaucrats, seem to have triumphed decisively in the construction of Russian culture, and when the countryside seems to have lost all relevance as a source of national identity.

PALEKH IN COMPARATIVE CONTEXT

While the Palekh story is uniquely Russian, it also is part of the history of the broader arts and crafts movement of the late nineteenth century. Writing about the arts and crafts movement in America, Eileen Boris has referred to the "craftsman ideal [that] sought an end to the division between the human spirit and material reality." That division emerged from the late eighteenth century and "separated the mental from the manual, city from country, individual from community, work from play." The craftsman ideal, she continues, was "a reaction against industrialization, urbanization, modernization—against what we can more precisely call the growth of a bureaucratized corporate structure in the context of capitalist social relations." Between 1880 and 1920, as the agrarian populist critique of the urban industrial order gained momentum, arts and crafts ideologues in America constructed visions of "a new sort of community." In that new productive order, the craftsman was "the characteristic citizen and craftsmanship [w]as the core value." The artisan's way of life would stand "in sharp contrast to the commercial values of 'the era of big business.'"[16]

The story in Russia before 1917 was in many respects similar.[17] Like their English or American counterparts, Russian craft ideologues were horrified by the perceived ugliness and alienation of the capitalist industrial order. A recognizably capitalist order—in the Dickensian sense—began to emerge in Russia in the second half of the nineteenth century. Russians witnessed urban squalor and working-class slums firsthand, and many were horrified by what they saw. For them, an idealized countryside, and a way of life rooted in a supposedly ancient past, was the antidote to capitalist modernization.

After the Bolshevik Revolution, arts and crafts advocates confronted the problem of craftsmanship in an entirely new social and political framework: the bureaucratized structure of the world's first industrialized anti-capitalist state. This was a unique challenge that sharply separated the Russian crafts movement from its western counterpart. After 1917, the focus shifted from survival in a capitalist order to survival in a socialist system. For folk artists, the problem of survival was made more pressing by a regime whose ideology treated the "somnolent" peasant, in Lenin's words, as someone "glued to his pile of manure."[18]

There were other similarities and differences between Russia and the arts and crafts movement elsewhere. Like William Morris and John Ruskin, the Russian craft idealists aimed to "achieve a world whose environment would be determined by beauty and necessity, harmoniously joined." In the Russian case, at least before 1917, this attempt at harmonious fusion in Palekh involved religious worship and nationalist politics. It was not just any craft, but the sacred craft of religious icon painting that inspired many of the craft ideologues of the reign of Nicholas II. For them, the Russian religious icon embodied sacred labor, natural materials, the national religion, and a living folk tradition, supported by the broad masses of "the people." So if Ruskin and his acolytes admired the Gothic tradition as authentic Christian spirit, their Russian equivalents, such as Fedor Buslaev, looked to the ancient Russian Orthodox icon and architectural style.[19]

Buslaev and later his student Nikodim Kondakov nonetheless saw in this sacred craft tradition something slightly different from the craftsman ideal in England. Focusing on Russian Orthodox icon painting, they idealized a traditional craft in which faithfulness to the canon was essential, in which the craftsman learned to discipline his individual identity within a strictly defined communal tradition. Discipline and collectivism, developed through the copying of supposedly ancient models discovered and vetted by the academic "experts," were thus as important as innovation and individual expression. In the view of the academicians this spirit of collective discipline would staunch the tide of social and political change and reinforce loyalty to the tsarist regime. The Englishman Morris, by contrast, decried copying of any kind and urged a broad democratization of culture and art. Central to Morris's craft vision, if not its practical implementation, was "the promise of individual autonomy."[20]

There are other critical distinctions between the Russians of this study and their western counterparts. In England, the focus on aesthetics in the 1880s "began with the aristocrat and dilettante as patron and it ended with the middle class as the main support of the arts."[21] Many Russian craft advocates started down this same path, adapting peasant crafts "to the needs of modern urban life and the laws of the new market economy."[22] Other Russians, however, took an alternative route. An alliance of expertise and bureaucracy, which first came together in the reign of Alexander III and continued across the revolutionary divide, stubbornly challenged the primacy of markets and consumers in Russian folk art. A robust spirit of anti-capitalism, fashionable in Russian educated and elite circles from the 1880s, created an ideal breeding ground for the growth of anti-capitalist utopias, conservative and radical.[23] This climate encouraged government attacks on market forces (before as well as after 1917), which would have been unthinkable in many parts of Europe and especially in the United States.

The comparison to the American example is especially instructive. If, as Eileen Boris suggests, the "original crusading impulse" of American arts and crafts "had been incorporated into the middle-class outlook and style," in Russia that crusading spirit was incorporated into the state.[24] Before and after 1917, the Russian state waged a long battle to save craft traditions from the market—and from a nascent middle class seen as hostile to the interests of "the people." Even though it ultimately failed, the length and intensity of this battle against capitalist control of culture was remarkable. It lasted from the early years of Nicholas II's reign, when he formed a special committee to control the craft of icon painting in 1901, through most of the Soviet era.

Adding to the spirit of anti-capitalism was Russia's long tradition of paternalistic statism, which melded seamlessly into the authoritarian socialism of the Bolsheviks. Russian elites tended to view centralized state power as a primary agent of change, and indeed from the time of Peter the Great it often was. Before and after 1917, Russian politicians looked skeptically upon the informal efforts of private activists. Suspicious of private initiative and civil society, many Russian craft ideologues believed artists and markets could never be left to their own devices. Only enlightened state power, they therefore concluded, could save art from the vulgarity and soullessness of modern capitalist society. The result was a distinctive statist attitude among many Russian craft ideologues. This statist attitude, which was hostile to culture as an autonomous private sphere, united many arts and crafts enthusiasts in Russia regardless of their attitude toward the tsar and revolution. Identity, for them, was a product of the state, and the collapse of the state in February 1917 meant that the successor state, and not the market, would have to take the lead in recreating Russian society.

Palekh's supreme challenge, as a producer and marketer of folk art rather than its theoretician, was survival in a political environment that aimed to incorporate all aspects of culture into an anti-capitalist state system. Before 1917, the peasant icon painters of Palekh had a well-deserved reputation as both religious icon painters and as traders and artistic entrepreneurs, a status of which they were justly proud, although it earned them the enmity of many of their would-be tsarist overseers. Indeed, the masters lacked the "collectivist" mentality and risk-averse nature so often identified with the Russian muzhik. The problem of survival, however, was particularly acute after 1917, given Palekh's continuing dependence on market demand and the regime's unshakable hostility to market culture and peasant "backwardness." Yet Palekh not only survived; it became a central site for producing Soviet Russian identity. This ironic outcome illustrates the determination and ingenuity of the Palekh artists as well as the ongoing power of markets to shape and transform culture. In the final analysis, Palekh suggests the limits of Soviet power and ideology, whose utopian goal of top-down planning met a challenge the authorities could not fully master and eventually had to co-opt: a Russian culture articulated as much by consumer tastes (foreign and domestic) as by state-sanctioned experts. Thus, alongside the anti-market mentality of the regime, which the Palekh masters themselves eventually internalized, the market, paradoxically, was critical in shaping modern Russian national culture.

CHAPTER ONE

Official Nationality and the Rise of the Icon Expert

"[Alexander III] called forth [the icon painters of Palekh] from the humble provinces for the glory of his holy coronation. [Such] loving devotion of the Sovereign Emperor toward Russian peasant icon painters inevitably brings to mind an old Russian saying: 'A prayer for God and service for the Tsar are not made in vain.'"

—*Izograf,* 1884[1]

In 1814, Maria Fedorovna, the empress mother, received an inquiry from the famous German writer Johann Wolfgang von Goethe. Goethe had been admiring Russian icons in Weimar, where he learned that peasant craftsmen near the ancient city of Suzdal painted holy images. How were the icons made, he asked? Did ancient Christian and Greek images serve as models? Did they paint images in a more contemporary style? "It would be especially nice," wrote Goethe, "to receive some typical examples of every type of icon . . . and if possible, from the best contemporary artists." He thought it "very instructive . . . that right up to our day an entire branch of art is preserved unchanged from the most ancient of times, thanks to an uninterrupted tradition passed down from Byzantium." Elsewhere, he lamented, "art . . . has strayed from its original, religious, and severe forms."[2]

The empress mother passed the request to the minister of internal affairs, O. P. Kozodavlev, who conveyed it to the governor of Vladimir, Avdei Suponov. Suponov answered on May 17, 1814, after gathering material from local informants. While he had little information on the history of icon painting in the region, he said the icon-painting traditions continued in the three villages of Palekh, Mstera, and Kholui. The masters of Palekh painted the highest quality icons. In the hamlet, approximately six hundred males (estate serfs who mostly belonged to the Buturlin family) worked full-time as icon painters. A strict division of labor governed icon production: some artists painted only the face and arms, others the clothing, and others the inscription and background. Greek originals served as models, "and although they are old, they are nonetheless preserved in churches and even in private houses." He passed on two icons from Palekh's best artists to Goethe in Weimar.[3]

Eager not to disappoint the great German writer, Kozodavlev asked the official court historian Nikolai Karamzin to research the history of Russian icon painting in the "Vladimir-Suzdal" region. Karamzin's terse and perfunctory response provided few new details—and suggested something less than keen interest in the subject. Suzdal icons (i.e., those made in Palekh, Mstera, and Kholui) "imitate the Byzantine style that entered Russia along with the Christian faith in the reign of Vladimir." The Greek icon painters "were our teachers," wrote Karamzin, who believed the manner and content of the icons had not changed for centuries "since the clergy demanded from painters an exact copy of Byzantine models, and innovation was considered a heresy." As proof, Karamzin cited a sixteenth-century church council (the 1551 Stoglav) that dictated the painting of icons "according to the models of Andrei Rublev and no other way." Karamzin was unsure how long the Suzdal icon painters had been working, but he guessed since the time of Andrei Bogoliubskii, who in the twelfth century "called to Vladimir the Byzantine artists." Karamzin could find "no further data on this topic." He suggested Goethe might turn to the Academy of Arts, stating, "I don't interfere in matters relating to the study of art."[4]

Karamzin seemed perplexed by Goethe's interest, but already by the 1860s, an influential group of Russian academics, collectors, and aristocratic enthusiasts (referred to hereafter as the icon experts) had transformed the icon into a thriving intellectual and political enterprise. The enterprise generated articles and books, a vigorous and lucrative trade in old icons among educated elites, and high-level patronage for the peasant icon painters of Palekh. Icon experts came to treat icons as political instruments as well as devotional objects; they believed that icon production and worship, if properly managed and vetted by expertise, could help to stabilize the modern Russian nation in an era of rapid change. One can trace this development through the exploration of three interrelated themes: the ongoing definition of Russia in comparison and contrast with the West; the paradoxical relationship of elites to "the people" whose interests the experts claimed to represent; and the exploitation of academic authority as an instrument of social and political control.

At the center of the experts' political agenda was a dilemma shared by all the dynastic orders of nineteenth-century Europe, namely, a concern over the spirit of ethnic nationalism, which located the ultimate source of political authority in the broad masses (or, from the view of the experts, in the peasant icon-painting traditions). Yet the experts remained loyal to a tsarist autocratic system based upon dynastic rather than popular legitimacy. Attempting to square this circle, the experts and their state allies tried to shape the people according to a utopian image of premodern Russian history and art. In that utopia, the "Holy Russian" masses worshiped a native art form (the holy Russian icon) that the experts believed would bolster tsarist authority and support a traditional estate order. Preservation of the sacred hierarchy of separate estates and privileges, in which peasants would remain humble second-class citizens, was thus combined with the search for a new source of legitimacy in the national traditions of the folk.[5] As a result, a peculiar attitude arose among the experts: if peasants were viewed as preservers of national folk traditions, they would have to be preserved in a manner deemed authentic by the experts—or risk being excluded from the confines of the regime's emerging national utopia.

THE FIRST EXPERTS

By the beginning of the seventeenth century the business of icon production, for reasons that are not entirely clear, had exited the walls of the monastery and entered the broader lay society. Peasant icon painters were now working throughout the Vladimir-Suzdal region. Icon shops in the Kremlin armory employed laymen as icon painters, most notably the master icon painter of the seventeenth century, Simon Ushakov (1626–1686), who began introducing western techniques of realistic painting and true perspective. This "fusion style," known as *friaz'* in Russian, combined western and Byzantine techniques. Along with the rapid growth of the state apparatus in the seventeenth century came also an increasing concern with surveillance and control. This concern was reflected in the controversial church reforms of Patriarch Nikon (1605–1681) and the persecution of those who rejected them (the Old Believers). To reject these reforms was tantamount to treason against the state. On the eve of Peter the Great's rule, the state attempted to impose bureaucratic control over icon production, to be administered by secular rather than church officials. The system included a centralized administration of the craft in the Kremlin armory and the ranking of masters throughout the realm. Icon painters were called to Moscow to paint murals or icons for new and old churches.[6] While this system of control did not resemble what a modern person would call censorship, it does suggest a state whose conception of its interests now extended beyond waging war and increasing its fiscal base.

With Peter's reforms, the state's budding interest in icon production and religion waned, though it never disappeared completely, as illustrated by the ongoing persecution of Old Believers and by Peter's own commandment to "improve the beauty and dignity of the holy icons." Nonetheless, the secular realm received the state's greatest attention. Even Peter's interest in icons was directed as much toward emphasizing modern western artistic techniques as toward preserving sacred Byzantine models. Peter also introduced a new idea into Russian governance—the imperative to reform Russian society along more western lines. Official ideology began to focus less on the symbolic linkage of Muscovy, Orthodoxy, and the tsar; instead, it viewed the tsar as a reforming European monarch. Emulating the early modern absolutist states of Sweden and Prussia, Peter and his successors wanted state servants to have a modern western education. The European-style academy of sciences served as Peter's model for learning and culture. The Imperial Academy of Arts, created by Peter's daughter Elizabeth in 1757, taught secular art according to the conventions of classicism and ignored the problem of religious imagery (even until the late nineteenth century). As a result, the production of icons, though not completely ignored by the state in the eighteenth century, became more and more the concern of the church and private producers.[7]

Over this same time period, the Palekh masters traveled far and wide, encouraged by their serf-owning family, the Buturlins. In 1705, one source notes ten Palekhians asking for permission to trade in icons in Serbia and Wallachia, followed by a similar request in 1706. A source in 1722 records Palekhians trading icons in St. Petersburg. By the end of the eighteenth century, Palekh, Mstera, and Kholui had become the main centers of peasant icon production. According to the Ministry of Internal Affairs, 640 males in Palekh produced nearly 500,000 icons in 1858. All told, the icon painters of Palekh, Mstera, and Kholui painted more than two million icons annually, providing a rare example of mass culture in a largely illiterate society. A special class of middlemen from the Vladimir province, with their own dialect and customs, sold the villages' icons throughout the empire and in the Balkans.[8]

The peasant icon-painting enterprise occurred against the backdrop of a thriving craft and industrial economy in the late eighteenth and early nineteenth centuries. "Millionaire serfs" working under the Sheremetev family in nearby Ivanovo (sixty kilometers to the northwest of Palekh) had shifted the center of textile production from Moscow to the Vladimir province following Napoleon's burning of Moscow and the decimation of its textile industry. Given the relative poverty of agriculture and the short growing seasons in the region, serf owners benefitted financially from the industrial entrepreneurship of their minions, many of whom paid hundreds of thousands of rubles to buy their freedom. In some cases, serf millionaires from Ivanovo, later known as the Russian Manchester, secured the latest equipment and training in England. In Palekh, the burgomeister, the serf hired by the Buturlins to manage the economic affairs of the estate, kept close tabs on the Palekh masters. One burgomeister, according to the memoirs of an artist from the 1840s, looked through the windows of the homes of Palekh masters at night. If he saw that the family was drinking tea out of a samovar, a sign of wealth, he raised the family's payment of quitrent (obrok). Palekh masters supposedly responded by hiding their samovars.[9]

While icons provided income to the Palekh masters (and their serf owners), icon worship continued to occupy a central role in Russian peasant life through the end of the Old Regime. Icons were passed down from generation to generation as part of a family's heritage. They adorned the iconostases and walls of Russia's omnipresent churches. Russian icons celebrated numerous leaders from Russia's past: Aleksandr Nevskii, who defeated the Teutonic Knights, Vladimir, the first Orthodox Russian to be grand prince, or Boris and Gleb, the princely martyrs. The icon thus functioned as a handicraft, a talisman, a family heirloom, a folk tradition, an object of Christian worship—and potentially a national political symbol.[10]

Meanwhile, in the post-Napoleonic era, Russian elites adopted a more positive attitude toward native culture and traditions. The first generation of icon experts in the reign of Nicholas I were the children of German Romanticism. They agreed with Herder "that since individuals were products of a particular time, place, and culture, all their acts, especially artistic endeavors, constituted an expression of the personality of the whole nation." Constructing their own identity in opposition to that seen in the more developed West, they exercised the "privilege of backwardness," taking peasant traditions defined by others as backward and using them to create a conservative utopia more authentic and ancient than its supposedly soulless counterpart in the West.[11]

Elites took their cue from the autocracy. In 1833, the minister of education, Count S. S. Uvarov, proclaimed "official nationality" and its banner of "Orthodoxy, autocracy, and nationality" the overarching ideology of the realm. The policy introduced the idea of Russia as a nation into official discourse, linking official Russian identity to Orthodox culture and the authority of the imperial family. Reflecting new priorities, Nicholas I attempted to reaffirm state control over the preservation and restoration of Russian Orthodox churches. "As a general rule," stated a new 1842 law, "the ancient appearance of churches, both internally and externally, must be assiduously preserved." The protection of a Russian Orthodox culture, firmly anchored in a distant past, thus became an explicit component of imperial politics. The policy marked a clear break with previous practices, whereby the restoration *(restavratsiia)* of a holy image had meant renovating *(obnovlenie)* it in accordance with the tastes and aesthetics of the present, which after Peter meant a more western manner of painting.[12] Beginning in the reign of Nicholas I, such renovations were increasingly seen as a western assault on Russia's sacred past.

To fulfill the new mandate of preservation the state hired experts in church art and archaeology to oversee the first restorations that embodied the more modern sense of restoring a work of art to its original state. In preserving the past restorers now had to possess expertise, the ability to determine in some objective sense what the original icon should look like, including the school it belonged to and the manner of its original creation. New opportunities emerged for academically trained individuals such as the architect K. A. Ton (1794–1881), creator of the mammoth Christ the Savior Cathedral in Moscow (built to honor the defeat of Napoleon), and the artist F. G. Solntsev

(1801–1892). Solntsev, the son of a peasant serf from Yaroslavl, had been enrolled by Count A. I. Musin-Pushkin in the Academy of Arts. After finishing
his program of study, Solntsev worked in the academy's division of archaeology and ethnography. During the 1830s, he traveled throughout European
Russia, copying and studying icons and frescoes, examining the date of their
creation and the styles in which they had been created. He became a favorite
artist of Nicholas I and a leading figure in state-sponsored restorations of
church art in the 1840s.[13]

The new emphasis on state-funded preservation dovetailed with growing
elite interest in Russian history and culture. Debates between Slavophiles and
Westernizers highlighted the problem of Russia's distinctiveness. Historians,
philologists, and archivists began gathering and publishing documents about
Russia's folk customs, habits, language, art, and history.[14] Moscow was a locus
for much of this activity. Separated from the daily business of empire management since the time of Peter the Great, Moscow, an ideal breeding ground for
retrospective visions of the Russian people, stood in stark contrast to the bureaucratic, planned capital of St. Petersburg with its neoclassical architecture
and imposing state structures. Moscow's ancient churches and monasteries
provided professors and students with living monuments to pre-Petrine Russia.
Thriving communities of sectarians, who worked in industry and trade in
Moscow, preserved forms of worship that predated the latter part of the seventeenth century.

The most visible manifestation of the new interest in Russian traditions was
a lively antiquarian trade, which spilled onto Moscow's winding alleys and
streets. Old Believer collectors, and the demand of prominent individuals such
as Count S. G. Stroganov (1794–1882), supported a lucrative antiquarian business in the reign of Nicholas I. During campaigns to seize Old Believer icons in
the 1840s, Count Stroganov successfully convinced Metropolitan Filaret to let
him review a warehouse full of seized icons (which were to be burnt) and take
those he deemed worthy for his personal collection. The willingness to see Old
Believers as possessors of a purer and uncorrupted Russianness marked a grad-
ual redefinition of the Russian nation around a group formerly excluded from
its boundaries.[15] This redefinition flowed logically from an official policy that
was developing a more positive view of the pre-Petrine cultural heritage.

Reflecting the new interest in Russian culture and history, Moscow University in 1835 began teaching Russia's first university courses in Russian history
and literature. Mikhail Petrovich Pogodin (1800–1875), the son of a serf, occupied the university's first chair of Russian history. A tireless promoter of patriotic ideals, he believed the historian's job was to bring a people "to an understanding of itself," an understanding that linked popular life, Orthodox
worship, and the ruling dynasty. According to his student Fedor Ivanovich
Buslaev (1818–1897), Pogodin railed against "cosmopolitans who preached . . .
universal human interests, the striving for which . . . should eliminate . . . any

distinctions between nations." Like the many icon experts he inspired and encouraged, Pogodin also combined the profession of history professor with that of antiquarian, amassing a huge collection of ancient manuscripts, books, and Russian icons (which he eventually sold back to the state for a huge profit).[16]

In addition to Pogodin, a visitor to Moscow's bazaars in the 1830s might have encountered Ivan Mikhailovich Snegirev (1793–1868), a pioneer in imperial icon studies. While working as Moscow's top censor and giving occasional lectures at Moscow University, Snegirev wrote numerous articles on icons in the 1830s and 1840s. These articles were based on observations from countless walking tours of Moscow's cathedrals and monasteries. In 1848 he published the first secular monograph on holy images, *On the Significance of the Fatherland's Icon Painting.* The book was the first to examine icons as artistic monuments and not merely objects of religious worship. The "mysterious symbolism" of ancient Russian icons, wrote Snegirev, "gives food for thought and imagination, it leads us into the sphere of the soul, it familiarizes us with the views and conceptions of our ancestors."[17]

Following Snegirev, I. P. Sakharov (1807–1863) attempted to place the nascent study of the Russian icon on a more solid scientific foundation. In the 1830s and 1840s, Sakharov published numerous works on Russian folk language, his travels among the Russian people, and fairy tales. He concluded his romantic musings about the Russian people with his most famous work, *Investigations into Russian Icon Painting,* published in two volumes in 1849. He said he took up the theme because of a growing aversion to "the emptiness of the West." The first volume was republished in 1850 and the fourteen hundred copies were almost immediately sold out. The most critical legacy of Sakharov's work was his call for a new field of icon studies. As envisioned by Sakharov, scholars working in this new field would provide biographies of the greatest icon painters, analyze Russian and Byzantine icons, investigate archival sources, and explain the proper techniques of icon painting. Most importantly, Sakharov urged the creation of a new *"podlinnik,"* literally "a prototype," as a compilation of the correct images and styles of icon painting to guide modern icon painters and restorers. Following Sakharov, the *podlinnik* would become the Holy Grail of icon expertise, a mechanism for defining and controlling the ancient traditions as well as their modern practitioners.[18]

The term *"podlinnik"* in Russian means a prototype or something authentic. In the case of icon painting, it refers to style manuals with an illustrated part *(litsevoi)* showing the saints and festivals of the church according to the church calendar, and an explanatory *(tolkovyi)* section describing the technique and significance of the icons. The peasant icon producers had used these style manuals for centuries, though just what they contained was not clear to many icon experts. Icon experts hoped the *podlinnik* would reveal the authentic images of early Christianity and their preservation by Russian masters. Combined with the more general romantic quest for cultural authenticity (as opposed to the "falseness" of modern culture), the idea that icon painters must follow a genuine Christian style gave the *podlinnik* special significance for conservative Russians. In subsequent decades, icon experts attempted to realize each aspect of Snegirev's agenda, culminating in the first state-sponsored *podlinnik* in 1905.[19]

Paralleling Sakharov's and Snegirev's work, Ivan Egorovich Zabelin (1820–1908) began developing a vision of icon worship as a common link between Russia's rulers and subjects. Of plebeian origins, and raised in a state orphanage, Zabelin owed his education and livelihood to the patronage of Count Stroganov and the historian Pogodin. Beginning in 1837, Zabelin worked as a clerk in the Kremlin armory archive, sifting through ancient documents about Muscovite Russia, organizing and summarizing them, and formulating ideas about their meaning and importance. He believed the physical objects of everyday life in Muscovite Russia reflected a unified style, a common spirit, that linked ruler and subject. Along with other aspects of everyday life, the worship of icons provided "the foundation of the entire social structure of the land." Zabelin made retrieval of these objects of past unity a lifelong endeavor. Eventually, as curator of the State Historical Museum (opened in 1881 just outside the Kremlin), he became the nation's chief antiquarian.[20]

Zabelin also stimulated the budding field of icon studies with new revelations from the archives. With Count Stroganov's help, Zabelin from 1847 to 1850 published fourteen groups of documents from the armory archive, most concerning the life and times of the pre-Petrine tsars. The most important appeared in 1850 under the title "Materials for the History of Russian Icon Painting, 1551–1623."[21]

Using Zabelin's documents and the work of previous icon experts, D. A. Rovinskii (1824–1895) attempted to reconstruct the official system of icon production in Muscovy (the term for the Russian state before Peter the Great). Rovinskii's intellectual interests, like those of his good friend Zabelin, linked Russian folk art, Orthodox worship, and state power. On long walks with Zabelin, Rovinskii gathered observations from Moscow's cathedrals, monasteries, and chapels. His 1856 work on religious icons posited an extensive system of patronage for holy images in late Muscovy. In this work, he highlighted for example the importance of the Stoglav Council of 1551, one of several councils held in Muscovy to set matters straight among the clergy and laity. The Stoglav (literally one hundred chapters) laid out these chapters of reformation (including the forty-third chapter on icon painting) with the provision that disobedience would result in transgressors being forever accursed. The Stoglav, wrote Rovinskii, condemned the artless painting of holy images and lambasted any departure from sacred models. Rovinskii believed the Stoglav laid the foundation for state icon supervision in the seventeenth century, and he located such supervision in the Kremlin armory. According to Rovinskii, the armory's patronage helped to forge a distinctive Russian style for the realm. The tsar, rather than church officials, thus played a critical role in creating a distinctly Russian style, becoming a supreme arbiter in the production and worship of icons.[22]

By way of contrast, Rovinskii implied that the modern Russian state had orphaned icon painting, but some Russian painters had strayed. He saw the Palekhians as direct descendants of the icon painters condemned in the 1551 Stoglav council for painting icons "without any learning, in a facile and self-satisfied way, and not according to a model, and these icons are sold cheaply among simple and ignorant people." He cited a complaint to Tsar Aleksei Mikhailovich in the seventeenth century about the icon painters of Palekh and Kholui for "painting icons without method and without fear." Subsequently, "untrained icon painters continued to paint 'improper icons' and sell them cheaply to the impoverished people." Rovinskii had a more positive attitude toward the icons in the collections of Old Believers, whose images he discussed in his original manuscript. The references were excised by censors amidst Nicholas I's crackdown on Old Believers (the 1903 reprint cited here included the icons and positive references to Old Belief).[23]

Rovinskii's contrast of sixteenth- and seventeenth-century state patronage with the absence of state support in the present became a central theme in Russian icon studies, as did his positive representation of Old Belief. Like Snegirev, Rovinskii placed high hopes for the future of icon painting and for the purity and holiness of Russian culture on the *podlinnik*, a seemingly reliable instrument for regulating the production of holy images.

With Rovinskii's work, which integrated historical analysis, aesthetic critique, and a search for the historical roots of a distinctive Russian style, the imperial icon expert was in full blossom. After the emancipation of the serfs in 1861, investigations into the past and present of Russian icon painting intensified, accompanied by new calls to purge the icon-painting traditions of harmful influences. These calls reflected a more general concern to maintain control over the peasant estate, now liberated from the private control of its aristocratic owners. As in Europe, "the greater the fear of change resulting from social mobility, the greater was the need to uphold the value of traditional institutions, to subordinate the individual to the group and to anchor both to some eternal and objective scheme of things."[24]

THE PROTOTYPICAL ICON EXPERT

The belief that icon painting was "medieval" and therefore threatened by modern civilization gave icons a renewed dynamism in Russian educated circles. Buyers were anxious to distinguish authentic antiquity from its artful imitation. Icon producers attracted the attention of the growing state bureaucracy, which like most modern states, was concerned with censorship, mass culture, and the protection of endangered national customs. Riding the crest of these trends, the icon scholar supplied cultural expertise, a new kind of authority that could negotiate the treacherous shoals of mass markets to rescue authentic culture from the storm of modernity.

The prototypical icon expert of the Great Reforms was Fedor Ivanovich Buslaev. A professor of philology and history at Moscow University, Buslaev's path to academic prominence began in the provincial backwater of Penza, where his father had worked as a low-level bureaucrat. After finishing the gymnasium in Penza, Buslaev passed Moscow University's entrance exams and matriculated there in 1834, joining its historical/philological faculty, just as the university prepared to teach its first courses in Russian history and literature. With Pogodin's help, Buslaev won a state stipend to finance his education. In addition, Buslaev received the patronage of Count Sergei Stroganov, who oversaw educational institutions in Moscow in the 1830s and 1840s. In 1839, one year after Buslaev finished Moscow University, Stroganov invited the young man to be a tutor for his children on a two-year trip to Germany, Austria, and Italy. Following Goethe, the twenty-one-year-old Buslaev called this period his *"Wanderjahre."* These years marked his transformation from apprentice scholar into seasoned master. The works of Johann Winckelmann, the eighteenth-century German archaeologist and pioneering art historian, introduced Buslaev to Italy's monuments of art and antiquity. Buslaev now imagined the classical and medieval ethos as an essential antidote to the alienating forces of modern society and culture.[25]

Many years later, on the strength of Count Stroganov's recommendation, Buslaev became tutor to Tsarevich Nikolai Aleksandrovich (in 1859). Buslaev's lectures to the tsarevich also influenced the tsarevich's younger brother, the future tsar Alexander III. Buslaev combined the preparation of lectures for the tsarevich with the writing of a book on ancient Russian literature and art, published in early 1861 as Buslaev completed the tsarevich's tutoring sessions. The two-volume collection of essays provoked a lively debate in educated circles, drawing the ire of some critics and the praise of others. As Buslaev boasted in his memoirs, his detractors "looked at Russian antiquity and nationality [narodnost'], at the eternal customs and habits, which constituted the subject matter of my monographs, as worthless and useless junk to be tossed out the window." His supporters, who included the empress, applauded Buslaev's examination of "nationality, with its ancient principles as one of the most important and critical issues of the day, in light of the emancipation taking place before our eyes."[26]

Buslaev's more general view of the West—praised on the one hand for its technique yet damned for its betrayal of "true" Christianity—profoundly colored his critique of Russian icons. Buslaev admitted that Russian icons were aesthetically inferior to western art, because they lacked proper perspective and realism. Yet "the lack of development of our iconography, in an artistic sense, constitutes not only its distinguishing characteristic, but also its superiority before western art." By remaining faithful to ancient models, Russian icon painters exhibited the proper spirit of Christian discipline. Individual creativity, as emphasized by the forty-third chapter of the 1551 Stoglav, was a product of pride and willfulness, "which violates the cleanliness of the holy enterprise of icon painting," wrote Buslaev. Traditions of rote copying in icon painting preserved "the primitive purity of iconographic principles" against "the erosion of morals, the naked materialism and senseless idealism that reigned in western art from the middle of the sixteenth century." The icon, he concluded, reflected "the determined independence and uniqueness of the Russian nation, in all its indestructible might, raised for centuries in backwardness and stagnation, in its unwavering faith in the long-ago accepted principles."[27]

At the same time, Buslaev demanded a more sophisticated technique from Russian icon painters. The nation, in his view, had to be both modern and primordially Russian. His model was Russia of the seventeenth century, when the Romanovs, he argued, successfully combined Orthodox culture with new western techniques. The greatest seventeenth-century icon painter, Simon Ushakov, presented a prototype for the modern icon painter. Following Ushakov, contemporary Russian icon painters should paint in a more realistic style yet somehow avoid the "naturalism" that had corrupted western religious art since the late Renaissance. "Obsessed with anatomy, Michelangelo distorted the figure of Jesus Christ in his representation of the final judgment." It was improper, as Catholics supposedly did, to show holy figures clean-shaven, in modern clothing "dressed like Catholic priests," or to show Christ "as betrothed to marry or be engaged with some maiden." Rembrandt reduced holiness to "cynical triviality" when he dressed holy figures "as Dutchmen in the clothing of the time. . . . How pathetic and senseless are the caricatures of holiness, which even great masters such as Rembrandt and Rubens pass off as icons to be worshiped in church altars."[28]

Buslaev ended his analysis with a formula for adapting western artistic technique to sacred icon-painting traditions. The vagueness of the prescription highlighted the challenge of defining Russian icons as distinct from, and yet part of, western aesthetic traditions:

> The concept of nature in art is assumed to be a faithfulness to reality in the drawing of figures, in their position and movement, and especially in the expression of spiritual movements, and finally in coloration. This demand should be acknowledged as lawful and reasonable on the basis that only through the naturalness of all external forms of representation, only through a faithfulness of spiritual expression, both in the entire figure and particularly in the face, can the artist instill the ideas that inspired him to the viewer. A faithfulness to nature and naturalness have to be strictly distinguished from so-called naturalism, which has acquired predominance among the most recent artists, especially in our fatherland. Raphael was always true to nature, but none would accuse him of naturalism.[29]

Determined to preserve the distinctiveness of Russian icon painting, and yet to update it in a way that would not corrupt those traditions, Buslaev gathered together the nascent community of experts in the first years of the Great Reforms.

Speaking at the newly opened Rumiantsev Museum in Moscow (the oldest building in the former Lenin Library complex), Buslaev in 1863 proposed an "icon-painting brotherhood" to apply his notions to reality. The brotherhood, said Buslaev, would be unlike any organization devoted to antiquities in the West, "because icon painting for the Russian people constitutes an essential, and to this day surviving modern element of life, just like other moral interests that define the national physiognomy." Peasant icon painters, whatever their aesthetic shortcomings, still exerted a broad influence among the masses, spreading ancient religious ideas "just like the tsarist school of icon painting in the reign of Aleksei Mikhailovich." Reflecting the ongoing reassessment of sectarians, Buslaev said the Old Believers, "who are not deprived of a certain aesthetic taste," had helped develop icon painting within the framework of the old style. Russian icon painting, he concluded, was a living part of culture that struggled with the "new secular art" and the doctrine of godless materialism it propagated.[30]

To wage this struggle, the proposed brotherhood would give "the icon painter the means for an aesthetic education" and the secular artist a thorough grounding in "the national traditions of Russian icon painting." This fusion of the academically trained artist, who had turned away from national traditions, and the peasant icon painter, who had stagnated in them, symbolized a broader reunification of Russian culture. The idea was seconded by G. D. Filimonov, a close associate of Buslaev. Since the time of Peter, Russia's elites had lost contact "with the firm ground of the people's spirit." They not only stopped patronizing icon painting but mistakenly viewed it as "some kind of Old Believer craft." On the contrary, Old Believers should be thanked for preserving authentic Russian traditions.[31]

Rounding out his agenda, Buslaev proposed a new *"podlinnik"* that would help icon painters understand the proper technique and meaning of the icon. Though it was unclear which icon-painting traditions would comprise the style manual (the icon experts were keenly aware that much work remained to be done in the science of icon studies, hence the vagueness of many of their proposals), the art of the catacombs was a safe starting point. Drinking deeply from the well of ancient Christian art, Russia would absorb the uncorrupted spirit of early Christianity, along with the aesthetic principles of Greco-Roman civilization.[32]

Meanwhile, the brotherhood would help icon consumers distinguish authenticity from its cheap imitation. Critical reviews from the brotherhood's publications, including advice on how to identify a counterfeit icon, would help "purge and direct artistic taste." To avoid becoming an "oppressive cen-sor" the brotherhood vowed to rely on the "precise data of science" as a guide for establishing canonically correct models. With the authority derived from its selfless and scientific labors, the brotherhood would enjoy broad rights of control in the icon-producing community, thus obviating the need for com-pulsion and fiat.[33]

Curiously, Buslaev's proposal excluded the one institution already formally endowed with oversight in the spiritual sphere, the Russian Orthodox Church. Buslaev and the many icon experts whom he inspired believed the church had been deeply compromised, because of what the brotherhood perceived as the ignorance of the church's priests and hierarchs. Exclusion of the priestly hier-archy, which was already likely to reject lay expertise, guaranteed the religious bureaucracy's hostility to the proposals of icon experts. As early as 1857, church officials had voiced concerns about academics controlling icon produc-tion. They were deeply troubled by the emerging conception of the icon as an object of academic and secular expertise. In early 1863, the Holy Synod flatly rejected a proposal from the Academy of Arts, a proposal approved by the Min-istry of Internal Affairs and likely inspired by Buslaev, to establish a special committee overseeing all holy image production. The committee, having made no provisions for the participation of church officials, envisioned a sys-tem of inspectors to control production in the icon-painting villages. The pro-posal was rejected for, among other things, usurping the prerogatives of the church censors.[34]

Another key player was also not included during Buslaev's 1863 presenta-tion: the actual peasant producers and distributors of icons from Palekh, Mstera, and Kholui. Although icon experts frequently condemned the supposed ignorance of the icon painter (in terms that were always vague), few had ever actually talked to one. Like their radical counterparts, conservatives often pre-ferred to view the people through the lens of their own political agendas.[35] A handful of articles, to which the discussion now turns, displayed the aesthetic and political preferences of icon expertise. These articles were penned by the economist and state servant V. P. Bezobrazov (1828–1889), a widely read author who developed an interest in the culture and life of peasant Russia in the wake of the emancipation of the serfs, and by the art historian G. D. Filimonov (1828–1898), one of Buslaev's students and a close associate of Zabelin, with whom Buslaev continued to develop the nascent field of icon studies. The au-thority of both authors was bolstered by their direct contact with the icon-painting villages, which they presented in published articles as an objective representation of the current state of icon painting. While solidifying romantic images of peasant icon painters, the articles sounded increasingly shrill alarms about the dangerous influence of market forces and mechanization—two ideas central to the political mobilization of icon expertise in later years.

THE LAND OF THE *OFENI*

Bezobrazov journeyed to the region of peasant icon painting in the summer of 1861. He traveled by horse to Viazniki from the provincial center of Vladimir before visiting Mstera, Kholui, and finally Palekh, and produced a detailed account of his trip in the journal *Russkii vestnik*. Bezobrazov's account became a standard point of reference for all subsequent experts on the contemporary state of peasant icon painting.[36] The three villages ran south to north, separated from each other by approximately thirty kilometers. Mstera, a center of Old Belief, occupied the southernmost part of the Suzdal icon-painting industry and was closest to Vladimir. As Bezobrazov traveled north past Kholui to Palekh, he noticed the thinning of the population, which he believed marked the transition from a primarily craft-based economy (including the production of icons but also other industries) to one with a mix of crafts (almost exclusively icons) and agriculture. The town in the middle, Kholui, hosted a bustling peasant market, which in the summer served as a gathering point for a class of peddlers known as the *ofeni,* many of whom were Old Believers. The *ofeni* specialized in the region's icons, purchasing them from local producers in the summer and reselling them the remainder of the year throughout Russia and even into the Balkans. As Bezobrazov noted with great curiosity, the *ofeni* were unlike any other people he had encountered in Russia, and he wondered, with some trepidation, if they might harbor the future spirit of the Russian nation. He contrasted Russia's "broad, massive features, its spaciousness and lack of discipline, the broad sweep of its movements and idleness of life," with the "miniatureness" of the icon peddler's physique. The *ofeni* built their houses "in the rural gentry style with various pretensions and decorations." Family life was merely a diversion from the all-consuming demand of business, a brief opportunity for the icon peddler to be "the boss of the home . . . [and] have someone to order about." In these peddlers, Bezobrazov encountered a kind of Russian he did not believe existed. "You don't know how to place [this type], ahead or behind the pure Great Russian peasant, and similarly you are puzzled: who will advance further in success in national life—the peddler or his neighbor peasant farmer."[37]

If Bezobrazov was unsure if the icon peddler "was ahead or behind the pure Great Russian peasant," his comments nonetheless suggested something unseemly and unstable in their lifestyle, something delicate, not quite manly, and distinctly un-Russian. For Bezobrazov, as for later investigators and state officials, the icon peddler stood in for the small peasant trader, famously disparaged by Marx as part of the petty bourgeoisie. Hostility to the *ofeni* also was fueled by a pervasive Old Regime discourse about people whose way of life did not fit the standard role assigned to their estate; it was widely assumed that physical and spiritual corruption would follow from their behavior.[38] The *ofeni* were thus stingy and lacked the hospitality supposedly so common to Russians, wrote Bezobrazov. They had their own dialect, which they used to deceive clients. A peddler, according to Bezobrazov, bragged about his money once he came home, even though he might travel thousands of miles on foot, hiring horses for the last leg of the trip to impress his neighbors. Unlike the Great Russian peasant, the peddler had "awkward features, dark hair, and an inaudible voice." Through the end of the century, published reports increasingly presented the *ofeni* as the exploiters and kulaks of the icon painters, an emblem of everything polluting, tawdry, and corrupting in the rule of money.[39]

Of the three towns, Bezobrazov believed Palekh was indisputably the premier center of icon painting (reflecting the same view presented to Goethe in 1814). Icon painters worked both in their own homes and for studios, the largest of which had fifty icon painters and was owned by the former icon master Safonov. Safonov, Bezobrazov noted, had an immense collection of icons as well as copies taken from ancient icons by his best masters, who restored and painted holy images throughout Russia. For specialists such as Buslaev, these collections represented a potential treasure trove of ancient Russianness. Any effort to create a new *podlinnik* would require their careful examination and analysis.[40]

For all his suspicions of the icon peddlers, and his outrage at the drunkenness and poor quality of production among some painters (especially in Kholui), Bezobrazov nonetheless felt he had encountered a world where religiosity, trade, and work were intimately bound together. He had experienced a way of life that was "real, genuine, national," where heavy-handed state intervention was not required. Even the poorest peasants, he imagined, would "sooner go around without a piece of bread, even vodka, than live without [worshiping icons]." Impressed by the seeming spontaneity of icon production and worship, and yet appalled by the lack of artistry and dominance of commercial interests, Bezobrazov was unsure whether it was a good idea for outsiders, even with the best of intentions, to interfere.[41]

Bezobrazov's indecisiveness echoed a broader dilemma for many educated Russians in the 1860s. On the one hand, many believed the "people" and their customs should be respected. State interference in peasant economic and cultural matters should be minimized, a point reflected in the emancipation itself, which preserved supposedly traditional institutions for the peasantry such as the peasant commune and the cantonal administration. On the other hand, conservative Russians wanted the masses to conform to elite conceptions of an ideal Russian citizen (humble, pious, and loyal to tsar and country), an ideal often contradicted by reality. The appointment of the conservative Dmitrii Aleksandrovich Tolstoi (1823–1889) to head the Holy Synod in 1865 and the Ministry of Enlightenment in 1866 marked a new conservative willingness to intervene in peasant society.[42] Haunted by the specter of revolutionary terrorism, conservative activism would gain momentum with the assassination of

Alexander II on March 1, 1881, and dovetail, as will be seen, with the demands
of icon experts.

Meanwhile, Bezobrazov's portrait of the icon-painting villages was soon followed in 1863 by another travelogue, this time from the scholar and icon collector Filimonov. Filimonov, a close associate of Buslaev and Zabelin, came from a
gentry family in Poltava. He studied history and philology at Moscow University, specializing in Russian church art. Beginning in 1858, Filimonov worked as
chief archivist at the Kremlin armory, continuing Zabelin's explorations into the
pre-Petrine history of icon painting. Like Buslaev and others of his time, Filimonov saw the seventeenth century as a golden age—and the artist Simon
Ushakov (about whom he would write a biography) as its model icon painter.[43]
Ushakov had created a balanced synthesis of old and new, of Russia and the
West, which was supposedly abandoned by many Russians after Peter.

A visit in 1862 to the Moscow Sukharev bazaar stimulated Filimonov's interest. Inspiration came from his colleague Zabelin, who during one visit to the
bazaar, had stumbled upon two thousand tracings from a brigade of Moscow
artists run by the Sapozhnikov brothers at the beginning of the nineteenth
century. Finding another cache of Sapozhnikov tracings, patterned after
Ushakov icons, Filimonov learned that the brigade had collaborated closely
with Palekh masters. Intrigued by the connection, Filimonov decided to travel
to Palekh himself in the winter of 1863.[44]

As he inquired about the hamlet before his departure, he discovered that
Moscow was home to many icon painters from Palekh. They restored and
painted icons across Russia, copies of which they then deposited in their studios as *podlinniki*. Self-taught, with only a year or two of schooling, "many are
at a higher level of education than our merchants," said Filimonov. Some masters even read newspapers and journals and cultivated reasoned views on a variety of topics. For Filimonov, the painters were not merely passive and largely
unconscious carriers of an ancient tradition, desperately in need of drawing
lessons and general enlightenment, but respectable craftsmen, and at times
even artists. They seemed to be the living embodiment of the seventeenth-
century ideal.[45]

Filimonov's article revealed new details about the more recent development
of Palekh's style. The Sapozhnikov brigade had fled Moscow during the
Napoleonic invasion, spending two years in Palekh and painting the frescoes of
the town's central cathedral. Filimonov theorized that the Sapozhnikov sojourn
in Palekh imparted to Palekh's art a more realistic style of painting, including
the use of proper perspective and a mix of oil and tempera paints. Filimonov applauded the development as paralleling Ushakov's infusion of fresh technique
and western learning into Russian icon painting in the seventeenth century, creating the so-called *friazhskii* style. This was precisely the kind of natural style
(though not naturalism) that Buslaev had been advocating, a measured and organic combination of native Russian traditions and modern western learning.[46]

Filimonov concluded that Palekh was "the leading force of Russian nationality *[narodnost']*." He called Palekh "a kind of academy," using the term ("academy") that subsequently became part of the myth of Palekh in Russian culture. Thus, the myth of Palekh as a village academy was born, and it survived into the Soviet era, when Palekh switched to the new medium of lacquer miniatures and folk motifs. According to this myth, Russia would be one part academy and one part village, thus representing the fusion of intelligentsia and peasant culture that many elites now envisioned.[47]

Filimonov's discovery of the village academy, however, was tempered by sobering developments. Instead of Christian virtue, many masters now worshiped the almighty ruble. "Unfortunately, in Palekh, I often hear the expression, 'I paint for the money,' an expression, of course, that is impossible to justify in church art." Many younger artists, in their travels "far away from their homeland," had removed themselves "from the soil of old traditions and native customs." They had become "indifferent to the old ways" and clearly reflected a secular rather than religious approach to art.[48]

Filimonov also linked the division of labor in icon painting to contemporary capitalism and its relentless quest for efficiency and profit, although such divisions had existed for centuries. Icon painters, for example, were divided, as Goethe had discovered, into those who painted the exposed parts of the body, especially the face (these painters were called *lichniki),* and those who painted the clothing and less holy parts (they were called *dolichniki).* Filimonov intimated that these divisions were the product of a more recent capitalist development. Cheap production from Kholui, known for producing shoddy icons, supposedly forced owners in Palekh to introduce an ever-increasing division of labor among the masters. In doing so, the owners reduced resources and time for training future artists and prevented masters from developing the skills to paint icons outside the context of the peasant icon studio. All of this was done "for the selfish goal of making profit," wrote Filimonov, but the process was binding the master to the owner, destroying the integrity of the artistic process, and profaning sacred medieval traditions.[49]

Admittedly, there was some truth to the idea that profit motives had cheapened the quality of icons and the integrity of the painter's labor, especially in Kholui. But many studios in Palekh and Mstera, while retaining the long-standing division of labor between *lichniki* and *dolichniki,* had a reputation for high-quality production. Moreover, contrary to the expert's story of capitalist exploitation and degradation, talented masters in Palekh through the last half of the nineteenth century frequently broke away from the supposedly iron-fisted control of their bosses to start up their own studios, often in Moscow and St. Petersburg.[50] Though no expert dared to admit it, perhaps capitalism and a division of labor were compatible with the maintenance of traditional practices; it was the fantasy of the integrated medieval master, under the tutelage of academic expertise, which was thoroughly modern.

AN IVORY TOWER UTOPIA

After returning from Palekh in January 1863, Filimonov became the first head of the Rumiantsev Museum's division of Christian and Russian antiquities, which immediately began collecting icons. The religious function of the icon seemed a secondary concern. Betraying his academic roots, Filimonov treated icons as national symbols and archaeological artifacts. By taking the icon out of the church and into the museum hall, Filimonov unwittingly challenged a core aim of icon expertise: the recreation of a unified medieval worldview, in which religious worship and aesthetics were tightly integrated. His activities thus embodied the spirit of secularization that many experts condemned.

Meanwhile, the experts continued to rely on foreigners to clarify the Orthodox and hence Russian image.[51] In the 1860s, Viktor Butovskii, director of the Stroganov School, enlisted the help of a French scholar to write the first comprehensive history of medieval Russian church art. In 1867, Filimonov arranged the first major exhibition of Russian religious icons in the West, submitting Russia's distinctiveness for western review. He later praised foreigners for appreciating the originality of Russian medieval art. "It was precisely from these same foreign scholars that we finally began to discover that our art should be national in character."[52]

In addition to collecting icons, the Rumiantsev Museum hosted the Society of Ancient Russian Art, the next iteration of Buslaev's 1863 icon-painting brotherhood. Like its predecessor, the society's aim was to integrate "Russian nationality and Orthodox antiquity." By the mid-1870s, its membership represented a who's who of patriotic forces. At the pinnacle stood Grand Prince Mikhail Nikolaevich and Grand Princess Maria Nikolaevna, the society's central patrons. Count S. G. Stroganov, Count A. S. Uvarov (son of the creator of official nationalism), and Prince V. F. Odoevskii provided critical material and moral support. Filimonov edited the society's publications, which he used to showcase his own research as well as Buslaev's. Dozens of other academics and icon experts also joined the society.[53]

While the society gathered together a broad cross-section of conservative elites, it also reflected the experts' national utopia. At the summit were the secular experts, who served as analysts and protectors of the national traditions. Their authority was sanctified by the patronage of the upper nobility and the royal family. Icon collectors and merchants (with connections to wealthy Old Believers) supplied the society with access to their collections and to the pre-Petrine expertise of the sectarian communities. Church officials remained on the margins of icon expertise, relegated to a largely honorary role as part of the "symphony" of state and religious power envisioned by the earlier Slavophiles. At the bottom of this utopia's hierarchy were the actual owners of icon studios and the peasant painters: their primary role was to follow the advice of the experts.[54]

The experts' first opportunity to realize their utopia came during the reign of Alexander III. His reign produced the notion of a "people's autocracy," a political system that would simultaneously derive its legitimacy from God-given and popular assent. In the view of the icon experts, the peasant icon-painting traditions stood at the intersection of both sources of authority: derived from Orthodox religious traditions yet sustained by popular demand. The key was to link these forces to autocratic power and to ensure that they were not overly influenced by foreign tastes.

Standing in for the holy Russian people during the 1883 coronation ceremonies was Palekh's most prominent icon studio, the Safonov icon studio, whose ties with elite consumers had long attracted the attention of the experts. According to local lore, a certain Nikita Safonov, a *lichnik,* started the Safonov icon business in Palekh at the end of the eighteenth century. His son began hiring masters from outside the family, following a system of apprenticeship in which students were divided into those who painted the face and those who painted other portions of the icon. At the same time, Nikita's nephew, Lev Mikhailovich, left Palekh sometime before the war of 1812 and settled in St. Petersburg, where he opened an icon studio. The Buturlins, who owned most of the serfs in Palekh, were so impressed by Lev's managerial abilities that they sent him back to Palekh in 1830 to administer their affairs. Lev nonetheless maintained the lucrative icon shop in St. Petersburg.[55]

Lev's two sons helped expand the icon business in the 1840s, receiving a number of prominent restoration and icon-painting jobs. When F. G. Solntsev, on orders from Nicholas I, directed state-sponsored restorations of religious frescoes in the 1840s, he hired the Safonovs to restore and paint icons in Vladimir's twelfth-century Dmitrii cathedral and elsewhere. The masters and studio owners of Palekh thus secured state and church patronage at the very dawn of the concept of official nationality and its linkage to the policy of Orthodoxy, autocracy, and nationality.[56]

Lev's son Nikolai managed the business throughout the 1860s, absorbing a number of smaller icon studios in Palekh. At the beginning of the 1870s, Nikolai's nephew Nikolai Mikhailovich took over the family's growing icon empire, which included a lucrative operation in Kiev. He shrewdly cultivated contacts with both church officials and academic societies to exploit the growing elite market for icon services.

By all accounts Nikolai Mikhailovich Safonov was a talented artist and businessman. His ability to paint an entire icon, combined with his self-cultivated literacy, impressed educated elites and attracted high-level patronage. According to one journalist, Safonov was an exceptional figure, "an educated and enlightened man" in a sea of poverty, ignorance, and hack craftsmanship. "Familiarity with Moscow and St. Petersburg church art gave him a refined taste and an understanding of antiquity." Despite lacking a formal degree, he was attempting to return icon painting to its roots, thanks, noted one journalist, to the demands of sophisticated buyers.[57]

The Safonov studio's greatest triumph came in 1881, when its best masters were selected by the tsar himself to paint the murals of the Kremlin's Palace of Facets. The restored murals were to serve as a backdrop for the tsar's 1883 coronation, which would elaborate a new relationship between tsarist power and the Russian people, without, of course, reducing the power of autocracy. Like his predecessors, Alexander III articulated the ruling ideology through a series of rituals. The coronation established a tsar's "scenario of power" that symbolically unified the tsar and his ruling elite. Alexander III's scenario, among other things, attempted to subvert the populist vision of the revolutionary Russian rebel with a vision of the humble icon-worshiping Russian Orthodox people. It was therefore the first coronation scenario to reserve an honored place for "the people," as exemplified by the selection of the Safonov studio for the Palace of Facets job.[58]

Selection of the Palekhians for the prestigious job immediately followed the March 1881 assassination of Alexander II. Instead of sparking a great uprising of the Russian masses, as the assassins had hoped, regicide encouraged greater state control and police surveillance. The so-called Temporary Regulations of August 1881, which remained in force to the end of the empire, gave the authorities expanded power to shut down newspapers and commercial ventures, remove local officials, and jail individuals.[59] Simultaneously, the assassination lent a greater sense of urgency to the search for unifying symbols and myths, ideas that would link the tsar to the people and make autocracy a popular as well as divinely sanctioned institution.

Art historians, including icon experts, helped lead the search for new instruments of social integration. Alexander III, who considered himself a connoisseur of art, followed and appreciated Buslaev's work and apparently recalled Buslaev's lessons in art history to his older brother Nicholas in 1860. Buslaev, in turn, "was well aware of the Sovereign's warm relationship to questions of art," remembered Count Sergei Dmitrievich Sheremetev.[60]

While Buslaev had cultivated the sovereign's appreciation of icon painting, it was Filimonov who first suggested that the icon painters of Palekh be hired for the Palace of Facets job so that Russia would be directed "onto the correct path of national development in all aspects of the life of state and society." Following the assassination of Alexander II, Filimonov delivered a "passionate speech" to the St. Petersburg Society of Lovers of Ancient Literature, urging that the Palekh masters be given the contract to restore the Palace of Facets. The proposal was passed on to Alexander III, who approved the idea and subsequently met with Filimonov to discuss the details, including the hiring of the best Safonov masters, V. E. and I. V. Belousov (whom Filimonov had met during his 1863 trip to Palekh).[61]

Costing nearly half a million rubles, the renovation of the Palace of Facets was designed to transport viewers "far back into the historical past." Built in the reign of Ivan III by Italian architects (1487–1491), the Palace of Facets in the pre-Petrine period served as a major venue for receptions of visiting dignitaries and merchants, as well as for gatherings of the tsar and his boyars. The reign of Ivan IV's son Fedor produced the first mention of frescoes in the spacious main hall. After numerous fires and neglect and the ravages of the Time of Troubles, the frescoes deteriorated, prompting a major repainting in the reign of Aleksei Mikhailovich in 1667 and 1668. Tsar Aleksei chose the chief artist of the Kremlin armory, Simon Ushakov, to lead a team of artists in repainting the murals as they appeared in the late sixteenth century. In 1677, under instructions from the tsar, Ushakov also provided precise descriptions of all the frescoes and their location, fortuitously as it turned out, since the restored murals were whitewashed in the reign of Peter the Great and covered with tapestries.[62]

The discovery of Ushakov's descriptions in the public library archive in the 1870s (which Filimonov then published in the Society of Ancient Russian Art's proceedings) created something of a sensation in the community of icon experts. While these descriptions furnished the Palekhians with a precise guide for the restoration, they also allowed the great seventeenth-century icon painter to participate directly in Alexander III's retrospective utopia. The use of Ushakov's descriptions as a *podlinnik* thus connected the Muscovy of Ivan III (when the palace was built), Ivan IV's son Fedor (when the murals were painted), the much beloved seventeenth century (when the murals were restored), and modern tsarist autocracy.

Tellingly, though Filimonov instructed the Belousovs to paint the murals strictly in the style of "the sixteenth century"—that is, the era of Ivan IV—he did allow the artists "some alterations in favor of a more realistic style and correctness of drawing, which accords with the current state of development of modern church and folk art." As earlier, the demands of modernity, "of a more realistic style and correctness of drawing," tempered Filimonov's (and Alexander III's) idealization of Muscovy. The fusion style *(friaz')* was now the official style of the regime.[63]

As for the murals themselves, the images represented biblical stories of creation, original sin, and Christ. Shifting from the ceiling to the walls, one traveled from the heavenly to the earthly kingdom, with the tsar as intermediary. The frescoes illustrated medieval legends about the derivation of the Romanov dynasty from Vladimir, Muscovy, and the Rurikid princes, who in turn supposedly traced their roots to the Roman emperor Augustus.[64] The murals drew connections between the modern Russian state, with the tsar at its head, and its pre-Petrine predecessors, the Roman emperors, and Christ himself. In this elaborate staging of modern tsarist power, the tsar's handlers made Christian icon-painting traditions a foundation of official nationality and tied both exclusively to the authority of the Romanov dynasty.

Alexander III expressed his gratitude to Filimonov and the Palekh masters (who were awarded medals for their efforts) and believed the restoration was a

"useful and desirable" precedent. By reaching into the plebeian ranks for aesthetic guidance, and verifying it with the expertise of trained scholars, tsarist
autocracy had illustrated its ability to rise above estate and class divisions. In
the jingoistic spirit of the time, a journalist applauded the coronation of
Alexander III in Moscow, "the heart of Russia," and predicted the reestablish-
ment of "our national distinctiveness . . . and the rejection of harmful western
influences."[65]

The coronation's ritualized representation of social harmony nonetheless
masked deep tensions and social divisions. While fear of market contamination caused many elites to doubt the bona fide national credentials of peasant
icon painters, they also believed the Palekhians (often referred to by elites deri-
sively as *bogomazy,* or god-daubers) lacked sufficient education to fulfill such
an important political and aesthetic task.[66] Jealousy also played a role. Many
professional academic painters were accustomed to receiving the big state
commissions for high-profile religious paintings in places such as St. Isaac's
Cathedral in St. Petersburg and the Cathedral of Christ the Savior in Moscow.
Consequently, elite criticism of the supposedly inferior work of the Palekh
masters continued during and after completion of the murals, "primarily," recalled one aristocratic patron of Palekh, "from those who mostly speak foreign
languages." The peasant masters, for their part, were equally disdainful of the
patronizing attitudes of their academic overseers. If elites often referred to the
Palekhians as "god-daubers," many Palekh masters, in the words of one journalist, "harbored the typical disdain of the practical worker for the theoretician." Not one academician painter, remarked a Palekhian, could wield a brush
with the aplomb of a peasant master. As the experts continued their quest to
"popularize" autocratic power, and to make Palekh Russia's village academy,
tensions between elites and Palekh would come into even sharper focus. Un-
derscoring the seemingly unresolvable contradictions of the late imperial political project, those tensions would widen in the reigns of Alexander III and
Nicholas II.[67]

CHAPTER TWO

The Commercialization of
Russian National Culture and Its Malcontents

"Love of the old ways is laudable and understandable; it
is an essential element in patriotism, but it is impossible to exist on such love alone. One must temper it
with reason. Everyone knows that everything changes,
that only that which is obsolete or dead does not
change, and that if a living organism does not change,
it soon begins to decay."

—Sergei Witte[1]

In 1900, the celebrated artist Viktor Vasnetsov penned a missive to the minister of internal affairs in which he lambasted "the new intrusion of industry
and the machine in the sphere of icon painting." In the realm of holy images,
"there can be no room for the stillborn machine."[2] New technologies corrupted Russian spiritual life, inserting their

> lifeless nature into the soul. . . . The phonograph is constantly being perfected and
> now clearly and accurately conveys a choir singing. Why not . . . replace the . . .
> untalented singing of a deacon with the clear and perfect singing of the machine?
> The . . . apologists of everything new would no doubt have nothing against this
> blasphemy. Electric light—the light of the streets, squares, bazaars, theaters, cafes,
> and various entertainments—has even been permitted in our cathedrals! It is hard
> to imagine the degree to which the clever technological devices of industrialists
> and secular enterprises will invade our cathedrals.[3]

According to Vasnetsov, attacks on traditional methods of icon production
in Palekh, Mstera, and Kholui posed the gravest threat to Russian spiritual and
national life. The threat was compounded by the ignorance of the peasant

masters themselves (the "god-daubers"). To counter these dangers, the state must ban foreign and machine-made icons, which entered the Russian icon market in the 1890s. Peasant artisans had to be retrained in state-run schools. Icon production had to be reorganized to "remove the yoke of kulaks and speculators. . . . In a time when industry and speculation rule, in an age of bowing down before the deathly furnace of profit, it is extremely difficult to defend the interests of spiritual life and everything that strengthens and supports it."[4]

Vasnetsov's view could not have differed more from the perspective of many Palekh masters. They especially resented the intelligentsia's habit of calling the peasant masters "god-daubers." If there was a crisis in Palekh, many Palekhians believed it was a crisis of elite perception, which in their view, had grossly misrepresented the real state of icon painting in the village.[5] It was a reasonable complaint, for Palekh circa 1900 emerges from the historical record as a vibrant community of entrepreneurial artisans, whose own identity arose from the very commercial values condemned by the experts. Displaying (and profiting from) their own unique system of artistic production, the masters were as determined to prove their worth as bona fide artists as the experts were to insist on their status as lowly god-daubers, whose only path to national redemption was to obey the academician's command.

THE VIEW FROM PALEKH

For a lad of ten or so, the road to becoming a master began with a six-year apprenticeship. A successful apprenticeship offered a young Palekhian mobility and financial means; it also guaranteed support for parents in their dotage, who therefore took a keen interest in their child's training.[6] Nikolai Mikhailovich Zinov'ev (1888–1979) began attending the village school in Palekh in 1896. "You've learned to read," said his father, who pulled the younger Zinov'ev from school after two years. "Now you will learn to paint." To give the boy a head start, the elder Zinov'ev began teaching his son the trade. The young Zinov'ev watched and copied his father's careful and precise brush strokes. After a year under his father's tutelage, Zinov'ev was taken by his mother to one of the local icon studios and accepted as an apprentice.[7]

Studio owners appointed apprentices as either *lichniki,* the most prestigious and talented artisans who painted the faces and exposed body parts of icons, or as *dolichniki,* who painted less "holy" parts of the icon. Through endless repetition, apprentices such as Zinov'ev gradually mastered the motifs and stylistic elements of their specialization. Students also had to learn the tools of the trade: the care of delicate squirrel-hair brushes, the preparation of primer *(levkas),* the mixing of egg yolks and natural pigments, the application of paints derived from silver and gold, the employment of wolf's teeth for polishing, and the use of varnishes. Depending on the studio, apprentices might also work the fields of their teachers, look after their children, clean house, collect mushrooms, and fetch vodka. At the end of the six-year apprenticeship, the *lichniki* apprentices were paired with *dolichniki* and painted a graduating icon *(otkhodnaia ikona)*, which they then used as a calling card to find work. A finished work represented the final rite of passage of an apprentice into mastership, providing the primary illustration of potential for future employers.[8]

While a handful of studio owners lived in two-story brick buildings—a rarity for peasant Russia and a sign of wealth and prestige—the majority of icon painters lived in small wooden houses, with a garden in back and often a larger patch of land to farm. Land provided supplemental food and income to the Palekh masters, an essential cushion during cyclical downturns in icon demand. It also sustained the myth of Palekhians as "peasant artists," although many masters would have preferred simply being called "artists."[9]

While some studio owners in Palekh shamelessly exploited their masters, others had a reputation for paying artists well and taking care of them should they become ill or their eyesight go bad, the most tragic of occupational hazards for the icon painters. It was a seller's market for the most skilled Palekhians. Masters had the freedom to move from one employer to another—provided they had talent. Even artists who survived (and thrived) after 1917 described their life in the late imperial period in surprisingly positive terms and rejected official characterizations of their prerevolutionary life as one of grinding poverty and ignorance.[10]

Although some studios used oil paints, most worked in the traditional tempera, which many elite consumers considered more authentic and natural. Because tempera paints, unlike oils, tended to run on vertical surfaces, icon painters had to lean directly over the horizontal surface of their work, which they often placed in their laps. One visitor to the village in 1901 observed that the Palekians had "a hellish capacity for industriousness *[adskaia usidchivost']*."[11]

The best masters spent much of their time, especially in summer, working on restorations or mural paintings in Russia's major urban centers.[12] Like the tradition of seasonal peasant migration to work in factories *(otkhodnichestvo)*, the itinerant labors of Palekh icon painters brought Palekhians into contact with the latest fads and developments in St. Petersburg, Moscow, and various provincial centers. Many Palekh masters met academically trained artists and absorbed various artistic styles and philosophies—not to mention the obsession of the intelligentsia with the acquisition and display of culture. When the peasant masters posed for the camera at the turn of the century, they wore dapper suits and ties. Many Palekhians, especially younger masters, were well-coiffed and clean-shaven, in contrast to those educated elites who in the manner of Leo Tolstoy began to rusticate themselves by sporting long beards, an outward sign of their connection with the common muzhik. Reflecting new secular aspirations, many Palekhians decorated their homes with lithographic reproductions of the work of Repin, Vasnetsov, and other Russian national artists.[13] "Everything new impressed me," recalled the Palekh master Ivan Vakurov regarding his first visit to Moscow. "Observations, people, theaters, museums—all of this facilitated my development as an artist."[14]

To illustrate their cultured status, younger Palekh masters improved upon a rudimentary literacy from the local parish school with a program of self-development and cultural uplift. Among the most talented of Palekh's itiner-ant restorers was Aleksandr Ivanovich Zubkov (1885–1938). While painting and restoring icons in the last years of the Romanov dynasty, Zubkov traversed the length and breadth of European Russia.[15] He knew all the major styles of icon painting. Belying the intelligentsia's view of the masters as uniformly uncultured and ignorant, he read the classics of Russian nineteenth-century literature. An impeccable dresser, he participated with other masters in collective subscriptions to a number of journals, including the popular science journal *Vestnik znaniia,* whose highbrow tone attracted culture seekers from Russia's small but growing lower middle classes.[16]

Other Palekhians moved from icon painting to secular art, taking classes at the Moscow College of Art, Architecture, and Sculpture. A. M. Korin (1865–1923) packed his belongings and moved to Moscow to make a living as a secular artist. In the 1890s, he began exhibiting in Russia with the Peredvizhniki (Wanderers) and frequently returned to the village, where he painted portraits of his relatives and friends. He was a hero to many masters, and his landscapes and portraits circulated among young Palekh artists, who copied his work and took inspiration from his example. Other Palekhians began working in the field of arts and crafts, including the filling of orders for the famous Fabergé—presaging the later Soviet transformation of the Palekh masters into folk art specialists. The Palekh masters and their art were thus becoming increasingly secularized, and after the pattern of the educated elites they met in the capi-tals, many Palekh masters aspired to membership in the rarified ranks of the Russian artistic community.[17]

By 1900, Palekh natives managed five icon studios in Moscow as well as shops in St. Petersburg, Nizhnii Novgorod, Samara, Kiev, and elsewhere.[18] Ex-patriate Palekhians frequently returned to the hamlet, hiring masters and keeping houses and land. Some new studios built in Palekh around the turn of the century were spacious and bright, with high ceilings and large windows, giving Palekh a prosperous and industrious look exceptional for rural Russia. Even experts commented on Palekh's affluent appearance, observations that complicated their own story of Palekh's precipitous decline in the face of predatory capitalist exploitation.[19]

Palekh's icon studios produced icons in various styles, each suggesting a particular conception of Russia's place in the world. Some styles were more western and Italian, while others linked modern Russian identity to ancient roots such as Muscovy, Vladimir, Kiev, or Byzantium. As noted in chapter 1, Nikolai Mikhailovich Safonov (1846–1911) operated the largest and most famous of Palekh's studios, employing nearly 250 masters at the turn of the century. Safonov was Palekh's leading citizen, a literate man and accomplished artist whose power and prestige far eclipsed that of the local nobility.[20] Until the 1870s, the Safonov studio worked primarily in an "Italian" manner that used a more realistic technique and brighter colors. This style reflected the cosmopolitan tastes of many of Palekh's elite consumers, who had little sense of the need for a distinctly "Russian Orthodox" manner. In the 1880s, the Safonov studio began producing more "Greek" icons in a neo-Byzantine style. The new production echoed the growing popularity in ruling circles for Byzantine and Greek relics, which were considered more authentically Orthodox and hence Russian. As the conservative newspaper *Sankt Peterburgskie vedomosti* put it in 1901, authentic holy images must avoid "Catholic" imagery with "ruddy-cheeked" figures and "beautiful maidens with sensuous lips, in bright and festive conditions." Painted figures should reveal the effects of constant fasting and show "an immovable gaze," "simple clothing," and "a lack of bright colors and brightening effects."[21] So-called *starinshchiki* (from the Russian root for old) at the Safonov studio catered to this segment of the icon market, in which Old Believer merchants also participated (see illustration 6, a Palekh or Mstera icon of *Christ of the Wrathful Eye*).[22] This shift in demand coincided with an increasingly retrospective turn in court rituals, which looked toward pre-Petrine Russia, rather than western Europe, as a model for Russian society and culture.[23]

By contrast, Safonov's main rival, the Belousov studio, specialized in the fusion style known as *friaz'* (the founders of the Belousov studio being the former Safonov masters who had restored the Kremlin Palace of Facets). The style used brighter colors and integrated elements of naturalism such as rounder faces, chiaroscuro, and true perspective. The Belousov icons applied generous amounts of gold paint to fill in the background and highlight features. Those who specialized in this style were known as *friazisti*. They often painted the background using oil paints and a more realistic style. Masters then switched to tempera to paint the face, hair, eyes, and certain other aspects of the icon in a more traditional manner.[24]

Whereas the Greek style catered to a purely Byzantine vision of Russianness, the *friazhskii* manner satisfied a related though distinct current of demand among elites: a technique that integrated Orthodox aesthetic traditions with post-Renaissance, western influences. As seen in the previous chapter, icon experts such as Buslaev and Filimonov in the 1860s considered the *friazhskii* style an ideal synthesis of tradition and modernity, and they traced its roots to the much-beloved seventeenth century and especially the rule of Tsar Aleksei. Rounder faces, bright colors, and a more realistic technique (including the use of oil paints) highlighted the possibilities of life in this world and suggested a culture closer—though not too close—to that of modern Europe. The Belousov *friazhskii* style also matched the growing spirit of conspicuous consumption in the village: richly decorated with gold ornament and enamel, bright colors, and saints with colorfully round and full faces.[25]

The Belousovs embodied the spirit of economic enterprise in the hamlet, where it was common practice for talented masters to break away from their former bosses and start their own businesses. In the mid-1880s, the three Belousov brothers gave up the security of a guaranteed salary in the Safonov studio, after restoring the Kremlin Palace of Facets for Alexander III's coronation. In preparation for the launch of their own business, they decided to paint an icon of the tsar, hoping to leverage his royal person as a potent marketing tool. In preparing the icon, the Belousovs designed an image that the tsar's family could worship in a more private and intimate setting. They decided on a two-part icon, divided by borderlines in "brilliant gold" and combining religious iconography, family portrait, and political portraiture. The upper part showed the tsar sitting on his throne, in his imperial vestments "and all the kingly paraphernalia." Archangels and angels surrounded the throne. The Russian saint Aleksandr Nevskii flanked the sovereign's right side and Mary Magdalene his left side. The lower portion of the icon represented the patron saints of the tsar's children. In the center were St. Nicholas, St. George slaying the dragon (the patron saint of the imperial Russian army), and St. Kseniia. The Belousovs described the ornament as done in the manner of the sixteenth century, a time of Russia's "renaissance" under Muscovy, which continued a cultural flowering supposedly cut short in Vladimir and Suzdal by the Mongol invaders. Alexander III was so pleased with the image that he wrote on the back of it: "To be blessed and placed in the [red] corner of the Palace of Facets," where it resided until the Bolshevik Revolution.[26]

Subsequently, the Belousov business expanded rapidly, enjoying support from wealthy patrons. According to one contemporary, the oldest brother, Vasilii Belousov, was "incredibly talented in everything," a jack-of-all-trades, who excelled as a mechanic, joiner, and painter. He was deeply religious, serving as the village's church elder for twelve years and before that as the village elder. When he died in 1890, at the age of sixty-two, his son Ivan Vasil'evich took over the business, "developing it into a large operation" and opening a shop in Samara specializing in the production of iconostases for the many new churches built by industrialists, church authorities, and state institutions in the south and east. "He was very talented at finding work," remembered one icon painter. He traded on the studio's high-level patronage, which he used as testimonial to the studio's deeply Russian and Orthodox nature. Like his father, he also served as church elder—and was elected to the Viaznikovskii district zemstvo. With the money earned from state and church orders in Moscow, St. Petersburg, and elsewhere, the Belousovs built a large two-story brick studio on Palekh's main street, thus keeping up with the other Ivans in Palekh, most notably the Safonov empire from which they had sprung. (The Soviets later converted the building into the State Museum of Palekh Art.)[27]

Lev Parilov also worked for the Safonov studio before starting his own business in the late 1890s. Among Palekhians, Parilov was known for his tireless travels around Russia in search of business. Parilov secured much of his business by lowballing the bids of his competitors for state and church orders, a practice that earned him the ironic epithet among Palekhians of Lev the Most Wise *(Lev-premudryi)*. For Parilov and his many paying customers, icons were not simply religious images, but artistic objects that could be displayed and admired for their elegance and craftsmanship. In April 1897, Parilov placed a six-page advertising supplement in the newspaper of the Vladimir eparchy. In great detail, he listed the many sizes and prices of all the saints, festivals, mothers of God, and saviors done by his new studio. Reflecting the growing demand for objets d'art, he offered icons in a variety of nontraditional media, including cloth, zinc plate, copper, glass plate, and mirror. Customers could pick and choose from a menu of Russian styles and themes and have the images ordered and delivered by mail. "The holy objects mentioned in this list," wrote Parilov in one ad, "can be done in various styles: ancient Greek, Stroganov, *friazhskii,* and realistic *[zhivopisnyi]*." Parilov also offered his services in icon and mural restoration, paying obligatory homage to the growing cult of academic expertise by promising to work "in strict accordance with scientific archaeological rules."[28]

Demand for Palekh's icons reached into the highest levels of Russian society. In July 1901, Count Sergei Sheremetev escorted Russia's minister of internal affairs, Dmitrii Sipiagin, to an exhibit of peasant arts and crafts in the textile town of Shuia (thirty kilometers north of Palekh). The aristocratic party spent much of its time surveying the large collection of peasant icons from Palekh. Eight artists from Palekh displayed their work, including the Belousov brothers, who marketed an *Apostle Peter* for one hundred rubles and a *Savior* for eighty rubles. In Palekh holiness did not come cheap, and along with a growing sense of national identity, its price was on the rise.[29] (For examples of the kind of icons typically produced in peasant icon shops in Palekh in the late 1800s, see illustrations 7, 8, and 9.)

The market for Palekh icons extended beyond the Orthodox East. Like many Russian elites, foreign consumers envisioned Russia as having an exotic mélange of religious icon-painting styles, the art of Russian realism, and Russian arts and crafts. On Nikol'skii Street in Moscow, one icon shop at the turn of the century advertised its wares in French. Alongside peasant-made icons from Palekh, Mstera, and Kholui, the shop displayed papier-mâché boxes from the village of Fedoskino. These boxes employed copies of works by Russian realist painters in their decoration. Palekhians would later draw upon this same market for Russianness as Soviet lacquer specialists.[30]

Other Palekh studios, such as the Karovaikov and Korin studios (the latter linked to the famous People's Artist of the Soviet era Pavel Korin), specialized in miniature painting *(melochnoe pis'mo)*, cramming dozens of saints in incredibly minute spaces. These painters were known as *melochniki*. On an icon scarcely larger than the size of this page, miniaturists could cram thirty figures into each of twelve frames representing the months of the year and their accompanying church festivals—with a face of Jesus in the center surrounded by 360 Mothers of God! Such icon painters contributed to a growing reputation of the Russian peasant as a master of painstaking craftsmanship.[31]

Some Palekhians diversified into new businesses. The founder of the Korovaikov studio, N. T. Korovaikov (d.1886), used profits from icon sales to buy up the land of impoverished nobility in the region, whose power and authority the peasant entrepreneurs of Palekh were rapidly displacing. His business interests spanned the sacred and the profane. In addition to producing and re-selling icons, Korovaikov operated taverns throughout the area and ran a liquor factory in the district center of Viazniki. His son (d.1910) concentrated on expanding the icon production business and around the turn of the century opened an icon studio and store in St. Petersburg. Another son, who owned seven homes in St. Petersburg, committed suicide in 1918 at the age of forty after being dispossessed by the Bolsheviks.[32]

Church figures in Palekh also caught the entrepreneurial bug. One of Palekh's central priests, Nikolai Petrovich Chikhachev, exhibited a flair for organizing elaborate church services as well as financial operations. According to one of his contemporaries, he was a "good priest," with a "delicate tenor voice," who conducted church services "artistically," although too long for many of the parishioners' liking. He also had "a hunger for money," producing and selling silver and gold tinsel for icon painters, reselling icons in Vladimir, manufacturing and hawking candles for the Vladimir eparchy, and lending money (with interest). He was a vain man, who publicly celebrated the anniversaries of his service, during which he "forced children to throw flowers at his feet as he walked from the church to his home."[33]

Regardless of a studio's style, Palekhians in the reigns of Alexander III and Nicholas II won prestigious icon restoration and church mural contracts. The Safonov, Belousov, and Parilov studios worked in all the nation's most important cathedrals and monasteries. While restorations were lucrative, they also integrated Palekh into the representation of tsarist ideology. Like other court rituals, restorations articulated the aims and goals of the regime.[34] In 1884, Safonov received the contract to restore the twelfth-century Uspenskii cathedral in Vladimir. Given Vladimir's status as a forerunner to the modern Russian state, the contract had great symbolic importance. The celebratory blessing of the completed restoration was an occasion for displays of civic pride and social and political integration. City residents dressed in their best clothing and packed the cathedral and square outside. As church bells rang across the city, a military band played "How Glorious Is Our Lord in Zion." The ceremonial procession from the church *(krestnyi khod)* included leading church, state, and military officials from the province, as well as secular and parochial educational administrators. Honored citizens and guests feasted afterward at the assembly hall of the provincial gentry. Organizers claimed the celebration was for "all of Russia," since Vladimir and the cathedral had provided an inspiration and model for the rise of the Russian state. "The glorious Princes of the Russian land, those who suffered for it, marched again . . . among the holy relics of Vladimir."[35]

Perhaps the most interesting variation on the restoration ritual came in Palekh itself. In 1900, the leading citizens of Palekh began restoring the murals and iconostasis of the town's central cathedral, long recognized as a valuable national treasure. The Belousov and Safonov studios set aside their rivalry to complete the job, which ultimately cost twenty-five thousand rubles. The Belousov studio restored the church's icons and produced a new frame for the iconostasis in its Samara division, in the manner of the rococo. Equally bold was the style of restoration, which avoided the Greek manner so popular in many conservative elite circles. The restored murals, with the help of Safonov masters, aimed to convey a style that fused "the demands of realistic painting [*zhivopis'*] with those of icon painting in the manner of the best Palekh masters of the eighteenth century." According to one observer, "the realistic representations in general depart somewhat from the strict religious icon style and are similar to secular pictures, but without the extremes of Italian painting." A more realistic style "enlivened the lifeless walls [of the cathedral] and in the language of captivating images evokes the construction of the house of human salvation." At least in their own backyard, the Palekhians preferred a more natural style, which, as will be seen shortly, ran counter to the growing preference among certain well-placed elites for a supposedly more authentic and Russian "Byzantine" style.[36]

Eventual completion of the restoration in 1907, like all major restorations, was accompanied by a celebratory blessing, which also served as a critical vehicle for defining and integrating the local community. Leading studio owners gave the keynote speeches, noting their contributions to the restoration and their ability to overcome competing interests for the sake of a higher goal. They received icons as gifts of thanks by parishioners. Nikolai Safonov thanked all involved, noting that their efforts ensured that future generations would not accuse them of "carelessness and a lack of attention" to Russia's artistic legacy. A member of the Vladimir archive commission attended a feast afterwards at the home of the Belousovs and confirmed that Palekhians were indeed great restorers and icon painters. He said he hoped the restoration would eliminate once and for all the incorrect view of the Palekhians as god-daubers and confirm Palekh's status as "the heart and soul of Russian icon painting." Palekh not only "loves the ancient images," he said in a toast, "but knows how to preserve them."[37]

Not everyone, however, was so impressed by Palekh's system for preserving and reproducing the ancient images. While some elites proclaimed that academically trained artists "have no place in the Orthodox church," others begged to differ.[38] Individuals such as Vasnetsov gave pride of place to academic expertise rather than the god-daubers. The experts also condemned the role of markets and consumer tastes in shaping Russian culture. Citing their own archaeological and aesthetic training, the icon experts in the 1880s and 1890s gained increasing confidence in their right to interpret national traditions and dictate the conditions of their future development.

ASSIMILATION OF THE *NAROD*

In the post-emancipation era, conservative Russian elites searched for common symbols and cultural practices to counteract a perceived breakdown of traditions. Folk culture, in their view, was the last gasp of a supposedly harmonious premodern world, which they were determined to resurrect. Similar to the radical Russian populists who in 1873 went to the people (where many were turned into the police by the peasants they encountered), academically trained artists thus made Russian peasant life the focus of their creative expression.

The neo-realist Viktor Vasnetsov spearheaded this elite appropriation of Russian folk culture. The son of a village priest, Vasnetsov studied at the Academy of Arts in St. Petersburg in the heady days of Alexander II's reforms. Guided by the studies of scholars such as Zabelin and Buslaev, he began drawing folk tales and epics and then branched into Orthodox religious art. For Vasnetsov, art was not just a pretty picture but the embodiment of a living national spirit that the artist embedded in every facet of daily life, from the design of furniture to the ornamental flourishes in one's clothing. Armed with such ideas, Vasnetsov in the 1880s transformed the estate of his patron Mamontov into a kind of cathedral of Russian folk art. While painting religious icons, he literally appropriated the *narod* with the famous depiction of the three Russian knights (*Bogatyri*, 1881–1898). He derived the central figure of Il'ia Muromets in the picture from a living muzhik, a certain Ivan Petrov from the countryside of the Vladimir province.[39]

Parallel to the development of Vasnetsov's interests, the Russian state began funding various efforts to promote peasant artisanal industry *(kustarnaia promyshlennost')*. Partly, these efforts were motivated by practical concerns, since Great Russian peasants in central Russia relied on nonagricultural pursuits to supplement poor soils and short growing seasons. State support of arts and crafts also evoked romantic notions of the medieval rural craftsman of the Russian heartland—an unalienated laborer who fully controlled the instruments of his production.[40]

As the holiest of the folk arts, peasant icon painting received special tutelage, and the Aleksandr Nevskii Brotherhood became the state's first protector of peasant icon painting. Created in the reign of Alexander II to battle the supposed "infection" *(zarazhenie)* of alien faiths in the Russian heartland, the brotherhood collaborated with the Academy of Arts and its newly formed museum of Christian antiquities to reform peasant icon painting. Its mission was to create "model icon-painting studios," which would "paralyze the work of the *ofeni*" (icon traders), reduce the price of icons for consumers, and "terminate trade in icons that do not meet the demands of the Orthodox religion." As defined by its charter, the brotherhood was proscribed from managing the production and distribution of icons as "a commercial enterprise," reflecting the elite view that sacred national symbols should be set apart from profit considerations. Justifying its program, the brotherhood referred to icon painting as suffering from an acute crisis of "decline" *(upadok)*. The imperial conception of *upadok* in icon painting (integrated into later Soviet propaganda) implied a number of threats. Profit motives and capitalism were the greatest menace, embodied by the abstract figures of the "speculators and kulaks." The "decline" also involved the supposed ignorance and backwardness of peasant Russia. According to one report from the brotherhood, icon painting in Palekh, Mstera, and Kholui "is striking for its vulgarity . . . both in relation to its content and to its execution. . . . It is hard to believe there could be demand for such things among the simple people." The combination of "illiteracy with the general ignorance [of the masters] allows incredibly crude icons to appear for sale." Especially dangerous were icon painters who fancied themselves to be creative artists. "Thus, the splendid idea occurs to some ignorant god-dauber to surprise the world with a new icon . . . stunning in its absurdity and at the same time arousing a smile for its naiveté."[41]

Focusing on Kholui, which among the three icon-painting villages was believed to be most in need of aesthetic and spiritual rejuvenation, the brotherhood opened Russia's first state-funded icon-painting school in 1882.[42] Although the brotherhood stressed that the school "should satisfy demands of a non-academic nature," it hired a professionally trained, secular artist to run the program.[43] Students learned proper perspective, drew from nature, and sketched geometrical shapes. More advanced students copied the icons of professional artists who had begun dabbling in religious art. In keeping with the broader movement to bring culture to the masses, the teacher explained the symbolism of icons, the lives of saints, and the history of icon painting in Russia, including the works of artists such as Andrei Rublev and Simon Ushakov.[44] The need for state control over icons was emphasized by the study of the forty-third chapter of the 1551 Stoglav. The books of the original icon experts Rovinskii and Buslaev were required homework reading. While mastering the icon expert's scientific point of view, the students also learned how to paint in tempera as well as oil, so that "icons, while being artistic creations, also remain icons, that is, holy images."[45]

The *ober-prokuror* of the Holy Synod, Konstantin Pobedonostsev, one of the few dissenting voices on the new school, captured a fundamental contradiction in the brotherhood's effort to modernize yet preserve the tradition of icon painting. "Instead of reviving ancient icon painting," he noted, placing an academically

trained artist in charge of the school "should have the result of completely displacing it, replacing it with the new, contradictory techniques and even new
content." The first lessons in painting, he added, would involve "drawing the
heads of Apollo, Bacchus . . . , the torso of Hercules . . . or, finally, the Catholic
Madonna. The figures of antiquity, which make up the ABCs of [academic]
training, will appear very strange and inappropriate in a Russian folk icon-
painting school." Either the teacher would have to abandon his training and
experience, or the icon painters would have to jettison the ancient traditions.
Even worse, the school's program treated icons as objects of archaeological investigation rather than of religious worship.[46]

Undeterred, and believing it had found in Kholui a workable template for
both transforming and preserving a sacred national tradition, the brotherhood
set up a similar school in Mstera in 1889. With the help of the Vladimir zemstvo, it then turned to Palekh.[47]

Palekh, however, turned out to be far more problematic. In the brotherhood's own words, the school "was dead as soon as it was born." As far as
Palekh's leading citizens were concerned, their own system of training, confirmed by commercial success and high-level patronage from the tsar himself,
was more than adequate. They chafed at the very notion of *upadok* that had
inspired the brotherhood's efforts, especially since many masters had close
contact with cultural and artistic life in the capitals.[48] And so the school was
opened in Palekh—and no one came. From the debacle the brotherhood concluded: "We all know how the simple people relate to any innovation with
suspicion and frequently hostility. That is especially true in the recently
opened drawing schools staffed by outside teachers, and, what is more, teachers from among the educated. Of course, by long established tradition, the locals will say they will agree, that it is no big deal, that it is a good thing, etc.,
but they will never send their children to this school."[49]

The icon experts nonetheless persevered, led by an energetic young archaeologist from Vladimir named Vasilii Timofeevich Georgievskii (1861–1923).
Georgievskii had played a critical role in the brotherhood during the 1880s
and 1890s.[50] Trained in art history at the Orthodox seminary in Kiev, he was
determined to complete the full appropriation of Russia's national traditions
from the *narod* and to recycle those traditions, à la Vasnetsov, in a purified and
updated form, in which authentic Russians could safely enjoy them. Penetrating and controlling the Palekh system of artistic production became his personal mission.[51] In the 1890s, Georgievskii aggressively marketed himself as an
essential link between academics and officials in St. Petersburg and the icon
painters of the Vladimir province. Fawning and flattering by turns,
Georgievskii impressed the famous Byzantinist Nikodim Pavlovich Kondakov
with his knowledge of local matters and his passion for church archaeology.

Like the other experts, Georgievskii had a paradoxical attitude toward Russian peasants. The people were caretakers of sacred national traditions, yet

hoarders and exploiters of those very same resources. "All provincials," he proclaimed, "generally consider it necessary to hide the truth as much as possible
[from] archaeologists, scholars, and writers." The Palekh masters, he wrote in a
letter to Kondakov, "by nature are extremely suspicious and secretive. Not for
any kind of money would they reveal that which provides their daily bread,
which they received as an inheritance from their ancestors."[52] He continued:

> In addition to the mistrust which one encounters here, . . . one runs into the
> purely ignorant fear of the average craftsman who believes he will lose something
> by giving away 'the secrets' of his craft. . . . And perhaps they have a point. Try to
> put yourself in the place of an icon painter and imagine that some interviewer has
> fallen from the sky into your office—perhaps even a famous person. Then he be-
> gins to interrogate you about your current work, what kind of sources you use and
> could he just take some of these sources for some goal that is entirely abstract and
> confused for you. It is understandable that you would try in a delicate way, not
> having given him what he wants, to get him to go back from whence he came. Al-
> most everywhere such a fate threatened me and my helpers from among the abo-
> rigines, even in circumstances where the owner was not infected by such preju-
> dices. In the latter case, the owner had fears of a mercantile nature: perhaps he
> would sell things for less money than his neighbor and thus appear in his neigh-
> bor's eye as a simpleton and a fool.[53]

In the established tradition of icon experts, Georgievskii traveled to Palekh
in the summer of 1894. He published his balance sheet on Palekh the following year. On the positive side of the ledger, peasant icon painters produced a
kind of art that was distinct from that done in the West and therefore superior.
"Real Russians," wrote Georgievskii, rejected "the so-called artistic icons of
contemporary academicians," which "contradict all the traditions of national
Russian church iconography." Yet Georgievskii said most peasant icon painting
was "anti-artistic, crude, and tasteless in execution" and thus justified the pejorative term "god-daubers" for the Suzdalites. Endorsing the academic approach
he simultaneously condemned, Georgievskii cited the work of Vasnetsov as an
example for peasant icon painters to follow.[54]

Whereas Buslaev and Filimonov had earlier praised the *friazhskii* style as an
ideal synthesis of western post-Renaissance technique and Russian Orthodox
art, Georgievskii preferred a more ancient "Greek" manner. Palekh's *friazhskii*
mix of tempera and oil paints, and a realistic and stylized manner, created "the
impression of something eclectic and undefined." The Palekh masters "feel
this lack of definition and thus try to distract the viewer's attention from the
manner of the icon with an elegant gold background, decorated with the most
intricate ornament." Holy images with bright colors and crude figures, he
added, catered to the corrupt tastes of "Little Russians," *(malorossiiane)*, reflecting the creeping influence of "Catholicism and Uniates." Such icons were

"surrogates of authentic religious art" and no doubt appealed to the head of a monastery "with little developed aesthetic sense" or "the less developed" trading classes, who could only understand cultural value in purely financial terms, based on the quantity and brilliance of gold ornament. Meanwhile, the few masters who painted icons in the superior "Greek style" were gradually dying out, pushed aside by the growing influence of vulgar tastes.[55]

Georgievskii expressed his disdain for Palekh's cultural achievement during a conversation with his guide from Palekh, the local priest Nikolai Chikhachev. As reported by Georgievskii, the two had the following chat:

> —Well, Father Nikolai, show me your much-praised masters.
> —With pleasure, with pleasure. I've long ago wanted you to visit our Palekhians. As you know, Palekh is a people's academy.
> —And you think such a nickname suggests something honorable for Palekh?
> —Of course. Iurii Dmitrievich Filimonov himself, having come here more than once, called Palekh an academy. How could you not call it such a thing, since our Palekhians had the honor of painting even the famous Palace of Facets before the coronation [of Alexander III]? They didn't invite your academically trained painters for this job, but our muzhiks. And what happened? Our painters certainly didn't fall on their face.

Challenging the worthiness of the work on the Palace of Facets, Georgievskii said that things had changed in the last decade. Academically trained artists were reacquainting themselves with ancient techniques and "Russian antiquity," so the Palekhians had no exclusive claim over icon painting. "Let's not waste time," said Georgievskii, cutting off the debate. "Let's look at your 'academic studios' and see for ourselves."[56]

Georgievskii was unimpressed. With regard to the Belousov studio, which worked in the *friazhskii* style, he said his previous negative comments on this style applied completely: one is struck by the "excess of gold ornament" and the almost total ineffectiveness of the depicted image. Supposedly testifying to the Palekhians' ignorance of the traditions they claimed to represent, the studio allowed tracings of ancient icons to gather dust in a heap. Only a lack of culture, noted Georgievskii, could prevent the studio owner from compiling these tracings of ancient icons into an album, thus making them available for archaeological investigation.[57]

The famous Safonov studio was no better, said Georgievskii. He condemned the studio owner's neglect of the masters' working conditions and health. His guide for the Safonov studio, the son of the owner N. M. Safonov, was "a young man, dressed foppishly, who, it seems, no longer paints icons and at the very least, in our view, knows little about them." When he inquired about the *"podlinniki"* used by the Safonov studio, the owner's son said they had no such things, "which can hardly be the case," wrote Georgievskii. Instead, Safonov showed Georgievskii photos of religious paintings by academic painters, seemingly reflecting Georgievskii's own endorsement of recent academic religious art as a model for the painters. Georgievskii was again unimpressed. It was one thing for icon experts to suggest models for academic painters to follow, but quite another for peasant icon painters to make these choices on their own.[58]

Though Georgievskii had plans to visit other icon studios in the town, a sudden downpour discouraged him from continuing his investigations. He had had enough of Palekh, which seemed determined, or so he thought, to pull the proverbial wool over his eyes. Before leaving, he huddled in the central cathedral to wait out the storm and acknowledged the presence inside of high-quality older icons. (As a matter of civic pride, Palekhians donated many of their best icons for display in the church). These valuable icons, he added in a parting shot, appeared in the church due to donations from local residents, who offered them in exchange for new icons. Those who made the donations, said Georgievskii, "for the most part know nothing about icons," since they had traded such valuable relics for new works in the stylized Palekh manner.[59]

Georgievskii concluded that the Palekh masters "do not deserve to be so proud of their work." It was "simply ridiculous and completely without basis" that the Palekh masters called themselves "artists" *(khudozhniki).*[60] Citing the condemnation of icons with "ruddy red faces" by the Old Believer martyr Avvakum, Georgievskii called for a new system of censorship. It should be modeled after the system of icon supervision that existed in Muscovy and disappeared in the post-Petrine malaise. Modern-day censors should be located on the premises of the icon studios, enforcing strict observance of a new *"podlinnik."* "It is time to put an end to chaos in this arena," said Georgievskii.[61]

In the meantime, Vasnetsov continued his project of appropriating the traditions of the folk. In 1896, after a decade of labor, Vasnetsov completed the murals of the Vladimir cathedral in Kiev, whose construction had begun nearly three decades earlier. The cathedral honored the baptism of Kievan Rus'. Vasnetsov used a style that was considered to be "Greek," combining Byzantine religious forms with classicism, including the correct proportions of figures and dignified poses and gestures. The first Christian rulers of Rus' occupied honored positions as the initial caretakers of the Byzantine heritage. Russian folk legends and traditions were featured, along with the medieval Russian monk and scribe Nestor. Vasnetsov invited a group of artists into an artel in which the collective spirit of Rus' (the Slavophile notion of *sobornost'*) would be revived through the joint manufacture of Orthodox religious art. He studied murals from early Christianity in Italy, before Christianity's apostasy in western lands. He examined the art of pre-Petrine monasteries and churches as well as Old Believer icon collections in Moscow.[62]

With Vasnetsov's painting, many elites, as well as Georgievskii, believed that the program of mastering the past had been completed. On the occasion of the 1896 blessing of the Kiev cathedral, which Nicholas II attended, one journalist described Vasnetsov's work as a thorough assimilation of the best of the icon-painting traditions and thus "a source for a new direction of all our religious art." Vasnetsov had appropriately adhered to the "Greek" rather than "*friazhskii*" manner. The latter style was rightly shunned because it emphasized "an abundance of gold and valuable gems," which encouraged "earthly passions." Reviewers waxed ecstatic. The press reproduced the murals in countless publications. Critiques of Palekh's own services grew, accompanied by claims that only academician painters such as Vasnetsov were qualified for serious religious artwork and restoration. Churches began requesting that painters produce copies of the Vasnetsov murals.[63]

In the meantime, Georgievskii expanded his search for patronage. He wrote to Professor N. V. Pokrovskii of the St. Petersburg seminary on April 5, 1897, offering his services as a collector of the *podlinniki*.[64] Pokrovskii was keenly interested in publishing a new style manual for icon painters. Georgievskii sent him proofs for an article on Vasnetsov in which he characterized the great artist as a prototype of the ideal Russian icon painter. The article, he added, is "an echo of your scientific opinions and those of F. I. Buslaev about our church art."[65]

In a letter of February 6, 1898, Georgievskii told Kondakov it was still not too late to save Russian iconography. He offered to be the great Byzantinist's factotum.[66] Intrigued by Georgievskii's commitment and contacts, both Kondakov and the powerful Count Sergei Dmitrievich Sheremetev (1844–1918) began planning a trip to the land of peasant icon painters for their own onsite investigation. Simultaneously, they sketched out an article calling for a new "*podlinnik*." The trip and the article, they hoped, would consolidate support within the sprawling imperial bureaucracy for a new committee to control and censor icon production. Sheremetev, who frequently met with the tsar, revealed his plans to Pokrovskii in March 1899:

> When . . . our article will be published, I am prepared to present a note to the sovereign emperor. . . . I am absolutely sure of the sympathy of the sovereign and on the basis of that sympathy I have reason to hope that following the example of his [Muscovite] predecessors he will render us his all-powerful help in this matter. Thus, the question will be decided and we will acquire the firm basis that we need for realizing the substantial plan we have conceived. But just leave this between us for now.[67]

THE NEW BREED OF ICON EXPERTS AND THEIR PATRONS

As patron of a new generation of icon experts, Count Sheremetev fit in perfectly with what Richard Wortman has called the "revival of Muscovy" in tsarist court rituals. Serving as adjutant to Emperor Alexander III, he cultivated the ideal of the aristocrat who countered the narrow interests of bureaucratic administration with nobler concerns. On cultural matters he briefed Nicholas

II at Tsarskoe Selo. During these visits he offered advice to Nicholas in the tsar's billiard room, perhaps imagining himself as a Muscovite boyar, whose style of dress he frequently imitated for costume balls. He so loved his adopted personae that he made a postcard of himself as a seventeenth-century boyar and sent it to his friends, writing on the back: "There you have my image!" In 1888, Sheremetev became chairman of the Society of Lovers of Ancient Literature, which had been created in 1877. While underwriting the society's many studies of icons, he also published sentimental portraits of his visits to Russia's holy shrines (1895) and penned a series of essays on his family's personal collection of holy images (1899).[68]

Kondakov, meanwhile, was the student of the prototypical icon expert Buslaev, under whom he studied from 1861 to 1865. He came from humble roots, the son of a serf estate manager. With the help of Filimonov and Buslaev, Kondakov published his first studies in the Moscow-based journal of the Society of Ancient Russian Art. In 1869, Kondakov began teaching the history and theory of art on the Russian Empire's southern fringe, at Novorossiisk University in Odessa. He participated in dozens of archaeological trips to study the church architecture and art of the Black Sea region, the Caucasus, Constantinople, and Syria. In the mid-1870s, he spent nearly two years in western European libraries researching his doctoral dissertation, which was entitled "The History of Byzantine Art and Iconography in the Miniatures of Greek Manuscripts." It was published in 1877 in the midst of Russia's war with Turkey. The national struggles in the Balkans against Ottoman rule inspired Kondakov to examine ties between Russian culture and Byzantium, and he published the results of these investigations in an 1887 monograph.[69] After publication of this study, Kondakov secured a new position teaching the history of art at St. Petersburg University, as well as the job of senior curator for the Hermitage. Meanwhile, Kondakov continued to amass titles and contacts, becoming a corresponding member of the Academy of Sciences in St. Petersburg in 1892 (and a full member in 1900), a full member of the Imperial Academy of Arts in 1893, and a distinguished professor in 1894.[70]

When Kondakov retired from teaching in 1896 at the age of fifty-two, with a generous pension of three thousand rubles per year, he was determined to use his knowledge of ancient Christian art as a guide for Russia's surviving icon-painting industry. Splitting his time between St. Petersburg and Yalta, Kondakov, from 1898 to 1900, discussed his plans with a wide circle of influential figures, including the writer Anton Chekhov, whose relatives on his maternal side had worked as icon painters not far from Palekh. Kondakov also cultivated new allies in the imperial bureaucracy, especially the powerful minister of finance Sergei Witte, with whom he arranged a number of meetings to discuss peasant icon painters.[71]

As a proponent of modernization and the son of a Baltic Lutheran, Witte was a surprising convert to the experts' cause. He condemned mystical tendencies at court and detested Sheremetev's reactionary tendencies. Later, in forced retirement, he called Sheremetev "one of the covert chiefs of the Black Hundreds," "a pillar of mindless conservatism," a person whom "everyone knows . . . is not completely normal, but . . . is generally believed to have a noble character." He does not say how he felt in 1900, when he backed Sheremetev's efforts to resurrect Russian icon painting.[72]

Witte was by all accounts a devout Orthodox Christian. If he condemned the persecution of non-Russian nationalities, he also believed in the existence of "a pure Russian type, pure as a result of blood and history." Witte believed these Russians lived primarily in Russia's north, where geographical isolation and links with Old Belief helped them retain their purity. When he traveled to Murmansk in 1894 to research the development of industry and transportation in the region, he took along a young painter (A. A. Borisov) from the Academy of Arts, the son of a peasant who had learned icon painting at the Solovetskii monastery. Witte had earlier arranged Borisov's study at the Academy of Arts in St. Petersburg, thus encouraging his own synthesis of academic and folk-art traditions, much as the icon experts were contemplating in Palekh. Though Witte never said so directly, he seems to have viewed Orthodox culture as a kind of corrective to modernization. In the "pure Russians" of the north, Witte saw the promise of a new kind of cultural synthesis. While modern technique and science would buttress the imperial Russian state, a pre-Petrine ethos of monastic contemplation would protect Russia from the alienating effects of modern culture and its soulless cosmopolitan spirit.[73]

The emergence of Dmitrii Sipiagin as minister of internal affairs in the fall of 1899 provided another critical base of bureaucratic support for the icon experts. Sipiagin's appointment, Sheremetev wrote to Kondakov, "has significance for the question that interests us, or at any rate it is *very* promising." Indeed, it was promising, given the importance of personal relations in tsarist politics: Sipiagin's wife was Sheremetev's sister. In addition, icon painting presented another sphere of economic activity for the ever-expanding system of social control of the Ministry of Internal Affairs. Supporting worker claims against capitalist industrialists, the ministry advocated a policy of "police socialism," which attempted to incorporate the Russian working class into a traditional autocratic system. Until his assassination in April 1902, Sipiagin offered critical support for icon experts and their plans, countering resistance from other branches of the state, most notably the Holy Synod.[74]

By early 1900 many of the bureaucratic stars and planets thus seemed to be in perfect alignment. When Sheremetev scheduled a discussion on icon painting with the tsar on January 10, 1900, Georgievskii was ecstatic. Now, he proclaimed, they would vanquish "the ignorant kulaks and give the icon painters a decent wage and artistic leaders who can direct native forces and talents." After meeting with Sheremetev, the tsar arranged Kondakov's full membership in the Academy of Sciences, a mark of imperial favor, and asked for a chat with

Kondakov at Tsarskoe Selo. "One feels that our mission will be realized," wrote Sheremetev to Kondakov, who prepared for his presentation to the tsar by studying Georgievskii's 1895 report on icon painting.[75]

Sheremetev's hopes, however, were premature. When Kondakov traveled to Tsarskoe Selo on February 15, 1900, the tsar seemed distracted, having spent the entire morning receiving ministers.[76] Although disillusioned by the tsar's seeming indifference, Sheremetev and Kondakov continued working their contacts. Georgievskii sent two of the worst examples of shoddy icon painting he could find to the tsar's wife, "a person who respects and honors everything genuinely NATIONAL." These icons, he hoped, would show "what a Russian person worships and the degree of impudence and blasphemy of which the Russian kulak is capable for the sake of profit."[77] Meanwhile, Sheremetev noted the importance of publishing a piece in the Society of Lovers of Ancient Literature that would lay out the dangers facing icon painting and the necessary measures "for an explanation of the problem for certain persons not well versed in this matter but very highly placed." Soon after, the newspaper *Sankt Peterburgskie vedomosti* predicted the imminent demise of peasant icon painting and called for immediate state measures against the supposed invasion of "Jewish factory-produced [icons]." Kondakov presented Witte with a budget for a proposed committee to open new icon schools in the icon-painting villages and to censor icon production. To bolster their case, Sheremetev and Kondakov embarked on a fact-finding mission to the heartland of Russian icon painting in June 1900—a trip originally planned the previous year but cancelled due to inclement weather.[78]

STORM CLOUDS OVER PALEKH

As luck would have it, the weather again refused to cooperate, but Kondakov and Sheremetev could ill afford to delay their trip. Constant rain encouraged a dark mood. "The same deeply depressing view of mounds of dirt, with stagnant water and deep pools, logs and planks, presented itself in Kholui and Palekh," wrote Kondakov. To make the roads momentarily passable, the locals added more branches and garbage to the muck, which only expanded the growing morass. The mud stopped Kondakov's carriage in the middle of Palekh, and the experts had to step gingerly from their vehicle and proceed on foot through the backyards of homes, finally finding safe haven, as Georgievskii had done six years earlier, in the village's central cathedral. Disgusted, Kondakov remarked that the deeply ingrained habit of putting things off, or of "philosophically blaming it on the weather," had conquered the will to pave.[79]

Echoing Georgievskii's earlier findings, Kondakov blamed "the famous distrust of the icon painters" for the group's inability to gather precise statistics on the state of icon painting. Palekh's studio owners "lied" to tax inspectors and presented themselves as "master craftsmen icon painters" rather than "industrialists-traders in icons." Kondakov lumped the Safonov studio into "the camp of the kulak" *(kulachestvo)*, calling Safonov an "archaeological monster," whose restorations were a "pogrom of ancient monuments" and an "imitation of ancientness."[80]

Most offensive, however, was the recent emergence of French companies Jacquot and Bonnaker in the Russian icon market (which Sheremetev in October 1900 referred to as "the Israelite invasion"). Specialists in the production of tin cans for shoe polish, perfume, and other products, the firms adapted their technology for stamping out high-quality images on tin plates. Since the beginning of the 1890s, their icon operations, based in St. Petersburg, worked with the blessing of the Holy Synod and the Ministry of Finance. For the Holy Synod, modern techniques were an ideal way to spread canonically correct images among the population. For the experts, these techniques spelled "the death of Russian iconography."[81]

The conclusion of Kondakov's report doubled as a list of recommendations. Just as the people's daily bread was subject to inspection and control, so, too, should its spiritual sustenance be examined and approved. All mechanical and foreign production of icons should be outlawed. Native producers should receive access to credit and favorable rail tariffs. Teachers trained at the academy should teach the proper techniques of painting in new icon schools in each of the villages. The state should set up icon stores with a broad variety of icons done honestly, in good taste, "and not of an industrial character." Permanent exhibits of icons should educate the public about the proper kinds of icons to worship and spread an appreciation of authentic iconography in urban centers. Finally, the tsar should extend his direct patronage to the icon painters in order to restore "the glorious period" of iconography in the pre-Petrine period.[82]

Meanwhile, Nikolai Safonov, the patriarch of the Safonov studio, angrily rejected charges that he was monopolizing icon production in Palekh. "It is just the opposite," he wrote in a letter to Sheremetev after reading Kondakov's report. He rightly noted that many of his former employees now operated their own studios and had become competitors of his business. As for Kondakov's critique of Palekh's restorations, Safonov said special commissions of academics and state officials had overseen Safonov's work. "One can draw all sorts of conclusions," he added, "since every person has his personal tastes and convictions." The guiding role of archaeologists, however, guaranteed the "correctness" of his studio's restoration work. It was therefore a pity that Kondakov's views "in so many ways depart from reality." The professor's contacts were either unfamiliar with Palekh or were "driven by other motives." He offered to document his claims, noting that during Kondakov's trip to the village, "I was not in town and was not forewarned of the time of your visit."[83]

Ignoring Safonov's complaints, the experts strengthened their case with petitions from groups of icon painters in each of the three villages, to be presented personally by Sheremetev to Nicholas II. In the manner of the Muscovite period, the petitions presented "the people" as supplicants before the tsar, appealing to his wisdom to intervene on their behalf. The petitions contained two requests—that the tsar ban all mechanized and foreign icon production and that the state establish icon-painting schools in the villages authorized to produce icons for sale. As educational institutions, the proposed schools would be exempt from taxes. "And we icon painters," went a draft of the petition written by Georgievskii, "were forgotten and deprived of the blessings of enlightenment, which facilitates development and improvement. Lacking the ability to give our children a decent education, we had to teach icon painting to them ourselves, without the aid of schools in our own studios."[84]

Much to Georgievskii's dismay, the Palekh studio owners, led by the Safonovs, rejected the petition written by Georgievskii. In its place they offered their own amended version. The amended petition supported the proposed ban of machine-made icons, since Palekh studios specialized in handmade icons. But it struck out language requesting an icon school, which Palekh studio owners reasonably feared as state-sponsored competition. It also asked the state to treat Palekh's icon studios as "educational" institutions rather than "industrial" enterprises. The clever request, which was simply ignored, would have exempted the private studios from taxation as a business enterprise.[85]

If Sheremetev was infuriated by the audacity of the Palekhians, he nonetheless had gained the tsar's attention with Kondakov's report. On February 28, 1901, he and Kondakov met the tsar at Tsarskoe Selo, also in the billiard room, and placed offending tin icons from Jacquot and Bonnaker on the playing table. "Above all we must get rid of these," said the tsar angrily, waving his index finger at the offending images. "The Greek style must be supported." Greatly pleased and concerned by the presentation of petitions from the icon painters (the tsar seemed not to notice the deficiencies of the Palekh petition), he agreed to form a special committee to oversee icon production in the realm, with Kondakov and Sheremetev in charge. The tsar bid adieu to the two, who then rushed to Sipiagin's office to report the news. "Now," said Sheremetev triumphantly, "people will treat us differently."[86]

Shortly after the tsar's decision to create a new committee, Kondakov visited Grand Duke Konstantin Konstantinovich Romanov, a notorious anti-Semite (as was the tsar himself), who offered his congratulations. "I'm ecstatic," Kondakov reported the grand duke as saying. "We'll force out the kikes. They're running for cover in the Holy Synod." The comment reflected the bizarre notion that Jews who had converted to Orthodoxy had somehow come to control the Holy Synod. At least in the grand duke's view, the formation of the icon committee was thus a key moment in purging "Jewish" influences from within the Orthodox Church's bureaucracy.[87]

Under the personal "tutelage" (*popichitel'stvo*) of the tsar, the committee carried the official name Committee for the Tutelage of Russian Icon Painting,

Established by His Majesty. It was a non-ministerial committee, meaning that although it had representation from many major ministries (not, however, the Holy Synod, which refused to participate), it answered directly to the tsar.[88] The conservative press hailed formation of the committee as a decisive event in Russia's national rebirth. Orthodoxy, declared one journalist, was the foundation of Russian life. "Without it Russia would lose its independent character and our people would turn into a herd of western Europeans or Asiatics." Another journalist proclaimed: "By preserving the icon we are protecting Orthodoxy; by preserving Orthodoxy, we are strengthening the keystone supporting the Russian state." He urged the committee to move quickly to "purge this field of national art of all the garbage created by open and hidden enemies of Orthodoxy."[89]

CHAPTER THREE

Palekhians into Russians, 1901–1918

Broader currents in turn-of-the-century Russia and Europe profoundly influenced the Committee for the Tutelage of Russian Icon Painting. Religious belief, nationalism, consumerism, and modernism were all vested in the Russian icon, making it a powerful symbol of Russian culture and society, and of the profound changes Russian society was undergoing.[1] Under the spell of the modernist vogue for the primitive and irrational, many Russian elites sought nonrealistic and symbolic modes of representation, of which the icon seemed the quintessential representation. As in Europe, reactions against realist and utilitarian doctrines stimulated curiosity in exotic folk practices, which became the subject of avant-garde as well as traditional artistic creativity. Steeped in the aesthetics of the so-called Silver Age of Russian culture, many educated Russians viewed art as an agent of social and personal regeneration, a view that complemented the religious conception of icons as reflections of the Holy Spirit. The praise of Russian icons by prominent artists from the West, especially the French impressionists, further legitimized Russia's growing reputation as the last of Europe's primitives. Icons were thus consumer items, collectibles, national treasures, objects of worship, and objets d'art.[2]

It was in this climate that Tsar Nicholas II created the new icon committee. In the committee's view, the fragmentation of traditional society and culture, fueled by the forces of capitalist consumerism, had endangered sociocultural cohesiveness. To restore social harmony, the committee's program included a state-managed system of icon painting in which masters from Palekh and elsewhere would follow the dictates of an authentic Russian style and canon. The committee's retrospective utopia drew upon idealized notions of pre-Petrine Russia. In that utopia, the estates of ancient Rus' labored selflessly and in the spirit of collective endeavor *(sobornost')*, inspired by a fervent desire to serve the ruling dynasty and its autocratic ruler. "For so many decades," said Kondakov, the committee's chief administrator, "we have affirmed the harmful break of Russian educated society with the people. Here is a chance to unite the two diverging sides in a common endeavor, and having begun to take care of the people's needs, to set on its feet a general national mission."[3]

That national mission, it should be noted, did not offer equal rights and powers. While the peasant traditions of icon painting became a source of political legitimacy for elites, the peasants who followed these traditions did not receive a voice in their own affairs. The privileged estates, especially the tsar's servitors and advisors, would now dictate the authentic forms that national aesthetic traditions should follow. The committee's politics were therefore nominally populist, since they privileged traditions preserved by the "people." But they remained deeply elitist, because they rejected the idea of a political nation of free and equal citizens to replace the tsarist hierarchy of privileged estates and monarchical power.

At the same time, the committee's vision bore the mark of a more modern age. The committee attempted to give the peasant masters the tools and techniques of the modern artist—to bring them the blessings of enlightenment. These tools, in the committee's view, would transform the masters into creative individuals and personalities, along the lines of academician artists such as Viktor Vasnetsov, who was the committee's model Russian artist. A journalist from Vladimir commented: "It wasn't our 'Suzdal god-daubers' who brought icon painting and church art to such a state of decline; rather, it was our Russian lack of culture and national poverty that created god-daubers in the first place." The committee must therefore protect sacred national tradition (and hence "the people") against capitalism, yet give Palekh decent health care, roads, and educational institutions. Icon painters must follow ancient Byzantine and Russian models, yet conversely express themselves as creative artists. Palekh, in short, must be both modernized and de-modernized. Thus it mirrored the broader dilemma of the regime itself, which aimed both to resurrect Muscovy and to create modern factories, schools, cities, and armies.[4] In transforming the Palekhians into Russians, the regime was torn between the Charybdis of perceived tradition and the Scylla of modern European civilization. In the final analysis, the tsarist system was unable to navigate this treacherous part of Russia's journey into the twentieth century.

A CONSERVATIVE UTOPIA

Emboldened by the tsar's enthusiastic pledge of support in 1901, Sheremetev and Kondakov performed a kind of triage on the nation's holy traditions. Hoping to relieve competitive pressures on the peasant masters, they sought an immediate ban on all foreign and machine-made icons. Acceptance of the proposed ban, however, required more than the tsar's signature. The many bureaucracies involved also had to agree, including the Holy Synod (which had originally allowed the mechanized production of icons by foreigners in the early 1890s) and the Ministry of Finance (which received tax revenue from the sales of machine-made icons). The committee had no choice but to wait for the proposed ban to go out to these ministries and then to await their response.

In the meantime, the committee began planning icon-painting schools in Palekh, Kholui, and Mstera to replace the private system of apprenticeship. In these schools students would fill orders for state and church customers and eventually, it was hoped, for all icon consumers. The committee also intended to hire masters away from private studios and include them in a new system of cooperatives. The committee called these cooperatives artels, in deference to the communal form of labor that supposedly distinguished Russia from the West. Committee stores in Moscow, St. Petersburg, and Kiev would distribute icon orders to this growing network of state-supervised production brigades.

Georgievskii hoped that the committee's alternative system of production and distribution would ultimately "liberate the master icon painters from [native] exploiter-kulaks, the industrialists of the Safonov ilk." A 1901 committee report on Safonov's large branch operations in Ukraine called Safonov a "kulak" who had a rapacious grip on the icon business in Russia and especially in Ukraine, on the sensitive border with Catholic lands. Partly to counter Safonov's Ukrainian operation, and the growing influence of Catholic imagery in the south, the committee planned an additional icon-painting school and shop in Borisovka (about eighty kilometers north of Kharkov).[5]

In each of the committee schools, a graduate of the St. Petersburg Academy of Arts held the position of director. He taught drawing, true perspective, and anatomy. Under him served two teachers of icon painting, chosen from among local masters, who taught the techniques of traditional icon painting. One was a *lichnik* and the other a *dolichnik*. Adherence to a set canon of sacred images, passed down from the beginnings of Christian worship, was meant to circumscribe creative urges within a tradition of collective authorship and piety. To ensure that students understood the significance of the images they painted, the committee schools planned to hire a teacher of church history from the ecclesiastical estate.[6]

The troika of academician directors, folk-icon painters, and the ecclesiastical estate symbolized the committee's hoped-for regeneration of the Russian nation. Absent from this new community were Palekh's icon-studio owners. It was a telling omission. Excluded from administration of the new schools, merchants and traders were by extension banished from the committee's national mission.

Since the committee was taking over the icon-painting schools already established by the Aleksandr Nevskii Brotherhood in Mstera and Kholui in the 1880s, it focused mostly on Palekh. The committee pursued a carrot-and-stick approach, attacking the private system of production in Palekh and promising state patronage for all who supported its efforts. Kondakov summed up the main strategy for penetrating the village. The committee, he noted, should play "Safonov against his [local] enemies."[7]

At first, the attempt to divide and conquer yielded few results, since the Safonov studio was the most powerful economic and political power in the village. If a Palekh master crossed Safonov, he risked exclusion from the icon-painting profession. Social and class tensions also thwarted committee efforts. Many Palekhians were offended by the habit of the intelligentsia (and the committee) of referring to peasant icon-painting masters as "god-daubers" who lacked the most basic training in art and church archaeology. Finally, the studio owners feared the committee school would deprive them of apprentices and take away their business.[8]

Stymied by local resistance, it took a year of negotiations (until April 1902) for the committee to find a Palekhian (the Belousov studio, Safonov's main competitor) willing to rent them a building. The building leased by Belousov, little more than a cramped shack, could barely accommodate a dozen students and was hardly the oasis of culture that the committee had promised its schools would be. From the start, the school faced "serious resistance." Banding together, the studio owners

> took all possible measures to convince the master icon painters that an icon school was not needed for them, that they were the best icon painters and they knew themselves how to teach their children, that, finally, the school that the committee wanted to open could harm the local industry, teaching secular painting rather than icon painting. It was not easy for the committee to convince the local population of its mistakes and explain that all the measures of the committee were directed exclusively for raising . . . ancient-Russian icon painting to the highest possible level, and not toward imposing "academic" painting.[9]

To make matters worse, months after formation of the icon committee in March 1901, the Palekhians, unlike their colleagues in nearby Mstera and Kholui, had still not produced a petition explicitly asking for a new icon school. The petition debacle violated a central pretense behind the committee's formation, namely, that the peasant masters themselves had actually requested the tsar's help in overcoming their benightedness. The committee therefore scrambled to secure a new petition from Palekh, which it finally received in November 1901, eight months after the committee's formation. Palekh's new petition, like the previous one penned by Palekh before the committee's creation, nonetheless fell far short of the draft crafted by Georgievskii. In no uncertain terms, the petition rejected the main rationale for the schools—that Palekh was part of the supposed decline *(upadok)* of icon painting. "Among our master icon painters," noted the new petition, "icon production did not weaken and fall to a low level." Equally offensive for the experts, the revised petition again requested that the government remove classification of the private studios as "industrial enterprises," so that their tax burden could be eliminated. The committee simply ignored the latter request. Saving icon painting was one thing; reducing tax obligations for kulaks quite another.[10]

As specified in the charter for the committee schools, a graduate from the Academy of Arts, E. I. Stiagov, accepted the position of director of the Palekh school. Father Nikolai Chikhachev, another Safonov enemy and the top priest in the village, was hired to teach church history and doctrine. Notorious in Palekh for his business acumen, Chikhachev eagerly played the role of middle-man between committee orders and local icon painters—and no doubt took a cut for himself.[11] At the same time, he became the central informant for committee members back in St. Petersburg.

In the meantime, the first cohort of twenty-three students came primarily from the families of masters who had been let go by the Safonov studio and thus had a gripe with the leading opponent of the icon committee's school. Finding local icon painters to work as teachers in the new school was equally challenging. Committee members wanted the best local masters, so they had to compete with wages paid by the private sector.[12] The two locals who eventually took the job in Palekh treated the job as an opportunity for personal enrichment, steering committee orders to their own private business and using their students as free labor.

With its apparatus finally in place by June of 1902, the committee marked the opening of the school in Palekh as the birth of a new era in Russian icon painting. Reports on the school's official opening said the school would break down the dependence of masters on "the foremen" of the private icon studios. The private studio system, it claimed, had divided the masters into *lichniki* and *dolichniki* to prevent them from becoming "independent master icon painters." "Everything here is reduced to the mechanical exercise of slavish copying," a kind of paint-by-numbers approach that prevented masters from "acquiring the knowledge of icon painting."[13]

Father Chikhachev played the role of chief choreographer for the school's official opening. On the morning of the ceremonial event, he gathered the twenty-three students in the new school. To freshen the cramped quarters, he had the children scatter fragrant flowers and garlands inside and outside the building. Promptly at 8 a.m., church bells accompanied the marching of the students to the town's central cathedral, followed by parents and other participants, including Georgievskii and the district and village elders. After an elaborate service and blessing of the students, the entire group performed the ceremonial procession from the church to the school *(krestnyi khod),* carrying the most valuable icons from the cathedral. Once the group assembled in the cramped studio, Chikhachev explained the purpose of the new school. The committee would teach students the correct models of church art, to which "barely literate rural icon painters" formerly had no access. Whereas Chikhachev in his first meeting with Georgievskii in 1894 had proudly cited praise of Palekh as a "people's academy" expressed by the expert Filimonov, the priest now chose a different quote from the venerable dean of church archaeology. When the Palekhians were painting the Palace of Facets for the coronation of Alexander III, Filimonov supposedly quipped: "Oh, brothers, if only I could attach my head to your hands, imagine the wonderful things we could do!" Chikhachev added that "our homegrown icon painters" had little reason to be so proud of their images, based as they were on "suspect models or . . . lithographic works not always of an Orthodox character."[14]

Georgievskii then gave the keynote speech. He began with the threat posed by foreign producers of machine-made icons, promising that beginning January 1, 1903, all machine-made icons in Russia would be banned by the Holy Synod. He proceeded to speak about icon painting's domestic enemies, those local residents who had resisted the opening of the school, who wanted to keep the masters in a state of "semi-darkness."

> These people frightened you with all kinds of terrifying stories, just to get you not to support the school. They told you the school was not needed, that you are the best masters on earth, that you can teach your own children, that perhaps schools are needed in Mstera and Kholui, but not here. They told you that an artist-teacher will not teach icon painting and that icon painting itself could be destroyed by the school. . . . Time will tell how evil and fallacious were these rumors and innuendo.[15]

Citing the 1551 Stoglav, he commanded the students to lead a clean life and to accept their calling as holy. After another round of prayers, the students each received a Bible and were sprinkled with holy water. The assembled crowd carried the icons back to the church, accompanied by another prolonged ringing of bells and more prayers. A select group then gathered at Chikhachev's house for a feast that lasted until four in the afternoon, and many toasts were made to tsar and empire.[16]

Celebrations notwithstanding, the committee's ambitions far outstripped available resources, the perennial bane of modernizing Russia. On opening day, the school had precious few teaching materials or art supplies. Chikhachev wrote to Georgievskii that "such a position, given the description of the opening of the school" would inspire "a devilish smile and ironic comments . . . among those who do not wish us well." Four months after the Palekh school's opening, the director of the committee schools remarked to Georgievskii, "You asked me to report what the locals are saying about the school. To your face they say it is a good thing, and what they say behind my back, who knows."[17]

Beyond material obstacles, the committee also faced serious pedagogical challenges. The committee struggled with a fundamentally contradictory urge to combine the methods and techniques of traditional icon painting with a pedagogical program modeled on the Academy of Arts. The committee member N. V. Sultanov (an architect) expressed this contradiction in a report to the committee in January 1902. Peasant icon painters, he noted, "preserved the ancient traditions," and their work "was devoid of any individual interpretation." Their icons were "stamped with a hieratic character," and the images provided sustenance to the people like "mother's milk." Nonetheless, the work of the peasant icon painter had numerous "deficiencies," including "the incorrectness of drawing and excessive conditional perspective, which acts in an unpleasant manner on the modern eye." The icons also contained "vulgar archaeological anachronisms," using backgrounds from Russian architecture in the representation of early church fathers or classical architecture as a backdrop for Russian saints. The schools, concluded Sultanov, must therefore combine training in church archaeology and secular artistic technique with the demands of "hieratic" art, a goal that Georgievskii, many years later, admitted "did not promise great success."[18]

Indeed, the committee's determination to teach academic techniques of painting encouraged enrollment by students who had little desire to continue as icon painters. Many Palekhians imagined their future as famous urban artists, and they saw the committee's icon school as a stepping stone to the secular art world of Moscow and St. Petersburg. The committee thus fostered a flight from the profession it was trying to preserve.

In the meantime, responses to the committee proposal to ban machine-made icons had arrived in February 1903. Shockingly for the committee, the *ober-prokuror,* Pobedonostsev, endorsed the rights of foreign capitalist producers and the limits of state control. Outlawing machine-produced images, he reported, would deny cheap images for the masses, force production underground, and put many icon traders and workers out of jobs. Furthermore, the state was not "in a position to enact surveillance at every step. . . . It is impossible for the police to be everywhere and follow all trade." An important subtext in such complaints was the church's resistance to secular and academic control over a previously sacred sphere. The ministry of finance also rejected the proposed ban on the grounds that it violated the rights of foreign producers and threatened tax revenues.[19]

Triumphantly, the producers of machine-made icons, the French companies Jacquot and Bonnaker, placed ads in Russian newspapers declaring that their icons had the endorsement of the Holy Synod. An outraged Georgievskii, citing the ads, condemned the "limp people" who had been unable to act against the "brazen foreigners" who were "spreading their Jewish manufactures" and "seizing everything and penetrating everywhere."[20]

Given the committee's promise to eliminate competition from foreign producers of machine-made icons (the one point on which all Palekhians agreed), the failure of the proposed ban certainly did not inspire confidence. Nor did the committee's pledge to make the new icon school in Palekh a model of culture and civilization in the countryside. In 1903 the school lacked sufficient firewood for heating, was dirty and cramped, and still was desperately short of art supplies. Students sat almost continuously from eight in the morning until seven at night, eating their lunch at their desks. "It is inhumane to leave children all day in suffocating conditions," remarked one committee member. To curious visitors who wanted to see the fruits of the committee's efforts, the school's administrators had to plead that the conditions were only temporary and would soon improve (they did not). The committee's opponents, according to Chikhachev, had a field day ridiculing the school.[21]

Tensions quickly flared, as parents of committee school students began to wonder about the future employability of their children. To assuage concerns, Georgievskii in late 1903 suggested that Kondakov might hold a public meeting of the icon committee in one of the three villages. Kondakov dismissed the idea out of hand. "From [the locals] we won't hear anything but the typical Russian complaints about everything under the sun. There is nothing we could learn from them." Two weeks later, in another letter to Georgievskii, he said that the committee's biggest challenge was to force the icon-painting villages "to fight with their own inertia."[22]

Plans for a system of state-coordinated icon cooperatives faced an equally inauspicious beginning. Both within and outside the schools, the committee planned to patronize a network of icon-painting artels. However, the plan received weak support from ecclesiastical authorities, who preferred to place orders with private producers. Moreover, the committee gave little thought to how orders should be distributed—to the artels attached to the schools or to other artels it was also encouraging in the broader community? Should these other artels work exclusively for the committee or be permitted to work on the side? Could their members simultaneously receive salaries working for the private studios?[23]

The lack of clarity in committee business operations sowed local doubts about the committee's motives. A committee report from August 1903 was concerned that students were spending too much time working on orders directed through the committee and not enough time learning drawing and the other subjects taught at the school. Students had become cheap sources of labor for their own icon teachers at the school, painting icons virtually for free. Locally hired icon teachers, especially M. P. Parilov in Palekh, bypassed the school completely and took the most lucrative orders for themselves, facts that were widely known in the village. By 1906, Parilov arranged with the business manager of the icon committee in St. Petersburg (who was also a Palekhian!) to steer committee orders to his private studio. His private studio thus thrived, using the free labor of students to fulfill such lucrative orders purloined from the icon-committee network. Eventually, Parilov gave up teaching at the school altogether, devoting himself full-time to his growing icon business, which had the committee's unwitting patronage to thank for its success.[24]

While the mixing of academic and business pursuits compromised the school in the eyes of many locals, it also raised concerns among the school directors. A focus on trade, complained one school director, introduced into the schools "a commercial orientation dangerous for children." Rather than creating a cathedral of God, the committee seemed to be transforming its schools into temples of commerce. Students were acquiring "undesirable tendencies from a moral point of view." Monetary considerations promoted "a destructive atmosphere in the society of children."[25]

In the meantime, the outbreak of war with Japan, and the political crisis the war generated, only widened the gap between the committee's aims and the resources and political will with which to achieve them.[26] As the "little, victorious war"[27] commenced in 1904, Nicholas distributed icons to soldiers headed for the Far East theater. General M. I. Dragomirov, in response to the icon distributions, supposedly remarked: "We were answering Japanese bullets with icons." True or not, the story gained wide currency in elite circles, where icons were now more than banners of Holy Russianness; they also symbolized Russia's military ineptness and technological backwardness.[28]

The committee's operations ground to a halt as the disastrous war fomented revolution. Kondakov left St. Petersburg, and fellow committee members had no idea where he was and when he would return. Sheremetev retreated to his country estate in October 1905. Under the present circumstances, he wrote, little "movement" in the committee's goals could be expected. To console himself, he asked Georgievskii to hire icon painters in Palekh to paint an iconostasis for the church at his country estate, "something in the manner of the beginning of the seventeenth century, very canonical and without the slightest bit of Italianness [ital'ianshchina]."[29]

Back in Palekh, long-standing tensions between the academically trained artists/directors of the schools and the teachers of church history and canon had erupted into what one committee informant called a "war." The teachers of church canon and history chafed at the domineering attitude of the directors and the downgrading of icon painting in favor of more conventional academic approaches to art and drawing.[30] Things went from bad to worse as the first cohort of graduates from the Palekh school received the title of "master icon painter" in the summer of 1906. The committee lacked the resources to support graduates in artels, and the private icon-studio owners refused to hire them, claiming they were unqualified. "We were distraught," remembered one graduate. "On the one hand the private studios boycotted us, and on the other we did not see an application for the traditional icon painting we had been taught." Indeed, many Palekh studios, in response to market demand, had begun painting in a more realistic manner. Because graduates of the committee's school could not find work either in Palekh or in the numerous icon shops run by Palekhians outside Palekh, many masters gave up the profession or moved into secular art. "Thus ended [the program] for the first group of graduates," remembered one Palekh alumnus. He received the title "master icon painter" and immediately became unemployed. "Almost all of us were forced to find work in other cities."[31]

The parents of some students responded by asking that the curriculum of the school be expanded to include the more modern style practiced in many of Palekh's studios.[32] They also wanted the school to downgrade the teaching of theoretical issues regarding the history and practice of religious and secular art. Georgievskii was livid:

> What can our student-masters do in such a situation? Accept bitter necessity and abandon everything that the school gave them . . . to work the way the local market demands? This is sad, offensive, and ridiculous. What kind of school is it that teaches something that one then has to abandon . . . ? And what of the position of the deceived parents, who gave away their children to a profession and received in return unemployed youth who sponge off them? Funny also are the comments of those insolent jokers who said enough already with a school that teaches poor illiterate icon painters how to draw correctly for free, at the expense of the state treasury, and yet they have to find work themselves.[33]

Reflecting a growing resentment after the 1905 revolution, when the gentry attempted to reform peasant life, parents in 1906 demanded the right to participate in a permanent advisory committee in each of the schools. The committee reluctantly granted the latter request, although it specified that the parents' committee, consisting of three elected locals, could not issue binding resolutions. As Georgievskii put it: "If we give them a binding vote, then they'll think they are the bosses and ruin everything."[34]

While the Palekhians earlier had resisted sending petitions to the tsar, the 1905 revolution, and a deepening economic crisis, changed Palekh's attitude, as it did that of thousands of other Russian peasant communities, who deluged the tsar with petitions after the October 1905 manifesto in which he reluctantly granted limited representative government. Bypassing the committee, a group of Palekhians sent requests directly to Nicholas II demanding an end to machine-made icons. Once again, the tsar promised to outlaw such icons (as he had in 1901), instructing the committee to come up with measures to lead the battle. And once again, the committee was unable to convince other ministries—not to mention emerging representative institutions—to follow the tsar's command. Given the downturn in the icon market, the committee thus missed a key opportunity to win potential local allies.[35]

Strapped for cash, and unable to enact its proposed ban on machine-made icons, the committee contemplated its own mechanized icon production plant in Moscow. To reduce the blasphemous nature of the plan, which it developed in strict confidence (or so it thought), the committee aimed to produce holy images on wood rather than tin. Nonetheless, word of the plan spread to the icon-painting villages in late 1906, where rumors affirmed that the committee was now going into direct competition with local producers. "The rumors emanating from the cradle of icon painting are not good," wrote D. K. Trenev, a committee participant, in a letter to Kondakov. Many parents of students in the school had stopped sending their children to classes. "A similar relationship is forming between the committee and the icon painters it is protecting [as between] the government and . . . liberal society," wrote Trenev. The committee must understand "the growing antipathy . . . on the part of a segment of Russian rural society." Trenev urged a democratization of the schools, including a parental school board empowered to determine curriculum and to elect the school's teachers. "I urge you to strike while the iron is hot!"[36]

Sheremetev, a committed opponent of any assault on autocratic power, ignored the advice even as he lamented the seeming helplessness of the entire imperial edifice. The state, he wrote the architect Sultanov in August 1906, "does not inspire confidence." Compounding a constant lurching from left to right was "a complete misunderstanding of the national spirit, a complete disrespect for history, a complete ignorance of the basic issues of church life." Only a miracle, he believed, could "save Russia from destruction." Two months later, Sheremetev received what he called "an unpleasant surprise": the iconostasis he had ordered through Georgievskii had arrived from Palekh. "I got modern icons, ruddy-cheeked and saccharine. . . . I have received nothing for all my efforts! With us the simplest things are so difficult. I would not have expected such a thing from the Palekhians. To whom shall I turn now?"[37]

By February 1907, Sheremetev no longer believed that "when lightning strikes the muzhik crosses himself." The state, he said, was "neither constitutional nor autocratic—but decadent and despotic—in a Venetian manner." He visited the Kremlin in April 1907 and noticed that the buildings were dirty and disheveled, a "disgusting" reflection of "the attitudes and directions of modernity."[38]

As if to prove Sheremetev's fears of a godless revolutionary peasantry, a number of Palekhians became active revolutionaries. Many had emerged from the icon committee's school and its first group of graduates in 1906. One such graduate was Aleksandr Vitsyn, whom the local studios refused to hire. He chopped firewood for a living by day and conducted revolutionary terror by night. He cultivated a simmering resentment of the Safonov studio and attracted a following of unemployed masters. Sometime in 1907, the group torched the warehouses of the Safonov and Karovaikov studios and unsuccessfully attempted to assassinate the son of Nikolai Mikhailovich Safonov, its chief foreman. Palekh's would-be revolutionaries splattered graffiti on the entrance of the village's main cathedral, announcing their intention "to hang all the priests, landowners, and the Tsar." On the wall of the state-run liquor store, the group wrote: "Down with the Tsar-winetrader!" The police apparently had little trouble rounding up and arresting the organization's ringleaders, who served a number of years in the Vladimir prison. Many members of the group survived into the Soviet era and became committed servants of Bolshevik power.[39]

In May 1907, Kondakov had had enough. While he lamented the state's lack of commitment to his plans he detested the weather in St. Petersburg, which greatly aggravated his tuberculosis. At his own request, he was relieved of his duties running the committee in the summer of 1907. He spent most of the rest of his time abroad or in Yalta conducting research for the committee's icon style manuals, leaving the day-to-day operation of the committee to Georgievskii.[40]

In dire need of resources to help its graduates, the committee unsuccessfully appealed for more money to the newest player in Russian politics: the Russian Duma. In its budget request in 1909, the committee said, "it is unthinkable to leave [the graduates] to the whim of fate." Throwing them "into the arms of large icon producer-industrialists," would be even worse, subjecting them to "merciless exploitation" in which their "artistic education . . . in correct icon painting" would be a complete waste.[41]

By 1910, the committee admitted that the artels attached to the schools had failed; the teachers were taking all the orders for themselves. "The fate of artels formed outside the schools is no less sad," said one report to the Duma, blaming the failure on the insurmountable obstacle of competing with large private studios, which took all the best business. In the end, the effort only "provided much bitterness and material losses" for those who had sided with the committee.[42]

Amidst the committee's many disappointments, Sheremetev had one last hope: he believed the *podlinnik,* the style manual and canonical guide for icon painters that had fascinated icon experts since the 1850s, could save the committee's program. Along with the attempt to outlaw machine-made icons and create a state-run system of icon painting and training, a newly compiled style manual constituted the final plank in the committee's program for saving Russian icon painting.[43]

AUTHENTICALLY RUSSIAN

Although motivated by a desire to enforce tradition, the committee's style manual was a very modern phenomenon. The committee wanted to transfer control of icon painting from peasant and private producers to the care of experts.[44] To achieve this goal, Kondakov used his expertise to determine the origins and cultural context of holy images, the various styles that emerged over the centuries, and the stylistic and chronological boundaries of Russian Orthodox iconography. Reinterpreted and codified through the prism of science, the newly vetted traditions, like finely tuned machine tools, would guide worker/icon painters in the committee schools, much as the new science of management in the West aimed to transfer control over the work process from laborers to managers.[45] Kondakov's images, compiled in a handbook for icon painters, would thus help to propagate authentically Russian traditions, and in the process define and preserve Russia's national distinctiveness.

In preparation for publication of the first volume of the *podlinnik* on the iconography of Christ, the committee in 1902 clarified the stylistic parameters of Russian authenticity. What were the historical roots of the Russian icon-painting style? In which periods of Russian history had the style developed and matured and at what point had these traditions become corrupted? To answer these questions, the committee focused on icon painting at the tsar's court in the seventeenth century, which the committee believed represented the most modern example of truly Russian icon painting. "The ancient *friaz'*," noted a committee report, "came to us from Italy at a time when individual creativity had not yet torn away from the understanding of the collective principle *[sobornoe nachalo]*." By way of contrast, "pseudo-classicism" and "artificial sentimentality" began to penetrate Russian church art in the eighteenth century, directly contradicting the demands of Russian Orthodox icon painting. Only the Old Believers had resisted the forces of modernization. They were "jealous defenders of pre-Nikonian antiquity" and thus protectors of a purer ancient style, especially in the icon-painting village of Mstera, which catered primarily to Old Believer consumers. The committee was much more skeptical of Palekh (whose artists were not Old Believers, at least openly). In the eighteenth century, according to a committee report, the Palekhians attempted to combine aspects of pre-Nikonian painting with western influences, thus continuing the trend of *friaz'* from the seventeenth century. However, their synthesis was purely mechanical and ventured too far into the terrain of Catholic and secular art.[46]

The process of collecting materials for the first volume of the *podlinnik* on the iconography of Christ reflected these general guidelines. When Kondakov began accumulating sources in 1901 and 1902, he focused on images produced during the rise of Muscovy from the cathedrals of the Kremlin, Novodevichy convent, and Holy Trinity monastery. Emphasizing Russia's Byzantine roots, Kondakov surveyed the collection of the Kiev Religious Academy, with its large collection of icons from Greece and the Near East. He selected tracings of icons that Filimonov had purchased forty years earlier at Moscow's antiquarian shops, which contained the *friaz'* style from the reign of the seventeenth-century tsar, Aleksei Mikhailovich. Finally, Kondakov analyzed the collections of Old Believer communities in Mstera and in Moscow (Rogozhskoe and Preobrazhenskoe), where he found "a few hundred valuable monuments of antiquity for reproduction" in the new style manual.[47] In stark contrast, the *podlinnik* did not contain a single image of a Palekh icon.

An essay by Kondakov accompanied the images in the new style manual. According to Kondakov, the fourth crusade's sacking of Constantinople marked a watershed in the decline of Christian authenticity in the West. During the conquest of Constantinople, the Venetians removed a number of craftsmen and their enterprises to Venice, including enamel, icon-painting, mosaic, and silk producers. Having absorbed these craft traditions, the Venetian "factories," like modern-day producers of tin-plated icons, flooded the

Orthodox world with "a mass of fake Eastern products, which did not permit the native production of those items in the East." Subsequently, Italians began assimilating the Byzantine iconography of Christ, but in the process they abandoned its guiding principles. Giotto's *Christ,* for instance, marked a first departure in the West from Byzantine iconographic types. "[W]hile exalting the real world [Giotto] at the same time diminished the timeless attraction of art to the representation of a higher, religious ideal." By the time of Rembrandt, the western image of Christ had "devolved into base vulgarity." Russia, meanwhile, followed the proper canonical dictates of authentic painting up through the end of the seventeenth century, at which time the same forces that had corrupted western art also emerged in Russia.[48]

Though ready for publication since 1903, a number of factors prevented the appearance of the first volume of the *podlinnik* until the spring of 1905. First and foremost was the privileged status given to Old Belief icons. Church censors objected to the presentation of icon models from the collections of Old Believers showing the sign of the cross with two rather than three fingers. Such images, noted the censor, "will greatly encourage" Old Believers "and be met by them with joy." Compared to fifty years earlier, however, when D. A. Rovinskii's references to Old Believer icons were censored, ecclesiastical authorities were more inclined to compromise. This was especially true after the events of 1905, when pressures to relieve remaining restrictions on Old Belief grew in ruling circles. Thus, when Kondakov's *podlinnik* on the imagery of Christ was finally published in April 1905, it contained many Old Believer icons, which now, much more than Palekh's *friazhskii* style, were considered to be the real thing.[49]

Curiously, the committee paid little attention to the actual mechanisms that might compel icon painters, not to mention their own schools, to follow the new *podlinnik*. Sheremetev felt the mere act of publishing the new style manual would "force people to take us seriously" and help "vanquish our enemies."[50] He believed peasant artists and private producers would be so impressed by the academic authority and elegance of the new definition of canonical icons that they could not possibly resist its strictures.

The committee's elitist impulses also limited the style manual's impact among the peasant masters. While the committee sent hundreds of free manuals to famous artists, academic societies, museums, and very important persons, it initially charged peasant icon painters for the book—albeit sometimes at a half-price discount. The style of Kondakov's introductory essay similarly contradicted the intended function of the style manual as a guide for icon painters with only a primary education. One church censor remarked that the work was less "a style manual than a scholarly examination. . . . For such a publication I have been designated the censor from the Holy Synod?"[51]

As with so much else the committee had been planning, war and the revolutionary events immediately overshadowed the publication. Sheremetev, in June 1905, thought it unfair that "such an important work . . . remains unnoticed by the entire press." To create the impression of a "sellout," the committee pitched the style manual to libraries and museums throughout Russia and even began marketing the publication in Europe, with an accompanying text in French. "The style manual will make a nice adornment," went one of the committee's marketing pitches.[52]

The committee, meanwhile, had counted on revenues from sales of the first style manual to finance the research and writing of subsequent volumes on the Mother of God and all the many revered saints of the Russian Orthodox world. By 1910, however, the committee had received only 2,112 rubles in sales (against a possible 25,000 rubles for all one thousand printed copies). Since each of the one thousand published copies cost 24 rubles to produce, the committee in 1910 carried a loss of nearly 22,000 rubles on the venture, and the state of Russian finances precluded the possibility of further subsidies.[53]

Kondakov's research strategy for the second volume, which was to identify the roots of the Russian Mother of God in comparison with its western representation, also presented ideological problems. Sheremetev believed that Kondakov had developed an unhealthy obsession with the art of the West. In late 1905, he commented to Georgievskii that Kondakov, "apparently is carried away with Roman representations of the Virgin Mary. I'm not sure it is advisable to give them preeminence over Eastern [images]." Indeed, Kondakov was so focused on comparisons of Russian iconography with its western counterpart that he spent far more time in the West than he actually did in the center of Russian icon painting in Palekh, Mstera, and Kholui. As an example, in the first three years of the committee he spent a total of less than twenty-four hours in Palekh, while in the same period he spent twenty-five days in Florence, Rome, Milan, and Venice for research on the style manual. In 1912, Kondakov was still in Rome researching the western Madonna, which he increasingly viewed (to the horror of many other experts) as a source of inspiration for the Russian Mother of God.[54]

Discouraged by the style manual's limited impact, which had become a kind of coffee-table book for icon aficionados, Sheremetev drew a new group of icon experts into the committee's plans. In 1912, the historian S. F. Platonov responded to Sheremetev's request for his views on the future of the style manual. Mocking the disappointing sales of the publication, Platonov condemned the committee's members as "monopolists" in the sphere of church archaeology.[55] Judging by Kondakov's essay, he wrote, one could only conclude that the study of icons had not developed since the work of Rovinskii in 1856. Amateurs and collectors continued to dominate the agenda of icon research, concealing the true secrets of icon painting so that the "`experts'" (in reference to the committee members, Platonov put this term in ironic quotes) could manipulate the lucrative antiquarian market. The committee, Platonov concluded, was holding back the science of church archaeology, playing into the hands of antiquarians who wanted knowledge of the icon's true nature to be "a commercial secret." Platonov's alternative program included the scientific registry of all existing icons, in which only professionally trained archaeologists could participate. He wanted the study of icons to become a bona fide science *(ikonovedenie)*, whose meaning would be defined exclusively by professionally trained academics—not by worshipers, church officials, amateur enthusiasts, and especially not by the icon painters themselves.[56] Sheremetev, to Kondakov's chagrin, endorsed Platonov's views. Facing increasing pressure from a new breed of icon experts, Kondakov reluctantly gave up control of the committee's style manual in 1912.[57]

An incident on the eve of the war illustrates the challenges faced by the committee, not only in producing the new style manual, but in forcing producers and consumers to follow its advice. The newspaper *Novoe vremia* in August 1913 published a long critique of the committee's icon store in St. Petersburg. Western nations, wrote the author, all had their own national saints, yet both the Russian church and state were indifferent to the issue, as was even the icon committee itself, whose style manuals had yet to progress beyond the imagery of Christ. By way of illustration, he went to the committee's icon shop in St. Petersburg in search of an icon of the medieval Russian warrior-saint Iaropolk, for whom his friend had named his son. "I thought that surely I would find what I needed there." To his surprise, an uninterested clerk at the store said they had no such icons and could not produce them. "It is not in the style manual," was the reply. When he asked for a St. Gleb, another quintessentially Russian saint, the evasive clerk said: "What about something in the Vasnetsov style," and offered him a photograph of Viktor Vasnetsov's image of the saint from the Vladimir cathedral of Kiev. When asked if the committee could get its icon painters to hand paint a copy of the Vasnetsov image, the clerk said he could not guarantee that the copy would be reproduced in exactly the same way. The author ended the story with a rhetorical question. "So in what does the tutelage of 'Russian icon painting' consist?"[58]

The committee's new chief operating officer at the time, the artist and architecture expert K. K. Romanov (1882–1940), took great exception to the article and published a response. Kondakov's work on the style manual, given the enormity of the undertaking and its "scientific significance," was not yet complete. It was not possible, furthermore, to simply point at an icon in Kondakov's style manual and have the peasant masters reproduce it, since few of those masters actually owned a copy of the publication. And when local icon painters did paint an image after the manner of Vasnetsov, elements of the local style and tradition would regrettably prevent an exact reproduction.[59]

Indicative of the committee's inability to control even its own system of production was another incident from 1913. As a result of orders from customers, images in the much detested "Palekh *friaz'*" began to appear in the icon committee's own shop in St. Petersburg. Rather than stocking up on more of the images, which were apparently popular, the committee issued a scathing report condemning the development as "pathetic."[60]

The committee's style manual thus had an extremely limited impact in the community of icon producers, to say nothing of the broader society. Unable to outlaw private producers, the committee had to devise noncoercive mechanisms that might encourage producers to follow its vision of truly authentic Russian imagery, and consumers, with pocketbooks in hand, to abide by it. In short, the committee had to muster the will to do the one thing it most detested: learn the rules of a market in which consumer demand was becoming increasingly diverse.[61] As the imperial era came to a close, the pull of consumers, rather than the push of tsarist committees and bureaucrats, was exerting the more decisive influence on modern Russian culture.

THE FINAL YEARS

If marketing and customer satisfaction were not the committee's forte, finding enemies was. Speaking before the Russian Duma in 1910, a committee representative concluded that nearly everyone had betrayed the sacred national traditions save one group: the Old Believers. True Russianness was now embodied by a group that the state had banished from the nation since the late seventeenth century. It was a curious reconciliation, inspired as much by narrow-mindedness as by a new spirit of toleration. Sheremetev, for instance, based his post-1905 political program on "a conciliatory, heartfelt, and careful rapprochement with adherents of the 'old rite,'" but he also urged a merciless "struggle with cosmopolitanism and indifference hiding under the cover of the word 'tolerance.'" In everything, Sheremetev once commented, "there are two currents. One purely Christian, from a native wellspring, ready to sympathize with a sincere desire for resurrection. The other is foreign, stinking of garlic. It is nourished from the international cesspools on which we greatly hope to pour fresh water from that pure, bright and silent well."[62]

To prepare for battle against "the international cesspools," Sheremetev reorganized the committee leadership. In the beginning of 1912, he handpicked the architect K. K. Romanov and the historians V. G. Druzhinin and S. F. Platonov to guide the committee's activities. He also pushed Georgievskii out of an active role. "Well to hell with them," Georgievskii commiserated in a letter to Kondakov in 1913. "It hurts when people who don't know what they are doing so impudently and shamelessly begin to destroy something which cost so much of our blood and declare themselves experts in an area where they have no competence."[63]

The change in the committee's leadership, meanwhile, did not improve its ability to provide patronage for icon painters. When the committee encouraged peasant icon painters from Palekh to participate in the three-hundredth anniversary of the Romanovs in 1913, the Duma, overseeing the production of icons for the jubilee, rejected their sketches. It chose an artist from the Academy of Arts instead. For perhaps the single most important event in the

Romanovs' modern history, the "people," as represented by the peasant icon painters of Palekh, played no visible role. The lack of patronage for the peasant holy-image producers stands in stark contrast to the high profile of Palekhians in tsarist ceremonies in previous decades, and it suggests the unwillingness of political elites, both in the Duma and the tsarist autocracy, to expand the tsar's base of social support.[64]

The exclusion of the Palekh icon painters from a celebration of the Romanov dynasty is all the more remarkable since it occurred against the backdrop of high-profile exhibits of Russian icons in 1911 in St. Petersburg and in 1913 in Moscow. The latter exhibit was a major cultural event in elite circles, solidifying the growing identification of Russianness with the painting and worshiping of icons. The exhibit inspired a new generation of icon experts, who had many differences with the old experts but agreed with them on one crucial point: modern peasant icons, with the exception of those produced by peasant Old Believers, were outside the boundaries of authentic Russian national culture. Such modern icons, according to the new experts, lacked the requisite artistic quality and were too tainted by the forces of European modernity to be linked to the positive legacy of Russian artistic culture.[65]

Reflecting the growing rift between elites and the masses, the committee in its final years devoted much of its attention to eradicating the Palekh style, that is, the hamlet's interpretation of *friaz'*. Predictably, the Palekhians refused to obey the command. When the director of the Palekh school, on the orders of the committee, attempted to purge the icon-school curriculum of all lessons in the local *friaz'*, the icon-painting instructors, hired from the local masters, refused to comply, saying "that's how we paint the *friaz'* in Palekh."[66]

While the committee grew increasingly hostile to Palekh, it showered scarce resources on the Old Believer icon painters of nearby Mstera, believing they were less tainted by the forces of modernity.[67] At the same time, Mstera was increasingly viewed as the only possible way to stave off Palekh's irrevocable decline. When one of the committee's icon-painting instructors from Palekh died in June 1914, the committee refused an application from the Palekhian I. M. Bakanov to take his position. (The director of the Palekh school remarked that Bakanov "is new around here and does not know how things are done.")[68] In its rejection of the application, the committee noted that, "despite his decent work, at least by Palekh standards, mister Bakanov would be . . . a teacher of the existing direction of the Palekhians, adding nothing new." Violating the committee's own school charter, which dictated the hiring of a local person for the job of icon-painting instructor, another artist from the Old Believer community of Mstera was chosen instead, because "he would introduce a current of old and noble traditions so necessary for the Palekhians." Justifying the decision, the committee affirmed that only Old Believers "are able . . . to strictly adhere to the style. . . . The central thing . . . was [to show icon styles] in their pure form, without any of the local corrections in general and the Palekh 'improvements' in particular, as a result of which the style loses its clarity and the icon is depersonalized, even if it is made more correct in respect to drawing and form."[69]

In the meantime, as World War I commenced, the state seemed to have no coherent plan for mobilizing cultural resources, a complement to its ineptitude in the military theater. The regime's one clear ideological principle, the official linkage of Orthodoxy and Russian patriotism, seemed out of step with the ongoing secularization of Russian society, not to mention the technological nature of modern "total" war. Perhaps it was true, as one scholar has suggested, that "Holy Russia and the saints of the Orthodox Church were no longer so convincing," at least as far as defending the imperial system was concerned. While many Palekh masters envisioned their future as secular artists, the military leadership was moving, in fits and starts, toward a more secular and inclusive definition of the Russian nation. Facing a dearth of recruits to fuel the meat grinder of the trenches, the military began to de-couple the link between Russian nationalism and Orthodox religious affiliation, for millions of imperial subjects were non-Orthodox and thus exempt from military service. As a result, the foundation of official ideology since the reign of Nicholas I, the ideology of official nationality, was losing its practical as well as its cultural significance, even as Nicholas II ordered the icon *Mother of God named Vladimir* transported to general headquarters. The decline of official nationality was also exacerbated by a growing popular alienation from official ecclesiastical structures. Amidst attempts to rejuvenate and modernize Russian Orthodoxy, religious believers began taking back their faith, openly challenging church and state officials who attempted to define it for them. The development mirrored the same processes that had separated church from state during the Protestant Reformation. It is hardly surprising, then, that state attempts (largely desultory) to exploit religious belief for patriotic purposes elicited little popular, or even bureaucratic, response.[70]

More attention seems to have been paid to cultivating romantic images from secular Russian folk culture, most of them popularized and even invented in the mid-nineteenth century. Such images included Russian folk heroes, operas based on Russian folk themes, and various folk choirs and ensembles. As Hubertus Jahn has shown, Russian folk themes played well among imperial audiences during the war, supplying a myth of a unified, harmonious, and heroic national past that seemed relevant to the struggle at hand, at least in the first and relatively successful year of the war. Already considered by some to be "folk artists," Palekhians would later draw on much of this folk material during their Soviet-era transformation into secular folk artists.

No amount of patriotic sentiment, however, could overcome Russia's technological and mobilizational backwardness. As the war effort flagged, conservative elites experienced a growing sense of hopelessness. Sheremetev captured the defeatist spirit of the icon experts in a November 1916 letter to Platonov. His comments were emblematic of a broader loss of will among the Old Regime's most ardent defenders: "I have completely lost the ability to understand what is going on, when and how we will be able to get out of this sad rut. I don't know . . . there is some kind of confusion and breaking of the spirit that does not instill confidence. A great nation needs great people, with talent and strong character, and above all honesty. Meanwhile, we are unable to distinguish authentic value from its imitation. Now is an age of imitation in everything."[71]

By the end of the imperial era, this view of modernity as an age of imitation became a leitmotif among conservative elites. Adding to the sense of imitation, the experts discovered that many supposedly ancient icons were actually elaborate fakes produced in the Palekh, Mstera, and other peasant icon-painting workshops. The academicians had been duped by the very people they were attempting to save. Experts argued about the true nature of the Russian icon and accused each other of false expertise.[72] Unable to distinguish authentic culture from its vulgar imitation, and lacking a seemingly objective guide for their own studies, many experts simply gave up on Russia, essentially leaving the struggle for the nation to other forces.

The abdication of the tsar and the revolutions of 1917, rather than marking a dramatic turn of events, provided a kind of euthanasia for the committee. When Sheremetev died in late 1918 on his country estate (having spent his last days reading Kurbskii's correspondence with Ivan the Terrible), Platonov, who reorganized the icon committee, read a eulogy before the newly reformed group.[73] He praised Sheremetev's continuing efforts to save the committee.[74] The committee, he announced, had preserved its status as a state organization under the new tutelage of the Commissariat of Enlightenment. "One hopes that it retains this status in the future," affirmed Platonov, noting that upon the solid foundations built by Sheremetev the study of icon painting would have "a bright future."[75]

Georgievskii, who had long since ceased to play an active role in the committee, saw in the change of regime a new opportunity. Appearing before the committee to eulogize Sheremetev, he believed the committee was in secure hands with Platonov. He applauded Platonov's aim to steer a new course "primarily in a scientific direction." He noted Sheremetev's frustrations in attempting to continue the publication of new style manuals and hoped that in the sphere of academic publishing the committee could find a new mission. He then announced that volume two of the *podlinnik* was ready for publication.[76] All of this, of course, was wishful thinking. In February 1919, Platonov informed the Palekh school's leadership that the school now belonged to the Commissariat of Enlightenment (Narkompros), which had no money in its budget for them. The school, noted Narkompros, "cannot enjoy any kind of material support from . . . a socialist state." Palekh's last graduating class of state-educated artists, a total of four masters, thus entered the ranks of icon painting in the summer of 1918. The committee itself survived into 1922 as a purely academic society, a place where Byzantinists and medievalists who had not fled the Bolsheviks could wax nostalgic about the historical significance of ancient Russian art. Its trading operations and schools, however, were jetti-soned, and volume two of the *podlinnik* remained but a gleam in the icon ex-pert's eye, deposited in the committee's archive, where it remains to this day.[77]

Back in Palekh, there was little nostalgia for the passing of the Romanovs. Immediately after the abdication of Nicholas II, Palekhians dismantled a statue to Alexander II, the Tsar Liberator, and tossed it unceremoniously into the pond in front of which it stood (a statue of Lenin raised in the 1950s now stands in its place, having survived the collapse of Soviet power). Meanwhile, the weakness of the consumer market during World War I, aggravated by the privations of war, had sapped the vitality of the once mighty system of private icon producers in Palekh. By 1917, the icon studios of Palekh had virtually dis-appeared. On the eve of the tsar's abdication, all sources of public and private authority had effectively collapsed in Palekh.

CONCLUSION: PALEKH AND NATIONAL IDENTITY IN THE IMPERIAL ERA

What, then, can be concluded with regard to Russianness and Palekh in the late imperial period? Beginning with the early experts in the reign of Nicholas I, the study of the icon had been tightly tied to the policy of official national-ity. That policy linked Russian identity with Orthodox Christianity and the Romanov dynasty. Following the lead of the state, experts attempted to define the nature of this Orthodoxy, an effort that included a positive reappraisal of a group formerly banished from the confines of the Russian nation: the perse-cuted Old Believers. The more positive assessment of Old Belief marked a key shift in official and elite conceptions of Russian identity in the mid-nineteenth century. This change in attitudes resulted from a growing critique of modern life, which the experts shared with similar critics in the West such as John Ruskin and William Morris. Since Old Believers seemed to reject the forces of modernization, which many experts had come to condemn, the schismatics were no longer considered pariahs and dissidents, but potentially a source of authentic Russian national culture.

This turn to Old Belief was at first tempered by a continuing recognition of the need for a Russian style that was nonetheless more modern, an ideal mix of western and Russian traditions embodied by the *friaz'* style of the official court icon painter of the seventeenth century, Simon Ushakov. For a time at least, the Palekhians (who were not Old Believers) seemed to be living embodi-ments of that seventeenth-century ideal. Equally important, the linkage be-tween expertise and political power eroded the boundary separating the study of icons from tsarist politics. As a result, the study of icons became a political as well as an academic profession.

Along with the development of expertise came demands to establish a new state-run system of icon painting. This academically managed system of surveil-lance was based on resurrecting the idealized estate-based society of Muscovy.

The experts' reading of pre-Petrine Russian history, along with their critique of modern civilization, thus helped the regime craft an ideology for integrating and controlling Russia in an age of rapid economic and social change.

Buslaev's proposal for an icon-painting brotherhood provided the first blueprint for preventing the loss of Russia's national distinctiveness. Buslaev's plans were finally realized in the tsar's new committee for the protection of Russian icons. It attempted to use religious art to shore up the authority of the Old Regime and create a distinctively Russian national culture. This effort involved the suppression of homogenizing market forces and, by implication, the power of consumers to determine their own national identity and culture of religious worship. It also reflected the patronizing attitudes of some educated elites and tsarist bureaucrats toward many of the peasant masters over whom the tsar's icon committee exercised tutelage, especially those considered tainted by profit motives and non-Orthodox values.

As the conservative critique of modernity gained more popularity, the Old Believers, who seemed to be the antithesis of modernity, acquired new authority in official circles, especially after restrictions on Old Believers were lifted during the 1905 revolution. Consequently, the icon committee turned away from the *friaz'* style endorsed by a first generation of experts and turned toward an explicit embrace of Old Belief as the most authentic expression of the Russian nation. Palekh, which was considered too corrupted by modernity, was pushed to the periphery of the committee's increasingly circumscribed national vision.

If the policy of official nationality had collapsed by the end of the imperial era, betrayed by the inability of its followers to overcome their own elitist impulses, the lines between icon scholarship and political power also blurred completely. This was true not only among the icon experts of this study but also among other educated elites, as Yanni Kotsonis argues in his research on agrarian specialists.[78] Far from resisting an erosion of their autonomy by the state, the icon scholars tore down the boundaries between politics and academic expertise. Academicians such as Kondakov eagerly invited the state into their field of study, consciously developing the ideas and agendas of the earlier generations of experts. In exchange, these scholars hoped to receive the kind of power necessary to graft their own vision of Russian culture onto Russian society. Among other things, their activities anticipated a new (and equally confused) effort by the Bolsheviks to fuse art, expertise, and power.

In the meantime, the Palekh masters took away from their experiences with tsarist power two key attitudes. First, they harbored a keen resentment of the Old Regime and its elitist policies, which would make many receptive to the new regime. Second, they had an equally ardent desire, begrudgingly accommodated by the Bolsheviks, to prove that they had never been god-daubers in need of expert tutelage. The tables were now turned. Educated Russians, in their view, were the ones who required aesthetic guidance, and the masters would attempt to provide it.

CHAPTER FOUR

The Last Shall Be the First

Although no Soviet law explicitly banned the painting of religious icons, the risk of political trouble combined with the collapse of the icon market, due to economic depression, forced most masters to abandon their craft in the first years of the revolution. Holy Russia was no more, and it was unclear what kind of Russia would replace it. The collapse of the icon market presented a profound dilemma for the most ambitious Palekh masters. They could either return to the soil and thereby descend to the status of peasant, from which many had been attempting to escape, or they could somehow find a new artistic medium in a ravaged economy. Complicating matters was the regime's rabid atheism, which heightened suspicion of anything connected with the legacy of Russian Orthodox culture—a point underscored by the arrest and execution of Palekh's leading priest in 1922.

The years of revolution and civil war were thus frustrating ones for the Palekh masters. From 1918 to 1922, surviving masters were involved in various failed efforts to produce and market folk art, including matryoshka dolls, spoons, wooden plates, and small wooden items. These failed efforts were a tremendous blow to their self-respect and seemed to confirm that the masters were indeed "god-daubers." Even loved ones back home offered little support. "Before our wives made preserves," complained one former icon painter. "[N]ow they torment us and make fun of our profession, they mock us for not bringing home the bacon."[1]

The Palekhians nonetheless persevered, relying on sheer determination, market savvy, and an informal network of patrons to assert what they believed to be their rightful place in the artistic profession.[2] At first, the most important Palekh artist was Aleksandr Glazunov (1884–1952), rightly known among Palekhians as "an able businessman who knew everyone and everything in Moscow." Before 1917, Glazunov marketed icons from his Moscow studio (opened in 1908) to state officials and well-to-do buyers. He also branched into secular decorative and folk art, to capitalize on the growing fame of Russian objets d'art and arts and crafts abroad. In the 1920s, during the regime's New

Economic Policy (NEP), Glazunov reopened his shop and resumed his marketing of all things ancient and Russian. A tireless networker, he quickly established links with the Commissariat of Enlightenment and its efforts to save
Russian icons and other church artifacts from revolutionary zealots. With the
help of the revived crafts museum (formerly run by the Moscow zemstvo, and
reopened on November 26, 1921), he and his brother-in-law Ivan Ivanovich
Golikov (1887–1937) enjoyed their first successes as icon painters turned
miniaturists.[3]

While Glazunov provided marketing resources and contacts, Golikov supplied the original artistic inspiration. In addition to receiving the traditional
training of an icon painter (a *dolichnik*) at the turn of the century, Golikov
studied secular art at the School of Technical Drawing of Baron A. L. Shtiglits.
Even as he restored numerous major church frescoes and icons in the late imperial period, Golikov had aspirations of becoming a celebrated artist and was
hardly the instinctive "peasant artist" of later Soviet propaganda.[4] He was also
determined to prove that Palekhians had never been god-daubers. In 1922, he
had arrived at Glazunov's doorstep in Moscow from the town of Kineshma,
where he had worked as a set designer for the theater. Inspecting shops and
museums in Moscow in 1922, he and Glazunov were impressed by decorated
papier-mâché boxes at the Moscow Crafts Museum. These boxes were from Fedoskino, where painters had been creating papier-mâché lacquer boxes with
folk images and copies of Russian realist paintings since the nineteenth century.[5] Golikov and Glazunov were confident they could produce such items
and approached the museum's management. The museum shop director, however, refused to extend to the "god-daubers"—as he called Palekhians after the
manner of prerevolutionary icon experts—materials and unpainted boxes for
their endeavor. Insulted by the slight, Glazunov fashioned black-lacquered surfaces from papier-mâché photographic plates for Golikov to paint on in his
studio. "And so I began to work," said Golikov, at first only with gold paint,
and then with red, green, and silver. Rather than using oil paints, Golikov used
the traditional pigments and tempera of icon painting. He fused traditional
icon-painting techniques with new themes, replacing the white-gesso background of the religious icon with a black-lacquered papier-mâché surface. "I
was driven by my wounded ego," said Golikov, who was as determined to enter the ranks of the artistic intelligentsia as he was to avoid descending into
the muddy realm of agricultural toil. He took the finished plates to the museum, where his ego was sated and his pocketbook enriched when an agreement was reached for the museum to buy the works and to supply more unpainted papier-mâché boxes.[6]

Albrecht Dürer engravings, rather than traditional Orthodox models, had
inspired Golikov's first creation, *Adam in the Garden*.[7] Golikov also produced
his first secular theme, a depiction of a bear hunt. Soon after followed *Peasant
Chess Players, A Stroll in the Countryside, Harvesting, The Peasant Seamstress*, and

Cocks. The Ploughman showed a Russian peasant behind a horse-driven plow. Filled with fantastic detail and gold-paint ornament, the figures of the horse and ploughman, unlike the Dürer-inspired religious scene, borrowed the style of the Russian Orthodox icon. Golikov began calling the same box *The Red Ploughman* to signify the change in political power (if not in manner). Still under the spell of the Great War, in which he had participated in nearly two dozen battles on the Prussian front, the former icon painter produced his signature Soviet-era theme, *The Battle,* which he would repeat hundreds of times before his death in 1937.[8] In creating the battle scene, Golikov said he was inspired by his hatred of the tsarist order. "I saw the deception of the priests who blessed us for death," he remarked. "The children of the rich were not on the front, but in the rear, and they were occupied with drunkenness and perversion. Our brothers were not spared. They killed them like cattle. I heard how officers talked about us: 'Many such pigs can be found.'" Although Golikov's anti-tsarist rhetoric fit nicely into the new order—and also reflected the profound resentment of many Palekh masters toward the previous regime—his visual representation of warfare nonetheless evoked the romance of medieval chivalry. His first battle scene showed two medieval warriors in the style of Orthodox religious saints. Rather than machine guns and grenades, they wielded harquebuses and spears. Golikov rechristened his knights *Reds versus Whites.*[9]

Word of success quickly traveled to Palekh as foreign visitors eagerly bought Golikov's creations. By trial and error, Glazunov's studio refined the application of traditional icon-painting methods to papier-mâché: tempera, the use of wolf's teeth to polish surfaces, and above all the various iconographic styles that the icon studios in prerevolutionary Palekh had so adeptly marketed. Glazunov provided consultations in adapting these styles to new media and new subject matter, as did the art critic Anatolii Bakushinskii and workers at the crafts museum.[10]

Bakushinskii's enthusiastic support of Palekh marked the emergence of one of the most important early patrons of Palekh art. A leading figure in the world of Soviet art criticism before his death (from natural causes) in 1938, he assumed the role of "expert" occupied before 1917 by Kondakov and Georgievskii, whose works he studied closely. Born in 1883, Bakushinskii was a native of the Palekh region. After attending the Vladimir seminary, Bakushinskii studied at Iur'evskii University (formerly Dorpat University in Estonia) from 1907 to 1911. His dissertation, entitled "The Historical Conditions of the Appearance of the Gothic Style in the Architecture of Northern France," explored medieval art and its relationship to social and economic trends. The Silver Age of Russian art, in which many Russian artists held the "conviction that Russia was destined to fulfill a messianic task in social, political, and artistic life," left a deep imprint on Bakushinskii's outlook and training.[11] Art, in his view, was the most essential tool for reshaping Russian national identity and consciousness. Working as a curator at the Tret'iakov Gallery during the October Revolution,

Bakushinskii (who remained a religious believer, though not openly) wisely threw his expertise behind the new regime. In May of 1921, he became chairman of the scientific-methodological division of Narkompros's committee for museums and the preservation of monuments and antiquities.[12]

Inspired by the party commandment to make the Soviet Union "national in form but socialist in content," he arranged exhibits of Palekh's new lacquer boxes, consulted with the masters on how to adapt their traditions to new secular themes, and wrote brochures and articles on the hamlet. Attempting to preserve what he believed to be the best of the cultural heritage for Soviet culture, he remarked that socialism was intimately "connected with the *Russian soil* [Bakushinskii's emphasis] and the paths of creative national will." In a 1923 speech, he said the masses had scoffed at the "uselessness" of constructivist experiments. "Machine idol worship" transforms "a living person . . . into a mechanized object . . . the devil machine demands obeisance before itself." A fan of Oswald Spengler's *Decline of the West,* Bakushinskii echoed suspicions about modern urban life frequently heard in the aftermath of the Great War, "the humanity deafened by the thunder and steely clang of factories and plants . . . , the mindless rush, without life's beauty and a minute of spiritual repose."[13]

By contrast, the natives of Palekh lived in an idyllic spot in central rural Russia and had a naïve and touching innocence, born of isolation and blissful ignorance. Infused with the spirit of "primitive folk idioms," the Palekhians plied their trade, spreading the nation's joyous colors and spirit across the land. They were, as Bakushinskii put it in his diary, the "last 'Mohicans' of Russian icon painting and medieval art," ancient yet pure and unadulterated. If socialists would only listen, they could teach urban Soviets to look beyond steel, concrete, and cold reason for socialist values.[14]

A growing vogue for the Russian primitive nurtured Palekh's budding venture. By 1922 the prewar market for Russian exotica had reemerged, phoenixlike, from the ruins of World War I. Russian refugees from the Bolshevik Revolution, especially the many artists who had fled Soviet power and were living in Paris, had turned to the production of Russian handicrafts to make a living in their new homelands. They joined an already established community of émigré Russian artists, many of whom were affiliated with Sergei Pavlovich Diaghilev and his famous Ballets Russes. Russian émigré artists, such as Nikolai Konstantinovich Rerikh and Aleksandr Nikolaevich Benois (a former iconcommittee member), catered to the demand for Russian exotica, as did the legions of lesser-known artists who went into the handicraft production business. Much of their production ended up in the United States, where the beneficiaries of a booming stock market eagerly snapped up artifacts from a premodern world they believed to be in terminal eclipse.[15]

Lenin's New Economic Policy, and the limited opportunities it provided for private enterprise, encouraged Russians within the Soviet Union to join this

1—This icon is typical of the highest quality icons produced in Palekh icon-painting shops in the late 1800s, favored by prosperous merchants as well as conservative elites. *Saint Gurii, Saint Samon, and Saint Aviv*, Palekh or Mstera, Russia, late 1800s, Tempera on wood with gilding. H. 12 5/16 in., W. 10 7/16 in.

2—This scene, characteristic of the kind of box bought by foreign consumers in the 1920s and early 1930s, adapts many of the distinctive elements of the Palekh icon to secular folk themes. *Scene of Young Man and Woman in Forest,* Palekh, USSR, 1935, Vladimir Mikhailovich Baranov (1901–1977), Lacquer, papier-mâché. H. 1 in., W. 3 7/8 in., D. 3 1/8 in.

3—The workspace circa 1905 for a Palekh painter. It is preserved in the Pavel Korin museum in Palekh.

4—The Palekh master Ivan Petrovich Vakurov (1885–1968) around 1905, who later became one of the most celebrated Soviet Palekh artists.

5—From left to right the icon painters and later Soviet lacquer miniaturists Aleksandr Ivanovich Zubkov (1885–1938) and Ivan Ivanovich Zubkov (1883–1938), with their father, Ivan (dates unknown). The caption on the photograph reads: "My grandfather with father and uncle Ivan, 1904."

Мои дед с отцем и дядей Иваном
1904 г.

6—This icon was typical of the growing demand among conservative elites in the reign of Nicholas II for icons believed to be untainted by Western, post-Renaissance influences. *Christ of the Wrathful Eye,* Russia, about 1900–1917, Tempera on wood with gilding, silver gilt, and enamels. H. 13 5/8 in., W. 11 in.

7—A popular Orthodox icon produced in a Russian peasant icon-painting shop in the late 1800s. *Dormition of the Mother of God,* Russia, late 1800s, Tempera on wood. H. 12 3/8 in., W. 10 1/4 in.

8—One of the most popular Orthodox icons produced in a Russian peasant icon-painting shop in the late 1800s. *Descent into Limbo*, Russia, late 1800s, Tempera on wood. H. 12 1/2 in., W. 10 9/16 in.

9—Another popular icon produced in a Russian peasant icon-painting shop in the late 1800s. *Baptism of Christ*, Russia, late 1800s, Tempera on wood. H. 12 5/16 in., W. 10 9/16 in.

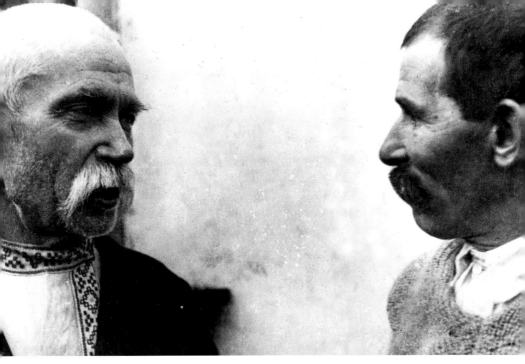

10—On the left is Ivan Mikhailovich Bakanov (1870–1936) and to his right Ivan Ivanovich Golikov (1887–1937), both highly skilled icon painters before 1917 and later celebrated as "Honored Art Workers of the Soviet Union." The photo was taken sometime in the early 1930s.

11—A photograph taken in the early 1930s of Palekh masters and their patrons. From left to right: the poet Dmitrii Semenovskii (1894–1960), Aleksandr Vasil'evich Kotukhin (1886–1961), Ivan Vasil'evich Markichev (1883–1955), Aleksandr Ivanovich Zubkov (1885–1938), Aleksei Ivanovich Vatagin (1881–1947), the writer Efim Fedorovich Vikhrev (1901–1935), Ivan Ivanovich Zubkov (1883–1938), Dmitrii Nikolaevich Butorin (1891–1960). The children are unknown.

12—This Box, titled *Red Army*, represented Palekh's fusion of Soviet power and Russian Orthodox forms, the symbolic transformation of the Orthodox saint into a Red Army fighter. Palekh, USSR, 1934, N. Blokhin, Lacquer, papier-mâché. L. 16 cm., W. 9.5 cm., H. 4.5 cm.

right—13—Here the Palekh artist equates the Soviet vanquishing of "whites" during the Civil War with Muscovy's successful drive to free itself from Tatar invaders. Palekh, USSR, 1936, Sergei Ivanovich Khazov (1883–1936), Lacquer, papier-mâché. H. 1 5/8 in., W. 6 5/8 in., D. 3 3/8 in.

14—Typical of Palekh's emerging canon was this 1925 adaptation of Saint George slaying the dragon by the former Palekh icon painter Ivan Petrovich Vakurov (1885–1968). Lacquer, papier-mâché.

15—While some artists attempted to paint more explicitly "Soviet" content, most preferred Russian folklore themes. *Box with Man and Woman on Flying Carpet,* Palekh, USSR, 1935, Nikolai Aleksandrovich Korovaikov (1883–1967), Lacquer, papier-mâché. H. 1 3/4 in., W. 3 3/4 in., D. 6 1/4 in.

16—An example of the kind of box that angered Palekh's ultra-leftist opponents in the 1930s. *Box with Mythological Scene,* Palekh, USSR, 1935, Boris Vasil'evich Terekhin (1914–1941), Lacquer, papier-mâché. H. 2 1/4 in., W. 3 3/4 in., D. 3 3/8 in.

17—Boxes such as this representation of a mythological folklore scene frequently prompted attacks on Palekh's art as irrelevant to Soviet revolutionary culture. Palekh, USSR, 1935, Ivan Konstantinovich Myznikov (1871–1961), Lacquer, papier-mâché. H. 1 in., W. 3 7/8 in., D. 3 1/8 in.

18—Aleksandr Ivanovich Zubkov (1885–1938), the first chairman of the Palekh art cooperative, before his arrest and execution in 1938.

19—Palekh artists often avoided the charge of "formalism" by illustrating the folktales of the great nineteenth-century poet Aleksandr Pushkin. *Box with Three Scenes from Aleksandr Pushkin's "The Stone Guest,"* Palekh, USSR, 1936, Sergei Dmitrievich Solonin (1892–1952), Lacquer, papier-mâché. H. 1 3/4 in., W. 13 1/4 in., D. 6 3/16 in.

20—In this box, Soviet power is embodied by the quintessential Russian bear, who drives the equally iconic troika of Russian society. Scene from the nineteenth-century poet Nikolai Nekrasov's "General Toptygin," Palekh, USSR, 1939, Stashkov, Lacquer, papier-mâché. H. 1 1/2 in., W. 5 1/2 in., D. 3 5/8 in.

21—Ivan Petrovich Vakurov (1885–1968) during the Great Terror, whose work was publicly praised in 1936 by Stalin's notorious associate Vyacheslav Molotov.

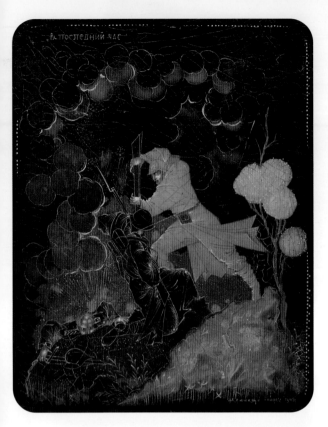

left—22—During World War II the focus on an external enemy, which was such a welcome relief for the masters, was represented in this box called *The Final Hour.* Palekh, USSR, 1943, F. I. Kliushkina (1918–1975?), Lacquer, papier-mâché.

below—23—During the war Palekh's art reflected an intense longing for the idealized comforts of home and native soil. *The Berry Pickers,* Palekh, USSR, 1943, Aleksei Mikhailovich Dushin (1894–1982), Lacquer, papier-mâché. H. 1 3/8 in., W. 5 7/8 in., D. 3 7/8 in.

above—24—In this box, titled *People's Revenge,* the anonymous Russian people of the countryside rise up to defeat the Nazis. Palekh, USSR, 1948, A. Palikina, Lacquer, papier-mâché. L. 20 cm., W. 14.5 cm., H. 6 cm.

right—25—In this box, titled *The Battle,* a Palekh artist after the war echoes the iconic St. George slaying the dragon. Palekh, USSR, 1948, E. Krylov, Lacquer, papier-mâché. L. 12 cm., W. 10 cm., H. 2.5 cm.

26—As the 1950s came to a close, Palekh responded to a new nostalgic yearning for an identity firmly anchored in a mythological past. Box with a scene from the Russian medieval epic *Slovo o polku Igoreve* (The Lay of Igor's Campaign), Palekh, USSR, 1958, V. Rygin, Lacquer, papier-mâché. H. 2 1/2 in., W. 8 5/8 in., D. 6 1/4 in.

27—In the Brezhnev period Palekh artists celebrated the triumphal spirit of Medieval Russia (Rus'). *Box with a Scene of Ruslan and the Head from Aleksandr Pushkin's "Ruslan and Liudmila,"* Palekh, USSR, 1969, Mikhail Pavlovich Kuvshinov (b. 1922), Lacquer, papier-mâché. H. 1 5/8 in.,W. 5 7/8 in.,D. 3 7/8 in.

rapidly growing market for the Russian primitive. Soviet authorities counted on handicrafts to revive the economy of central Russia that due to poor soil and long winters had always depended heavily on craft industries. The regime also needed foreign currency to buy machine tools and engineering expertise, and handicrafts were one of the few finished products the Soviet regime had to sell. The reliance on selling folk arts had an ironic outcome, at least so far as the ultra-modernizing aspects of Soviet ideology were concerned. The very craft skills that helped finance industrialization were sharpening an image of Russia as a land of medieval masters and premodern craftsmanship.

While export policies and the business acumen of the artists helped build new markets abroad, Palekh's expanding system of domestic patronage offered ideological support at home. Patrons were inspired by Anatolii Lunacharskii, the commissar of enlightenment and Bakushinskii's protector, who viewed Russia's "pre-capitalist" survivals as a potential advantage for the revolution. Because capitalism had not thoroughly destroyed craft forms of labor in Russia, the revolution, he argued, had inherited premodern forms of labor that could help overcome the degradation and alienation of labor associated with industrial capitalism.[16] He thus turned what had been a liability for Marxism—a proletarian revolution in a largely agrarian society—into a cultural asset. Relying on the folk art legacy, Soviet culture would avoid the bourgeois descent into a "decadent" morass of cubism and futurism.[17] Lunacharskii's comments echoed Trotsky's and Lenin's famously negative view of the proletarian culture movement; they condemned modernist attempts to glorify the factory milieu, arguing instead that Soviet artists must first master the aristocratic and bourgeois artistic legacy. Reading the tea leaves of official proclamations, Palekh's patrons treated the hamlet and its traditions as a weapon for combating the "industrial fetishism" of urban avant-garde artists. Worship of the machine, said I. A. Tugendkhol'd, art editor for *Izvestiia* and then *Pravda* before he died in 1928, attacked "the very soul of the Russian artistic industry." Craftsmen such as the Palekhians, he proclaimed, were "the romanticists of modernity." Following the party's commandment to fill national forms with socialist content, these craftsmen would help Soviet Russia proceed down "the path to the International . . . through the stage of national development . . . [by] protecting the collective, spiritual-national elementalness."[18]

The first All-Union Agricultural and Craft Industry Exhibit in Moscow in the fall of 1923, which followed a smaller exhibit on arts and crafts in Moscow the previous spring, provided another boost for Palekh. *Izvestiia* declared that Russian arts and crafts provided an edifying contrast to the decadent modernism of the bourgeois West (and of Russia's own avant-garde).[19] Palekh items on display at both exhibits featured mostly "everyday peasant" themes done in the distinctive icon-painting style: a shepherd tending a flock, two peasant men playing chess, a country lad courting a country lass, the reaping of a harvest. One million visitors attended the fall exhibit, convincing the organizers that Palekh had both "great significance for export" and could be applied "to the conditions of the new life" in the Soviet Union.[20]

Emboldened by Palekh's initial success, the Soviet state promoted the hamlet at an art exhibit in Venice in the spring of 1924. Emerging from its isolation in the cultural sphere, Soviet Russia was now offering its wealth of both modern and traditional art for western judgment. Mussolini was certainly impressed. Following the Venice exhibit, the head of the All-Union Society for Cultural Contacts, Ol'ga Davidovna Kameneva, learned that four Palekh masters had received a gold prize from the Italian exhibit committee. Il Duce offered to bring the masters to the land of Giotto to start up a school of icon painting, where they would receive permanent residence and a full retirement pension.[21] Confident in Palekh's value, Madame Kameneva categorically rejected the offer.[22]

Foreign praise turned out to be a revelation for the Soviets themselves; along with the market, it helped to shape their developing conception of the socialist cultural project, for which the classics of Marxism-Leninism seemed to provide no clear guide. Trotsky in the fall of 1924 called Russian arts and crafts a *van'ka-vstan'ka,* a traditional Russian toy that always returns to an upright position. The metaphor, in a positive sense, connoted the perceived dynamism and indestructibility of the ancient traditions (an ironic characterization coming from the leader who had coined the term "trash bin of history").[23] Even Soviets, it seemed, could enjoy "the privileges of backwardness."

Palekh's most critical international success came in May 1925 at the first major display of decorative arts in Paris since the turn of the century. The French organizers defined the theme of the exhibit as "a new style for a new time." Madame Kameneva headed the selection committee for Soviet items. According to *Izvestiia,* the exhibit "should play no less a role than the international exhibit in London following the Franco-Prussian war, which became a competition for worldwide hegemony in the sphere of art." While Soviet organizers included the latest experiments in the Soviet avant-garde, they also gave to Palekh (as the leading edge of other folk artists throughout the Soviet Union) a primary role in defining "the new style for a new time."[24]

With orders for the Paris art exhibit in hand, and the beginnings of a papier-mâché plant in Palekh, eight Palekhians formally registered a new artel on December 5, 1924, thereafter the official birthday of "Soviet" Palekh. In Soviet culture, the formation of the new artel became the founding event of the Soviet Palekh collective. The event was elaborated in subsequent years of press coverage during the many jubilees of Palekh's art. The founders dubbed the new organization the Palekh Artel of Ancient Painting and prepared dozens of items for the Paris show. The choice of name had great symbolic significance, for it signaled a clear commitment to preserving traditional forms of Russian art for Soviet revolutionary society. As Bakushinskii put it in early 1925, Palekh provided great possibilities "for the future mighty development of Russian artistic culture, not from western transplants, but from our own strong, vital, and beautiful roots."[25] The comment, incidentally, seemed to align with the party commandment to build socialism in one country—Russia.

The Parisian exhibit committee awarded the entire group of Palekh masters a Grand Prix, an ironic commentary on the search for "a new style." One box in the traditional style of Russian icons was called *Pioneers*. It showed five young girls carrying revolutionary banners, including "Glory to the Pioneers" and "Toilers of the World Unite!" Another box depicted a cat by the old oak tree, the narrator of many of Pushkin's fairy tales. A complex layering of national symbols, Palekh's interpretation of the Pushkin folktale integrated Russian folk motifs, a tribute to Russia's greatest poet, and stylistic elements from the Russian Orthodox icon. In great demand both at home and abroad, the Pushkin fairy tale quickly dominated the new Palekh canon.[26]

Parisian praise further legitimized the regime's embrace of Palekh. The "humble lacquers" of Palekh, proclaimed the art critic Tugendkhol'd, "testify to the synthesis of ancient technique with new ideas. Not in vain did the Palekh lacquers make an immense impression on the French and receive the Grand Prix." Only the USSR, he concluded, could "combine its striving for international and socialist culture, its reliance on scientific and technical progress, with complete respect for national tradition."[27]

The Parisian success and the first robust sales of Palekh lacquers put the artists in a festive mood. In the fall of 1926, the Palekh collective, seventeen masters strong, gathered to celebrate. Aleksandr Kotukhin made the first toast, calling upon "all members of the collective to unify in one harmonious family, to respect and help each other under any circumstances, and to not abandon what we have begun." Golikov followed: "Don't lose heart, friends. Soon we will be making lots of money and will live well." Meanwhile, Ivan Bakanov, one of the oldest masters, whose application to teach at the tsar's icon-committee school had once been rejected, echoed the hopes of many other artists, proclaiming that the former icon painters of Palekh, "will not become tillers of the soil, but will labor in the field of their new Soviet art."[28]

THE NEW PALEKH CANON

In the meantime, the masters continued to create new thematic content to replace the Mothers of God, saints, and apostles of the previous canon. In this way, the masters believed they were carrying out the party command to fill national forms with socialist content, while simultaneously earning a living. Thus, just as icon painters before 1917 produced variations on a fixed repertoire of holy figures, the younger Soviet Palekh artists of the 1920s copied themes done by the first Soviet Palekh masters, themes that were themselves based on many standard images of Russian folk culture from the late imperial era. These copies honored the original's mastery, honed the technique of the artist, and (often most importantly) provided images likely to sell. The less certain the themes appeared, the less likely they were to be copied and the more likely they were to exit the emerging canon. The market's lack of interest in certain industrial and revolutionary themes, combined with an almost total absence of state patronage until the late 1920s, thus excluded many seemingly Soviet themes from Palekh's oeuvre (and, by extension, from the new society it was representing). As a result, Palekh banished proletarian topics to the margins of utopia, finding beauty, as Golikov once put it, "where other [Soviet artists] do not."[29]

A shipment to Paris in late 1925 reflects the content of the emerging canon, as well as the artists' understanding of the Soviet political project in the 1920s, in which ideological confusion reigned.[30] One of the best sellers was *Stepan Razin*, based on the peasant rebel from the seventeenth century who was first immortalized in lacquer by Golikov in 1924. The rebel embodied the Russian quality of "elementalness" *(stikhiia)*, which in Russian connotes a chaotic rather than party-directed rebellion. A staple of revolutionary populist imagery, *Razin* symbolized the countryside as the locus of revolutionary activity. By contrast, Bolshevik leaders considered peasant "elementalness" a four-letter word, something to be tamed, controlled, planned, and, if need be, violently suppressed. Moreover, *Razin* ignored the notion of the party as the ultimate organizer of revolutionary activity (the "spark" in Leninist terminology) and the builder of socialist industry.

While proletarians and party planners were absent from Palekh's emerging canon, so too was a staple of Soviet poster art from the 1920s and 1930s: the kulak and shifty trader. Instead of icons of the greedy NEPman, a box called *Korobeiniki (Peddlers)* supplied the central image of the trader in Palekh's repertoire. The image reflected the continuing influence of populist ideology from the earlier era. Golikov first produced the box in late 1924, inspired by a poem of the same name by the nineteenth-century populist poet Nikolai Nekrasov (1821–1878).[31] Nekrasov wrote the poem in 1861. In a series of songs modeled after folk ballads, Nekrasov told the story of peasant Russia through the eyes and ears of two traveling vendors in the Russian heartland, who meet a tragic end when they are robbed and murdered. The poem evinces nostalgia for the past, for a way of life and a tableau of picaresque characters that seemed destined to pass forever into history.[32] True to Nekrasov's poem, Palekh's *Korobeiniki* was a neutral and even positive figure. *Korobeiniki* provides a stark contrast to the Marxist stereotype of peasants as hopelessly ignorant, superstitious, drunk, and requiring intense "de-bourgeoisification."

Palekh's first representation of a Soviet figure, a Red Army soldier, came in January 1925 as part of a shipment that also included *Card Players, Reaping, Hunting, Fishing, The Shepherd, The Dance, The Weaver, Processing the Flax,* and two of *Stenka Razin*. The Red Army figure on a horse was an obvious rendering of St. George slaying the dragon and was one of the few explicitly Soviet themes to enter Palekh's Soviet canon. It combined a familiar figure from the Orthodox tradition with the Red Army soldier, the most visible symbol of Soviet power in the countryside.[33]

Although the *smychka* (the alliance of peasant and proletarian) was a central slogan of Soviet power in the NEP period, it also was one of the least prominent themes of the Palekh repertoire in the mid-1920s. Other new themes, however, soon became standards: the troika, the firebird, and the knight *(vitiaz')*, all conventional images of Russian folklore from the prerevolutionary period. The knight provided a Palekhian interpretation of Viktor Vasnetsov's famous *Knight at the Crossroads,* a medieval Russian warrior facing the eternal Russian question of which of many equally undesirable paths to choose.[34]

By September 1925, boxes based on the Russian medieval epic *The Lay of Igor's Campaign* first appeared, one month after the first *bogatyr'* Il'ia Muromets (a mythological Russian knight errant). While the figures on both of these themes became hallmarks of the Palekh canon, themes on the Red Army, the Komsomol, the alliance of peasant and proletarian, pioneers, and Soviet power had largely disappeared and would not reappear through most of the rest of the 1920s.[35] The artel's records make no mention of why, nor does correspondence between the artel and its export agents. The artel most likely stopped producing these items because they did not sell (or because it was thought they would not sell).

Finally, the masters painted endless variations on the Pushkin fairy tales. With the active encouragement of Palekh's Soviet patrons, Pushkin fairy tales seemed to constitute the primary "socialist" content of the Palekh lacquer box. One journalist suggested that Pushkin's fairy tales were particularly important for Palekh's Sovietization because they involved non-Christian, pagan themes (witches, water sprites, and tree spirits) with which to counter the Christian influence on the traditions.[36]

In surveying Palekh's body of work one is struck by the almost complete lack of concern for identifying enemies, in stark contrast to Soviet poster art.[37] Palekh's attention to positive imagery reflected the tastes of many of the hamlet's customers, but it was also influenced by the masters' own aesthetic traditions. Russian religious icons, given their hagiographic focus, traditionally contained few representations of evil. One of the only representations of the "evil" kulak in Palekh art of the 1920s and 1930s was frequently called "a peasant man" rather than a "kulak." Few masters copied the image, and no records indicate an explicit order for its reproduction. The master who originally painted the box in 1926 died before he could finish it, and many artists were unsure if it was a positive or negative image.[38] This single likeness of the kulak constituted the "crowning" achievement of Palekh's contribution to Bolshevik demonology—in the 1920s and later. It was a meager addition to a perverse new Soviet iconographic tradition that differed so fundamentally from its Orthodox predecessor, and from Palekh's own vision of utopia.

Palekh, meanwhile, attracted a growing domestic market for its repertoire of rural motifs, *bogatyri*, and Russian folktales, despite the high cost of its products.[39] Many customers, such as Bakushinskii, Boris Pil'niak, and Aleksei Tolstoi, bought lacquers for their own collections.[40] A lacquer box became a kind of currency among the intelligentsia and in certain political circles, one that gained material value in Soviet Russia, as it did abroad, from its supposedly primordial Russianness.

Authorities staged exhibits of Palekh's art in Shuia in 1926 and again in 1927 for a regional conference of soviets. Moscow exhibits displayed Palekh art in 1928 and 1929, in addition to the permanent exhibit of Palekh lacquers at the Moscow Crafts Museum.[41] An exhibit of Palekh lacquers in December 1926 at Leningrad's State Russian Museum put Palekh on the cultural map in the cradle of the Russian Revolution. The Russian Museum had two sections, one for Russian fine arts and the other for the folk arts of the various peoples of the Russian Empire. Palekh anchored the museum's ethnography of the Russian nation. At the 1926 Leningrad exhibit, the art critic A. S. Gushchin called Palekh "one of the most significant artistic events of our day." In a letter to the artel, Gushchin said that Ivan Markichev's *Zhnitvo (The Reapers)* enjoyed the most popularity among viewers. This box, which quickly became a Palekh trademark (depicted today on a prominent line of Russian chocolates), showed three peasant women reaping hay in the fields. They are doubled over in hunchbacked positions, in deference, one assumes, to the toil and suffering of Russian women.[42] Thanks to Gushchin, Palekh's customer base in Leningrad expanded rapidly.[43]

Once again, the state followed the market's lead. The first recorded state order came in May 1926, a transaction amounting to three thousand rubles from the Supreme Council of the Economy. In a letter confirming the order, the vice-chairman of the Ivanovo Executive Committee wrote: "I am not familiar with you, comrades. But based on rumors about your work, which drew attention with its elegance at the Paris exhibit, you should be given as much support as possible." In 1927, Bakushinskii sat on a commission at Narkompros with Lunacharskii that ordered nearly a dozen Palekh boxes to honor the revolution's tenth anniversary. Along with the famous artist Vera Mukhina, who did a statue of a peasant woman, the Palekhians received the top prize of one thousand rubles at the exhibit. Lunacharskii, the exhibit's main organizer, dismissed attempts by city artists at "proletarian" art, reserving his greatest praise for the Palekhians. "This is an immense treasure in our midst, and it is high time to acknowledge this fact loudly and come to the aid of the amazing masters of Palekh, who without our help could be swallowed completely by the river of time."[44]

While the Palekhians were preparing for the tenth-anniversary exhibit, they received their most prestigious order to date: a commemorative desk-set for Soviet premier Aleksei Rykov.[45] The desk-set for Rykov, done by the master

Golikov, contained a rare lacquered image of Lenin. Golikov painted a similar desk-set for Maxim Gorky in Sorrento, as part of an intense campaign to entice Gorky back to the Soviet Union. Upon receipt of the desk-set (which throughout the Soviet period sat on Gorky's writing desk at the Gor'kii-apartment museum in Moscow), Gorky became Palekh's most powerful patron.[46] The masters now had the support of the ultimate champion of Soviet culture, who despite his disdain for peasant ignorance, nonetheless held a special place in his heart for the masters of Palekh, with whom he had worked as an icon's apprentice before the revolution.[47] Ivan Golikov's son, Nikolai, said that the masters and their traditions might very well have perished without Gorky's support.[48] On June 5, 1928, the old Bolshevik Iakov Ganetskii, a top trade official, traveled by train with Gorky back to the Soviet Union. A number of prominent Soviet editors shared Gorky's compartment. During the trip Ganetskii showed Palekh drawings to his traveling companions and described the artists' supposed plight. "I took advantage of the festive atmosphere to extract some money for you," he wrote to the artel.[49] Instructed by Gorky to protect the artists from their many attackers, Ganetskii sent a letter to Shuia in early July 1928. "You probably do not know that a whole series of senior comrades are very interested in the activities of the Palekh cooperative artel and are trying to undertake a number of necessary measures for its strengthening." He demanded that Shuia provide building materials for the Palekhians, mentioned Gorky's interest in the Palekhians, and requested a car, so that Gorky could travel in comfort to meet the masters in person. Gorky's support prompted positive coverage of Palekh in the press, generous subsidies for the growing Palekh art school and library, and a very big name for the artists to drop in Ivanovo and Moscow.[50]

Meantime, in the 1920s, a loose association of authors known as Pereval (mountain pass) also lent Palekh their support and expertise. Pereval's leaders saw the revolution as an intense spiritual and cultural movement, a new Renaissance that embraced all of Russian educated society. The "mountain pass" was the transitional moment in which they lived. Russia was thus ascending from the old capitalist culture to vistas that revealed a new world, just as the Renaissance looked up from the medieval period to the next cultural formation.[51]

Like Bakushinskii and many other Soviet crafts advocates, the *pereval'tsy* looked for signs of the emerging new culture beyond the factory and the machine, in a world that synthesized the cultural heritage in both its rationalist and romantic guises, its urban and rural dimensions. Abram Lezhnev (1893–1938), one of Pereval's theorists, wrote at the height of the first five-year plan: "For us, socialism is not a gigantic worker home, as it is imagined by the maniacal supporters of productivism and defenders of factology. It is not a depressing barracks from '*klop*', where people are identically dressed and die from boredom and monotony. . . . Socialism is not dressed up in grays but is filled with warmth and color."[52]

Lezhnev defended art as a specific way of understanding and transforming reality, one he contrasted with the coldly rational, inorganic approaches of engineers and scientists. "If the production of things is conditioned only by the demands of utilitarianism, as defined by science and technology, then there is no place for applying the specific methods of art." Lezhnev called the artistic understanding of reality "experimental" as opposed to "descriptive" realism, "organic" rather than "mechanical."[53]

Lezhnev was originally inspired by the proclamations of Aleksandr Voronskii, editor of *Krasnaia nov'*. In his 1924 book *Iskusstvo i zhizn'*, Voronskii proclaimed that the new culture must be a "combination of realism with romanticism and symbolism." He called this doctrine "neo-realism," in which "the symbol is given a realistic character, and realism becomes symbolic and romantic." The writer should strive for the "organic combination of everyday life with romanticism and an artistic 'philosophy.'"[54]

Before editing *Krasnaia nov'* in Moscow in the mid-1920s, Voronskii had edited the Ivanovo daily newspaper *Rabochii krai*. Around him gathered a circle of young writers from the Ivanovo region, some of whom later became the most enthusiastic members of Pereval. One of those young writers was Efim Vikhrev (1901–1935), a native of Shuia who joined the Pereval group in the mid-1920s. Along with the art historian Bakushinskii, the new "expert" Vikhrev became the most important popularizer, patron, and interpreter of Palekh's art during NEP and the first five-year plan.[55]

The son of a provincial clerk, Vikhrev was born in 1901 in the textile town of Shuia, about halfway (thirty kilometers) between the city of Ivanovo to the northwest and Palekh to the east. Along with his brother, who became a prominent Soviet engineer, Vikhrev was studying in *gimnaziia* when the tsar abdicated. Vikhrev adored Pushkin, Lermontov, and especially the early symbolist poet Balmont. Although Vikhrev regretted that Balmont did not support the October Revolution,[56] he remained deeply influenced by Balmont's striving for the infinite, his belief in the world-transforming mission of the poet, and his opposition to realistic and rational trends.[57] In this respect, Vikhrev, like Bakushinskii, was very much a product of the Silver Age of literature in late imperial culture.

Unlike Bakushinskii, however, Vikhrev preferred to aid the revolution as a party member rather than as a fellow traveler. He helped organize the Komsomol in Shuia in 1918 and joined the Red Army in October 1919.[58] After demobilization in 1922, Vikhrev returned to Ivanovo and joined the Ivanovo newspaper *Rabochii krai*, where he ran a section on worker life, handled worker correspondents, and wrote satirical pieces lambasting corruption and inefficiency. It was here that he befriended the poet Dmitrii Semenovskii, a client of Gorky's from before the revolution.[59] Both later identified with the Pereval group and formed the core of a "brigade" of writers sent by the Union of Writers to protect and promote Palekh in the mid-1930s.[60]

Vikhrev's introduction to Palekh came in the summer of 1925 while he was visiting his parents in Shuia. There he met Elizaveta Safonova, the daughter of an icon painter from Palekh. They fell in love and married that fall (Vikhrev's younger brother Vasilii later married Elizaveta's younger sister).[61] Vikhrev's first major article on Palekh came out in *Rabochii krai* in late 1926, titled "From Generation to Generation." In it Vikhrev recycled one of the most enduring myths about Palekh from before the Russian Revolution, namely, that the Palekhians are living embodiments of Nikolai Leskov's "The Left-Hander." Leskov's story concerned an artisan from Tula in the reign of Nicholas I. The artisan demonstrated his incredible skill by putting a horseshoe on a mechanical flea created by English craftsmen. While Leskov's story was a legend, said Vikhrev, the Palekhians were a "fact that speaks to the organic genius of the self-taught Russian."[62] Vikhrev also believed the Palekhians embodied the refined Russian sense of irony. The irony-loving Palekhians, wrote Vikhrev, "sent the Mother of God to you know where *[po rodoslovnym instantsiiam]*" as they painted shoddy icons and laughed at the "fools who worshiped" them. As prototypes of the ideal Russian, Palekhians had: "[a]n internal pride, which does not reveal itself in external demeanor, a calm assurance in the correctness of one's business, self sacrifice and meticulous conscientiousness in work. Also characteristic is an element of irony that is inserted, as if from an anciently born wisdom, into the object of mastery."[63]

In 1926, Vikhrev took his young bride back to Moscow, where the couple kept company mostly with Pereval writers: Nikolai Zarudin, Semenovskii, Ivan Kataev, and others. Vikhrev was eager to devote himself to the topic that he believed was his last chance to make his mark in the Soviet literary world: Palekh. As he wrote in a letter to his family in April 1927, he felt he had failed in his first chosen calling, to become a great revolutionary poet. As a prose specialist, however, he hoped Palekh would provide income and glory. "If I will fail at prose as I did in poetry, I'll have nothing left but to turn to criticism, give up everything, and eke out a pathetic existence as a mediocre journalist."[64]

As Vikhrev focused on Palekh, his wife provided introductions into the homes and lives of the masters, whom Vihrev commissioned to paint lacquers for his growing private collection. Working his contacts at *Rabochii krai* and in Moscow, Vikhrev began publishing detailed articles on Palekh. After spending most of the summer of 1928 in Palekh, he contemplated a monograph, an idea he floated among the community of Ivanovo writers. On December 6, 1928, he read a series of his essays on Palekh in Ivanovo before the Ivanovo local history society. The first of those essays linked a key component of Palekh's pre-revolutionary reputation with its growing myth in Soviet culture, to wit, "Goethe's Interest in Palekh." Other essays included "The Neglect of Palekh," "A Contradiction: Palekh in Ivanovo-Voznesensk: the City of Economic Projects and the Village of Artistic Ideas," and "The Professional Tragedy of the Icon Painter."[65]

Vikhrev encountered harsh criticism of his readings. Some viewed the topic as frivolous, others saw it as possibly counterrevolutionary, and still others were "coldly indifferent." "So you're going to write about the god-daubers," said Boris Kut'in, a playwright and proletarian culture activist. "What a topic! What kind of art is this? They put a helmet with a red star on St. George and say: 'There's a Budennyi soldier for you!' The meeting of the village soviet looks exactly like the Last Supper. The chairman is Christ, the peasants the apostles. All that's missing is Judas. You've really come up with a great idea, Efim." Lev Nitoburg thought that the idea, at the very least, was untimely and the topic outdated. "Imagine that some agitator would come up to some workers and start explaining things in Old Church Slavonic. It's absurd! Your Palekh is simply a fiction." One writer said Vikhrev should be kicked out of the party for even coming up with the idea. "People are fulfilling the five-year plan, thinking about industrialization, and you're off talking about god-daubers."[66]

Admittedly, Vikhrev occasionally experienced reservations. "From time to time I had doubts: Is Palekh really so great and is it worth talking and writing so much about it? But again and again I conquered my doubts, and again it flowed into my consciousness that Palekh is a beautiful song." For Vikhrev, the road to socialism was not straight and narrow, leading through the proletariat and factory to socialist culture, but curved, often turning in on itself (to an Orthodox, peasant culture), much like the meandering rivers, streams, and rivulets that pass through the heartland of medieval Rus'. The young writer's doodles in his notebooks are revealing. He drew intricate mazes turned in on themselves—a reflection, perhaps, of the paranoia and fear experienced by cultural entrepreneurs such as Vikhrev. Like the Palekh masters, he operated in a dangerous ideological no-man's-land, where there was no party line—the creation of Russian socialist culture. Vikhrev wrote inside one of the corridors of a maze: "No Exit."[67] Would he be able to find an exit to the new socialist world under construction? Where was "the mountain pass"? An idealized Palekh, the Russian countryside, the dream of a dacha: these were Vikhrev's exit from the confusing and often frightening maze that the Soviets called the road to socialism.

Even Vikhrev's closest allies marveled at the boldness of his apparent contrarianism. In January 1930, a party mentor wrote a note to Vikhrev: "Aren't you afraid of falling . . . under the charge of right deviation? In our time of fast tempos, industrialization, and collectivization, Palekh sounds like an anachronism."[68]

Vikhrev's ever-growing patronage network boosted his confidence that Palekh lay just beyond the mountain pass of socialist modernization. Semenovskii and Mikhail Shoshin, both prominent figures in the Ivanovo literary world, supported him. Vikhrev wrote and personally delivered a letter to Gorky on September 24, 1928, pleading for support; Gorky immediately composed an answer promising patronage for him and the Palekhians.[69]

To prove his political loyalty, Vikhrev in December 1928 wrote a long essay about Lenin's life for *Krasnaia niva*. In the next months, Vikhrev was careful to share his ideas with as many writers as possible, knowing, in addition, that he had Gorky's support as an ace in the hole.[70] Tapping his contacts, Vikhrev landed a job in November 1929 at the Nedra publishing house, which agreed to publish his Palekh book.[71] It was to be published following the purge of his party cell on January 1, 1930. In the hall, as he waited his turn, his enemies gleefully taunted him. "You won't be in the party for long," said one. "At long last we'll be rid of this Palekh scum." Though even his friends expected him to get a reprimand, Vikhrev passed the purge with flying colors, and his book came out on January 6. Vikhrev immediately sent a copy to Gorky in Sorrento, "the court of last resort," as he put it, and nervously awaited the master patron's verdict. Gorky's response from Sorrento was all Vikhrev could have hoped for. "The book is excellent," wrote Gorky. "This art is fully worthy of a wider and more literate evaluation than it has so far had, and of a much greater appreciation in a material sense. You will be able serve the cause of popularizing the works of the Palekh masters among us, in the Soviet Union." Gorky assigned him an article on Palekh for his journal *Nashi dostizheniia* on the theme "How the 'god-daubers' turned into genuine artists."[72]

In the meantime, Palekh lacquers continued to star at Soviet exhibits in Leipzig, Copenhagen, Milan, Berlin, Vienna, Paris, Tokyo, and New York. When the Soviet Union trumpeted its cultural and economic successes before the American public in early 1928, Palekh stole the show, as it had three years earlier in Paris. Palekh items on sale were almost immediately sold out. A year later, as the campaigns of collectivization and industrialization were getting under way in the Soviet Union, Soviet authorities capitalized on the success of the previous exhibit in New York, sponsoring the "Soviet Russian Art and Handicraft Exposition" in the city's Grand Central Palace. A Soviet brochure called Palekh "a significant factor in raising the cultural level of the peoples of the Soviet Union," one that "mingled the refinements of the Byzantine influence with the vivid colors of the native Volga engravings." The *New York Times* reviewer proclaimed that shifting from religious to secular subjects "for milady's dressing table does not seem to have interfered with the artistry or skill of the workers."[73] A review in the *New Republic* waxed ecstatic, noting the "exquisite Byzantine charm of line and color . . . adapted to modern, sylvan and fantastic subjects. These little [Palekh] boxes are probably the loveliest things being made by unselfconscious artists anywhere in the world. That this ancient tradition should have survived, through war and revolution, in one small village, is a most singular and arresting fact."[74]

With friends in high places and a stable and growing market at home and abroad, the Palekh artel continued to grow. On May 20, 1928, Ganetskii wrote in *Izvestiia* that the "self-taught" artists of Palekh had endured the double yoke of victimization by revolutionary extremists and capitalist mechanization. Only the artists' devotion to art, and the far-sighted patronage of Soviet power, had resurrected the traditions (he conveniently omitted the crucial role of markets). The article framed a photo of the artel masters, now twenty strong, in sheepskin coats and fur hats, against the backdrop of a peasant cottage. It was time, said Ganetskii, for "planned, organized help" to aid the expansion of Palekh's art and the ongoing Sovietization of the masters themselves.[75]

A "PLAN" FOR PALEKH

The call for "planned, organized help" foreshadowed immense new challenges during the period Stalin dubbed the Great Break. The Soviet Union had caught its breath during NEP and was now preparing for an all-out sprint toward socialism. The mad dash to socialism materialized in the first five-year plan, forced collectivization, and the "liquidation of kulaks as a class." What all this meant for Palekh was unclear. On the one hand, Palekh provided valuable foreign currency. On the other hand, many believed that Palekh's art had nothing to do with the creation of a revolutionary culture.[76]

Palekh's marching orders were thus contradictory from the start. At times, the All-Russian Council of Industrial Cooperation (Vsekopromsovet), Palekh's new Moscow overseer in 1929, suggested that Palekh should focus on exports and forget about the socialist content. Yet even as Vsekopromsovet drove the export whip, it shrilly demanded greater attention to "Soviet themes" and condemned "a lack of ideological control."[77] The lack of ideological guidance accentuated Palekh's ambiguous status. The classics of Marxism-Leninism were silent on critical issues, including the role of markets in cultural production and the relationship between national tradition and socialist modernity. Party leaders also confronted the dilemma of a Soviet society that was supposedly created by the proletariat yet was inhabited mostly by peasants and a large minority of non-Russians. At the intersection of these tensions, Palekh became a central arena for defining the socialist cultural project.

A late 1931 meeting in Moscow on Palekh typified the regime's unclear conception of its cultural mission. The chairman of the meeting, a certain Koval'skii, believed Palekh's stubborn refusal to transform the religious artistic forms proved the style was not yet proletarian. Koval'skii asked: "So do we bury [Palekh] or do we restructure and reeducate it?" While many foreign bourgeois artists were "becoming revolutionary, everything is just the opposite with us. This is unnatural." The old Bolshevik I. S. Unshlikht was even less sanguine about Palekh's relevance. The "broad sweep" of Soviet reality, its "power" and "strength," could not be captured "in miniature." However, he realized Palekh earned foreign currency, and for this reason Palekh should be left alone. Furthermore, since copiers of the Palekh style had already emerged in the West, only by preserving Palekh could the party protect "the lucrative brand name that the Palekhians have acquired." The comments confused other attendees: so was Unshlikht for or against Palekh? A certain Aristova interjected: "That means you deny that Soviet themes can be represented in miniature?" Unshlikht: "You can't build the future from dregs."[78] The ultimate result of such discussions for the masters was that they "became confused."[79]

Their confusion was also shared by the Soviet viewing public. In late 1931 and early 1932, Vsekokhudozhnik (the body overseeing Soviet art production in the 1930s) exhibited Palekh lacquers next to an exhibit of modern art by a group called Brigade 13. The leadership of the Palekh artel composed this description of its art for the Moscow exhibit:

> The most interesting aspect of the Palekh exhibit is . . . the application of artistic craft form to Soviet ideas. One painting shows a tractor, bathed in brilliant rays of golden light, which in the old days surrounded the heads of saints. Another painting at first glance evokes the old Russian theme of St. George slaying the dragon. If one looks more closely, however, it becomes apparent that St. George is a Red Army figure who pierces with his lance the dragon—a counterrevolutionary officer on a white horse. The First of May demonstration on the Palekh box is similar to an old church festival, the so-called *krestnyi khod* [a procession of the cross].[80]

Viewers seemed alternately drawn by the romantic and Enlightenment sources of the revolutionary project as they gazed upon the otherworldly figures, brilliant colors, and intricate gold ornament of the Palekh boxes. One visitor, echoing a statement from many attendees, said: "What poverty of brush and thought among the neighboring [artists of Brigade 13] compared to Palekh." A certain Tsaregorodtsev disagreed: "You can't make modern workers and peasants out of Madonnas and saints. You can't represent Soviet themes with the old forms of the Russian icon. . . . It turns out naïve and false." He had no doubt the Palekhians were highly skilled masters, "but it doesn't express Soviet subject matter. . . . They are playing on the elegance of form and a bright decorativeness of painting. And everyone likes it. But one has to look more closely—does it achieve the goal of a clear expression of content?" No, he concluded. "On the contrary, it is funny but also unpleasant to see saints carrying the slogans of Soviet life." Nonetheless, he allowed that Palekh's Pushkin fairy-tale themes were "original and interesting."[81]

Many visitors seemed to want the same face Palekh presented to the West: a quaint rural Russia, defined by the rural milieu, and connected (if only through "style") to Russian Orthodox traditions. One artist, who had just come from the Brigade 13 exhibit, urged patience in dealing with the Palekhians. The artists needed to be treated "carefully and with love," as they searched for the appropriate way to marry their artistic traditions to the demands of modernity. Palekh, he believed, provided a sanctuary from the impersonal work of self-styled revolutionary artists. It was no accident, said the artist, that crowds of visitors "go right past the gray canvases [of Brigade 13], which in a cold and official way depict the life of the factory, and linger in the

Palekh hall, in which the living source of national creativity flows." Directly below this remark an unsigned comment proclaimed: "Bring a brigade of workers and you will hear a completely different opinion about this art. I do not think that it would be possible to show something worse than Palekh."[82]

A perceived conflict of form and content deeply disturbed another visitor, who saw Palekh as the carrier of a hostile ideology. In its geographical and cultural isolation Palekh was surprised "by the social revolution, industrialization, the five-year plan, and by the emergence of new themes in farm labor." The Palekhians had a petty bourgeois psychology and were therefore unable to embrace new themes in a concrete manner. "Surrounded by idealized peasant lone farmers, the tractor seems as miraculous as the first steamship." The visitor concluded that either Palekh's artists, under the pressure of social changes, would find new content and new forms, or the art would survive as an exotic curiosity, cut off from the march of progress and time, "which would have no broad social significance. One assumes that sooner or later the artists will figure this out and will not want to remain a tiny island in an ocean of living reality."[83]

For every visitor who wanted Palekhians to flee their tiny island, another living in the "ocean of living reality" seemed eager to crowd into a tiny lacquer box of his or her own: setting up a dacha, planting a garden, watching the sunlight reflect through the birch forests. One visitor called Palekh "amazing exotica" that should constitute "a great contribution to the emerging culture of the proletariat, of a classless society, both for the high artistic value of its content and for the remarkably refined elegance, in the highest degree, of its cultural form." A conference of official experts at the exhibit repeated the ambivalence of viewer reactions.[84]

While museumgoers debated Palekh's art—and the socialist cultural project more generally—the artists had to wage a nearly constant rearguard action against local opponents. Officials responsible for liquidating kulaks as a class identified the artists as the most obvious candidates. From its inception in late 1929 and early 1930, the collective farm Red Palekh coveted the artel's labor and resources. As with all of the Soviet Union's newly formed collective farms, Red Palekh lacked the material resources and expertise to realize the frequently extolled advantages of mechanization and socialized labor. Long-standing resentments among the non-artists around Palekh, who were indeed a kind of underclass, also fueled the conflict. Links with religious traditions and foreign markets only seemed to confirm suspicions that the former icon painters were producing "kulak art." Tensions exploded in January 1930, when Red Palekh informed the artists that they would be forced to work in the cattle and milking section of the collective farm (a job traditionally performed by women, and thus calculated to highlight the intended lowly status for the male masters).[85]

The masters immediately mobilized their extensive network of patrons, including the Soviet president Mikhail Kalinin, who supposedly had sympathies for Russian peasant life. In January 1930, Ganetskii and Bakushinskii personally visited the commissar of agriculture, Nikolai Muralov (1877–1937), to protest the artel's absorption into the Palekh collective farm. A sympathetic Muralov attempted to work out a compromise: the artel would retain its independence but pay a sum equal to labor lost to the kolkhoz. Each member would also mow hay five days a year.[86]

Ominously, according to a stenogram of a general meeting of artists on February 4, 1930, the collective farm had not responded to Muralov's proposed compromise, "which greatly disturbs and upsets the masters." The artel general assembly met again on February 21 and came up with a carrot to sweeten the offer for the local collective farm. They released money from the general fund to purchase a tractor for the farm, in exchange, they hoped, for being left alone (it would take a year for the Palekhians to pull strings in Moscow to get the tractor delivered). Although Stalin's famous speech "Dizzy with Success," published in *Pravda* on March 2, condemned the excesses of collectivization, the leadership of Red Palekh was not paying attention.[87] That article put the brakes on the collectivization campaign, blaming the increasingly disastrous program on overzealous locals.

Outraged by what it perceived as an attempt by the Commissariat of Agriculture to seize resources belonging to the system of industrial cooperation, the All-Russian Council of Industrial Cooperation issued an edict on July 8, 1930. "The Palekh artel," noted the edict, "has exceptional importance as an organization that produces objects of high value of an export character. Thus, in conducting the collectivization of agriculture, the members of the artel must be guaranteed an independent status in the future development of their productive activity." Simultaneously, Gorky discussed Palekh's plight with the prominent party member Georgii Piatakov and organized a fund to provide material support for the Palekh artists.[88]

As the kolkhoz geared up for spring sowing in 1931, a general meeting of the collective farm in early March made a new bid for the artel's assets and labor. The chairman of the kolkhoz, a certain Kalmykov, said the Palekh artel was only needed as long as the Soviet Union was dependent on foreign currency for the purchase of foreign technology. Once the Soviet Union began producing its own tractors "we will spit on them." Predictably, Palekh appealed again both to the Ivanovo Executive Committee and to Vsekopromsovet in Moscow and Ivanovo. Only on July 31, 1931, did Muralov send a telegram (again) forbidding the collective farmers from forcing the artists to work on the farm. None of this, however, changed the situation, as local officials continually pressed their attacks through 1933.[89] Only in early 1934 did the artists' situation finally improve, the result of a decision to integrate Red Palekh into a number of other collective farms, which reduced the farm's labor shortage.[90]

If the struggle against Red Palekh dispirited many of the masters, in retrospect it also provided an unexpected boon to the hamlet's political position. In response to attacks, Palekh's patrons during the first five-year plan created an impressive body of popular and specialized literature devoted to Palekh's art. These stories provided political justification for the hamlet's art, which complemented Palekh's value as a source of foreign currency. As before 1917, these stories celebrated Palekhians as native self-taught geniuses—a village academy—who thanks to enlightened state power had successfully overcome their legacy as god-daubers.[91] The stories also made ingenious use of the conflict with the local collective farm. Taking a cue from Stalin's "Dizzy with Success" article, the Palekhians and their patrons crafted a story of national martyrdom. Palekh's artists became heroic victims—and the collective farm Red Palekh became an amalgam of class enemies and destroyers of the Russian nation.[92] Collectivization in Palekh was thus respun as the story of powerful patrons intervening to save Palekh's art from uncultured revolutionary extremists. Like the cavalry in American mythology, Soviet commissars saved the day, protecting a defenseless Russian nation and its ancient traditions from evildoers and Trotskyites.

Tales of suffering and woe, of course, lie at the heart of so many modern nations: genocide for Israel and Armenia or supposed Soviet attempts to wipe out the Ukrainian nation in the collectivization-induced famine. Among some historians, it has even become commonplace to cast the Soviet Union in the role of destroyer of nations.[93] In stark contrast, Soviet power appears in stories about Palekh as Russia's savior, ironically, against the very forces that the revolution had unleashed. Collectivization thus provided a powerful foil against which the masters of Palekh, as defenders of distinctly Russian traditions, continued to advance their social status. Palekh had survived the Great Break.

In the meantime, the hamlet's patrons continued to interpret and elaborate the meaning of the new Soviet Russian culture. Especially critical were Vikhrev's writings. Republished throughout the 1930s, they acquainted a large segment of the population with Palekh and validated the artists as bona fide Soviet heroes. According to Iurii Melent'ev, a high-level party official and ardent Russian nationalist in the 1970s and 1980s, Vikhrev's musings on Palekh helped establish an early link in Soviet culture between "national aesthetics" and rural Russian landscapes and lifestyles. In this sense, Vikhrev anticipated the "village prose" of the 1960s and its romantic infatuation with the countryside.[94]

Emphasizing the importance of rural contributions to revolutionary society, in July 1930, Vikhrev called a display of Palekh lacquers in Moscow a "gift" to the sixteenth party congress. The gift, he claimed, ranked alongside the gigantic factories and blast furnaces of urban Soviet Russia. At a time when "worker muscles are in shock-worker tension," he wrote, Palekh presented "a humble and unusual gift . . . delicate and elegant. . . . Its name is also unusual: The First Exhibit of the Palekh Art of Ancient Painting. . . . So you probably wonder: Palekh and peacocks, what does this have to do with the revolution, construction, modernity? Now wait, don't laugh so skeptically. One first has to become familiar with the gift."[95]

The gift, in Vikhrev's retelling, was to give Soviet Russia the soul that modern life desperately needed—not a religious one, but a romantic spirit not yet depersonalized and alienated by urban lifestyles. For Vikhrev, the Palekh master Ivan Golikov embodied this spirit. If Vikhrev was the Lorenzo de Medici of the Russian Renaissance, Golikov was its Michelangelo-cum-muzhik. When Golikov smiled, he exposed but one tooth in his upper mouth. "You look carefully at this man of medium height and suddenly, after a moment's reflection, you understand that before you stands a medieval master, a man with a big soul and a capacity for work." Poverty had ennobled rather than destroyed Golikov's spirit—and that of the other artists. Golikov did not work for money or fame (questionable claims), and could therefore easily "reconstruct himself." Golikov's connection with precapitalist craft traditions gave him special powers of creation. He was a "hypnotist" who worked "according to cabalistic principles beyond comprehension." Golikov was a real muzhik, as much a model to be celebrated as the "worker muscles in shock-worker tension."[96]

Golikov was also the medium through which Vikhrev projected his fantasy of Russia as a land of elemental peasant rebellion, patriotic bloodletting, and uncontrolled passions. Vikhrev identified with Golikov's single-minded obsession with battle scenes. The battle *(bitva)* was an idée fixe for Golikov, repeated hundreds of times on lacquer boxes until his death in 1937. He freely mixed images of medieval Russian warriors on stylized horses, rifles, lances, Budennyi hats with red stars, and other Soviet symbols. In October 1926, Vikhrev ordered the first of many Palekh boxes from Golikov, an item called *Burial Ground,* which depicted a postbattle scene littered with Russian warriors, an echo of the famous Vasnetsov painting on the same theme. Vikhrev had penned the poem that inspired the box. In 1932, Golikov stayed with Vikhrev in Moscow after the master was commissioned (at Gorky's suggestion) to produce illustrations for *The Lay of Igor's Campaign.* Vikhrev was his constant companion and consultant on the first major Soviet effort to illustrate Russia's medieval heroic epic, previously attempted in the late imperial era by the great neo-realist (and earlier Palekh mentor) Vasnetsov. Also in 1932, as Vikhrev noted approvingly, Golikov produced two miniatures for the Red Army. One showed a Red Army soldier as a modern-day Stenka Razin. The other depicted Aleksandr Blok's famous poem "The Twelve," in which twelve Red Army soldiers march through Petrograd, led by a Christlike figure, symbolizing the destructive chaos of the revolution and its apocalyptic dimensions.[97] For Vikhrev, the ethos of the medieval Russian warrior, the great peasant rebels, and the violence and paranoia of the revolution were all linked (see illustration 13 for one Palekh artist's representation of these themes, a scene depicting Reds and Whites in the civil war).[98]

Vikhrev attached to this fantasy of permanent peasant rebellion a vision of the Palekh master as the Russian Holy Fool. Golikov was everything the ideal shock worker was not: clumsy, unkempt, slump-shouldered, imprecise in his physical movements. He had an enormous mustache. He went days without working, only to produce dozens of boxes in a furious sleep-deprived stretch. Vikhrev celebrated Golikov's illiteracy: the artist's barely literate autobiography was so authentic that it required virtually no editing, said Vikhrev. Golikov's manner of speech, wrote Vikhrev, was almost incomprehensible, "his words jumped over each other." Frustrated by his own incoherence, Golikov would often fall silent. When lacking for inspiration, Golikov's wife sang folk songs to him. "Only having understood his tortured grimace and rapid shaking of his moustache will you understand how poor is his language, how chaotic his speech, and how rich his internal world." Vikhrev believed, "it is our fortune that he is barely literate, that knowledge does not disturb him."[99]

In Vikhrev's retelling, Golikov ultimately became a model of inefficiency and irrationality. He was illiterate, wrapped up in his own internal muse, blissfully unaware of the surrounding world, and thoroughly intuitive and emotional in his approach to socialist reality. Vikhrev's portrait of the "master-muzhik" Golikov, which the poet Semenovskii called an "enchantment" and "significant cultural event," challenged the idealized, plan-focused, efficiency-mongering industrial manager and worker.[100] In short, Vikhrev's socialism was not built by planners and technocrats, but by artists/rebels and dreamers, steeped in the elementalness (stikhiinost') of Russian peasant life.

The writer Boris Pil'niak, an avid collector of Palekh lacquers beginning in 1930, elaborated the connection between Palekh, the revolution, and peasant elementalness. After visiting the village in 1934, Pil'niak was fascinated by the apparent contradiction between the revolution and Palekh, which he concluded only proved the revolution's chaotic nature. He delighted in making this point to foreigners during his last trip to the West before his arrest and execution in the Great Terror. Hunched over Palekh boxes that Pil'niak had brought along, his hosts on the sixty-seventh floor of the Chrysler building in New York asked: "This is ancient, right? No," said Pil'niak, "this is Soviet Russia." Upon his return to the Soviet Union he brought the anti-fascist Norwegian writer Nordahl Grieg to Palekh. Pil'niak explained to the perplexed Grieg, who seemed unable to grasp the connection between socialism and Palekh: "Sometimes in the mining industry new and unusual minerals appear in the slag and cracklings of the slag heap. Nobody could have predicted that in the blast furnace of revolution the castaways of religious tradition would be transformed into an alloy of great art. . . . Unexpectedly for the revolution itself, [this alloy] was done in the blast furnace of the revolution."[101]

If many found Palekh's contested and contradictory nature a constant source of irritation, Palekh supporters eagerly trumpeted these qualities before readers. Nikolai Zarudin, another Pereval member, said the Palekhians were "free slaves." Vikhrev believed the multiple linguistic variants used to describe Palekh suggested, in a positive sense, the ambiguity of the hamlet as a site for cultural synthesis: "Foreigners pronounce the word Palǝkh, Muscovites PalEKH, peasants PALekh. *Intelligenty* speak of Palekh objects as palekhovskie. But rural people know their language better and say: 'paleskie,' abandoning in speech the letter '*kh*'. *Intelligenty* call Palekhians palekhovtsami, palekhtsami and even Palekami (`well, how are the paleki doing?'). Often, regarding miniatures, people say: 'How many palekhov do you have?'"

These variants, said Vikhrev, showed that many considered Palekh "something abstract, distant, and mysterious: not quite a village, not quite an artist, not quite a handicraft." He concluded that "Palekh presents itself under the misty sign of a question mark,"[102] one that provided seemingly endless opportunities for dialectical struggle and ironic synthesis. Was the lacquer box an art or craft? Was it religious icon or socialist propaganda? Was it progressive or reactionary? Was it bourgeois or socialist? Was it kitsch or high art? Socialist culture was to be synthesized from the dialectical tensions raised by such questions, in a form that nobody (including Vikhrev) could predict, except that it would probably appear ironic.

VIKHREV'S FINAL IRONY

As befits a Bolshevik romantic, Vikhrev's romance with Palekh had a tragically ironic ending. In 1934, Vikhrev was joined by a brigade of writers that included the former *pereval'tsy* Ivan Kataev and Nikolai Zarudin. As if embarking on a perilous journey to the jungles of Borneo, the brigade in the summer of 1934 led an expedition into the Russian heartland (the Gor'kii oblast') in search of authentic Russian peasant artists. Gorky planned a special issue of his journal *Nashi dostizheniia* to unveil the discoveries of the brigade, prefaced by a series of essays on Palekh. Among the folk artists, Vikhrev encountered widespread confirmation of the broader significance of his patronage of Palekh. The many folk artists he visited "all know me," he wrote to his brother. "They know my book about Palekh. It turns out that [Palekh] has a leading role among the artels." The tour culminated in a visit to Palekh for the triumphant tenth-anniversary celebration of Palekh's Sovietization (see illustration 11, showing Vikhrev with prominent Palekh artists).[103]

Not yet thirty-five years of age, and imagining a life ahead as self-appointed commissar of romantic craftsmanship, Vikhrev in late 1934 could barely contain his excitement. He could now entertain a cherished fancy, his version of Oblomov's famous dream. From dacha command posts, writers would join the artists in celebrating the beauty of Russian nature and the triumphs of socialism reflected in the cupolas, lacquer boxes, lacquered wooden trays, clay whistles, decorated distaffs, Tula flintlocks, intricate laces, window-frame ornaments, and icons of Great Russia. He joined a cooperative of writers planning a gated dacha community at the Vnukovo train stop. He wrote to his brother about his dream of a village academy:

We are living with one dream now. We want to build our dacha. . . . I am on the front of the list, just like Kataev and Zarudin. We each will have one hectare of land with a garden plot, with a good stand of trees (pine, oak, linden, and aspen). We will each have our own house as a permanent residence winter and summer, a house with electricity, running water, four rooms, two stories, with a balcony and veranda. If our dream will come true, we will live there permanently.[104]

And then something terribly ironic happened in Palekh. Ending his triumphal folk-art tour in Palekh in January 1935, Vikhrev suddenly and unexpectedly contracted blood poisoning and died the next day in a hospital in his native Shuia. By his tragic death, Vikhrev became a martyr for the Palekh cause and has been the source of endless conspiracy theories to this day among Palekhians.[105] In the dead of winter, a funeral procession took his body the thirty kilometers from Shuia to Palekh, to be buried on the east side of the main church there. As if to scare away the saints, canons were fired above the cupolas of the church as the commissar of Palekh was laid to rest. One of the irony-loving Palekhians said at his graveside: "He didn't make it. Not once did he get to go on the metro!" which had just been completed in Moscow.[106]

Perhaps he never rode the metro, but Vikhrev's writings on Palekh got quite a ride, reprinted and quoted throughout the Soviet Union. These writings created memorable and enduring stereotypes of socialist Russian man, including the Holy Fool, the primordial peasant rebel, the master medieval craftsman, and the lover of irony. The myth constructed by Vikhrev stressed the chaotic and elemental quality of the revolution. It opposed an urban, proletarian, and technocratic vision of socialism.[107] Soviet Russians in Vikhrev's socialism wore peasant costumes rather than suit and tie. They wielded paint brushes, harmonicas, and balalaikas rather than hammers and pneumatic drills. Above all, Vikhrev stressed Soviet Russia's ability to produce the unexpected, not as a betrayal of the socialist ideal but as a mark of socialist Russia's ironic nature, "inserted, as if from an anciently born wisdom, into the object of mastery."[108]

Finally, Vikhrev had introduced a large community of writers, Stalin's "engineers of the human soul," to the art and artists of the now-fabled village, which he dubbed (or rather redubbed after the example of imperial icon experts) a "village academy." In addition to the American journalist Albert Rhys Williams, Vikhrev helped to arrange visits to Palekh of foreign fellow travelers such as Paul Vaillant Couturier, André Malraux, and Nordahl Grieg. Gorky introduced Romain Rolland (who met with Palekh artists at Gorky's dacha) to Palekh through Vikhrev's essays, which were translated and published in foreign journals, along with other Soviet studies of Palekh.[109] Sensing that Palekh had become a trendy topic among editors, many of Vikhrev's writer-friends published their own articles about Palekh. Despite Vikhrev's death, the myth of Palekh as a "village academy," which in turn was appropriated from the imperial era, thus endured. Most critically, that myth reintroduced elements of Russian populist ideology back into the Soviet political project.

ROMANTIC RATIONALISTS, SOVIET RUSSIANS

So what does Palekh suggest about the development of Russian identity in the early Soviet period? Despite a policy of cultural and economic autarky, of building socialism in one country, the style and thematic content of much of Palekh's work was forged in the crucible of western bourgeois demand for Russian exotica. To the extent that Palekh introduced new socialist themes into its art, these efforts were almost always one-time orders for exhibits, and the new topics rarely entered the mainstream canon. Even when the artel switched almost exclusively to domestic markets in the mid-1930s, the legacy of the bourgeois market lived on in the Palekh canon, which remained largely unchanged from a decade earlier (and in many respects from the canon of Russianness developed in the late imperial period). With Palekh in the role of intermediary, foreigners thus participated in the "invention" and imagining of Soviet Russian culture, just as western engineers and capital had helped design and finance Soviet industrialization.

Domestic tastes were also crucial in Palekh's success. For Palekh's patrons and consumers, the village was a safe haven from monumental art and the depersonalized aesthetic experiments of the avant-garde. Palekh brought out the romantic in its political supporters, who integrated the masters into a broader policy of cultural preservation in the 1920s. These romantic tendencies, which conveniently validated market demand, seemed incompatible with the vehemently anti-peasant and urban-based spirit of Soviet modernization, especially during the first five-year plan. Yet doubts about Palekh's art were never sufficient to convince party leaders to shut Palekh down. Partly, this was a result of Palekh's ability to generate foreign currency. Yet Palekh's successes also reflected a soft spot in certain party circles for Russian national traditions, even those associated, if only stylistically, with Russian Orthodoxy.

Among other things, Palekh's Soviet triumph suggests the enduring legacy of European romantic nationalism, which was integrated, however awkwardly, into Soviet Russian culture. Resting uncomfortably alongside the Marxist urge to rationalize, modernize, and urbanize, romantic strivings created a split personality in the revolution: the enlightened/romantic Bolshevik, who both idealized and excoriated Russian rural traditions.[110] Faustlike, the romantic and enlightened Bolshevik often resided in one and the same person, creating a tension that was reflected not merely in competing factions, but in one mind.[111]

While the Soviet project of rationalization and standardization has received much attention from scholars, the influence of romantic strivings on Soviet revolutionary thinking has attracted less interest. Nearly five decades ago, Jacob Talmon noted the Rousseauian tendency to see cities as condemning "one portion of the people to overwhelming toil, and the other to demoralizing inaction." Talmon also contrasted "totalitarians of the Right," who operate "solely with historic, racial and organic entities," with the hyper-rationalist "totalitarians of the Left." Martin Malia has recently revisited the role of

Romanticism and the Enlightenment in the European revolutionary tradition and refers intriguingly to romantic influences on Marxism and Leninism. Nonetheless, he emphasizes the imprimatur of technocratic impulses in Stalin's program of socialist construction and largely ignores the romantic strivings that contributed, at least in part, to Soviet cultural policies. Palekh suggests that the situation in the Soviet Union was more complex. Tensions between rationalist and romantic impulses became a permanent feature of Soviet cultural life and production, just as they had shaped the tsarist icon committee's attempts to both "enlighten" the Palekh masters and preserve their traditions in a pristine and pure state. It was around these tensions that Soviet national cultures (in Russia and other Soviet republics) grew and developed from the 1920s onward.[112]

The masters, for their part, played an active role in the hamlet's triumph. They were hardly the instinctive and unconscious "peasant artists" of later Soviet propaganda. Long before 1917, Palekhians had catered to the aesthetic and spiritual needs of Russian elites. They quickly adapted to the demands of new domestic patrons, who were inspired by many of the same romantic inclinations that had intrigued Palekh's prerevolutionary customers. This entrepreneurial spirit survived the revolution, and along with the ambitions of the artists, it played no small role in reestablishing the Palekh brand name.

All these factors—foreign market demand, romantic strivings, local ambitions, and entrepreneurial traditions—ultimately made Palekh a privileged site for producing Soviet "Russianness." Notably absent in the story of Palekh is any hint of a coordinated state policy, much less one that discriminated against Great Russians for their "dominant-nation chauvinism," as some authors have argued was the overarching cultural policy of the 1920s and early 1930s.[113] According to the accepted scheme, the Soviet state in the 1920s and early 1930s actively discriminated against Great Russian culture. It encouraged non-Russian "indigenization" to exploit non-Russian resentment of tsarist Russification policies. At the same time, Soviet Russians were limited to the production of cosmopolitan revolutionary imagery, which was deemed more appropriate for Russia, supposedly the most advanced and revolutionary nation in the Soviet federation. By the late 1930s, according to many scholars, the Soviet regime abandoned its earlier policies and for practical rather than ideological reasons promoted a revival of patriotic Russian culture, with a heavy reliance on folk motifs and the tradition of Russian statism.[114] While this explanation may make sense from the perspective of non-Russian peripheries or official policy statements, it does not work in Palekh. With state sanction, the hamlet thrived in the 1920s, producing many of the images of Russian folk culture and heroic myths typically associated with the supposed shift to Great Russian chauvinism a decade later. Moreover, from the late 1930s to the late 1950s, the village faced frequent attacks for its focus on Russian folklore and epics and its inability to develop new "Soviet" style and content. If Soviet cultural policies were increasingly Russocentric after 1935, one would expect such demands to disappear, above all, in the Russian heartland. They did not.

Palekh suggests a more nuanced picture of Soviet cultural construction. Party leaders were fundamentally confused on issues of national culture and identity, for which the classics of Marxism-Leninism provided little guidance. The resulting ideological crisis that emerged with the revolution itself and lasted well beyond the death of Stalin created a constant stream of conflicting signals for culture producers in the Russian heartland. Beyond the vague commandment to fill national forms with "socialist" content, the lack of clarity set the tone for the production environment in Palekh (and probably elsewhere, though studies are lacking on this topic). As a result, Palekhians occupied a kind of ideological no-man's-land. They constantly had to weigh the risks and potential benefits of this or that image or style, as well as their own need for money. True, they knew that the national cultural heritage provided legitimate inspiration, and was also supported by most consumers, but which aspects of that heritage were "progressive" and which were "reactionary" and "bourgeois" were often unclear. More often than not, they had to risk making this decision on their own and let consumers decide whether the decision was worthy. One result of this system of production was that the market ultimately decided cultural issues that the party itself could not resolve (a development that did not sit well with many party ideologues). Another result was that the artists became active participants in cultural construction rather than mere fulfillers of some party directive. Each new lacquer box added to the ongoing project of socialist cultural construction, whether it was an original work or an interpretation of a troika, firebird, or Pushkin fairy tale already in the Palekh canon. Forced to create the images that ideological overseers could not clearly define, the producers and consumers of Palekh's art, rather than planners in Moscow, unexpectedly assumed the role of chief cultural architect in the Russian heartland. In the process, the masters asserted their identity as artists rather than god-daubers, achieving a goal that had eluded them under the previous regime.

To be sure, the Soviet system had not embraced Palekh because of a commitment to full and open participation in its cultural project. Soviet leaders were as hostile to markets and peasants as were the experts of the previous regime. If the Soviets tolerated Palekh, it was more a result of their own ideological confusion and need for foreign currency than because of any commitment to allowing bourgeois consumers or former god-daubers to dictate the contours of Soviet Russian culture.

The Palekh masters were keenly aware of their tenuous hold on the regime's loyalties. As the 1930s commenced, they believed that the party might revoke its sanction for the hamlet's art at any moment. They therefore felt both a sense of empowerment under the Soviet system and profound fear and self-doubt. Perhaps more than anything, it was this perverse combination of fear and empowerment, of celebratory inclusion coupled with the threat of expulsion from the new society, that continually shaped Soviet Russian identity in the early Soviet period. Driven by fear and an intense desire to prove that they were not god-daubers, the masters (along with their patrons) presented their own ideas and traditions for party inspection. And in stark contrast to the hostility of many tsarist elites toward Palekh in the previous political order, the new regime seemed to be receptive. The revolutionary inversion of making the last the first had been realized, or so it seemed from the perspective of the early 1930s. If the Soviet Union had become a bit more Russian because of Palekh, the masters also had become a bit more Soviet.

CHAPTER FIVE

Palekh in the Age of Terror, 1933–1941

Through the 1930s, there was no master plan to guide Palekh's production, just as there was no master plan for the construction of Soviet Russian culture. The lack of state direction contrasts with the sprawling Soviet system of censorship that required, above all, some sense of what it should actually control.[1] In the absence of clear guidance, masters came up with their own themes and submitted finished boxes for monetary evaluation to a committee in the artel. The artel then submitted these themes for approval to an ad hoc evaluating committee of "experts" in Moscow, which usually included Bakushinskii and Vikhrev. The hamlet's situation partly reflected its unique status as a producer of art for export. Because its goods were primarily made for export, no coherent institutional structure controlled its style and content during the first five-year plan. Yet even later, when the hamlet turned toward domestic markets, Palekh's expert overseers in Moscow remained deeply divided over Palekh's art and, more generally, over the nature and purpose of socialist culture.

While the center's lack of consensus greatly troubled the masters, it also violated a general premise of culture-building in the 1930s. The forging of a socialist base after the first five-year plan and collectivization required such a consensus for the cultural superstructure that this new order had created. The time for creative debates had ended. The path from socialism to communism, which the Bolsheviks equated with historical progress, demanded a total merging and harmonizing of points of view. Anything less suggested a detour, perhaps permanent, from the progressive revolutionary path. Consequently, as the storm clouds of terror gathered in the mid-1930s, there was less and less tolerance for the one thing everyone agreed Palekh represented: chaos and contingency in the cultural sphere. Combined with suspicion of Palekh's link to markets and to the Russian traditions Palekh celebrated, this confusion convinced many party officials that the village's art (along with the masters) had no place in Soviet society.

A late 1933 meeting in Moscow, hosted by the All-Russian Union of Cooperative Workers in the Visual Arts to which Palekh belonged, epitomized the growing stalemate. The Gorky protégé Efim Vikhrev opened the meeting with an attack on his fellow Palekh patrons, especially the art critic Bakushinskii. He said the utility of an artistic object was not in the object's function (the "bourgeois" conception and Bakushinskii's too) but in the art's ability to convey a revolutionary message. That message was enhanced by the elegance of the Palekh technique. Equally misguided were attempts by "the art historians" (i.e., Bakushinskii) to trace the roots of the Palekh style to this or that century. Such an approach was "wrong," as were those individuals who attempted "with no apparent reason or rationale to say that Palekh's art is kulak art."[2]

Bakushinskii took the podium next, having furiously scribbled notes in red pencil during Vikhrev's presentation. Bakushinskii detested Vikhrev as a dilettante and opportunist in the field of folk art. Few were surprised, therefore, by his attacks on Vikhrev, but they were all stunned by his changing view of Palekh—a result, it seems, of his growing fear that Palekh could cause him serious political problems. Collapsing categories of class and nation, Bakushinskii said he saw in Palekh "a catering to foreign tastes . . . the unfolding of the style and influence of a . . . foreign class." By its association with foreign markets, Palekh had lost its "authenticity" *(podlinnost')*, becoming "sterile, deprived of any feeling of joy. The color is the color of a funeral. [The boxes] are imprisoned in gold leaf." While real folk art had "manly" *(muzhitskii)* peasant roots, Palekh's art was not "manly enough" *(po-muzhitski krepka)*. Art-for-art's-sake effetes such as Vikhrev, allied with foreigners, had emasculated the traditions. "Everything that is closer to modernity, to our Soviet images, either destroys [the Palekh style] or is conquered [by the style]." The style had to be "corrected for Soviet consumers." Only by embracing a more realistic manner of representation could Palekh avoid becoming "an island unto itself," cut off from the march of history.[3]

Bakushinskii's attacks on Palekh, given his earlier defense of the art, scandalized the gathering. The old Bolshevik Iakov Ganetskii admitted the masters should focus more on the internal market and were too slow in embracing new themes, but "what Anatolii Vasil'evich Bakushinskii said about Palekh today shares nothing in common with what Anatolii Vasil'evich Bakushinskii used to say." While Palekh's art troubled Bakushinskii, "it deeply pleases me." Another attendee (a certain Sletov) said Russian Orthodox traditions contained much that was valuable and progressive. If older folk such as Bakushinskii were offended by the Palekh style and mistakenly associated it with the nonprogressive aspects of Orthodoxy, "for the future generations [these false associations] won't exist."[4]

As for the attending masters, Golikov was "very depressed" by the proceedings. As far as he could tell, the debate was less about Palekh than about the rivalry between Vikhrev and Bakushinskii. Rather than providing coherent expert advice, the two patrons reminded him of "our women who gather around the well and exchange vicious gossip. One needs to speak more concretely. . . . Criticism is a good thing, but only a fair critique." Another angst-ridden master seconded his comrade:

Our artists already are beginning to waver and feel that there is not something quite right in our business. We came here to solve this problem and go back and work peacefully. . . . We came here to [settle this issue] once and for all. . . . If this is not art, then let them tell us if it is worth continuing our enterprise. Should we continue this art or not? We, the old masters, listening to this debate, are coming to a certain conclusion. Tell us, are our iconographic works valued, not simply as icons, but as works of art?[5]

Moscow's inability to answer such questions took a toll in frayed nerves and self-doubt among the masters, who were keenly aware that their fate as "artists" depended on a system whose inner workings were opaque and capricious. Without central direction, they feared that they might lapse into counterrevolutionary deviation and in the process forfeit their hard-won status as national artists. "It was terrifying and difficult to work without being guided by anything," lamented one master in a letter to Bakushinskii.[6]

A constant stream of conflicting signals from the Moscow committee responsible for reviewing Palekh's art only reinforced this sense of insecurity. Through the mid-1930s, boxes on new themes frequently evoked the critique of *"dvusmyslennost'"* (double entendre), the belief that the figures or events portrayed, due to the archaic Palekh style, did not clearly convey the proper meaning. A review of a box called *Reprisal (Rasprava),* one of the few attempts to show revenge against the kulak, said, "there is no justification for the represented image. The subject speaks more in favor of the enemy than of the revolution." By late 1933 attempts to paint new themes elicited a harsh rebuke for the artel leadership, which was told that henceforth all artists contemplating Soviet subject matter (especially of Soviet leaders) should present sketches for preliminary approval. Given the constant production pressures faced by the artists, and their own need for money to buy essential yet expensive goods in the quasi-private kolkhoz markets, securing preliminary approval greatly increased the already tedious and time-consuming process of producing a finished painted lacquer box. And there was no guarantee that the sketch would be accepted. To survive as an artist producing originals rather than copies, a master had to produce at least two high-quality originals a month, a near impossibility given the demands of the Palekh technique and the need for preapproval of sketches and themes (a process which was itself unclear). The artist Pavel Parilov, in October 1933, complained that "in order to create something unique one has to risk spending a lot of time, but living requires rubles. A vicious circle is created and there is no exit."[7] It was easier, and safer, to simply repeat themes already established in the canon. (See illustrations 15, 16, and 17 for common themes from the middle 1930s.)

If the experts remained deadlocked over Palekh's art, they were nonetheless determined to continue transforming the former god-daubers into cultured artists and citizens. In this way they would distinguish themselves from their tsarist predecessors. As part of this effort, the state embarked on an aggressive campaign to modernize the village and popularize its art. Outpourings of state largesse were initiated by the tenth jubilee of Palekh's "Sovietization," marked ten years after the Soviet artel's founding in December 1924. Jubilees played a key role in Soviet cultural construction. Like ship ballast, jubilees gave stability, legitimization, and chronological context to Soviet cultural policies in the 1930s. Celebrations of Pushkin, anniversaries of the revolution, the Stalin constitution, Lenin's death and birth, and Stalin's birthday elaborated the official social hierarchy and values of Soviet society following the first two five-year plans.[8]

Palekh's jubilee became a highlight of cultural construction in the Russian heartland. According to one attendee, "famous writers, social and political activists, party and government bureaucrats" visited the fabled hamlet. They were "enchanted by the exotic combination of old and new." Nearly twenty autobiographies of the leading artists were published (with Gorky's approval) on the eve of Palekh's jubilee. Before the jubilee two Palekh artists, Ivan Golikov and Ivan Bakanov, received the title "Honored Artist of the USSR," and the head of Narkompros announced the conferral of the same title on three additional Palekh artists. The Palekhians were god-daubers no more. Marking its transformation, Palekh received a major upgrade in the Soviet administrative hierarchy, becoming a district center. As a *raion,* Palekh could now publish its own newspaper *(Tribuna Palekha),* thus securing a local medium through which to discuss and popularize the art.[9]

Palekh's jubilee also supplied the cooperative with a "foundation event," a context for constructing a narrative that linked the artists to the revolution and to their participation in Soviet society. This foundation story contained two elements. The first recounted the village's abuse by uncultured bureaucrats and self-appointed commissars during collectivization. During the festivities in early 1935, Palekh's patrons recalled the village's struggle against revolutionary thugs in the Russian heartland, who had attempted to "de-kulakize" the artists. Palekh's victory, in this retelling, was the victory of the progressive Russian nation against reactionary factions within the revolution.[10] The second element wove a tale of Palekh's victimization and degradation in the late imperial era. Soviet propaganda now asserted that the former god-daubers, thanks to Soviet power, were able to break free from the chains of a capitalist system that had supposedly thwarted their ambitions and talents at every turn. The typical Soviet narrative about Palekh's history thus had all the elements described by Hayden White as a romance, "a drama of the triumph of good over evil, of virtue over vice, of light over darkness, and of the ultimate transcendence of man over the world in which he was imprisoned by the Fall." Wiping away the positive memory of the imperial era, and accepting the notion that in their past they had been god-daubers, was one of the costs of Palekh's entry into the Soviet intelligentsia.[11]

Tellingly, many Palekhians privately considered the darkness-to-light romance of Bolshevism an insult to their own prerevolutionary accomplishments, just as they had earlier rejected the tsarist experts' claims that they were god-daubers. But now they muted their objections, since challenging the official line threatened the status they had begun to achieve. Limited economic opportunities encouraged their public silence. In contrast to the prerevolutionary period, when talented masters could sell their services to multiple employers, the Soviet masters could either work as artists in the one and only organization employing Palekh artists, or join the collective farm and become peasants, the lowest rung in the Soviet social hierarchy. The absence of alternatives, combined with their own ambitions, thus restricted the ability of Palekh masters to challenge publicly the story of their prerevolutionary benightedness.[12]

The carrot of patronage, combined with the stick of possible arrest, also convinced the Palekhians to keep their complaints to themselves. The establishment and expansion of three organizational structures provided patronage opportunities that far eclipsed anything provided by the tsarist state. The largest was the production cooperative, which had grown to 110 full-time artists in 1935. The school serving the cooperative, upgraded from a professional or trade school *(profshkola)* to a technical secondary school *(tekhnikum)* in the same year, helped shape the tastes and views of young masters independently of the older masters in the cooperative. Following Gorky's advice, Narkompros opened a museum in Palekh in 1935, setting the stage for one of the most impressive provincial museums in the Soviet Union.[13]

The appointment of German Zhidkov (1903–1953) as the museum's first director marked the emergence of an important new patron for Palekh. The son of an accountant, Zhidkov had graduated from Moscow State University in 1922 with a specialization in philology and medieval history. In the 1920s, he helped preserve and defend Russian historical monuments. As the newest state-sanctioned expert to visit Palekh, Zhidkov was responsible in 1935 for enacting the myth of Palekh as a "village academy" *(selo-akademiia)*. The village academy envisioned Palekh as "a unified scientific-production and museum conglomerate" that would generate and propagate Palekh's traditions in murals, book illustrations, playing cards, animated films, theater sets, and a wide variety of decorated papier-mâché (and even plastic) items. Working closely with the cooperative's leadership, Zhidkov had to coordinate the sprawling apparatus of control and production set up in Palekh after the tenth-year jubilee. This apparatus included the cooperative, school, and museum, as well as the ever-shifting matrix of officials in various ministries, museums, and party organizations to which they were independently attached in Ivanovo and Moscow. Given the lack of agreement about Palekh's art and its relationship to socialist Russianhood, one can appreciate the challenge of turning this lumbering ship of artistic production toward the glorious future.[14]

Meanwhile, officials attending the tenth-anniversary jubilee seemed unsure whether to celebrate Palekh's art or to call in the secret police (the two often went together). An article in the central journal on Soviet culture charged that Palekh "has little connection with our time. The style is decorative, conditional. . . . Spinning around endlessly in a circle of its old themes, the Palekhians continue the line of 'fairytaleness' [skazochnost']." New content "in the old canonized form could not be resolved." Palekh presented a kind of false dialectic incapable of productive synthesis. Perhaps, concluded the author, the Soviet Palekh experiment would end "tragically."[15] The clear implication was that Palekh did not deserve the honors that it had received.

Most alarming, however, was Palekh's connection with bourgeois markets, which became an increasing liability for the hamlet. Building "socialism in one country" in the mid-1930s meant severing all contacts with the non-socialist world. Thus, while commentators in the 1920s and early 1930s sometimes cited Palekh's economic success abroad as proof of the art's value, markets were now Palekh's dirty little secret. The key role of the market was omitted from new writings on Palekh's post-1917 history. Reprints of earlier works on Palekh excised references to Palekh's ties with markets and foreign patrons—and foreign visitors were prevented from visiting the hamlet, a situation that would endure until the late 1950s. Henceforth, market dependence was carried as a badge of shame by the masters and periodically employed by the village's foes as a kind of cudgel to keep the artists in line.[16]

The campaign against Palekh's bourgeois contacts was also accompanied by a direct attack on the artel's business enterprise. In mid-1935, Moscow summarily terminated all of Palekh's export business, thus saddling the masters with unsold production totaling hundreds of thousands of rubles.[17] In retrospect, the cancellation was the first in a chain of interwoven economic and political crises that dominated Palekh from 1935 to 1941, as the intense stalemate about Palekh's art fed off a more general climate of paranoia, purge, and economic chaos. It is to this chain of events, and to the way it tainted Palekh's seeming triumph during the tenth jubilee of its "Sovietization," that the story now turns.

An odd hybrid of markets and planning shaped Palekh's art through the 1930s. While plans for Palekh only specified the required ruble value of production (the choice of theme was left to the artist), they were silent on where and how Palekh's production should be consumed.[18] Encumbered with production forced upon them by the plan, the artel leadership searched constantly for buyers, including publishers of illustrated books, museums, retail distribution outlets, and theater directors. Campaigns of cost accounting provided extra incentive to the artel's managers. Cost accounting, or khozrashchet as it was called, required that the cooperative balance its books and show a profit. Without balanced books, as in private businesses, the cooperative would face a liquidity crisis and thus be unable to pay its masters for works that had already been approved by its own art committee. When the cooperative was flush with cash, as in the early 1930s, the impact of cost accounting was

largely theoretical. The cooperative leadership could cover wages for artists before receiving payments from customers. But when sales slowed, as they did
dramatically in late 1935, cash reserves inevitably dwindled and inventories
rose. Unable to receive loans to cover debts and everyday operating expenses,
the cooperative had no choice but to stop paying artists, who logically stopped
working. These economic setbacks then provided fodder for charges of wrecking (subversion) and counterrevolution, as the leadership faced the prospect of
plan underfulfillment.

The rationale for canceling Palekh exports in mid-1935 was a frightening
puzzle for the Palekh masters, who were unable to separate the economics of
their situation from the political climate of the time. According to one rumor
going around the village, an outraged Stalin, following a visit to an exhibit of
Palekh lacquers, demanded termination of Palekh's business. Others saw the
cancellation as punishment for the cooperative's links to foreign markets.[19] In
fact, the stunning collapse of Palekh's export business was more prosaic, initiated by market conditions abroad. By the end of 1933, Soviet exporters had
saturated the limited western market for Soviet products. A decline in sales and
growing inventories in warehouses, for which rent in precious foreign currency had to be paid, began to threaten export plan fulfillment, with predictable consequences. From 1933 to 1935, nine high-level officials in the
Commissariat of External Trade were arrested as Trotskyites. Memoranda began
referring to "contamination" in the trading apparatus, and the resulting organizational chaos further intensified a snowballing economic and political crisis. A ban in early 1935 on using émigrés as sales agents only compounded the
problem. Working on commission, émigrés from the Soviet Union since the
NEP period had provided sales channels for the Soviet export industry, developing markets that Soviet officials were unable to exploit.[20]

An unshakable hostility to markets and trade only worsened matters.[21] Export agencies were more concerned with rooting out internal enemies than
with developing "socialist trade," a concern exacerbated by the very "capitalist" nature of their enterprise. Incompetence played a large role as well. Export
officials were unsure what kinds of exports, and in what quantity, lay unsold
in warehouses in New York, France, Germany, Holland, Belgium, and elsewhere. It was common practice among Soviet trade workers to toss all kinds of
goods into crates (including Palekh lacquers, carpets from Central Asia, and
matryoshka dolls) before shipping them abroad. As the backlog grew in these
countries, crates remained unpacked and trade officials could provide only
ballpark estimates of the amount of unsold inventory for a given product.
These estimates were critical, for they provided the basis for calculating the
value of goods still languishing in warehouse limbo before being shipped back
for distribution internally. Without precise figures, Palekh's beleaguered ac-
countants had little accurate material with which to write off debt and satisfy
the ongoing requirements of cost accounting.[22]

By December 1934, as a result of the broader crisis in Soviet exports, 164 crates of unsold lacquers were collecting dust in a New York warehouse. Letters from Moscow to New York in late 1934 demanded that the American Joint-Stock Company (Amtorg) take "all measures to liquidate these remainders." Amtorg reduced orders for Palekh lacquers, even as the artel continued churning out boxes to meet its own production plan. To eliminate remainders, authorities shipped crates back to the Soviet Union and dumped unsold inventory on the domestic Soviet market, despite orders that all goods sold domestically undergo a special process of political censorship and approval.[23] By the end of 1935, chaos afflicted the entire export system.

The dumping of Palekh goods on the internal market in 1935 and 1936 set off a chain reaction of unpleasant consequences. Dogged by concerns about the Palekh style, the masters faced renewed attacks as a foreign bourgeois contamination, since the items placed on the internal market were intended for foreign consumption. Dumping also saturated the already limited domestic market for lacquers, which was hampered by a lack of disposable income among Soviet consumers and primitive distribution and retail networks. In addition, Palekh had to meet growing plan requirements and a permanent state of *zatovarivanie* (unsold inventory), which provided enemies with seemingly palpable proof of wrecking activity. As if that were not enough, wages for artists were linked to the prices of lacquers on foreign markets. To sell export remainders (of all sorts) to Soviet consumers, trade officials had to lower prices to a point far below the cost of production. A capital shortage immediately gripped the entire trade system, exacerbated by periodic campaigns of cost accounting. As a result, Palekh was often unable to receive expected payments from trading organizations for past shipments, much less advances for ongoing production. The resulting liquidity crisis forced the cooperative to delay wage payments to artists, aggravating a climate of panic and mutual recrimination in the hamlet.[24]

Back in Palekh, the political and economic fallout of the export industry crisis fell squarely on the capable shoulders of Aleksandr Zubkov, chairman and all-around marketer for the cooperative. Zubkov's Sisyphean efforts to lift Palekh from its economic woes greatly expanded Palekh's presence in Soviet culture. Tragically, however, this could not prevent his arrest and execution, as Palekh was drawn into a broader political storm.

Zubkov was born near Palekh in 1885. Like his brother Ivan (also a founding member of the Soviet Palekh artel), he took the usual route for sons of icon painters, spending two years in grade school and then six as an icon painter's apprentice. Despite minimal schooling, Aleksandr had a great hunger and respect for culture, a trait he shared with many of the other supposedly "illiterate" peasant icon painters. If his Soviet-era autobiography is to be believed, Zubkov gained his first experience in politics in 1903, organizing local icon painters and orchestrating a reduction in the Palekh studio workday from twelve to ten hours. By 1905, he headed a circle of artists to discuss illegal revolutionary literature in the forest surrounding Palekh.[25]

Soviet power provided Zubkov with the kind of authority, responsibility, and respect he had long sought. The Ivanovo poet Dmitrii Semenovskii described Zubkov in 1935 as "a man with a confident stride. . . . He was one of the most qualified painters in Palekh, but the artists chose him as the chairman of the artel and Aleksandr Ivanovich traded the brush for the briefcase." Ida Treat, an American paleontologist who visited Palekh in the early 1930s, described Zubkov as a "lean and wiry" man with "shrewd peasant eyes and short-clipped mustache." The chairman "welcomed the occasional visitors to his village with the easy hospitality that characterizes his countrymen from one end of the Soviet Union to the other." Briefcase in hand, Zubkov tirelessly developed new markets and dunned delinquent payers. He attended conferences and Vsekokhudozhnik meetings in Moscow. When foreign visitors and patrons visited Palekh, they invariably stayed at Zubkov's house. Treat described the house as

> an *isba* of peeled logs, its facade decorated with scroll-saw lace, set back from the roadway in a grassy yard. Indoors the stove with the sleeping place on top and underneath, in a neat bundle, the forked sticks for pulling pots out of the oven. Against the whitewashed wall, broad shelves, which served as bunks. In their corner the household icons were still in place, but no lamps burned underneath. "The village is no longer pious," Zubkov hastened to explain. "To be sure, some of the women do still go to church, but the parish priest has lost all his influence in local affairs." On the wall, grouped like other icons, were family photographs— prominent among them the dead in their coffins and the chief mourner in a fitting pose of grief.[26]

If Zubkov had doubts about the political ramifications of Palekh's growing economic crisis, a mysterious letter in December 1935 from Vsekokhudozhnik clarified matters. The letter to Zubkov's attention contained a typed review of a Moscow Palekh exhibit held more than two years earlier. It came in two versions, one in English and one in Russian translation, and was supposedly based on a review printed in the *Sunday Times* (presumably of London). An accompanying note from Vsekokhudozhnik underscored the political importance of the article: "I hope that you understand what this means."[27] The anonymous review described Palekh in terms that the sociologist Timasheff would later call the "great retreat." Soviet exhibitors, wrote the author, claimed the Palekhians were liberated from religious subjects and were returning to an "earlier peasant inspiration." They had freed themselves from "formalism and tradition, so that they can interpret the new ideas in peasant life." As far as the reviewer could tell, "precisely the opposite is true . . . you will be struck by the very marked contrast between the secular subjects and the religious treatment." In representing peasants "either consciously or unconsciously" the artists had in mind the figures of Christ and the saints. "Is that what [Soviet power] means when it says 'returning to earlier traditions'?" Religion, the aristocracy, the world of the old merchant class—"this is undoubtedly the spiritual world in which these artists are still living." Palekh's art, concluded the reviewer, represented "the Russia of the Tsars and nothing else," and "communistic sentiments are by no means overbearingly allowed to run away with the formal design."[28]

Fear and desperation mobilized Zubkov into action. Aided by sympathetic officials from Vsekokhudozhnik, Zubkov crafted strategies to increase Palekh's role in decorating the "joyous" new socialist life, and hence in relieving the cooperative's growing surfeit of artistic production. To prepare students for work in new media, the school in Palekh developed majors in theater set design, graphics, ceramics, and lacquers. Looking forward to future jubilees and exhibits, Zubkov requested separate Palekh pavilions at the upcoming "Socialist Industry" exhibit and the 1937 World's Fair in Paris.[29]

It was the approaching 1937 Pushkin jubilee, however, that offered Zubkov the most effective guarantee of Palekh's political and economic survival (though not his own). Set for the hundredth anniversary of Pushkin's death in February 1937, plans to celebrate the jubilee had received official sanction in 1935. In the midst of a growing unionwide campaign to root out the "formalistic distortion" in Soviet art, Pushkin provided a seemingly surefire strategy for securing state patronage, a kind of fig leaf to hide the potential sins of "formalism." This was true for Palekh as well as for many other culture producers during the Terror. The panicked rush to Pushkin, the one indisputably safe topic for Soviet artists, gave the Pushkin cult added momentum in the terrifying years of the Great Purges.

Palekh was ideally positioned to exploit the great Russian poet's canonicity. Since the 1920s, Palekhians had focused much of their creative energy on the expansion and interpretation of Pushkin's legacy. While the artel produced eight different themes from the Pushkin oeuvre in 1925, the number reached eighteen in 1926 and sixty in 1930 (all part of a canon copied endlessly by junior masters). By 1933, Palekh produced more than fifty variations on Ruslan and Liudmila alone, inspired by the usually enthusiastic reception and evaluation of the boxes in Moscow, and thus the promise of higher wages.[30]

The new Soviet experts encouraged the hamlet's Pushkiniana, believing that Pushkin was beyond reproach as a uniquely Soviet artist. Bakushinskii's two monographs on Palekh in 1932 and 1934 presented detailed analyses of Pushkin and Palekh. Efim Vikhrev developed the theme in long essays in 1933 and 1935. The writer Boris Pil'niak cultivated a large collection of Palekh Pushkin miniatures. Publishing a lengthy tome on Palekh and Pushkin in 1937, Zhidkov consulted the masters on how to retain the Palekh style and fill it with Pushkin subjects. According to Zhidkov, Pushkin would help the artists throw off the double yoke of bourgeois decadence and religious obscurantism, thereby allowing them to complete their transformation from god-daubers into genuine artists. "[Palekh's] work on Pushkin," wrote Zhidkov, "turned out to be the most essential factor in the process of restructuring the consciousness" of the masters.[31]

As head of the State Museum of Palekh Art, Zhidkov commissioned dozens of boxes on Pushkin themes (and none on Stalin or any other Bolshevik leader). The orders provided the artel with sales and stocked the new museum of Palekh art almost exclusively with Pushkin lacquers. In 1937, M. P. Sokol'nikov, editor at the prestigious Academia press, also came to Palekh's aid, publishing a series of Pushkin fairy tales illustrated by the Palekhians. The Palekh artist Pavel Bazhenov animated the first full-length Soviet animated film, a production of Pushkin's "Tale about the Fisherman and the Fish."[32] From early 1937 to early 1939, the leading Palekh masters covered the walls of pioneer palaces with interpretations of Pushkin fairy tales in Moscow, Rybinsk, Voroshilov, Kislovodsk, Iaroslavl, Ivanovo, and Leningrad.[33]

The attempt to redeem Palekh with Pushkin did not go unrewarded.[34] On October 14, 1936, *Pravda* published a letter from Viacheslav Molotov to the Palekh artist Ivan Vakurov. Molotov praised the Palekhians for their profound insights into the Pushkin corpus. He sensed in Vakurov's work "the spark of talent and the broad social interest of the artist." His work, he promised, would occupy a central place in the upcoming Pushkin jubilee exhibits (it did). He personally expressed the hope of success for all the artists of Palekh "who with their labor and art serve the toiling masses of the Soviet nation and the construction of a new life."[35]

Alas, not even Pushkin's genius could undo the disastrous consequences of Soviet planning. While capitalism fired workers during crises of overproduction, Soviet planners kept production lines going and left the mess of accumulating inventories, unpaid wages, and delinquent debts to hapless managers such as Zubkov (who then had to answer, from 1937 to 1939, to the NKVD). The artel grew from 110 members in 1935 to 120 in 1938. There were 130 students waiting to become masters in the Palekh art school. Production rose from 429,800 rubles in 1935 to 737,700 rubles in 1936. To the 16,000 rubles of unsold production in 1933 were added 12,000 in 1934, 25,000 in 1935, and 126,000 in 1936. A memorandum from the artel sometime in 1938 said there were no prospects "in the near future" of relieving inventories, now worth 150,000 rubles and growing. From 1936 to 1938, the artel was forced to lower prices on boxes at least twice to stimulate domestic sales. The practice clashed with countervailing tendencies in cooperative payment practices, in which wages began to grow far faster than income, along with a growing differentiation between the highest- and lowest-paid members of the cooperative. Thus while polishers and other non-artist workers in the workshop earned as much or more than artists in 1930, in 1937 they earned on average one-fifth the wage of the highest-paid artists. By the mid-1930s, the artists thus earned more as *intelligenty* than did the artel's "proletarians," signaling a significant shift in the official social hierarchy away from the privileging of proletarian labor. The payment statistics, however, were more apparent than real. Faced with a liquidity crisis, the artel often failed to deliver wages, a practice that cast doubt on the raised social status of the masters in official rhetoric and policy.[36]

Meanwhile, evaluations of Palekh's art in Moscow remained as contradictory as ever, promoting a damned-if-you-do, damned-if-you-don't mentality. A Vsekokhudozhnik evaluator in the summer of 1936 complained that the masters depicted peasant labor "as a ballet" instead of showing the concrete reality of physical exertion and toil. Confronted with a box in May 1936 showing the purchase of consumer goods for distribution into the Soviet retail network, an evaluator remarked that "the central group seems to be engaging in the purchase and resale of goods for profit." Lamenting the continued impasse over Palekh's art, a journalist from the Ivanovo regional newspaper in early 1937 summed up the cooperative's dilemma. He declared that the masters "have disappeared, if one is permitted to put it this way, 'into the little Palekh box.' The box limits their horizons, stymies their creative personalities."[37]

While Zubkov soldiered on, trying as best he could to ignore the unresolved contradictions of the Palekh style, it was difficult for him to brush aside personal attacks. In late December 1937, the chairman traveled to Moscow to lobby for new business. He was met by a Vsekokhudozhnik official who "took an extremely rude tone" and began berating and insulting him like "the old type of bureaucrat." In a letter of complaint to the Committee for Art Affairs, Zubkov said he told the official that such rude treatment was impermissible "since it is illegal to violate the rights of a citizen in our Soviet Union, rights given to us by the Stalin constitution." The Vsekokhudozhnik official told Zubkov where he could put his citizenship and kicked the stunned chairman out of the office.[38]

How, one wonders, did the arrest of Palekh's most important patrons (and Zubkov's personal friends) affect the chairman's faith in Soviet citizenship? In early 1937, the NKVD arrested Boris Pil'niak and most of the other writers sent by the Writer's Union to patronize Palekh in the mid-1930s. In November 1937, Iakov Ganetskii, one of Palekh's most important Old Bolshevik patrons, was convicted and shot as an enemy of the people.[39]

A tax imposed in late 1937, the agricultural tax paid by collective farmers, presented Zubkov with another blow. Previously, the Palekh art cooperative had been exempt from the tax. On March 9, 1938, Zubkov sent a letter of complaint to the Central Committee, requesting that the impost be rescinded. The authorities, he said, were taking away with one hand the status and privilege offered with the other. "It is incomprehensible why we, the artists of Palekh, who live exclusively on our earnings as artists, for which [we pay taxes], should also pay the agricultural tax," wrote Zubkov. The masters of Palekh should be treated "like city artists. . . . The only difference is that they live in the city and we live here in a village." In defense of the cooperative, Zubkov attached copies of edicts from Moscow from 1932 and 1935 testifying to the upgraded status of the Palekh masters as artists and confirming their separation from the local collective farm. All these documents were signed by, or included mention of support by, individuals who had already become enemies of the people.[40]

DENOUEMENT

Combined with the cooperative's financial woes, the more general climate of terror in 1937 inspired the first serious local attacks on the masters since collectivization. The primary source of those attacks was the district party organization, which had been created along with the cooperative's tenth jubilee in 1935. Like the party apparatus more generally, the Palekh party organization was profoundly insecure about its ability to prevent Soviet society's contamination by counterrevolutionary elements. The cooperative's growing financial crisis, and the absence of party members among the top masters, only accentuated this sense of insecurity. When the Palekh party committee met for the first time on March 11, 1935, not one of the leading members of the artel was a party member, despite concerted efforts by leading Palekh masters to enter the ranks of party membership. To build up the district party organization's presence among the masters, the party focused instead on younger masters born after 1900, rather than the older artists. Simultaneously, younger party functionaries from outside Palekh emerged in administrative positions in the school and cooperative.[41] The party thus played on generational tensions to penetrate and control the cooperative's art, attacking the older male masters (the *stariki*) who traditionally commanded the greatest respect and authority. This divide-and-conquer strategy was now paying off.

The first direct attacks on the cooperative leadership began at a meeting of the Palekh district party committee in April 1937. A certain Kuz'minov, the young new director of the Palekh art school, noted the cooperative's "hospitable and friendly greeting, with prolonged hugs and kisses, of the inveterate Trotskyites Zarudin, Pil'niak, and Kataev." In the presence of the local leaders, the writers had staged drinking parties at Zubkov's house during the 1935 jubilee and chanted anti-Soviet slogans such as "Glory to Soviet Drunkenness." Under Pil'niak's influence, the artel leadership "produced painting foreign to us and tried to raise the beginning artists on such fare." These facts "illustrate the blunting of our vigilance."[42]

Party meetings in August 1937 continued the attacks. Zubkov's new young deputy was berated for "bowing down before the 'authority' of the [cooperative] leadership, groveling for their 'friendship' and resorting to non-party methods of bootlicking." (Presumably, party methods of bootlicking were preferable.) The visits of Pil'nyak, Zarudin, and Kataev "were not accidental," said Kuz'minov, and had led directly to many of the artel's present economic and political problems. He expanded his charges to Zhidkov, "a political exile" who had allowed "protectionism to flourish" and who was "politically unreliable." He demanded, successfully, that Zhidkov be transferred. Seconded by the regional head of the NKVD, a party representative from the collective farm complained about the privileged position of the artists. "The artists consider themselves a second power here. They have not acknowledged the authority of the district party. Whenever they can't get something, or when they get taxed for this or that, they go running off to Ivanovo or Moscow with complaints." He concluded that "all their production is wrecking activity with the goal of enraging the masses [against Soviet power]."[43]

A native Palekh master now joined the attacks. N. A. Blokhin, the cooperative's young cultural worker, condemned a strategy that the cooperative had used earlier to build patronage: the conferral of honorary memberships, accompanied by the presentation of a Palekh lacquer to the honoree. "The cooperative granted a number of honorary memberships, to Iagoda, Rykov, and Bukharin, all of whom are enemies of the people." As evidence of wrecking, he pointed out that "eighty thousand rubles-worth of finished production is lying around in the warehouse and nobody wants to buy it."[44]

A renewed campaign against religion accompanied the attacks. For the May Day celebrations of 1937, the League of Militant Godless demanded that all bell ringing stop at the hamlet's only remaining active church. Officials terminated services at the church, forcing worshipers to walk three kilometers to the nearest house of worship. The bells in the hamlet's two churches, after much effort, were heaved from their towers and hacked into pieces for scrap metal.[45] At a meeting in October 1937, Konstantin Evmenenko (hired to replace Kuz'minov, who had disappeared from the regional party proceedings) condemned the "priestly education of youth," especially the educational activities of a well-respected teacher of literature at the art school. He claimed she insisted on writing the word "god" *(bog)* with a capital B and chose phrases in her literary analyses that contained as many mentions of "the lord" as possible. The local NKVD official seconded Evmenenko, recalling a conflict with an old lady during the campaign to terminate bell ringing. Older masters are "our people," she supposedly said, and they "would not allow you to terminate bell ringing." Attendees shouted angrily, as the NKVD representative asked why the elderly artists had allowed anti-Soviet forces to spread poisonous church propaganda.[46]

Finally, on June 5, 1938, the NKVD arrested Zubkov at his house, where in happier times he had hosted Palekh's most important parties. Many of the famous revelers from those years were now enemies of the people: Pil'niak, Zarudin, Kataev, Ganetskii, Bubnov, and Guber, to name a few. Since 1935, visits of foreign dignitaries to Palekh had stopped. The street where Zubkov lived (Golikov Street) carried the name of the celebrated artist who, like Palekh's patron Efim Vikhrev in 1935, died mysteriously the previous year at the height of his artistic powers. The arrest order invoked memories of more doomed souls. Zubkov had supposedly participated with Aleksandr Glazunov (Golikov's brother-in-law and former inmate in the gulag) in spreading counterrevolutionary propaganda with the Palekh priest Rozhdestvenskii, arrested and shot in a show trial of priests in 1922. As proof that Zubkov was a spy, the order cited contacts with the American consulate in Moscow and with the American fellow traveler and Palekh lacquer enthusiast Albert Rhys Williams. Meanwhile, the NKVD seized and destroyed all printed materials in the Palekh museum that mentioned Zubkov's name, including copies of the autobiographies written by Palekhians in 1934 (thus eradicating an important confirmation of the masters' hard-won status as official artists).[47]

Zubkov maintained his innocence for the first three weeks of interrogation, although his admissions of frequent contacts with "enemies of the people" only hardened the NKVD's resolve. After beatings and threats Zubkov finally admitted to being a spy for Germany, recruited by the Palekh aficionado Georgii Baier, a German director of a pencil factory concession during the NEP period. The signed confession was, like most Soviet confessions, absurd. Zubkov admitted that during a trip to Moscow in 1930 he could not find a place to stay and happened to run into the American journalist Albert Rhys Williams. Williams arranged that he meet Baier, who then recruited him as a spy for Germany. Zubkov's task was to reveal the production activities of the Palekh cooperative. When asked if this constituted counterrevolutionary activity, Zubkov categorically said no, that he simply provided information critical for developing business with a potential partner. Dissatisfied with the confession, the interrogations broke off for two months and resumed on September 15, at which point Zubkov said he had nothing to add. The interrogators then had him sign a fabricated and detailed account of his spying activities, in connection with another recent arrestee from the Ivanovo oblast'. If Zubkov's earlier protests and petitions are any guide, he probably believed, up to the moment interrogators beat him to a bloody mess, that he had rights as a Soviet citizen, that it was all a mistake.

Convicted as a foreign spy, Zubkov was shot on October 16, 1938.[48] The purge soon expanded to Palekh's prerevolutionary art. In early 1939, the new head of the Palekh museum, Iurii Bondarenko, was ordered to compile a list of all religious icons in the town's central cathedral that "lacked historical-artistic value." A blue-ribbon panel focused on icons from the last half of the nineteenth century and early twentieth century, since they were supposedly corrupted by the rise of industrial capitalism and its vulgar cultural tendencies. Bondarenko, in a letter to the Palekh regional party committee explaining the list of fifty-one icons to be purged, presented "the act regarding the artistic values *[khudozhestvennye tsennosti]*, which have no artistic value *[khudozhestvennoi tsennosti]*." Many of the older masters reviewed the process of selection (they very likely painted a number of the icons to be purged). Pavel Korin, the Palekhian who had moved to Moscow and received Gorky's patronage as a prominent painter in the capital, traveled to Palekh as an icon expert to sanctify the process. The local head of the NKVD presided over the proceedings, "arresting" the icons after all the appropriate inventories and documents were assembled on July 21, 1939. Interestingly, the icon purge focused especially on Aleksandr Nevskii—the most repeated item on the list and the subject, simultaneously, of much fanfare in Sergei Eisenstein's famous film.[49] While Eisenstein had appropriated Nevskii the warrior as a "gatherer of the Russian land" and symbol of socialist unity against outside aggressors, Nevskii the saint was taboo. Banished in Petrograd from the Aleksandr Nevskii monastery in 1922, Nevskii's saintly relics remained unserviceable for the construction of socialist Russia. Many masters probably imagined they might suffer a similar fate.[50]

ORIGINS AND AFTERMATH

Why was Zubkov arrested? Reviewing Zubkov's KGB file in 1990, a Russian journalist was perplexed. Almost apologetically, after poring over transcripts of interrogations and orders for arrest, the journalist offered the same explanations for the chairman's purge that Palekhians had whispered for decades. One version linked Zubkov with a previous case against the Palekh priest falsely accused of espionage and shot in 1922 and with Zubkov's continued defense of Russian Orthodox artifacts. Others pointed to his connections with foreigners and with enemies of the people such as Pil'niak and Ganetskii. While some thought anonymous denunciations triggered the arrest, others saw Zubkov as a scapegoat for the cooperative's economic woes, or simply as fulfillment of the NKVD's own plans for locating and excising enemies.

Despite the absence of a smoking gun, Zubkov's arrest is not surprising, given the nature of Soviet political practices during the Terror. In Palekh there was an inextricable link between economic insolvency and political unreliability. Beginning with the cancellation of Palekh's export business in 1935, a vicious and mutually reinforcing circle of growing political charges and economic malaise provided seemingly undeniable proof of wrecking. Palekh's connections with foreigners and Russian religious traditions confirmed the suspicion. Given these circumstances, Zubkov was purged because the builders of socialism in the Soviet Union demanded the rooting out and extermination of enemies, and in Palekh the hapless chairman and former icon painter met all the NKVD's criteria. Perhaps more surprising than Zubkov's arrest was that no other older masters suffered a similar fate, itself a testimonial to Palekh's "privileged" position in Soviet Russian culture.

If the precise mechanics of terror in Palekh remain a mystery (and probably will forever), its consequences are easier to discern. Many of the older masters denied the charges against Zubkov. When the old master Zinov'ev was first advanced to party candidacy in January 1939, he refused to admit that Zubkov was an enemy of the people, prompting the Palekh district party committee to reject his candidacy. When pressed, Zinov'ev said Zubkov was a capable leader up to the very moment of his arrest. "When he was taken by the NKVD I thought there was a mistake, that Zubkov got drunk and said something [stupid] and that he would soon be returned." As for the cooperative's financial problems in 1937, Zinov'ev thought they were caused by circumstances beyond Zubkov's control. In answer to the question, had he "ever thought about the conditions that created the scandalous practices" in the cooperative, he answered: "No, I never thought about this question and to this day I do not think about it." True, he did admit drinking vodka with former enemies of the people and hunting and fishing with them, but everyone in the cooperative did these things. Only a year later, on February 14, 1940, did Zinov'ev "confess" that he was wrong, thus clearing the way for his own party membership. "I am now convinced that Zubkov was really an enemy of the people and was correctly and in a timely fashion taken away by well-known organs." Zinov'ev added that he always considered himself a "non-party Bolshevik," but he lacked the requisite "political literacy" to become a party member. The Terror apparently gave Zinov'ev the necessary schooling in Bolshevik political principles.[51]

Zinov'ev's change of heart (and it was almost certainly not genuine) marked an important watershed in Palekh's Sovietization, a transition from the heroic phase of the revolution, which attempted to paint all struggles as battles between good and evil, to something far more complex and far less heroic. Zinov'ev's great-grandson in an interview in May 2000 described his great-grandfather as a "complex man" who understood quite well the cynical spirit of the time in which he lived and the necessity of choosing one's battles.[52] In this new post-terror phase, Zinov'ev chose to "not think about" certain things. He recognized the limits of honesty and idealism (without necessarily rejecting them outright) and the necessity of cynical calculation. He now understood, as Zubkov never seems to have realized, that party prerogatives always trumped Soviet legality and that retaining his status as a Soviet artist required the explicit recognition of this fact.

Equally important, Zinov'ev's decision to join the party, even while knowing the falseness of charges against his friend Zubkov, suggests a sense of inevitability about compromising one's beliefs. Outside of the party, the most ambitious masters had almost no way to realize their dreams of artistic glory and their intense desire for public acclaim, especially at a time when the future of the cooperative seemed in grave doubt. The perceived absence of any alternative to the one-party dictatorship thus made the decision to join the party more palatable, both for Zinov'ev and for the many older masters who also joined the party in 1940 and 1941.

While Zubkov's purge solidified a growing cynicism among many artists, it also aggravated social tensions in the hamlet. In the spring of 1939, a generational war engulfed the village's art school. It was exacerbated by the continuing stalemate about Palekh's art. While older masters and younger masters traded accusations, instructors "undermined each other in front of their students." Enrollments were down, as many prospective students believed Palekh's art had no future.[53] "I remember this dangerous time for Palekh's art and for the Palekh art school," wrote the master Zinov'ev. His comments cast doubt on the common notion that the late 1930s marked a decisive return to Great Russian chauvinism and a glorification of Great Russian traditions. If there was a glorification of Great Russian traditions, it was highly selective and far from emphatic.

> At the time there were more than a few writers, artists, art critics, and leaders of our system who did not understand the new Palekh art. They wanted to steer Palekh's art from the correct path and turn our art into formalistic art. These people said that Palekh lags behind, that Palekh is standing in one place, that it needs to restructure and renew itself. In the Palekh art school [some teachers said] it was not worth studying ancient Russian painting and that only drawings and painting from the classics of the Renaissance should serve as a model. They claimed the Palekh technique is a simple thing to learn, that one does not need to study it, and that the Palekh stylization is not contemporary. They called Palekhians falsifying money-grubbers, and the art of Palekh—reactionary. Such was the opinion of some of the leaders of our system, locally and in Moscow.[54]

The plan for 1939 allowed no respite, calling for 300,000 rubles-worth of lacquer boxes, 250,000 rubles-worth of mural painting, and 350,000 rubles-worth of work in other media. The cooperative had no idea who would buy this work, the themes they should paint, and whether they should retain the Palekh style or switch to a more realistic manner. Severe shortages of goods compounded a pervasive sense of gloom. In August 1939, tobacco and sugar vanished from the shelves in Palekh and in the oblast' center Ivanovo. Electricity and kerosene also disappeared, forcing the masters to work by candlelight in the evening, as before 1917.[55]

Amidst social and economic collapse, the calendar, of all things, presented the cooperative with one last chance to prove its socialist mettle: the critical fifteenth jubilee of Palekh's Sovietization at the end of 1939. It was "a question of life and death," said one artist, regarding the exhibit that was to precede the celebrations. With the memory of his predecessor's arrest to help the flow of creative juices, the cooperative's new chairman huddled together with Moscow overseers to compose a thematic plan for the jubilee exhibit.[56] Perhaps the most detailed plan ever composed for Palekh, it also bore little resemblance to the eventual exhibit. The gap between plan and execution was emblematic of the gulf separating the official values of planning and the actual processes of cultural construction. For instance, in a section on portraiture, the exhibit plan inscribed a predictable hierarchy of Soviet political and cultural figures, beginning with Lenin, Stalin, Molotov, Voroshilov, and Kaganovich. Given the association of the religious iconographic style with religious saints, however, retaining the Palekh style in portraiture was out of the question. The actual exhibit thus presented just two portraits of Stalin, one of Kirov, one of Frunze, and one of Kalinin—the only Soviet leaders portrayed. Lenin was passed over for three portraits of Suvorov, two of Kutuzov, and one of Ivan the Terrible. Victor Hugo, Pushkin, Anatole France (a non-communist sympathizer), and a portrait of the deceased Palekh artist I. M. Bakanov, uncle of the cooperative's chairman, completed the pantheon. One is struck by the randomness of this roundup, the blurring of a coherent narrative or message: a few portraits of the *vozhd'*, Napoleon's tormentors, a French communist, an insane tsar, Russia's national poet, a French romantic, and a relative of the cooperative's new chairman.

Another part of the exhibit plan called for twenty-nine original boxes to showcase the achievements of Soviet power, from the victories of Voroshilov and Budennyi in the civil war to the triumphs of collectivization and the Stalin constitution. The eventual exhibit, however, randomly mixed in a handful of achievements of Soviet power among the other displayed items. Eight boxes depicted the triumphs of collectivization, perhaps to offset the eight boxes of boyar-like figures hunting in the Russian countryside. The only box depicting an enemy in the more than three hundred exhibited items showed the capturing of a kulak-arsonist. Palekh never excelled at enemies, which may have helped the cooperative's former chairman become one himself just a year earlier.

The masters did faithfully execute parts of the exhibit plan dealing with the "heroic past": Razin, Kutuzov, Suvorov crossing the Alps, Nevskii's battle on the ice, the seventeenth-century copper rebellion, the seventeenth-century Russian patriot Ivan Susanin tortured to death by Poles, and the defense of the Kremlin from the Tatar khan. However, it ignored nearly all the themes suggested for revolutionary history, to wit, the childhood and youth of Lenin, Stalin's first meeting with Lenin in 1905, Lenin entering Petrograd, Stalin defending Tsaritsyn, the third conference of the Russian Social Democratic Revolutionary Party, and workers shot in a 1905 strike in Ivanovo. In the world according to Palekh, Soviet Russianness displayed a premodern pedigree. Old Believer peasant rebels substituted for professional revolutionaries leading the proletariat. Decorated tsarist generals and medieval warriors stood in for purged Red Army leaders.

Despite explicit instructions to tone down the number of folk themes (the plan imagined just seven such boxes), Pushkin fairy tales and folklore eclipsed all other themes, as they did in a display of Palekh lacquers at the 1939 World's Fair in New York.[57] Nearly 50 of the 180 lacquer boxes on display in Moscow were on Pushkin themes, and nearly all the exhibited sketches for Palekh's work in book illustrations and murals, sixty-three in all, were devoted to the great national poet.

What factors had so transformed the plan for the exhibit into the actual exhibit? In Palekh, at least, the turn to heroic prerevolutionary figures, Pushkiniana, and Russian mythological representations was less the result of implicit or explicit messages from the center than the chaotic system of production in the cooperative. To put on the exhibit, for instance, the cooperative estimated it had to spend 69,559 rubles for wages and materials. However, it was only guaranteed 50,000 rubles of payment from Vsekokhudozhnik (itself short on cash), to be received *after* completion of the exhibit. The Palekh cooperative would have to make up the rest of the money and hope to turn a profit by marketing the exhibited items to various museums across the Soviet Union. Given the cooperative's financial crisis, where would the cooperative get the money to finance the exhibition and pay the artists? And how would the cooperative continue to meet its overall production targets—and find buyers for this production—as it diverted precious time and resources to the exhibit?[58]

To mobilize the collective, the leadership cajoled some of the more prominent remaining older masters into special roles as "consultants" to meet with the individual artists and counsel them on how to execute their assigned themes. In keeping with the Soviet pretense of individual initiative, the leadership stressed that all consultations were to be undertaken by artists "voluntarily." Many artists took this edict seriously by volunteering not to be consulted. By the end of May, "not a single artist has begun working on sketches of compositions according to the agreed-upon themes." Instead of sticking to the plan, artists were producing "a repetition of old [themes]," a logical choice given previous experiences with the reviewing committees in Moscow.[59]

True to form, Moscow evaluators rejected nearly all works that attempted explicitly post-1917 topics, not because they frowned upon such topics (just the opposite was true) but because they feared the consequences of allowing these images in the Orthodox religious style. A joint meeting of the cooperative leadership and Moscow overseers on August 12 came up with an emergency measure to save the exhibit, now scheduled to open in Moscow in November. It ordered that fifty-nine works from various museums and in the cooperative's inventory (one-third of the more than three hundred items eventually shown at the exhibit) be gathered for the exhibit. Among other things, using older boxes saved money and avoided the challenge of getting the masters to follow the plan. Unfortunately, the older boxes almost uniformly invoked Pushkin fairy tales and pastoral idyll, themes the exhibit was supposed to prove Palekh had outgrown.[60]

How surprised the masters must have been when they learned that the exhibit had garnered decent if ambiguous reviews in Moscow. In the wake of the exhausting terror, political patrons seemed content to declare Palekh's iconography socialist (while admitting residual "contradictions" in the art) and leave it at that. The main newspaper on Soviet culture appropriately named its ambiguous but largely positive review after the famous Vasnetsov painting *At the*

Crossroads. To the surprise of many masters, the art critic Sokol'nikov said many Palekhians had acquired a false understanding of socialist realism. "Palekh has become afraid of its tried and true themes . . . fairy tales, *byliny*, legends, fantasy, romanticism." He concluded on the usual irresolute note, which also mirrored a *New York Times* review of the exhibit that questioned the compatibility of folk and industrial themes. "Palekh," said Sokol'nikov, "today presents a picture of . . . contradictions. Yet, it also has a deep vitality and the exhibit of Palekh art proves this."[61]

Despite the center's qualified praises, the windfall of expected contracts and orders did not materialize. By the end of 1940, the cooperative's unsold inventory exceeded two hundred thousand rubles. The cooperative had almost no operating capital. Nine of the young masters, who had been groomed as party members to step into the void left by the death of older masters and the arrest of Zubkov, were called up for military duty. A new leadership void thus emerged, at a time when many older artists, in a silent protest, simply refused to work.[62]

The final collapse of the local economy and supply system only aggravated social tensions. According to an April 1940 party report, most students at the Palekh art school suffered from severe stomach disorders. Students rarely received their meager stipends, and what they did receive they gambled, drank, and smoked away. The school and its dormitory had no art supplies, mattresses, electricity, or kerosene. Newspaper subscriptions no longer arrived. Older students physically abused younger students. The cafeteria had no heat. Lunch consisted of sugarless tea and a watery potato soup with no meat. Students used wallpaper torn from the walls for their drawing class. An informant reported a typical student comment: "As soon as I finish this torture I have no intention of becoming an artist. I'm going to study somewhere else in another specialty." An NKVD informer from the cooperative in June 1940 reported a similar collapse of morale among the masters. "They've taken the last shirt off my back," said I. A. Pershin, regarding taxes and obligatory government loan campaigns. "The state needs to live, and we need to die." While NKVD informants were apt to exaggerate problems in their search for internal enemies, it would have been hard to overstate the collapse of social and economic order in Palekh following the Terror.[63]

A report after World War II looked back on early 1941 as "a fateful [time] in the history of the cooperative. Production continued, but already at the beginning of the year it was clear that there were no buyers. The production life of the cooperative was experiencing the agonies of death," and even before the Nazi invasion, the cooperative had ceased to operate, its facilities picked apart like so many Roman ruins by locals.[64] The cooperative was bankrupt and had no choice but to shut its doors and leave employees to their own devices. The project of creating the village academy seemed to have ended in utter failure.

A BLESSING IN DISGUISE: THE NAZI INVASION

A lethal mix of economic and ideological factors ultimately triggered Palekh's prewar demise. First, the Terror's decimation of the state trading apparatus, compounded by a militant anti-trading ethos, exacerbated the dysfunctionality of Soviet consumer markets upon which Palekh depended. Second, amidst an unprecedented military buildup in 1939 and 1940, the Soviet state, along with most Soviet consumers, had run out of discretionary income for artistic purchases. Third, continuing disagreements about Palekh's art, and about the Great Russian national traditions it celebrated, cast further doubt on the socialist nature of the masters' artistic accomplishments. Finally, Palekh was denied access to foreigners and foreign markets, its main customer base before 1935. As a result, the Palekh cooperative descended into a financial hole from which it could not escape.

That same vortex also seemed to consume Palekh's gains in social status. With the closing of the cooperative, the masters had no pension, few savings, and no effective system of patronage. Joining the only other employer in town, the collective farm, meant relinquishing the status of "artist" and descending back into the position of "peasant"—the official status of the Palekh masters in the imperial period. From the standpoint of Palekh in May 1941, the bankruptcy of the cooperative thus symbolized the bankruptcy of their official identity in Soviet society. Soviet power seemed to have reneged on its promise of helping the masters transform themselves from god-daubers into genuine artists, just like its tsarist predecessor. The empty promise was all the more humiliating for the masters, since they had reluctantly endorsed the notion that they had been god-daubers in the first place. Rejected by the market, and facing withering attacks as a nest of counterrevolutionaries, many Palekhians now wondered if they weren't god-daubers after all.

And then Palekh experienced another ironic twist of fate. Hitler's invasion came to its rescue. The emergence of an external enemy was as uplifting for the artists as the Terror's earlier search for internal enemies had been demoralizing. Like an opened pressure valve, the war allowed Palekhians (like many other Soviets) to redirect their animosities from abstract internal enemies to easily identifiable external foes. When the state commanded the artists to reorganize the cooperative's operations in early 1942, the masters joyously redeemed a sense of communal and national solidarity that had been so elusive before the war. In the process, they reestablished their identity as genuine artists.

It helped, of course, that one major source of discord in the village, the generation of new Soviet masters born after 1900, marched off to war and death, paving the way for the old masters to reclaim control of the traditions. The war thus ended the generational conflict through which the party, with some success, had attempted to divide and conquer the community of Palekh artists.

Thanks to the blitzkrieg, Palekh's dramatic if contested expansion in Soviet culture was therefore more than a Pyrrhic victory.

As for Palekh's memory of the Terror, one point stands out in comparison with the other traumatic event of socialist construction related earlier: the campaign of collectivization. If the Palekh artists had turned attempts to "dekulakize" the masters into a story of heroic resistance against the forces of cultural nihilism, Palekh's total collapse during and after the Terror produced no narrative of triumph against ignorance and local excess. Partly, this was a result of the Terror's limited impact among the artists. Only the hapless chairman of the cooperative, Aleksandr Zubkov, perished as an enemy of his people (though a number of prominent artists died mysteriously and others committed suicide). But it also had to do with an understandable reluctance to dredge up painful memories and decidedly unheroic events, especially since Zubkov was a widely respected figure among the artists and a central reason for their Soviet successes.

The inadequacy of political terror as a basis for national historical memory is especially apparent against the backdrop of the Great Patriotic War. For instance, in rural Vinnytsia in the Soviet Republic of Ukraine the local elite during World War II had almost completely erased the memory of the Terror. They attributed atrocities to Nazi invaders rather than to the NKVD. Already by 1943, "the Terror had become a non-event."[65] As the next chapter will show, a similar process of wiping clean the memory of the purges occurred in Palekh. Indeed, memory of the Terror was so effectively erased by the far more heroic experience of fighting Nazis that the Terror also remains a nonevent in Palekh. For instance, in central Palekh today, as in most cities, towns, and villages of Russia, an elaborate memorial honors the hundreds of young male victims of fascism. One searches in vain, however, for a marker honoring Aleksandr Zubkov. Not even a gravestone or tiny plaque commemorates the chairman, who more than a decade after the fall of Soviet power remains largely beyond the pale of serviceable local memory. Keeping this thought in mind, the story now turns to Palekh during World War II, which despite its physical destruction allowed Palekh to resume its post-Terror transformation into Soviet Russia's village academy. Side by side, and thanks to Hitler, the Russification of the Soviet project also gained new momentum.

CHAPTER SIX

Saved by the War!

"Despite their advanced age the old masters are working productively and one must say they are doing a splendid job."
—The Palekh district party committee, December 1942[1]

In September 1942, Pavel Korin, former icon painter and celebrated Soviet artist from Palekh, echoed the thoughts of many Russians in the first grim stages of the war. "Although Soviet power has done a lot of bad things to me I am a patriot. I love my motherland. I hate foreigners and love my fields, villages, and churches. All this is close to my heart." The "German pig," he concluded, "underestimated the resolve of a Russian person." How gratifying it must have been to focus on an enemy of the people who was not of one's own race or community. Equally important, the artists were desperate after the Terror to prove their loyalty to the regime. As an act of political atonement, they therefore threw themselves headlong into the battle against the Nazis. If Hitler had counted on native resentment of the Bolsheviks to help conquer the Soviets and make Russia a Teutonic "lebensraum," his reading of Russian attitudes could not have been more mistaken.[2]

Hitler's miscalculation was accentuated by a dramatic shift in Moscow. In a moment of extreme hopelessness, the regime displayed an uncharacteristic spirit of clemency and political flexibility. The masters, according to one artist, no longer had "to endure all types of restructuring . . . that were foreign to the nature of our art." It was a remarkable ideological retreat, a complement to the rapid disintegration of the Red Army in the first phases of the war. The old concerns about contaminating socialist content with vulgar market tastes and Russian Orthodox forms suddenly disappeared. The Leninist bias against the peasantry but toward the privileging of class over nation receded further into the background. National unity became the new rallying call. Emboldened by the shift at the center, older Palekh masters saw the struggle against foreign invasion as an opportunity for redemption, both for themselves and for Russian national and rural traditions.[3]

Signaling the shift in policies, in early 1942, Moscow officials ordered the masters to restart their operations, wiping away the cooperative's previous debts. One of the cooperative's first state orders that year was to design the stage sets and costumes for the Bol'shoi ballet's production of *The Land of Miracles,* under the direction of the famous Soviet ballet master Leonid Iakobson. Iakobson, in consultation with the old Palekh master Zinov'ev, envisioned the stage as a gigantic lacquer box. In a Russian fairy-tale setting, the ballet was to show the triumph of good over evil. Through 1942, overseers in Moscow told the Palekhians to retain the unique Palekh style and to focus "on themes combining history with the modern period and many others of an historical nature that have relevance in the period of the heightened struggle against fascism."[4] Continuity with the past, rather than a radical break, was now official policy.

The masters responded enthusiastically to the first clear marching orders they had received from Moscow since the revolution. New boxes included *The Female Partisan—The Destruction of Enemy Tanks, The Defense of Moscow from Enemy Attacks, The Patriotic War of 1812, Attack!, "Bogatyri" of the Russian Land,* and *The Landing of Paratroopers in Crimea.* A celebration of the October Revolution in 1942 produced similar orders from the Committee for Art Affairs, the first major orders the masters had received for a high-profile exhibit in Moscow since the Pushkin jubilee of 1937. One box referred to the war as a "holy war" *(sviashchennaia voina).* Other boxes celebrated the victory over Napoleon, the heroes of the Time of Troubles, and Nevskii's defeat of the Teutonic knights, all painted by older masters.[5] Historical battle themes, of course, had already emerged in the late 1930s but were always ambiguously juxtaposed with Soviet triumphs during the civil war and depictions of so many Reds versus Whites. By contrast, Palekh represented Russia during the war as an internally unified nation with little legacy of class strife and division.[6]

Reflecting Palekh's favored status, the regime reaffirmed Palekh as a center of Russian artistic culture and the masters as bona fide artists. In November 1943, Ivan Markichev became a People's Artist. It was the first honorific for Palekhians since before the Terror. The older masters Aristarkh Dydykin, Nikolai Zinov'ev, and Dmitrii Butorin received the title Honored Artist of the Soviet Union.[7]

Relaxed trade restrictions, and a growing fad among soldiers and their loved ones for Palekh miniatures, complemented the increase in state support. The climate of relative tolerance for the private domestic market in lacquers harkened back to the NEP period, when Palekh often filled orders for clients without the mediation of state trading organizations and without the constant charge of contaminating their art with vulgar market tastes. In 1942 and early 1943, requests for portraits of sons and husbands on the front began pouring into the cooperative. The cooperative, said the vice-director of the Palekh museum, could not "refuse people that turn to the artel with a request to immortalize the image of a husband, father, or son who spares no effort battling the enemies of the Motherland." Some customers ordered boxes of loved ones who had died at the front, sending photographs of the fallen soldiers. "The image of our son, immortalized by you, softens the grief of our irreplaceable loss," went one letter of thanks to the cooperative. These images were framed by Palekh's elaborate golden ornament on small boxes that could fit inside one's pocket. One commander at the front in late 1942 sent a letter to the cooperative explaining that Nazi invaders had killed his family in Ukraine. His only physical memory was a picture of his daughter, which he sent to the cooperative along with money. "Draw a portrait of my daughter on a box, if you can." One old master drew a picture of a smiling child—curiously thin and elongated in the Orthodox iconographic manner. A father at the front had ordered the box after the image of his son, to be cherished "like a most valuable relic."[8]

The growing domestic trade in lacquers also proceeded through the gift shop of the State Museum of Palekh Art, which experienced a sharp rise in visitors in 1942 and 1943. Individuals evacuated from the western parts of Russia as well as soldiers on leave began visiting Palekh and its museum, drawing inspiration before returning to the battle. By the end of 1942, demand was "enormous," said the master Zinov'ev, and given the advancing age of the older masters and the death of so many young ones in the war, he was unsure the masters could keep up. Letters with orders continued to arrive from the front, where according to one Palekh party district report in December 1942, Palekh's art "enjoys enormous popularity among soldiers and their commanders." Commanders sent soldiers directly to Palekh to pick up orders.[9] It was a striking contrast to Palekh's situation during World War I, when there seemed to be virtually no attempt, directed by the state or otherwise, to link Palekh's artistic traditions to the war effort.

In the meantime, the Soviet state renewed Palekh's ties with foreign buyers, just as it had allowed the cooperative more latitude to exploit domestic market opportunities. The policy of reviving Palekh exports reversed the xenophobic backlash against Palekh's foreign trade in the mid-1930s. Palekh lacquers generated both precious hard currency and helped to build relations with new allies. In 1944, the cooperative fulfilled an order from Franklin Delano Roosevelt for the princess from *Swan Lake*. "It was stipulated that the female personage in the composition should have the likeness of one highly placed figure, whose photograph was attached." The Palekhians also painted the top of a large chest with the figure of Pushkin reading folktales to Russian peasants. Molotov presented the box as a gift to an American diplomat during the congress that formed the United Nations.[10]

While the Soviets used Palekh to impress the industrialized West, they also exploited Palekh's art in the developing world. Exhibitions of Palekh lacquers in Persia in late 1944, Mexico City in early 1945, and in Egypt immediately after the war projected an image of Soviet Russia as a land that valued its rural craftsmen and traditions. In nations with large peasant populations, this was an especially important selling point for the Soviet system. One Iranian visitor to a 1945 exhibit of Palekh lacquers in Tehran spoke approvingly of Soviet cultural policy as reflected in the preservation and development of Palekh's art. "If folk art is dying in the large capitalist countries, consumed by capitalist industry, then in the Soviet Union the preservation and development of artistic industries is guaranteed."[11]

THE NEW IMPERATIVE: PRESERVATION

Palekh's revival occurred against the backdrop of another striking change in Soviet cultural policies: a revived movement to restore and preserve Russian monuments of antiquity, which paralleled and complemented the emphatic embrace of romantic Russianness.[12] Preservationist policies had a complex history in the Soviet period. Struggles between advocates of a radical break with past artistic forms and conventions and those who supported aspects of the prerevolutionary heritage were a central dynamic of cultural debate in the 1920s. Building on the work of their tsarist predecessors, many Soviet preservationists considered the artistic forms of Russian Orthodox culture part of the "progressive" cultural heritage.

During the first five-year plan, the state's ambiguous commitment to preservation lost momentum. The dramatic dynamiting of Moscow's Christ the Savior Cathedral in 1931, built to honor the victory over Napoleon, initiated a wave of church closings and demolitions in central Russia. The main cathedral in Palekh was among the churches targeted for destruction after being closed. Only through the determined intervention of Gorky was it saved and turned into a museum of Russian culture. In 1934, Narkompros disbanded the State Central Artistic Restoration Studio and folded its personnel and functions into the Tret'iakov Gallery, a move that downgraded and decentralized (though did not eliminate completely) the restoration and preservation of Russian religious icons.[13] The downgrading of preservation, which at least in part belies the notion of a supposed great retreat to prerevolutionary values in the mid-1930s, was also reflected in a coordinated policy of selling off Russian cultural artifacts that intensified after the first five-year plan.[14]

It was one thing, however, for the Soviet state to destroy Orthodox culture and quite another when foreign invaders began dropping bombs on ancient Russian churches. The destruction of Russian monuments of antiquity by foreigners, like the destruction of the Russian people by Nazi invaders, thus turned the pendulum back toward a preservationist policy. In 1942, the Council of People's Commissars (Sovnarkom) convened a special commission to assess the damage done by Nazis to Russian historical monuments. In 1944, the Soviet state revived the State Central Artistic Restoration Studio, a move that coincided with the sober realization that Nazi occupiers had almost completely destroyed Peter's Summer Palace and countless ancient cathedrals in cities such as Novgorod. A concern for preservation coincided with relaxed state policies toward the Russian Orthodox Church, culminating in the famous concordat between Stalin and the church in September 1943. Intentionally or not, the policy shift reinforced attitudes toward the icon as a fundamental and legitimate part of Soviet Russian culture.[15]

The fate of Palekh's most famous son, the artist Pavel Korin, illustrates these dramatic and confusing swings in cultural policies. A graduate of the tsar's icon-committee school in Palekh in 1907, the young Korin moved to Moscow, where he pursued his dream of becoming a famous artist. In the 1920s, Korin's sketches linked Russian Orthodox culture, the landscapes of central Russia, and Russian national identity. They were part of a grander project he called *Requiem*, which depicted various church figures exiting the Cathedral of the Assumption in Moscow. Korin remained an openly devout believer throughout the Soviet era, but depending on one's point of view, his painting either symbolized the church's tragic demise or a potential rebirth of Christianity in the broader society.[16]

The artist's big break came in September 1931, when the writer Maxim Gorky visited Korin's Moscow studio. Korin's work on *Requiem* impressed the father of socialist realism, who urged Korin, for reasons of political safety, to change the title from *Requiem* to *Disappearing Rus' (Ukhodiashchiaia Rus')*. Korin subsequently traveled with Gorky to Sorrento in 1931 and 1932 and worked on a famous portrait of the writer that Gorky said was his favorite: a far from flattering vision that depicted a tragic figure, aging, with a deathly pallor and sagging folds of skin. Like Palekh itself, Korin attracted high-level patronage. He also ran the restoration workshop at the Moscow Museum of Fine Arts, where he restored religious icons and continued to amass his own collection of ancient holy images, building on his family's private collection.[17]

By the mid-1930s, Korin, like the preservation movement, fell on hard times. Denied state patronage, Korin was called upon to display his loyalty in the late 1930s by destroying the very objects he was employed to preserve. When the Palekh museum's collection of religious icons was purged of fifty images in 1939, Korin was sent to his native Palekh to preside over the process. One can imagine how hard it must have been for Korin to destroy items that represented not only his own artistic heritage but also his most cherished and sacred beliefs.[18]

The war gave Korin, like his fellow Palekhians, an opportunity for redemption. He again received state patronage as an artist, including orders for a triptych of Aleksandr Nevskii (the main subject of items destroyed in the Palekh icon purge before the war) and a portrait of Marshal Zhukov. State support also kept Korin busy restoring icons. During the war, he traveled throughout central Russia where he analyzed church murals and icons and initiated restoration procedures. Signaling the alteration in cultural policies, Korin, at a gathering in his honor before the Moscow Union of Artists on March 26, 1945, boldly proclaimed that his monumental painting *Disappearing Rus'* was "not a disappearing Rus', but a Rus' that still lives, an ancient Rus', an authentic Rus' that never died and will not die."[19]

In line with the new emphasis on preservation, the Soviet government during the war restored the State Museum of Palekh Art to the status of a republic-level museum rather than a regional museum, putting it directly under the control of cultural officials in Moscow. The All-Russian Cooperative Association of Artists (Vsekokhudozhnik) sent German Zhidkov, the museum's first director and subsequently the vice-director of the Tret'iakov Gallery, back to Palekh in August and September of 1943. Whereas the district party had earlier considered Zhidkov "politically unreliable," they now greeted him as an honored, patronage-bearing guest. Finding his own redemption in the war, Zhidkov inventoried the museum's icons and outlined a program of further development for the museum's collections of local religious art.[20]

Meanwhile, in June 1943 the head of the Palekh museum, K. Pomerantsev, issued a public call in the local newspaper to "preserve monuments of national creativity," especially icons and frescoes in churches. "It is the obligation of everyone in these historic days to take special care of cultural values and not to permit . . . even the slightest acts that might be harmful to monuments of national creativity." The newspaper article prompted a wave of activism as local citizens brought treasured icons out of their hiding places and abandoned churches and donated them to the museum. Throughout 1943, Pomerantsev met once a month with Pavel Korin in Moscow, bringing him icons to restore. He returned each time to Palekh with a load of freshly restored icons to deposit in the museum's growing collection of holy images. Those same images also inspired aspiring art students in Palekh, who assiduously copied the images as part of their training to become Soviet lacquer specialists. One summer day in 1943, the visiting vice-chairman of Sovnarkom approvingly watched the Palekh students at work. Ancient Russian Orthodox images, he remarked, "develop and guide the tastes of the young generation." Before the Nazi invasion, no high-level Soviet official would have dared to make such a remark about Palekh in public—and probably not in private either.[21]

Also unthinkable in the prewar period was a new religious icon acquisition program initiated in September 1943. Using funds released by Moscow overseers, the State Museum of Palekh Art acquired twenty-seven icons from the surrounding area in December 1943. The purchasing program gained momentum after the old master Nikolai Zinov'ev took over the museum's operations in early 1944. Zinov'ev was the first Palekhian and master to hold the position of museum director. He immediately restored the "old wing" of the museum, the central cathedral in Palekh that had been closed for church services in 1934 and nearly razed, to its previous interior arrangement (though not its function). The decision was a telling statement on the official shift in attitudes toward the Russian Orthodox heritage. When the church was converted into a museum in the mid-1930s, its icons had been taken out of the iconostasis and put on easels, accompanied by an exhibit explaining the fallacy of the Christian myths of creation and the resurrection. Other icons were removed completely from the walls and put in storage, along with church paraphernalia. Officials covered the walls with tarps. In 1944, Zinov'ev put the icons back into the iconostasis, took down the tarps, and restored the rest of the icons and other church paraphernalia to their original place. His aim, he explained, "was to show the best of Palekh in its Renaissance, on the basis of which the modern art of Palekh emerged."[22]

Preservation efforts also extended to Palekh's Soviet-era production, especially the sketches and works of the first Soviet masters from the NEP era. These works celebrated historical Russian battle themes, folk motifs, and village life, now considered classics of the Palekh medium. The program, backed by one hundred thousand rubles released from Moscow overseers, reversed an earlier trend begun during the Terror, when the local museum abandoned purchases of Palekh art and acquired mostly works from urban Soviet artists. The newly acquired works provided the nucleus of a traveling exhibit to introduce Russia's provincial centers to Palekh's art.[23]

THE ARCHAICIZATION OF CULTURE

Unforgiving demographic realities lent greater urgency to preservationist policies. Privileging continuity with the past, Soviet officials were greatly troubled by the possible death of the oldest masters. Of the cooperative members in November 1945, thirty-nine were born before 1900, twenty-five before 1891, and ten before 1882. Only twelve were born after 1900. Moreover, many younger masters, such as Ivan Golikov's talented son Georgii, died in the first days of the war. After finishing the Palekh art school in 1940, he was called up for military duty and was killed on the second day of the Nazi invasion. Four months later, nearly twenty young masters gathered to depart for the front in Rybinsk, only to die instantly in a Nazi bombing raid. Just like that, much of the new generation, which was attempting to absorb and adapt the traditions from the older masters, had disappeared.[24]

The fate of Pavel Bazhenov (1904–1941), killed in the bombing raid of Rybinsk in October 1941, illustrates the war's destructive impact on the younger generation—and on attempts to Sovietize Palekh's traditions. Bazhenov belonged to the so-called middle generation, those who had begun as icon apprentices in the tsarist period but only finished their apprenticeship as artists under Soviet power. Like many younger masters, Bazhenov was far more open to the aesthetics of urban socialist realist art than were his elders.[25] While he painted thousands of folklore images on boxes and theater sets, and even animated cartoons, he also embraced contemporary themes, drawing inspiration from urban artists such as Aleksandr Deineka, who excelled at modernist industrial and sport scenes. One of Bazhenov's most celebrated lacquers from the mid-1930s, a representation of a border guard, evoked the growing obsession with keeping out alleged enemies. The figure retained critical elements from the style of the Russian icon, including the distinctive dress and folds in the clothing. Yet it also contained images of factory silhouettes and urban landscapes. In 1940 Bazhenov joined other Palekh masters in painting murals in the new Ivanovo Pioneer Palace. Bazhenov tackled the murals on the second-floor hallway. Instead of the Palekh style and the hamlet's typical subject matter, he painted ten scenes from the history of the revolution in the manner of monumental Soviet art.[26]

The seeming ease with which Bazhenov moved between the traditional style and Soviet monumental art made him the darling of those who wanted to update Palekh's art for the revolutionary society. Uniquely, however, he was also popular among older masters. "Bazhenov was undoubtedly the best hope of Palekh," lamented the old master Zinov'ev in the spring of 1942. For Palekh's art, Bazhenov's death in the war, along with the deaths of so many of his younger comrades and protégés, thus complicated more than a decade of assiduous efforts to square the circle of Palekh's tradition with a Soviet modernity.[27]

Meanwhile, many surviving older masters, taking advantage of their newly dominant status, aggressively promoted a more traditional approach toward their craft. Anticipating the return from the war of surviving younger masters and students who had not finished their studies, they created a mandatory system of training for younger masters at the cooperative. Run by the older masters, these study circles were designed to preserve "the art of contemporary Palekh based on the many-centuries-old traditions of ancient Russian art and a direct continuation of the religious icon-painting art." The "value and significance" of Palekh's art, noted a cooperative report from 1944, lay precisely in "preserving the ancient traditions" of which only the "oldest masters" were the true carriers. The younger masters were "completely ill-prepared in their knowledge of the traditions and in their deep understanding of the basic particularities of the Palekh style," and such ignorance created "grave dangers for the further development of Palekh's art as a distinct art form."[28]

By July 1945, with the support of the regional party, Zinov'ev and other older masters pushed through a curriculum that made the teaching of Russian Orthodox icon styles the explicit core of Palekh art school pedagogy. This conclusion, added the Palekh cooperative chairman, came not only from the experience of the Soviet art school in Palekh "but also from the raising of this question in the prerevolutionary icon-painting school." The tsar's prerevolutionary school, he added, had struck a balance between tradition and modernity that should serve as an example in the Soviet period.[29] Nicholas II's art school in Palekh, founded in 1902 and shuttered in 1918, thus became an explicit model during World War II for the Gor'kii School of Palekh Art.

If the war had reinforced the power of the older generation, not to mention its traditional values and tastes, it also allowed women to assert themselves as masters. This shift represented an immense and permanent change in the social fabric of the Palekh art community, which had excluded women for centuries. In prerevolutionary Palekh, women had supplemented the income of their husbands by tending gardens and doing piecework for the region's robust textile industry, centered in nearby Shuia and Ivanovo. They were excluded, however, from the icon-painting profession. Women in Palekh first attempted to become masters at the time of the dramatic expansion of the Palekh art school and cooperative in the early 1930s, but they had limited success. Even the daughters of leading masters were rejected as candidates for the artel since, in the words of one older master, "that's the way it had been since time immemorial." Among the more than three hundred graduates of the Palekh art school in the 1930s, less than a half dozen appear to have been women. At least three of those graduates were refused work in the cooperative following their studies in the mid-1930s. Instead, they were assigned to work in the Red Porcelain factory just outside of Leningrad, a job they clearly did not relish.[30]

The war, however, opened new opportunities for women, who supplied the inspiration that young male masters at the front could no longer provide. Profoundly aware of the devastating impact of the war on Russia's male population, Palekh's women took advantage of the chance to represent Russia as a "motherland" and not just a "fatherland." Russia, in their art, became a fertile land capable of regenerating itself, an image that emphasized "organic" rural landscapes at the expense of urban spaces and technological prowess.

One of the first women to break the glass ceiling in Palekh was Anna Kotukhina (1915–), niece of one of the artel's founders and a 1940 graduate of the Palekh school. She was joined by Tamara Zubkova (1917–1973), a graduate from the Palekh art school in 1938 (and niece of the executed former chairman of the cooperative). Zubkova returned to Palekh in 1942 from the Red Porcelain factory to which she had been involuntarily assigned. Both artists, remembered one female master many years later, introduced into the art of Palekh "a feminine principle, especially in lyrical, folk, and popular-song theme," qualities that seemed to suggest a significant feminization of Palekh art that complemented the simultaneous "archaicization" of the collective. Kotukhina, in particular, reflected "the broad nature of the Russian feminine soul" in works depicting a birch forest, a day off, and the snow maiden, which "are distinguished by a bright decorativeness of image and a harmony of feelings." Beginning in 1943, Nadezhda Khomiakova (1918–1974) and Anna Khokhlova (1918–1982) also entered the ranks of masters, specializing in folklore themes. Together with Kotukhina and Zubkova, they created a strong nucleus of women masters considered by some art critics to be the cooperative's most influential younger members.[31]

The gender shift was dramatic, fueled by the same forces that had strengthened the role of the older masters: the decimation of a cohort of younger males on the front. When the Palekh art school reopened in April 1943, twenty-six of the forty-eight students (all ethnic Russians) were female. In November 1943, twelve of the male students were called up for the Red Army, thus changing the balance even more in favor of women masters.[32] With the influx of males into the ranks of the school and cooperative after the war, women retained a hold on these gains—a striking contrast to other societies during the war, in which opportunities for women frequently disappeared as soon as the men returned home. Paradoxically, therefore, the war strengthened one aspect of traditional Palekh, the role of the older masters, even while it decisively brought down another, the centuries-long exclusion of women from the icon-painting profession.

Women played more than a token role as artists and social activists. Anna Kotukhina, even today retaining a militantly atheist spirit, called herself a "nonparty Bolshevik." One artist remembered Kotukhina as a "decisive, complex personality who combined enormous emotion, expressiveness, a restless soul, lyrical subtlety, and masterful command [*masterovitost'*]." She exploited her artistic reputation during the war to earn a spot on the cooperative's ruling board and art committee, where she never hesitated to voice her opinion. She also became an official voice for the cooperative, writing and publishing articles for the local press. In May 1942, she wrote an account of Palekh, "In the Days of War," noting defiantly that "Palekh has not died." In "carrying the traditions of ancient Russian art," the masters acquired "greater and greater significance." She linked the preservation of Russia's medieval past with a defense of the Soviet motherland, not merely the fatherland. "We will not forgive the enemy for the shed blood of women, mothers, and children," she wrote.[33]

Beginning in the war, Kotukhina received some of the cooperative's most prestigious orders for exhibits, murals, theater set design, and graphics, including a contract to depict the greatest battle in Russian history: the Battle of Stalingrad. The suffering of the motherland seemed to require a mother to be its decorator and illustrator. According to one Soviet art critic, Palekhians believed that "romanticism and impulsive emotion" provided the foundation of "living art, and of life itself at the most tragic hour of extreme danger." With Vsekokhudozhnik's blessing, Kotukhina traveled to Stalingrad immediately after the Nazi defeat. Amidst the ruins of the battle, as corpses were being gathered following the momentous victory over fascism, she spent three weeks collecting impressions. She especially remembered a strange contrast: the stench of rotting flesh and the determination of residents to continue life and work in the rubble.[34] These impressions inspired her epoch rendition of Stalingrad in lacquer, done in the Palekh style but also under the clear influence of a more monumental approach. The Palekh art critic Vitalii Kotov, a resident of Palekh since the late 1940s, said Kotukhina partly drew inspiration from Vera Mukhina's famous *Worker and Collective Farm Woman*. He described the intended message of Kotukhina's large papier-mâché chest, which expressed the indestructible strength, energy, resilience, and spirit of sacrifice, the heroic *bogatyr*-like thrust of the defenders of Stalingrad. The heroic images are deliberately expressive. This is the exalted expressiveness of a broad decisive step, of powerful gestures, and of a monumental exaltation, which is infused with romantic pathos. . . . Anna Aleksandrovna traveled to Stalingrad to witness the evidence of the recent events and observed the ruins. But rising above the ruins were the *bogatyri* drawn from her imagination.[35]

Stalingrad earned Kotukhina fame and patronage in Moscow and additional respect in Palekh. Soon after, she began another large chest on *The Lay of Igor's Campaign*. She was the first female master, and perhaps Soviet Russian female artist, to tackle the great medieval epic of Russian national martyrdom. As in her chest on Stalingrad, she expressed "romanticism [and] emotion." Both jobs illustrated the willingness of the old masters to allow a woman to secure what were perhaps Palekh's most prestigious state orders of the entire Stalin era.[36]

Attaining the status of a celebrated master, however, did not mean sacrificing her nurturing role. Palekhians admired Kotukhina for her talents as an artist and housewife. She was noted for her skills as a cook and hostess, abilities that the author has witnessed firsthand. When her husband went off to fight the Nazis, she painted portraits on tiny lacquer boxes of their two children. Her husband carried the boxes through the trenches and back to Palekh after the war. Today, Kotukhina proudly displays the boxes as a testimonial to the tenacious spirit of the Russian people, and to her dual role as both mother-creator and Soviet Russian artist.[37]

One fan of Kotukhina's art, the Ivanovo writer Mikhail Shoshin, captured the war's new spirit of Russian patriotism. In a long paean to Palekh written immediately following the war, he elaborated the qualities that a leading Soviet journal on cultural affairs dubbed "authentic nationality."[38] The Palekh style was "in blood and body connected . . . with life in the countryside." The masters sang Russian folk songs, recited Russian folktales, "and constantly studied Russian history." The war had brought out the best in Palekh, which was guided by "determined creative strivings, . . . daily artistic labor, enchantment, most original talent, domesticity *[domashnost']*, and simplicity."[39] The emphasis on "simplicity" and "domesticity," so prominent in the works of the new women masters, was particularly striking. It reflected a growing nostalgia for the idealized comforts of home and family that was greatly intensified by the deprivations of the invasion. These longings encouraged a continuing transformation of the family into the primary social unit of Soviet Russian society, a trend that had begun to emerge in the late 1930s. The trend was so strong that the Palekh district party in August 1943 endorsed private family cottages as the ideal work environment for the Palekh master. Justifying the decision, the party said the masters' cottages, rather than the communal cooperative building, were most likely to give flight to Palekh's creative muse. This endorsement of cottage-based production stands in stark contrast to the substantial resources devoted in the mid-1930s to a new cooperative building for the artists, accompanied by constant attacks on the supposedly reactionary nature of cottage-based production. Consciously or not, the regime was now downplaying a central principle of Soviet Marxist ideology: the superiority of public and industrialized work spaces.[40]

PALEKH AND THE VOZHD'

In so many respects, then, the war seemed to liberate Palekh, providing the artists with a clear sense of mission and purpose. On one point, however, the war offered little clarity, namely, the depiction of Stalin. What was the relationship of Stalin to the victory over fascism? Should his figure eclipse the heroic efforts and sacrifices of the people? Would it now be appropriate to depict Stalin in the "Orthodox" manner instead of in a purely realistic style?[41]

Answers to such questions had eluded the Palekhians since the rise of the Stalin cult in the early 1930s. Numerous factors had discouraged Palekh's participation in the cult, including the conditions of production in the cooperative, market demand, and the specificities of the Palekh art form. Artists mostly repeated and elaborated a set canon of images, which had largely stabilized by the mid-1930s around the themes most in demand from consumers: rural idylls, fairy tales, and folk themes. Moreover, numerous reviews in the 1920s and 1930s made it clear to the masters that the explicit application of the Palekh style to Bolshevik leaders represented, at best, a mockery of the figure and perhaps even a counterrevolutionary intent.[42]

A curious social transformation among Palekh's artists also contributed to the relative paucity of Bolshevik leaders in Palekh art. Before 1917, the ranks of icon painters were divided between those who painted the face, the *lichniki,* and those who painted other portions of the icon, the *dolichniki.* While the *lichniki* occupied a privileged status in the prerevolutionary hierarchy of Palekh masters, after 1917 they became a kind of underclass, a sort of substitute kulak and exploiter. Meanwhile, the *dolichniki,* who lacked skills in portraiture, dominated the cooperative. "A few *[lichniki]* still remain in the box-finishing shop," noted the American paleontologist Ida Treat, who visited the village in 1933, "but most of them have returned to the land. Of late, it is true, an attempt has been made to provide the 'portraitists' with work for which they are fitted . . . but as yet there is little demand for miniatures of this type."[43] This situation continued through the end of the 1930s and the initial part of the war.

Only the regime's more relaxed policies during the war, including Stalin's concordat with the Russian Orthodox Church, encouraged the elite Palekh masters to tackle the Stalin theme. The masters believed the new policies meant they again could apply the traditions of ancient Russian art (the Soviet euphemism for Russian religious icons) to Bolshevik political figures.[44] A "saintly" icon of a Bolshevik leader pushed the war's hybridization of Russian Orthodox and Soviet identities even further. It also mirrored the Palekhians' ongoing linkage of Russian traditions and Soviet power, an almost universal feature of Soviet patriotic culture during World War II.

The Palekh artist Dmitrii Butorin was one of the first old masters to tackle the portrait of Stalin following the Nazi invasion. He began working on the image *Stalin, the Organizer of Victories* in late 1943. He was inspired by the new vice-director of the Palekh museum, the art critic Nikolai Bariutin, who counseled masters during the war (contrary to art critics before the war) to use the distinctive style of a religious icon in depicting Soviet leaders. Butorin continued working on the image of Stalin through 1944 and 1945, adapting each succeeding military victory to the portrait and to the increasingly favorable reception to the experiment.[45] The lid of the box represented Stalin as "the Marshal of Russian" (rather than Soviet) forces.[46] As in the Orthodox representation of saints, smaller images in separate frames surrounded the central figure of Stalin, depicting victories in Stalingrad, Sevastopol, Leningrad, and Kiev, and a salute to victors in Moscow. "This item is interesting also in relation to the artistic portrait itself," continued Bariutin, a religious believer. "The miniature portrait of I. V. Stalin is painted with the techniques of ancient Russian painting" that were familiar only to "the very oldest masters of Palekh."[47]

Immediately after the war, Palekh's experiments in *vozhd'* iconography continued. Rather than depicting Stalin in miniature, however, the masters depicted the generalissimo in a more appropriately monumental setting: a four-and-a-half-meter by two-and-a-half-meter portrait, by far the largest portrait Palekh had ever attempted. The portrait combined, as *Komsomol'skaia pravda* put it, "the conditional style of Palekh with the realistic features of modern art . . . ," an echo of the popular *"friaz'"* style of religious icon painting before the revolution. The signature gold ornament of the Palekh lacquer framed the portrait of Stalin in military uniform. Stalin's long coat and decorated chest contained the distinctive folds from the icon-painting tradition, and the leader's hands were likewise captured in the stylized manner of a religious icon. Fantastic plants, flowers, and other stylistic elements from Palekh's Orthodox past filled in part of the background. Connecting the center of Soviet power and imperial Russian power, not to mention Muscovy and the "cradle of the Revolution" in St. Petersburg, the artists depicted Stalin against the backdrop of the Admiralty and Catherine's statue of Peter the Great on one side, and the Kremlin and the monument to Minin and Pozharskii on the other. These images "recalled the great historical events of the past, against which Stalin's greatness shines even brighter." In July 1946, young athletes representing the Russian Federation carried Palekh's icon of Stalin through Red Square for the All-Union Physical Culture parade. One critical aspect of this synthesis of Russian and Soviet identities, however, separated Palekh's Soviet present from its Russian Orthodox past: Stalin was no saint, and contrary to Orthodox canon, Stalin was still living.[48]

Palekh's experiment in applying its own traditions to the cult of personality was nonetheless brief. Less than a month after the parade in Moscow in July 1946, the Politburo member Andrei Zhdanov launched his infamous attack on "formalist" and "bourgeois" art in the journals *Leningrad* and *Zvezda*. In Palekh, the attack resulted in a campaign against the Palekh style and links between Palekh's art and Orthodox religious traditions. Not surprisingly, Palekh's *vozhd'* iconography came to an end, and those who had advocated the innovation were purged from the ranks of art criticism. The portrait of Stalin in July 1946 thus completed the war's fusion of Russian Orthodox and Soviet traditions, after which Soviet authorities again attempted to distance Soviet Russia from many of the values and traditions propagated by Palekh's art.[49]

But even during the war, Palekh's wartime participation in the cult of Stalin should not be exaggerated. Most Palekh artists continued to ignore the father of all peoples. A long-standing theological prohibition against the representation of living figures (especially a most unholy figure such as Stalin) discouraged at least some of the older masters from attempting the leader's portrait. Other artists feared the ramifications of getting the details wrong. Still others believed that the perceived function of Palekh's art—to represent the supposedly joyous and festive spirit of the Soviet Russian people—seemed somehow incongruous with a figure (also a Georgian) who inspired a mix of awe, fear, and even hatred. As the architect of the Terror, Stalin was therefore inappropriate subject matter for the Palekh lacquer and, by extension, for Russian national artists.[50]

From the perspective of Palekh's overall production, the cult of Stalin, like urban landscapes and the proletariat, thus remained very much on the periphery of the hamlet's art. Just one portrait, *The Great Marshal*, was among the cooperative's twenty major creative themes listed for 1944, suggesting, as before the war, an extreme reluctance to marry Palekh's traditional style to the Soviet leader. Among the twenty-six Palekh works on display at the eighth regional art exhibit in Ivanovo in late 1945, not a single one showed a Soviet leader.[51]

Few consumers seemed eager to buy Stalin's image. Palekh's warehouse in late 1945, perhaps the best measure of the cooperative's mainstream production, did not contain a single portrait of Stalin, and it contained only one each of Lenin and Molotov. By contrast, the warehouse contained many portraits of the Napoleonic-era generals Kutuzov and Suvorov, the most popular figures among the Palekh masters. In early 1945, for instance, ten officers who had helped liberate territory from Nazi occupation received Palekh portraits of Suvorov and Kutuzov (rather than of Stalin). In late 1943 and early 1944, the Red Army placed orders with Palekh masters for portraits of Nevskii, Donskoi, Minin and Pozharskii, Suvorov, and Kutuzov—but not one for a portrait of Stalin, or even of Marshal Zhukov. Joining Palekh's pantheon in the warehouse was an odd mix of Russian military and cultural figures, which, with the exception of the civil war figure Chapaev and the writer Aleksei Tolstoi, concerned a pre-1917 past. Historical figures also dominated the canon in the cooperative's creative plan for 1944. The masters glorified Ivan Susanin's resistance to the Poles during the Time of Troubles, martyrdom in defense of the motherland in *The Lay of Igor's Campaign,* Ivan III's defiance of Mongolian rule, mythological *bogatyri,* and Bogdan Khmel'nitskii's "struggle against Polish oppressors."[52]

Meanwhile, a new hero, the Russian people themselves, seemed to upstage Soviet leadership. Besides historical figures, the Russian people, and the places they defended, now achieved cult status in Palekh's wartime production. *Glory to the Russian People* and *The Nation Victor* complemented a celebration of *The Russian Woman* and the *Hero-Cities* of Leningrad, Stalingrad, Sevastopol, and Odessa. Palekh's warehouse in 1945 contained numerous generic portraits, apparently done in the Palekh rather than realistic style, labeled simply *Boy, Girl, Woman, Man, Partisan Woman, Partisans,* and *Child.* As noted earlier, Palekhians also produced portraits of soldiers, sons, and daughters for individual customers. These images of individual citizens, rather than those of Soviet leaders, arguably represented the most valuable relics produced by the Palekhians during the war. Along with the spirit of prerevolutionary Russian generals, the anonymous Russian people thus became the true heroes of the battle against fascism.[53]

BACK TO "NORMALCY"

Palekh's wartime revival was as brief as it was dramatic. When the war concluded, the perceived dictates of Leninist ideology again took precedence. As a result, Palekh's art came under a cloud of suspicion, since it was derived from religious traditions, was focused on a sector of Russian life (the peasantry) defined by Marxist ideology as backward, and was critically dependent on market exchanges.

Reflecting the growing importance of ideological imperatives toward the end of the war, Palekh's Moscow overseers revived the prewar litany of complaints about the archaic and escapist nature of Palekh's production. Under pressure from the Ivanovo party committee and Moscow, the Palekh district party committee in late 1944 demanded the creation of a "red corner" at the cooperative, in which artists would study the biography of Stalin and acquaint themselves with the latest achievements of Soviet technology. Party officials dictated that the artists study the *Short Course,* the canonical text of Soviet history in which the proletariat and the party, rather than Russian historical figures, played the primary role. Moscow overseers also ordered the masters to abandon rural genre scenes. Such topics were thought to be insufficiently dynamic and therefore cut off from the dialectical movement of history and revolution, which the party seemed desperate to rejoin.[54]

In the meantime, the cooperative leadership began to realize it might have to answer for the lax conditions of 1942 and 1943 that had encouraged the cooperative to abandon detailed accounting reports. Through the 1930s, the yearly ritual of accounting had been an agonizing process. Soviet officials in Moscow judged the economic and political position of an enterprise, and whether its members were engaging in "wrecking," through the yearly accounting procedure. In the chaos of the Nazi invasion, however, the Soviet system of accounting effectively collapsed. "The cooperative worked blindly in the first years of the war," admitted the chairman Evmenenko at the end of the war. "We did not submit a single accounting report and there was not a single audit."[55]

Whereas Moscow authorities overlooked such omissions in 1942 and 1943, they were not willing to do so in 1944. The fulfillment of orders without Vsekokhudozhnik's permission had become "a matter of political and state importance," said one Vsekokhudozhnik missive in early 1944. Vsekokhudozhnik castigated Palekh for failing to submit thematic plans. It demanded financial reports for the artel's activities stretching back to the prewar period, when the cooperative was hopelessly mired in unsold inventory, delinquent wages, and debt. Concerned about Palekh's lack of accountability, Vsekokhudozhnik dispatched an official to observe meetings of the cooperative's party cell in November 1944. The official condemned the cooperative's improper accounting procedures and the lack of political work among some older masters. He suggested that a decline in output might be considered "wrecking" activity.[56]

In the meantime, Stalin's wartime shift in religious policies confused many Palekhians. The regime's willingness to entertain the reopening of churches closed in the 1930s was especially bewildering.[57] The new policy followed Stalin's so-called concordat with the Russian Orthodox Church on September 4, 1943. Though it has been argued that Stalin reconciled with the church to mobilize patriotic sentiments during the war, the concordat came after critical Soviet victories at Stalingrad and Kursk. Moreover, the bulk of church reopenings occurred after the war's outcome was no longer in doubt, and many took place after the war had already ended. More likely, Stalin's move was connected with attempts to use the foreign Orthodox community to assuage the West, to improve the Soviet Union's image in the international arena, and to force the earliest possible opening of the western front. At any rate, the immediate result of the concordat was to restore the patriarchate, to ease the persecution of priests, to permit the recreation of diocesan structures and seminaries, and to allow the reopening of some closed churches. Subsequently, between 1944 and 1947, believers submitted nearly 4,500 petitions to open churches, of which 1,270 were granted.[58]

The central cathedral in Palekh, the one nearly blown up but rather converted into a museum in the mid-1930s, was among those churches for which believers submitted a petition. When the church held its last services in late 1933, about half the adult population in Palekh listed themselves as believers. Despite the large number of believers in Palekh, it was not until just after the victory over Germany in May 1945 that Palekhians felt confident enough to submit a request to reopen the cathedral for religious services. The unsuccessful petition came ten days after a similar petition submitted by the head of the Ivanovo/Vladimir eparchy, who pleaded that Palekhians be permitted to "pray for our native combatant defenders . . . for our Red Army that creates momentous victories under the leadership of the genius commander, comrade Stalin." On June 4, 1946, Moscow also rejected another petition from Palekh, sent to Nikolai Shvernik, chairman of the Supreme Soviet. Twenty-two Palekhians signed the petition, including many elderly masters. Drafted by a woman kolkhoz worker, the petition promised that services would always be over before the museum opened for visitors and agreed to provide the material resources necessary to preserve the museum's murals and icons (the state, it implied, was letting the church fall into disrepair). It expressed the hope that the church could be opened for services by the next victory day celebration "to pray for the fallen soldiers and for the precious and dear victory sustained by the Generalissimo Iosif Vissarionovich Stalin." The petition was rejected because of concerns expressed by museum and cultural officials that a valuable architectural monument and its icons would be damaged by worshipers.[59]

Reflecting the growing dictates of ideological imperatives, local party officials in early 1945 emphasized the impossibility of any kind of retreat on matters of religious worship. A meeting of the cooperative party cell on June 4, 1945, harshly condemned one of the oldest masters, Aleksandr Chikurin, for attending the religious ceremony of his wife's death. She had made her husband promise that he would pray for her in church when she died. "Now I have fulfilled her promise and no one will ever see me in a church again," said Chikurin, when confronted by fellow party members. Chikurin's explanation only partially appeased his comrades in the cooperative, one of whom remarked: "Aleksandr Vasil'evich, it is one thing to remember a person who has passed away. It is quite another to visit a church with a party card and pray to God. This can never be reconciled. This amounts to going out of one's mind." Zinov'ev, one of the most vocal defenders of the Palekh style, called Chikurin's church visit "a blatant violation of party discipline" and recommended a "stern disciplinary measure." Chikurin escaped any disciplinary measures, but he no doubt spent the rest of his days far from the district's only active church (located three kilometers to Palekh's north in the village of Krasnoe).[60]

After the incident with Chikurin, the cooperative's leadership worked with district party officials to cleanse the cooperative and related institutions of religious elements. One of the first and most significant casualties was Zinov'ev's assistant at the museum, the art critic Bariutin, who became increasingly bold in proclaiming his religious beliefs by the end of the war. Zinov'ev refused to defend Bariutin from political attacks as Bariutin was forced to leave the hamlet sometime in 1946 (in a private letter to Bariutin in 1956, Zinov'ev apologized for his "cowardice"). While Bariutin's tenure as vice-director of the museum (1943–1946) had coincided with the center's embrace of Russian national traditions, his exile from the hamlet in 1946 reflected a growing discomfort, both in Moscow and Palekh, with a perceived backsliding from a revolutionary agenda.[61]

Much to the chagrin of the Palekh masters, the regime was thus taking back the compromises (its relaxed attitude toward both the market and religious belief) that had been such a welcome relief for the artists, and for millions of other Russians. There is perhaps no greater proof of the revolutionary impulses that continued to drive the regime. At the same time, the war had fundamentally changed attitudes toward Russian culture. The change of attitudes resulted from two important factors. The first was the destruction of Russian cultural monuments by Nazi invaders, which created an intense feeling of cultural loss. The new nostalgic turn added momentum and legitimacy to preservationist attitudes, even as it dampened enthusiasm for a new round of revolutionary restructuring. Palekh, as one central facet of traditional Russian culture, could not help but benefit from this trend. The second factor emerged from a general belief among Russians, a belief that was close to the truth, that ethnic Great Russians had carried the burden of defending the Soviet Union. Thus, just as many Soviet ideologues argued that victory in war had justified the earlier revolutionary sacrifices during the Terror and collectivization, others asserted that the victory had proved the loyalty of the Russians themselves. Since Palekh seemed to embody the same Russian spirit that had defeated the Nazis, many masters believed their Soviet patriotism was beyond doubt, that if the war had been a test of their revolutionary potential, they had passed it with the highest marks. It was a potent defense unavailable to the masters before the war—and one with which the father of all peoples seemed sympathetic. As the Palekhian Pavel Korin put it in July 1943, Stalin "was the only person who was able to correctly understand Russia. . . . The war showed that Russia will survive . . . and that the national minorities that make up the USSR [were] poor fraternal partners in this union."[62] Two years later, Stalin's famous toast to the Russian people on May 24, 1945, echoed these same thoughts.[63] Revitalized and redeemed by the war, the masters were thus in a far better position to defend themselves from a new campaign to replace foreign foes with domestic ones.

CHAPTER SEVEN

The Cultural Transformation Continues, 1947–1958

"The stimulus in our work is the ruble and not the high
consciousness of satisfying the growing demands of the
people. We have sullied the great glory of Palekh."
—Palekh artist G. M. Mel'nikov, January 6, 1953[1]

"I do not agree . . . that the artist should paint according to the dictates of his soul. Supporting this view we
might find ourselves in a situation where there would
be no one left to represent a modern theme."
—Palekh artist A. G. Bakanov, October 7, 1955[2]

Like a line of thunderstorms on the prairie, social engineering campaigns had
rolled continuously over Palekh since 1917. The relentless demand that the
Palekhians restructure themselves had disappeared only for a brief period during World War II, and the war turned out to be the eye of the revolutionary
storm. In November 1945, an official from Vsekokhudozhnik warned the older
masters that "they must be as humble as possible about their accomplishments," by which he meant the many honorifics and glowing press received
by the older masters during the war. He added: "Not only must the young
artists work on themselves, but the artists of the older generation."[3] As before
the war, Palekh again found that it was trapped between conceptions of a universal Soviet community and a community bound and restricted by the national forms of the folk. It was not clear to the Palekh masters if these two
lines could be combined, or if one line would emerge victorious.

Palekh's postwar dilemma resulted from an intense ideological crisis in the
highest echelons of the party. From the late 1930s and through World War II,
advocates of a more pragmatic approach to governance clashed openly with
party ideologues. Led by Georgii Malenkov and Lavrentii Beria, the pragmatists
gained the upper hand during the war when Palekh rebounded from its prewar
malaise. Following the lead of many of Stalin's wartime pronouncements, the

pragmatists tended to view Great Russian national traditions as the foundation of Soviet patriotism. Their opponents were the party revivalists, led by Andrei Zhdanov, who following the war attempted to infuse "party spirit" *(partiinost')* and socialist ideological relevance into all spheres of Soviet life and culture. Zhdanov sparked renewed attempts to eradicate "formalism" and "decadent" bourgeois ideas in the arts, echoing similar campaigns during the mid-1930s.[4]

The clash between these tendencies was exacerbated by an increasingly enfeebled Stalin. The generalissimo, as he now styled himself, was unable to negotiate the dialectical movement of history, or the competing factions of his inner circle, in his formerly resolute manner. In addition, campaigns for new construction and technological achievement, motivated by the dire need to rebuild thousands of cities and towns from the rubble of the war, increasingly competed with pressures to preserve the cultural heritage of the Russian past, also devastated by the Nazi invasion. There were simply not sufficient resources to pursue both goals. As a result, party priorities swung chaotically between the revolutionary impulse to wipe the historical slate clean and the more conservative desire to preserve ties with a supposedly primordial national past.[5]

As the ideological debate heated up, relations between artists were again marked by suspicion and the fear of another round of terror. One Palekh artist, who was exiled from the village for his religious beliefs in 1946, recalled a three-day visit to Palekh in the summer of 1946. "Wariness, wariness, and wariness—this is the main thing in Palekh. From it logically flows suspiciousness, distrust, caution, and surveillance."[6]

In the new climate, cultural officials branded Palekh's style "archaic" and too closely linked with religious traditions and foreign markets. Back in Moscow, the vice-director of the Tret'iakov Gallery (Palekh's erstwhile ally Zhidkov) condemned an excessive focus on historical themes and an idealized representation of prerevolutionary "leaders and tsars." At a 1947 conference on Russian folk art, he said historical themes had to engage the revolutionary traditions and not turn into "a flight from contemporary themes." He urged the Palekh artists to remember that many of its images, made for export, "were a prisoner to the petty-bourgeois ideals . . . in the Western European and American artistic industry." One artist in the audience asked the vice-director "how to combine the wonderful traditions, which have developed over the centuries, with contemporary content. Just a year and a half or even two years ago our art critics protested against filling these . . . traditions with any other kind of content. . . . How does one explain this?" The vice-director responded vaguely, "The combination of creative traditions in such a way as to preserve them and yet to create items that are genuinely modern in spirit and theme is the path of greatest resistance."[7] Highlighting the impasse, the Central Committee in 1947 redoubled efforts to standardize textbooks and pedagogical programs in art schools. It aimed to reassert the primacy of world socialist culture and an "ideological-political education," yet it also emphasized the centrality of Great Russian national culture, particularly the romantic Russian nationalist painters of the nineteenth century.[8] The Palekhians thus had to negotiate a postwar ideological climate that was one part Marxist and one part romantic nationalist, one part oriented toward revolutionary transformation and the other toward building a sense of community and loyalty around Great Russian national traditions. Indicative of these contradictory impulses, the masters in the late 1940s were hired to restore medieval religious icons and murals in the Kremlin cathedrals, even as they faced the charge of being "archaic."

Negotiating these slippery boundaries between the need for revolutionary restructuring and the desire to preserve the past was complicated by another factor, Palekh's continuing reliance on the market, which tended to favor a more traditional Palekh. To offset the influence of the market, the state attempted, with mixed success, to impose its influence on Palekh's art through a two-tiered system of production. For instance, by the war's end the hamlet's production studios formally distinguished between "creative work" (tvorcheskaia rabota) and all other art, known by the pejorative term "massovka." For Palekh's overseers, the master-copyist represented the ignorant peasant beholden to bourgeois consumer tastes, while the creative artist, working on supposedly more modern and relevant themes, was a fully conscious and cultured Soviet citizen, an intelligent. Creative artists, who received honorific titles from the state and exhibit opportunities, had to submit preliminary sketches and apply for consultation and up-front money from overseers in Moscow, thus ensuring (in theory) that the creative energies of the collective were subject to active party influence. By contrast, the vast majority of masters focused on massovka, the copying of the classics of the Palekh canon from the 1920s and 1930s for domestic and foreign consumers.[9]

The challenge, from the standpoint of Moscow experts, was to raise artists focused on massovka to the level of creative artists, thus manipulating the social category of "artist" to achieve Moscow's goal of increased control. The realization of this aim, however, was hindered by two factors. First, Palekh remained very much tied to massovka and the market that sustained it, both to generate revenues for the state and to provide work for the majority of artists. Second, Palekh could not escape the logic of the broader system of production that favored quantity over quality, since the system of pay was based largely on square centimeter of output. Desperately in need of money, even creative artists spent most of their time painting variations on the classic fairy-tale themes for their creative works (which took far less time) rather than producing completely new topics on modern themes.[10] Calls for the restructuring of Palekh, and the entire edifice of official social status, thus struggled mightily against the economic logic of the broader Soviet system of artistic production.

In the meantime, a dramatic and unexpected downturn in the Palekh lacquer business aggravated Palekh's growing political crisis, suggesting for the artists a haunting parallel to the earlier crisis of the mid-1930s. As in the mid-1930s, the robust expansion of Palekh exports had quickly saturated foreign markets, triggering the rapid growth of unsold inventory in mid-1947. By the end of 1947, half a million rubles of unsold inventory was piling up in the Palekh warehouse. Trading organizations in Moscow, Leningrad, and elsewhere were refusing to take additional Palekh lacquers. As sales ground to a halt in 1947 and 1948, the cooperative often failed to meet payroll, thereby, in the words of one cooperative report, "threatening the further survival of Palekh."[11]

Chaos in the state system of artistic purchasing aggravated the unpredictability of the market that Palekh served. According to a Central Committee report, organizations administering public buildings (movie houses, houses of culture, theaters, etc.) typically waited until the end of the year to purchase decorative art that "for some reason comes out of the budget for capital investment." If there was money in this budget at the end of the year, the organizations spent all of it on art, which meant "a real boom in art salons." It was catch as catch can: in November and December various clubs, factories, institutes, and universities purchased whatever was in the stores to decorate the gray interiors of Soviet public life. The vast body of artistic work, which ended up in private interior spaces or in the many public spaces created during postwar reconstruction, thus remained beyond the purview of party planners. As one Central Committee report noted, most of the art in a Soviet person's life had "a random" character, mostly standard Russian landscapes, folk themes, still lifes, and very rarely anything with explicitly Soviet content. Such was the reality of Soviet cultural construction: it was anything but planned.[12]

The entire situation was gravely aggravated by the infamous currency reforms of December 1947. On December 16, 1947, all Soviet citizens, factories, collective farms, and organizations were required to exchange ten rubles for one new ruble. Bank accounts with up to three thousand rubles were exempted from the exchange, but this was little comfort to most Soviets, who did not have such savings and lived from paycheck to paycheck. Government bonds, which Soviets periodically were forced to purchase, were also devalued at a rate of three to one, and interest rates for these bonds were dramatically reduced. (One Palekh master who complained about the situation was arrested and sent to the gulag.) If the aim of the currency reforms was to attack the rapid rise in speculation and the accumulation of wealth during World War II, the main impact was on the everyday consumer. As one Russian economic historian put it: "[The reform] was a genuine theft from the toiling masses."[13]

A crackdown on quasi-private economic activity accompanied the economic reforms. In the system of retail trade, this crackdown in mid-1947 meant an end to a critical wartime practice in Palekh: the use of independent "agents." Palekh had three such agents on its payroll in 1947, who helped grease the mechanisms of distribution for Palekh by seeking out retail and wholesale customers. The cooperative received more business, while the agents secured lucrative commissions ranging anywhere from 2 to 8 percent of the price of goods sold. Some individual consultants in the first half of 1946 made as much as forty thousand rubles. "The earnings of these individuals," went one irate Central Committee report, "have grown to immense proportions."

The committee, noting that such a distribution system "has nothing in common with Soviet art," finally abolished the practice of using middlemen in early May 1947. At a most inopportune moment, one of Palekh's main distribution channels was thus eliminated.[14]

Searching for a way out of the crisis, Palekh's leaders confronted a truly Sisyphean dilemma. If the cooperative leadership continued to increase production to meet plan requirements, it faced a growing stash of unsold inventory, which was considered a political crime. Yet if Palekhians cut back production and failed to meet the plan, they had to endure the equally lethal charge of "wrecking." The only solution was to shift toward new and cheaper types of production, and this meant simpler paintings on smaller functional items such as buttons, cigarette holders, and brooches. Here too the cooperative encountered problems. Given the lack of consensus in the center about the proper content of a Palekh lacquer, not to mention its style, the cooperative was at a loss to figure out what kinds of images to paint on these items.[15]

Equally troubling, the Palekhians could only lower costs by reducing the amount of labor, since the main cost of a lacquer was primarily in labor rather than materials. Reducing labor costs inevitably resulted in lower quality and hence a challenge to a master's "artistry." In May 1948, the chairman of the Palekh art cooperative complained to the Committee for Art Affairs about the cheapening of Palekh's reputation and brand name. He said Palekh's talents were far more appropriate for the production of high-quality museum pieces, icon restoration, and the painting of murals in public buildings and places of culture. Anything less cast doubt on the deserved status of the Palekh masters as Soviet artists. The "trading organizations," he complained, were compelling Palekh to abide by the principle "let it be shoddy, as long as it is cheap."[16]

The masters were distraught. In a stormy meeting of the cooperative members on February 12, 1949, everything and everyone was to blame—as was perhaps appropriate in a self-professed communist system, where collective guilt went hand in hand with collective triumph. One artist, a member of the cooperative's art council evaluating committee, frankly admitted that he "did not know what the hell was going on [in Moscow]."[17] Another older master remarked in frustration that "everything achieved [in Palekh] in the last 25 years of Soviet conditions . . . is being liquidated." Palekh had been a center of Russian culture for centuries before 1917, he protested. Was this not reason enough for the state's support?[18]

PALEKH, COSMOPOLITANISM, AND THE JUBILEE

Implausibly, Palekh also faced the potentially lethal charge of being a center of "cosmopolitan" art. The confusing campaign against cosmopolitanism had been launched in the postwar period to root out alien and bourgeois influences. Often, it focused on Jews in prominent professional and political positions, culminating in the famous "doctor's plot" on the eve of Stalin's death, when Jewish doctors were accused of plotting to kill Stalin. Yet the term was also more than an anti-Semite's shorthand for being Jewish; even Russian folk art could be considered a source of cosmopolitan contamination. A doctoral candidate in history, A. N. Pravdin, made precisely this charge against Palekh at a Moscow conference in June 1949. The newly minted expert on Palekh art began his paper with an analysis of the late imperial era, when the study of peasant icon painting, he charged, was dominated by the idle wealthy and "art critic aesthetes." The Great Russian icon painters of the Novgorod, Moscow, and Stroganov schools, he claimed, "proved the creative talent and independence of the Russian masters," yet icon experts such as Nikodim Kondakov "viewed them as part of 'the Byzantine heritage' and not Russian artistic culture." Such a position overlooked "the inexhaustible wealth of the Russian land" and "belittled the creative strengths of the Russian people." Palekh's early Soviet patron Bakushinskii, he added, was a direct descendent of such views, when he suggested the influence of both Byzantium and the Renaissance on Palekh and Russian icon-painting traditions. Bakushinskii's ideas were therefore "cosmopolitan" and encouraged the Palekh masters to travel down the same dangerous path toward counterrevolution. Pravdin concluded that improper direction from "cosmopolitan" experts had allowed bourgeois consumers to taint the authentic Russianness of the masters' artistry. As proof he cited the critical dependence of Palekh on foreign markets and consumer tastes—the hamlet's dirty little secret. Not everyone at the conference agreed with Pravdin (one art critic was outraged that Pravdin attacked experts who were dead and unable to defend themselves), yet the deadlock provided little consolation to the masters, many of whom heard haunting echoes of the Great Terror.[19]

While the experts and art critics searched in vain for a new party line, many Soviet viewers of Palekh's art were far less ambiguous, especially in comparison to reactions from before the war. Here one can detect a real change from the prewar period—a growing level of comfort in the population with the symbols and icons of Russian patriotic culture. With only a few exceptions, visitors to the State Museum of Palekh Art from 1947 to 1949 praised Palekh as a banner of quintessential Russianness. According to one Leningrader, the Palekhians preserved the "subtle, stern, and harmonious" art of the ancient Russian icon. Palekh's art, he added, represented "a national strength. This is our pride, which we must carefully preserve and develop." Another visitor proclaimed: "Just try, you cosmopolitans, to find such art in the West! Nowhere does such an art exist—except in our Motherland." Joining the chorus of praise, a group of students from the pedagogical institute in nearby Shuia wrote in 1948: "The exhibit of Palekh art is yet another confirmation of the profound originality of Russian culture in general: the wealth of forms, the unmatched combination of colors, the vibrant images, the dynamism of composition. Palekh is the Elbrus of culture compared to the cow-manure art of the West, the art of a depraved and rotting imperialism. Glory to our Russian culture!!!"[20]

Emboldened by popular support, many Palekhians counted on a critical event to open up state coffers and political patronage: the twenty-fifth jubilee of Soviet Palekh art, to be celebrated in December 1949. The Palekhians approached the jubilee with a sense of confidence and entitlement, proudly noting their services during the war in preserving the Russian cultural heritage. With the support of party and state officials in Palekh and Ivanovo, they boldly requested financial support, more money for artists, a series of exhibits, and honorific titles for leading artists. At the beginning of 1949, Palekh and its overseers proposed a date of June 6, 1949, for a retrospective exhibit in Moscow to showcase Palekh's accomplishments. Ominously, however, the date came and passed without any word from Moscow on approval for the event.[21]

Finally, on December 31, 1949, the Central Committee's section on art affairs passed its verdict: the jubilee was denied, along with the requested outpouring of state largesse to accompany the festivities. As the committee noted in a letter to Politburo member Mikhail Suslov, "the creative production . . . of the Palekh artists demands a significant improvement in the sphere of mastering the principles of socialist realism. The themes of the works of Palekh artists are limited and weakly reflect the socialist transformation of our country."[22] The Palekh artists, in short, had not finished their restructuring, although just how they should restructure themselves remained a mystery.

While the sources do not reveal the exact reasons for the jubilee's cancellation, they do suggest a number of explanations. Given the continuing stalemate over the roots of Soviet Russian national culture, to celebrate Palekh meant celebrating a national art form that might very well turn out to be "cosmopolitan," "formalist," and "anti-Soviet." For obvious reasons of self-preservation, nobody was willing to take the risk of endorsing Palekh. Equally important, it was the Palekhians' misfortune that their jubilee coincided with the mother of all Soviet jubilees: Stalin's birthday, which in December 1949 had grown to truly perverse dimensions. Even Pushkin could not provide a safe refuge for the masters, as he had during the Great Terror. In comparison to the celebration of Pushkin in 1937, the 1949 commemoration of Pushkin's 150th birthday was a relatively subdued affair. Testifying to the downgrading of the Pushkin cult, the Pushkin Museum of Fine Arts, where the Palekhian Pavel Korin continued to restore Russian religious and secular art, suffered the indignity of being renamed the Museum of Gifts to I. V. Stalin.[23] It was as if Stalin was compensating for the diminishment of his cult during the war.

The Palekhians scrambled, as did all artists, to immortalize the father of all peoples. They wanted to show the great leader "eternally young and wise, looking into the future, a bright future."[24] Seeking to atone for the supposed sins of their "reactionary" past, twenty-one masters labored four months to produce a "monumental" lacquer miniature, a gigantic, eight-sided papier-mâché chest the size of a small trunk devoted to the life and work of Stalin, titled *Comrade Stalin Is Leading Us to Communism*. In stark contrast to Palekh's "icons" of Stalin during the war, the chest was done in a strictly realistic manner. Presented to Comrade Stalin for his seventieth birthday, the box contained Stalin's portrait on the lid of the chest. On the eight sides, the Palekh masters represented all the significant stages in the development of the Soviet state. Those stages included Lenin and Stalin leading striking workers in Petrograd, Stalin at Tsaritsyn in the civil war, Stalin kneeling at Lenin's deathbed and taking an oath of loyalty to his cause, Stalin and the first five-year plan, Stalin and collectivization, Stalin and socialist construction in the various national republics, Stalin as generalissimo, and Stalin leading the postwar construction and "our movement forward to communism." On the basis of this work, the cooperative, in its annual report for 1949, noted somewhat unconvincingly: "The artists of Palekh are more and more mastering the modern theme and reflecting our Soviet reality in their work."[25]

THE VIEW FROM BELOW

At their lowest ebb since the Great Terror, the Palekhians seemed perilously close to losing their livelihood, not to mention their status as a crown jewel of Soviet culture. How did Palekhians react to their travails? Did they speak with one voice, or were they hopelessly divided, like their overseers in Moscow, by the obscure yet inescapable demands of the center? To hear Palekhians answer this question in later years, one might think that the artists were united in defense of the traditions. One typical recollection from 1993 noted that artists and students after the war were forced against their will to follow a strictly realistic style and "give up the traditions. Our ideological mentors told us: 'Study the history of the party and then you will become good artists.'" One of Palekh's main expert patrons in the 1960s and 1970s, the art critic Mariia Nekrasova, made Palekh's persecution in the late Stalin era a leitmotif of her analysis of Palekh. She coined the term *plakatnost'* (literally "posterness") to describe the demands for the posterlike "pseudo-realism" imposed by anti-national and anti-Russian forces from outside the village. In her depiction of Palekh during the last days of Stalin's rule, only the heroic intervention of far-sighted members of the intelligentsia saved the masters and—by extension—Russian national culture from extinction.[26]

While this version certainly contains a grain of truth, it also ignores the deep artistic and ideological divisions in the hamlet itself.[27] Demands for cultural transformation were not merely imposed from above but were also seconded by many masters, especially returnees from the front. Mirroring divisions over Soviet Russian culture in the party leadership, the artists waged fierce debates about the role of modern Soviet themes in Palekh lacquer and the future of the unique Palekh style in Soviet decorative art. The level of engagement is suggested by a telling fact: Palekhians frequently demanded the intervention of Moscow to decide who was right and who was wrong in their local disputes. It is to these creative debates in Palekh—the cultural transformation from below—that the discussion now turns.

Demographic factors profoundly influenced the tenor of debate in Palekh. As noted in the previous chapter, the war's decimation of the younger generation had temporarily reinforced the position of the elders *(stariki)* within the collective. Of the sixty active masters in February 1949, thirty-eight had received their training as icon painters under the tsarist regime. Only seventeen masters were under the age of thirty-five. Within the collective, older masters tended to provide the most vigorous defense of the Palekh style and traditions (minus, of course, the religious content). As one older master noted in April 1949, "Many comrades do not understand the Palekh style and believe that the artists should work on contemporary themes." Doing so, he added, would not "revive [the Palekh style], but completely destroy it."[28]

Meanwhile, younger masters and students who had survived the war began returning to the village in 1947 and 1948. The frontline servicemen, or *frontoviki,* vigorously advanced their views on the proper style and content of Palekh art, mirroring a broader phenomenon of the bold and confident war returnee in Soviet politics and society. The *frontoviki* launched a new wave in Palekh, inspired by what they believed to be a new party line in the center, to wit, a "move away from archaic elements and a striving for a more truthful representation of reality." One *frontovik* said his "generation was raised in the spirit of patriotism, of loyalty to the ideas of Lenin and Stalin. We genuinely believed in the bright future. We tried to express our sentiments in our works on the contemporary theme." The Palekh newspaper in May 1949 trumpeted the work of the "artists-*frontoviki*" as proof of a genuine reforging of Palekh humanity in the postwar period: realistic portraits of Stalin and of partisans of the Great Patriotic War, tributes to labor in the USSR as "a matter of honor, glory, and heroism," and depictions of labor in the mines.[29]

One of the most important *frontoviki* was G. M. Mel'nikov, who finished the Palekh art school during the Great Terror. When he returned to Palekh after the war, he said he wanted to overcome the central "error" in Palekh's art from the 1920s and 1930s, the inability to distinguish the old from the new. "It often happens that artists, drawing an image of a peasant from the old village and the image of a collective farmer of the new village, interpret them identically, simply adding a few incidental details, with which they want to distinguish the new from the old, thinking that this alone would add something new." Palekh artists, in his view, must depict Soviet men and women "so that they reveal the new era."[30]

Another *frontovik,* A. V. Kovalev, was associated almost exclusively with a group of other returnees from the front, who numbered 20 of the 130 students of the Palekh art school in 1948. Called up for military duty in 1939, he returned to Palekh in March of 1947 after helping to liberate and administer Berlin. In 1948 Kovalev painted a number of interpretations of the civil war hero Chapaev. "I was especially inspired by the military theme," he wrote in an unpublished autobiography. Eschewing the typical fairy-tale themes and the "stylized canonical forms," which he felt were "archaic," he moved on to *The Youth Brigade Collecting the Harvest, Song of the Tractor Driver, Glory to Miners, Moscow-Beijing, Stalin Is Today's Lenin,* and *In Defense of World Peace.* In one box depicting the martyrdom of young Soviet fighters executed by Nazis, he abandoned all "the usual stylized perspective and the application of archaic techniques" to show "fearlessness and determination in the face of death and the hatred for the enemy." Later, in the mid-1950s, with the rise of the Lenin cult after Stalin's death, Kovalev became Palekh's leading specialist on Lenin, studying the haunts and work of the revolutionary leader and embodying his image in dozens of lacquer boxes. He worked on one of his first lacquers on Lenin, *A Song about Lenin,* for three years in the mid-1950s.[31]

While Kovalev studied the biography of Lenin, his fellow *frontovik* A. Borunov tackled the topic of the *Slacker (Brakodel).* The 1953 work was a rare Palekh representation of a negative figure. The conflict in Borunov's lacquer echoed the battle of generations in the artistic collective. Borunov's slacker was an older tractor driver who carelessly allowed his plow to run too shallow. Vigilant young collective farmers, like the *frontoviki* in relation to their elders in Palekh, noticed the mistake, which they immediately corrected. Borunov, wrote one reviewer, was said to be "the first among the creative artists of the collective to depict the conflict typical of life in the kolkhoz, and he thus revealed the great possibilities inherent in the medium of the miniature." Few of the older masters, however, were impressed with the *Slacker,* or with the numerous creative works of his cohort, including *The New Agricultural Tax, A Happy Childhood, Brotherly Aid to China, The Obligations Are Overfulfilled,* and *The Youthful Brigade.*[32]

While the old-timers looked to a certain set of art critics for inspiration and defense, the *frontoviki* sought the advice of a new expert named Vitalii Kotov. A *frontovik* himself, Kotov arrived in Palekh in 1949 after finishing the graduate program in art criticism at the Repin Institute in Leningrad. Kotov was a great admirer of the nineteenth-century Russian realists (not surprising since he was a graduate of the school named after realism's leading figure), and in this sense he was a Russian patriot. As a militant atheist, however, he was also deeply offended by the religious elements in Palekh's art, which in his view were hostile to a materialist point of view and promoted escapist tendencies. As art critic–in-residence and vice-director of the State Museum of Palekh Art (where he worked until the mid-1990s), Kotov continuously preached the incomplete nature of Palekh's socialist transformation. Palekh's battle against cosmopolitanism, he proclaimed, began in the late imperial era, when Russian realists such as Repin developed a critique of the tsarist capitalist system and opposed the alien forces of impressionism, "mannerism," and the avant-garde. Since Palekh's Soviet art was so tightly linked to bourgeois markets, it had been infected by the latter tendencies, which were "anti-national" and hostile to "a materialist point of view." Only an intense study of the Russian realists, and a rejection of the reactionary canons and conventions of Russian religious icon painting, could integrate the Palekh artists into the mainstream of socialist realism and help them overcome their legacy as money-grubbing god-daubers.[33]

Kotov immediately became a lightning rod for controversy. In 1950 the chairman of the cooperative, Evmenenko, who had occupied the position since the beginning of the war, rejected claims by Kotov that much of Palekh's art was "reactionary, formalistic, . . . and contained elements of mysticism." Kotov, wrote Evmenenko, incorrectly concluded "that for Palekh to remain on its old foundations is a crime, that a complete rejection of tradition is necessary." Evmenenko followed up his condemnation with a denunciation of Kotov to Moscow, in which he accused Kotov of distorting Leninist principles, especially the foundation of nationality policies "about the dialectical relationship of form and content." To follow Kotov's reasoning meant "rejecting the Russian national art of the thirteenth through seventeenth centuries" and could not possibly represent a Leninist position.[34]

While experts at the center refused to clarify their position for Evmenenko (an indication of the ongoing ideological stalemate on Russian national identity), debates on issues of Soviet Russian culture and the Palekh style came to a head in the cooperative's central institution. This was the committee responsible for evaluating the works of artists and hence the size of their paychecks and status within the collective. Throughout 1951 the cooperative's committee for evaluating creative work was trapped in a kind of pincer movement. While Moscow overseers accused the committee of "nepotism" *(semeistvennost')* and a "lack of objectivity" in its evaluations, artists objected bitterly to the opaqueness of the committee's work. In October 1951, the older master N. M. Parilov, who had won the Stalin prize in 1946 for his decorations of the opera *The Golden Cockerel,* said he was "unclear just what the art committee is evaluating: the theme or the quality of the work." Boxes, he complained, had lately received higher evaluations simply because they attempted a more "contemporary theme." His own box, *The Golden Cockerel,* was the victim of one such biased evaluation. "Clearly, the amount of labor expended is not being taken into account." Rather than having his box receive a low evaluation, Parilov announced that he was withdrawing the work from consideration and demanded that it be evaluated exclusively in Moscow. At the same time, masters who attempted more contemporary themes also complained. In October 1951, two *frontoviki* said that their box *Stalin—The Lenin of Today* deserved to be evaluated at sixteen thousand rubles, more than twice the amount designated by the committee. Both these complaints—Parilov's and those of the two *frontoviki*—were resubmitted to the cooperative's evaluating committee at the same time. Interestingly, the committee granted Parilov's request and gave his work a higher evaluation, while it kicked the request of the *frontoviki* upstairs to

Moscow, wisely seeing Moscow as having far more competence to evaluate the value of *Stalin—The Lenin of Today.*[35]

The ideological impasse came to a head in another central institution in the Palekh system of production, the five-year Gor'kii School of Palekh Art that produced new masters. As in the icon shops, where the phase of apprentice-ship culminated with the production of an "exiting icon" *(otkhodnaia ikona),* Soviet Palekh masters spent their fifth and final year of schooling composing an original work known as their "diploma work" *(diplomnaia rabota).* By estab-lished practice since the 1930s, they developed their theme in consultation with older masters from the cooperative. The graduating ceremony, still in ex-istence today, involved the student's presentation and description of the work—its theme, style, and central ideas. Attending older masters from the co-operative and administrators and teachers from the school then peppered the student with questions, following which they graded the work. The parents of the students, many of whom were masters, watched and listened. The whole community, and its many competing interests, thus participated in the gradua-tion ceremony, more often than not proving, as one journalist put it in 1954, that although the school and cooperative were physically "next to each other, [ideologically] they are far apart."[36]

Kotov remembered one graduating class of mostly *frontoviki* from 1952. As the school year came to an end, Kotov received a visit from the distraught and frantic director of the Palekh art school, Mikhail Shemarov. "Vitalii Tim-ofeevich," said the director to Kotov, "there has been an uprising at the school! The graduating class refuses to paint their diploma work!" Students rejected the direction of the older masters and demanded the right to experi-ment with new styles and more modern themes. Kotov told the director to calm down. "Mikhail Ivanovich," said Kotov. "Don't use the word 'uprising.' News might make its way to the district party office and then we'll really have problems." Following Kotov's advice, Shemarov called an all-school as-sembly, at which he spoke of the need for mutual respect. He then turned to the *frontoviki,* who were sitting in a group. "So this means that you believe the old-timers have nothing to teach you?" A resounding chorus erupted from the *frontoviki.* "They teach us nothing! *[ne nauchat!]*" Kotov remem-bered looking over at one older master. His head was lowered, "with a silent and sad expression on his face."[37]

Neglected by ideologues at the center, teachers divided into opposing camps and berated their colleagues in front of students. The result, as one party com-mission reported, was "the loss of control over the pedagogical process." Ob-serving the Palekh collective's descent into a near state of anarchy, the art critic N. Sobolevskii in May 1952 could only tell the Palekhians to keep their chin up and satisfy the long-standing command to fill national form with so-cialist content. This approach was "the path of greatest resistance" and the only possible way out of the standoff.[38]

Frequently, ideological disputes in Palekh mixed explosively with alcohol, pettiness, personal grudges, and sheer stupidity. On January 25, 1952, leading advocates of new style and content joined Kotov at the Palekh art school for a drinking party. One was Nikolai Vikhrev, the head of pedagogy at the Gor'kii School of Palekh Art, who frequently clashed with the old-timers and with the art cooperative chair Evmenenko. Vikhrev, a shameless intriguer, used all means to advance his career and agenda. He knew that one of his drinking companions, a *frontovik* named Solov'ev who was the head of the party organization at the school, had an unstable personality. In Vikhrev's view, Solov'ev was too friendly with the old-timers and the cooperative leadership. So he got Solov'ev drunk and whispered conspiratorially in his ear: "During the years of the war, comrade Evmenenko slept with your wife." Infuriated, Solov'ev went directly to Evmenenko's apartment, started shouting obscenities, and called out Evmenenko for a brawl, which the chairman of the cooperative eagerly accepted. A district party investigation concluded that the entire incident was planned by Vikhrev in order to trigger the teacher's expulsion from the position of party secretary at the school and to compromise Evmenenko. Vikhrev, incidentally, had heard the rumor about Solov'ev's wife from the former director of the Palekh art school, who had earlier been expelled from the position for drunkenness and brawling (and would soon be reinstated). With some justice, an art critic in December 1952 said the center's inability to grapple with "the complex roots" of Palekh's art and "the lack of culture of many masters" had allowed social tensions in Palekh to explode. "We are stewing in our own juice," said the director of the Palekh art school in early 1953. "The artists . . . are forced to work blindly, guided only by their own intuition and taste."[39]

EVER SO FAINTLY, A PARTY LINE EMERGES

So far as Palekh and the problem of Russianness were concerned, the death of Stalin had surprisingly little impact. Through most of the 1950s, officials continued to insist that Soviet Russian society be revolutionary and urban-oriented yet derive many of its values from rural and prerevolutionary traditions. If there was a change in official attitudes toward Palekh in the 1950s, it was a matter of emphasis, and it actually predated Stalin's death. In 1952, for instance, cultural bureaucrats had begun to de-emphasize "monumental art" in Moscow and Leningrad. They argued for greater support of the "smaller art forms" of the provincial Russian heartland, by which they meant the various folk arts, along with their traditional forms and folkloric content. Rectifying the imbalance between monumental art at the center and "the small art forms" of the periphery and the rural heartland included greater resources and attention to Palekh.[40]

For Palekh this was a most welcome development. Palekh was thus allowed to celebrate the crucial thirtieth anniversary of its Sovietization in 1955, reversing the decision in 1949 that had prevented Palekh from marking its twenty-fifth jubilee. Soon after, eight Palekhians (mostly older masters) received the title Honored Artist of the USSR, the first such recognition since the end of the war. Indicative of the state's changing attitudes, Palekh also received a prestigious contract in 1955 to restore the "lacquer cabinet" in Peter the Great's Monplaisir at Peterhof. This cabinet was filled with oriental lacquer images supposedly painted in the era of Peter the Great by Palekh's icon-painter forerunners. The re-created lacquer panels (painted on Bakelite!) replaced those that had been destroyed by the Nazis. The local party in 1956 also unveiled a five-meter-tall bronze bust of Lenin, sculpted by a former icon painter from Palekh. As if to symbolize the final integration of Palekh into Soviet culture, the bust was placed directly facing Palekh's central cathedral, on the site of the previous monument to Tsar Liberator Alexander II, which had been torn down after the February Revolution.[41]

While debates about Palekh's style and content continued in the hamlet, the section of the Ministry of Culture of the RSFSR (Russian Soviet Federated Socialist Republic, also loosely referred to as the Russian Republic) responsible for museums and historical preservation embarked on an aggressive purchasing and exhibition program of Palekh lacquers in 1955. The move was part of a broader effort to promote Russian culture and gained even more momentum with the creation in February 1956 of a special bureau of the Central Committee to oversee cultural affairs within the RSFSR. This was the first Central Committee organization devoted specifically to Russian culture.[42] Within three years, fifteen museums in the RSFSR had received money to expand or create Palekh art collections, including the Tret'iakov Gallery, the State Russian Museum in Leningrad, and regional museums across the RSFSR. The state purchasing program mostly concentrated on buying the classic fairy-tale lacquers from the 1920s and 1930s, rather than boxes featuring more modern content and a realistic style. The "grand challenge" of the Ministry of Culture was to open a special section of Palekh art in every regional museum of the RSFSR, thereby making Palekh a central aspect of the regime's new resolve to Russify the RSFSR itself.[43]

The Palekhians also issued a new series of autobiographies in late 1954 to reaffirm their identity as national artists. The collection appeared twenty years after Efim Vikhrev, with Gorky's support, had published the autobiographies of more than twenty of the older Palekh masters (most of the volumes disappeared from library shelves because they contained a chapter on Aleksandr Zubkov, arrested and shot as an enemy of the people in 1938). Top billing in the new collection was given to the older masters, as was the case with the first collection, rather than to the *frontoviki*.[44] Perhaps the most striking element in these autobiographies is their treatment of the prerevolutionary era. In recounting their experiences in the prerevolutionary icon studios, the oldest masters expressed a clear nostalgia for life in the not-quite-so-good but increasingly not-so-bad old days before 1917. Rather than god-daubers, the older masters in this collection presented Palekhians on the eve of the Bolshevik Revolution as accomplished artists. It was a far cry from the earlier official view in place since the 1930s that Palekh had suffered from a dramatic decline *(upadok)* in the reign of Nicholas II.[45] The official story of the Palekh masters as god-daubers on the eve of the 1917 revolutions was weakening, eroded by a spirit of nostalgia that would soon come to dominate the cultural landscape.

Not everyone in Palekh, however, was so inspired by the new wistfulness. While the older masters rewrote their prerevolutionary history, the *frontoviki* continued to call for a radical break with the past. Khrushchev's secret speech of 1956, in their view, signaled a rejuvenation of the Soviet project, a return to the genuine roots of international socialism. If Palekh was to be a center of Soviet art, then they concluded that the masters had to be the equals of urban Soviet artists, free to choose their manner and theme independently of a traditional folk canon or style.[46]

The militant art critic Kotov again led the charge. Outraged by the seeming absence of socialist spirit in the Palekh lacquer, he arranged in October 1958 a conference and exhibit in Palekh, designed to offset the increasing emphasis on traditional forms and folkloric content in the dozens of other state-sponsored exhibits. He called it "The Soviet Theme in the Art of Palekh." Interestingly, despite Khrushchev's denunciation of the cult of personality, Kotov included Palekh's iconography of Stalin in the exhibit. For Kotov, as for many of the *frontoviki* who shared his ideas, comrade Stalin remained very much a positive part of Soviet modernity.[47] In his speech at the conference, Kotov elaborated the "progressive elements" of Palekh's prerevolutionary art. Repeating a favorite theme, Kotov traced the progressive roots of Palekh's art to increasing contacts in the late imperial period between the masters and the realist school of Russian painters known as the Wanderers.[48] These realistic strivings, which broadened the masters' worldview and acquainted them with the harsh realities of imperial Russian society, created a foundation for the new socialist realism of the Soviet era, and for the transformation of Palekh's god-daubers into fully developed socialist personalities. As evidence of that transformation, Kotov said the "best" work of Palekh in the 1920s *(The Demonstration, October in the Village, The Peoples of the USSR, Revolutionary Festivals,* and *May 1 in the Village)* was nearly identical to the program of Soviet artists in the capital. Palekh therefore proved that "the agitational forms of Soviet art" had entered "organically," along with Soviet power, "into the consciousness of the Russian village," displacing the reactionary worldview of the earlier period. For Kotov, the "organic" fusion of Soviet ideas and power into the Russian village thus meant that the revolution had not been in vain, that despite appearances to the contrary, the mentality of the prerevolutionary Russian village had not sabotaged the revolution.[49] Kotov's interpretation, of course, ignored the vast majority of Palekh's production, but such elements could be ignored because in Kotov's view they were the legacy of the past, to be discarded, forgotten, and, if need be, purged anew.[50]

FROM RESTRUCTURING TO PRESERVATION

Always the eager gadfly, Kotov and his exhibit triggered acrimonious debate in the collective. In retrospect, however, the exhibit was the last hurrah for the anti-traditionalists in Palekh. Two factors greatly complicated Kotov's revolutionary agenda. First and foremost was the legacy of the war itself. Kotov's traditionalist opponents benefitted from a popular sense of outrage at Nazi destruction of Russian national culture, which prompted a new nostalgia toward Russian traditions, even those associated with Russian Orthodoxy. Emphasizing the importance of continuity with the past, the spirit of nostalgia sapped the energy from postwar campaigns to continue Palekh's restructuring. The second factor was an emerging dialogue between Russian patriotic forces in the intelligentsia and many high-level party officials that added political legitimacy to preservationist tendencies. This growing alliance came at a time when non-Russian nationalities were more adamant about expressing their grievances. In response, a new course in nationalities policies followed the 1956 Twentieth Party Congress, in which Khrushchev denounced "gross violations of the basic Leninist principles of the Soviet state."[51] Although Khrushchev argued for greater independence for the Union republics, and earlier gave sunny Crimea as Russia's gift to the Ukrainian Republic, "the first direct beneficiaries . . . were the Russians. Because the entire Soviet state had been identified with them, their own Russian Federation had lacked some of the trappings of statehood possessed by the non-Russian republics." Along came a new newspaper devoted to the concerns of Great Russians (*Sovetskaia Rossiia*), the creation of distinct unions in the arts for the RSFSR, and a controversial educational reform that privileged the Russian language.[52]

Against this backdrop, Kotov's calls for revolutionary transformation (like Khrushchev's ultimately career-ending attempt to impose term limits on party officials) seemed increasingly old-fashioned, irrelevant, and out of step with the new preservationist spirit of the times.[53] If restructuring had been the rallying call of cultural practice in the late Stalin era and even much of the 1950s, preservation gradually became the dominant slogan by the early 1960s. The emergence of new attitudes toward Russian traditions, which reflected a broader yearning for stability, signaled that the cultural transformation in the Russian heartland was an accomplished fact. Palekh was entering the phase that Brezhnev called "developed socialism" and Gorbachev later dubbed "stagnation." In this new phase, Palekh was simply assumed, without need for further clarification or caveat, to be both Russian and Soviet. The priority now was to celebrate the hamlet, not transform it.

CHAPTER EIGHT

Triumph, Collapse, and Regeneration, 1958–2001

The growing alliance between the party and Russian nationalism built on the earlier wartime revival of patriotic Russian culture, whose "central features," noted Andrei Amalrik, "are an interest in Russianness, a belief in the messianic role of Russia and an extreme scorn and hostility toward everything non-Russian."[1] Symptomatic of the change, in December 1962 the artist Il'ia Glazunov told a sympathetic ideological commission of the Central Committee (whose members were nearly all ethnic Great Russians) about the shameful neglect of Russian national traditions, especially Russian Orthodox churches and icons. "How will we develop patriotic pride, what will we love," he lamented, if the regime allowed priceless treasures of church architecture and art to perish. "A genuine artist-creator should believe in the life-creating forces of his native country, he should search for creative inspiration in the bright well-springs of national creativity."[2]

Perhaps less surprising than the party's alliance with Great Russian nationalism was that this alliance had taken so long to emerge, especially given the surge of Russian patriotism during the war. The reason was Soviet ideology. Since 1917, the Palekhians faced wave after wave of hostile campaigns from Moscow, directed against the supposedly archaic and reactionary traditions of the Russian countryside as well as toward the hamlet's continuing links with the market. The Soviets also had to rule a multi-ethnic empire, and that meant imposing limits on Great Russian nationalist sentiments in order to maintain manageable relations between Russians and non-Russians. At the same time, the symbols and traditions of Great Russian national culture continued to attract popular support in the Russian heartland. The trend was bolstered by the cliché-ridden and formalistic rituals of Soviet culture, which seemed sterile and uninviting by comparison. Eager to shore up its waning hold over the hearts and minds of its citizens, the Soviets co-opted Palekh's vision of Great Russianness into the socialist project and declared the mission of cultural construction an accomplished fact. For the regime, it was a desperate gambit to exploit Russian patriotism to counter an increasingly moribund and apathetic Soviet public spirit—the hallmark of the late Soviet era.[3] For Palekh, it meant the dawning of a golden age of state patronage and acclaim.

The year 1958 marked the date when the state's turn to Russianness seemed to acquire a certain permanence. Signalling the shift, the native Palekhian Pavel Korin, an openly devout Orthodox Christian, received in that year the highest title for a Soviet artist: he was named a People's Artist of the USSR. Three years later the KGB finally closed their long investigation of Korin. After four decades of constant surveillance, the secret police concluded that Korin, like Palekh itself, no longer presented a clear and present danger to the Soviet state.[4] As if to sanction Palekh's prerevolutionary accomplishments, the Palekhians in 1959 were called upon to restore their greatest political triumph of the preceding period, the elaborate murals of the Kremlin Palace of Facets, which their forefathers had painted for the 1883 coronation of Alexander III.[5]

Equally telling, the Soviets abandoned the earlier notion that western demand constantly threatened to corrupt and debase Palekh. Instead, they now claimed that westerners loved Palekh so much because the hamlet conveyed a spiritual quality uniquely characteristic of Soviet Russian society and completely absent in the decadent West. In the new Soviet view, capitalist buyers consumed Palekh's art without influencing its style or content. It was a convenient way to square Palekh's dependence on the western market (which provided valuable foreign currency) with the regime's anti-capitalist outlook. Westerners, meanwhile, provided the ever-insecure Soviet regime with an important sanction for its emerging cultural policies. The American artist Rockwell Kent, a Soviet sympathizer and fan of Palekh art, called Palekh's art a "revelation" and said the lacquer boxes he had seen were "masterpieces of the art of all times," comments that the Soviets immediately trumpeted in reports on Palekh to their own population. Eager for more foreign acclaim, the Soviet regime arranged ten international exhibits of arts and crafts in 1957, thirteen in 1958, twenty-three in 1959, and twenty-five in 1961. This was the beginning of a systematic effort to display Palekh's art around the world, both in the capitalist West and, equally important, in the newly emerging third world. For the decolonizing nations, the Soviets used Palekh to craft a message designed to appeal to new nations with large peasant populations, like Russia itself in 1917. According to this message, only Soviet civilization could both modernize and preserve an intimate connection with vital national traditions—and protect them, so the line went, from the destructive and soulless forces of the capitalist West.[6]

Domestic tastes similarly aligned with foreign demand for Russian exotica. In 1960, retail outlets in Moscow and Leningrad signed contracts for the delivery of 745,000 rubles-worth of boxes and exports worth 300,000 rubles. Much of that went to special foreign-currency shops for the growing legions of foreign tourists, who were also allowed to visit Palekh in the late 1950s for the first time since before the Great Terror. Palekh miniatures were also available in retail outlets for Soviet consumers. In accordance with the increasingly stable

Palekh canon, these items, now officially called "souvenirs," depicted Pushkin fairy tales, rural idylls, Russian knights errant, troikas, Russian peasant dancers, and so forth. Domestic consumers of these items probably shared the sentiments of one group of college students from Ivanovo in 1961. Visiting the State Museum of Palekh Art, they said they saw in Palekh "the embodiment of the Russian people, its thoughts, feelings, and desires. [The art of Palekh] was born long ago, but just as long ago was born the optimistic and bright art form about which we are so proud, for only the Russian people could create such a thing." It was a typical reaction. The comment books for viewers in the State Museum of Palekh Art from the period reveal an overwhelming sense of pride and identification with the distinctly Russian traditions of the Palekh lacquer, its evocation of religious icon-painting traditions, the folk themes and bright colors, and the reference to idyllic rural landscapes. In no uncertain terms, a broad cross-section of visitors—from junior-high students and cosmonauts to powerful cultural officials and army generals—demanded that these traditions be preserved and propagated.[7]

Reflecting the decisive support of Palekh and its style, the Central Committee in June 1961 reviewed an ambitious plan to expand Palekh's art in Soviet society. The plan included a host of construction projects in the village. This outpouring of state largesse was designed "to further develop Palekh art and raise its role in the education of the toiling masses, and also with consideration of Palekh's inclusion in the list of sites for visitation by foreign tourists." At the same time, the State Museum of Palekh Art made tours of the central cathedral in Palekh, and the icons and religious murals that it contained, a centerpiece of the Palekh tour.[8]

Khrushchev's infamous attacks on abstract, foreign, and modernist art in December 1962 at the Manezh exhibit added further legitimacy to Palekh. After the outburst, Central Committee Secretary L. F. Il'ichev told a gathering of artists in Moscow that "the Leninist principles of the Party and folk nature of art are and will continue to be the foundation of our Party's policy in the sphere of the development of socialist culture." Khrushchev, in March 1963, noted that he grew up on Russian folk songs and culture, and that every nation should have a culture that is intelligible to its people. It was a message that was also conveyed abroad. In May 1963, the Academy of Arts of the Soviet Union offered forty of its most prized Palekh lacquers for display in three London galleries; Soviet authorities had earlier refused similar requests from the New York manager of the exhibition. The hamlet was thus aligned with cultural policies in which the Russian cultural legacy (minus its avant-garde and modernist strains) was increasingly, and uncritically, equated with socialism, both at home and abroad.[9]

Marking the end of the previous ambiguity, one of the last public critiques of Palekh's art was published on March 26, 1961.[10] The leading masters immediately penned a complaint to the party defending their honor and condemning the article, which apparently cut too close to the truth.[11] From the early 1960s to perestroika, at least so far as Palekh's public face was concerned, the hamlet appeared in the press as a picture of national perfection and harmony, and most masters wanted to keep it that way. All talk of Palekh's problems (like the market it depended on) were to be limited to closed-door meetings. Socialism had become developed. The title of one laudatory article devoted to Palekh in January 1964 embodied the new spirit of developed socialist culture: "It has the Russian Soul, It Smells of Rus'."[12] The appearance of such a headline in a newspaper of the late Stalin era, or even in the mid-1950s, would have been framed in ironic quotes. Almost certainly, it would have signaled an attack on Palekh's anti-Soviet character.

With growing acceptance came a search for an official emblem. By 1964, the cooperative created its own commercial and political logo: the mythical Russian firebird. In vain, the militant art critic Kotov protested the selection, arguing for a more modern symbol. In its official yearly accounting report to Moscow for 1965, the Palekhians incorporated the Palekh style into their bureaucratic correspondence. The report, which gloriously recounted the overfulfillment of the plan for generating foreign currency, came in a folder framed by elaborate red and black ornament. A troika in the Palekh style occupied the center of the report cover. Drawn in red, gold, orange, and purple colors, the classic Palekh troika was driven not by the party leadership but by the great nineteenth-century Russian poet Aleksandr Sergeevich Pushkin.[13]

THE NEO-TRADITIONALISTS

A new generation of artists enthusiastically embraced the latest party line, quickly establishing their dominance in the cooperative. For these new masters of the late 1950s and 1960s, de-Stalinization meant the celebration of ancient Russianness. They imagined the late Stalin era and the early Khrushchev years as a dark period in which deracinated and denationalized bureaucrats supposedly tormented supporters of national tradition. Confident of support from Moscow, they took the offensive against the previous generation of modernizers, the *frontoviki* and other artists who had demanded (with less than unanimous support in Moscow) Palekh's complete transformation. Self-consciously restoring the traditions that they believed had been threatened by the perceived imposition of socialist realism in earlier decades, new traditionalists looked to the Russian icon and Russian folklore as the foundation of their art. "We began to return to the essence of the style," said Aleksei Kochupalov, a student in Palekh from 1955 to 1961. He and his cohort "began to purge the rubbish from [our art] . . . the tractors, combines, and factories [that had] nothing to do with Palekh."[14]

Their ally in Moscow was the art critic Mariia Nekrasova, who believed the more realistic Palekh art of the earlier period was "a pedestal for loud and banal compositions." Resorting to classic Soviet techniques of argumentation, Nekrasova said Palekh images of Soviet construction projects and Stakhanovites, whose position in Palekh's production she grossly exaggerated, "were polluted with petty-bourgeois tastes" and "crippled the souls of people" who came to view such imagery at museum displays. She condemned attempts to find a new style and thematic content as "pseudo-innovation." In her view, the earlier Soviet period was the dark age of Palekh art, when "in essence . . . the language of [this] original art," like Russia itself, "was destroyed." Nekrasova's analysis is also notable for what it leaves out: the role of the market in Palekh's Soviet history (the dog that didn't bark), an omission also in evidence among the artists themselves. Denying market influence was critical in retaining what was left of the communist agenda, and it was now the key link between the Palekh artist and the Soviet order.[15]

While the art critics developed a new party line, the masters participated in a much broader revival of Russian culture. According to one Palekh artist, many masters after the mid-1960s considered themselves part of the neo-populist and *pochvenniki* (native soil) sentiments in some educated Russian circles. They read the works of the "village writers," authors such as Valentin Rasputin, Vasilii Belov, and Viktor Astaf'ev, who celebrated peasant folk culture and lamented the disintegration of Russian village life. They imagined themselves as defenders of bygone times and traditions. Through the 1960s, the thick journal *Molodaia gvardiia,* a bastion of Russian nationalism under high-level party protection, was obligatory reading for the new generation of Palekh masters. In 1966, the Russian nationalist Vladimir Soloukhin published in its pages a piece "that sought to dramatize the neglect of ancient Russian architecture and to cultivate an appreciation of Russian icons." After the journal subsequently published numerous letters inspired by Soloukhin's lament, the study of the Russian icon entered one of its most productive periods since the late imperial era. As one Palekh artist recalled, "there was created an entire direction of artists" singing the praises of Russian peasant life and folk culture. Anyone who disagreed with their position risked being branded anti-Russian and anti-Soviet.[16]

The new generation also drew inspiration from a popular movement to preserve monuments of Russian national culture that gained many adherents among the Russian youth of the 1960s. Preservationists believed, according to one scholar of Russian nationalism, that "preservation equals patriotism; anti-preservation equals national nihilism." Co-opting popular demands for preservation of Russian monuments, the regime in 1964 approved creation of the Homeland *(Rodina)* club to promote historical preservation. The Palekhian Pavel Korin spearheaded the effort, which acquired the name All-Russian Society for the Preservation of Historical and Cultural Monuments. Established by a decree of the Council of Ministers of the RSFSR, the group's first conference was held in June 1966. The ranks of this voluntary society grew rapidly, numbering seven million members in 1972 and twelve million in 1977, or nearly

10 percent of the population of the RSFSR. Among other things, the society published pamphlets and brochures on the importance of preservation, promoted indigenous tourism to Russia's so-called Golden Ring, and collected materials related to Russian folk culture. By the mid-1980s, the society had nearly forty million members.[17]

Although Palekh's earlier jubilees tended to emphasize the village's incomplete Sovietization as well as its triumphs, Palekh's jubilees in 1964–1965 and 1974–1975 were pure celebration. In 1964 the Palekhian and People's Artist of the Soviet Union, Pavel Korin, proclaimed that Palekh had a golden touch. While Midas turned everything into gold, everything the Palekhians touched became beautiful. Scores of artists received honorific titles. Municipal authorities in Moscow named a street after Palekh. Bards of the popular press composed couplets in honor of the hamlet and its art. A Soviet ship was named after Palekh; in a cruel irony, it sank in 1992. In the mid-1960s, a group of more than one hundred Palekh masters formed an amateur choir called the Folk Choir of the Town of Palekh. The Soviet record company Melodiia issued a collection of their songs. The group performed on unionwide Soviet television, dressed in traditional Russian peasant costume designed by local seamstresses. The popular journal *Ogonek* in 1974 summed up Palekh's secure status in the heartland of Soviet Russian culture. Noting the masters' many triumphs, the journal remarked, "it is hard to believe that not so long ago [Palekh] had many influential enemies."[18] The Palekhians, in fact, had become so confident of their status in socialist society that they referred to Palekh art as simply "Palekh realism" rather than socialist realism.[19]

Soviet officials, meanwhile, continued to pump resources into the village, giving it the required visage of plenty and comfort (in a sea of collective-farm poverty) befitting a Russian rural utopia. First on the agenda was a new production studio. For those who viewed cottage industry as a more backward and hence doomed system of production, a new studio was essential for continuing what was left of the communist agenda. The first studio in Soviet Palekh, used from the 1930s to the early 1960s, was situated in a building built by Palekh's prerevolutionary icon moguls, yet it was too small to accommodate the entire collective. Stymied by scarce resources, local party officials sanctioned the painting of lacquers in private homes during World War II, setting a precedent that the regime was unable to reverse. By 1960, nearly half the artists did most of their work at home—an environment many masters preferred, given the opportunity to avoid the gaze and comments of others.[20] Hand in hand with the privatization of housing in the USSR, the collective communal ideal thus kept losing ground, yet another sign of the waning influence of Marxist ideology.

Nonetheless, the regime would not give up its attachment to supposedly "higher" forms of production. At the insistence of Prime Minister Kosygin, work on the new studio began in the 1970s and dragged on through the beginning of the Gorbachev era. An immense structure made from quality Estonian brick, an extreme rarity in the Russian province, the new studio was to be the defining structure of the village, the realization of the long-standing dream to make Palekh a village academy. It incorporated a new hotel (to replace the old hotel built in the 1960s), workspaces for the more than two hundred masters, a conference center devoted to folk art, and a fitness center.[21]

Meanwhile, if Palekh was dependent on the market (a point still ignored in the public story of Palekh's Soviet history), it could not profit overtly from it, since private profiteering suggested, as Vladimir Shlapentokh once put it, "the withdrawal of human energy and emotion from work for the state and the absorption of people in their private interests." The KGB thus kept close tabs on the Palekh artists, scrutinizing them on trips to Moscow, Leningrad, and abroad to make sure that they did not sell their work privately. An incident in 1982 represented a last gasp of enforced Soviet anti-capitalism in the hamlet. Amidst Iurii Andropov's crackdown on corruption, the artist Valerii Konstantinovich Bokarev was arrested in late 1982 on trumped-up charges of speculation and sentenced to eight years in prison. The son of a prominent communist master from Palekh, Bokarev frequently participated in state exhibits and traveled abroad, where he also took orders from private clients. Perhaps his biggest sin was being too explicit about his consumption habits. He was the first Palekhian to have all the latest electronic gadgets, household amenities, foreign jewelry, and Levis. Luckily for Bokarev, the authorities cut his sentence in half, at the beginning of perestroika, and released him.[22]

While ideological reasons played a role in Bokarev's arrest, the regime also had other motivations: the hamlet had become a veritable machine for producing foreign currency. By the 1980s, nearly five hundred Palekh masters were earning the regime one million annually in convertible "gold" rubles. Upscale shops and department stores in New York City, such as Macy's and Brentano's, ran full-page ads in the *New York Times* pitching Palekh's lacquer boxes. "An Art of the Past Makes a Perfect Present," went one such ad placed by Brentano's on Fifth Avenue. Boxes featuring Pushkin themes at Brentano's were on sale for $425—a bargain compared to prices charged to foreigners for some lacquer boxes at the Moscow GUM department store, which were retailing for as much as $600 in the late 1970s. At Bloomingdale's, the French perfume company Payot began marketing a perfume and toilet water for $70 an ounce called "Pavlova," after the great Russian ballerina. It contracted with the Soviet state to have Palekhians make the elaborate decorated boxes to hold the perfume.[23]

THE MAGICIAN OF DIAGHILEV: SOVIET RUSSIAN, RUSSIAN SOVIET

As Palekh's status as a crown jewel (or, alternatively, a cash cow) of Soviet Russian culture solidified in the Brezhnev era, a native Palekh master took on the task of defining the traditions that now seemed to have such a secure future. The individual was Nikolai Mikhailovich Zinov'ev (1888–1979), known in press accounts as "the last of the Mohicans" and "the magician of Diaghilev" (a settlement one and a half kilometers from Palekh, where Zinov'ev lived).[24] Zinov'ev's personal story reflects a key factor behind the revival of Russianness in the 1960s and 1970s: a nostalgic turn that looked back beyond the 1917 revolutionary divide for identity and culture. As part of this nostalgia, Zinov'ev completed the writing of a new line on Palekh's prerevolutionary history in which the masters came to the Russian Revolution as fully developed artistic personalities rather than god-daubers. Among other things, this line consciously minimized the role of the revolution in the hamlet's artistic accomplishments. It was a telling reflection of newly permissible attitudes toward the prerevolutionary legacy—a harbinger of the coming end of the Soviet Union itself, along with the revolutionary spirit that had sustained it for so many decades.

Zinov'ev began his amazingly long artistic career in the 1890s as an apprentice painter of religious icons. Inspired by the example of many other Palekhians, he abandoned his apprenticeship in the private icon-studio system and entered Nicholas II's new icon-committee school in 1902. Like his fellow Palekhian Pavel Korin, Zinov'ev enrolled in the tsar's new icon school to hone his craft but also to learn the techniques of academic and secular painting. It was thus at the turn of the century that Zinov'ev, with the help of the tsarist state and conservative Russian nationalist intellectuals, began realizing his dream of becoming a national artist, rooted in a sacred and supposedly ancient tradition, yet also conversant with the demands of a more modern and secular art.

To realize his ambition, Zinov'ev traveled to Moscow and St. Petersburg in 1907, supporting himself by working in icon studios. In his spare time he studied secular artists, especially the Russian neo-realists Mikhail Nesterov (Pavel Korin's teacher) and Viktor Vasnetsov (a frequent overseer of Palekh's restorations of church art before 1917). Like his idols, he attempted to integrate the traditions of Russian religious art and folk culture with a more academic approach, an element of mastery that would prove once and for all that he was no mere god-dauber.[25]

Zinov'ev's prerevolutionary training prepared the young artist surprisingly well for the Soviet period. At the heart of Soviet Palekh's national synthesis, which Zinov'ev more than any other master helped create and sustain from the 1920s until his death in 1979, was the integration of Russian Orthodox aesthetic traditions, the modern technique and ethos of secular art (especially attribution of authorship), and Russian folk themes.[26] Of course, adding new socialist content to this art represented a significant departure from the last decades of the Romanovs. Yet even here, Zinov'ev drew on much of the emerging canon of folk motifs and ideas from the imperial era, especially the folk images popularized by artists such as Vasnetsov and I. Ia. Bilibin, and by the popular fairy tales of Pushkin.

At the time of his death in 1979, Zinov'ev had amassed numerous accolades and honorifics: a gold medal at the exhibit at the 1937 World's Fair in Paris for his Pushkin fairy-tale boxes, Honored Artist of the USSR (1956), People's Artist of the RSFSR (1963), Hero of Socialist Labor (1968), Laureate of the I. E. Repin Prize (1970), and at the age of 86 the highest of all honors for a Soviet artist, People's Artist of the USSR.[27]

More than any Palekhian or Soviet official, Zinov'ev helped make Palekh a "village academy." The term, as noted earlier, had first been coined for Palekh in the 1860s. Zinov'ev adapted the mission of making the village an "academy" as his own in the Soviet era. He ran the State Museum of Palekh Art from 1943 to 1955 and helped develop much of its vast collection of Russian religious icons and Palekh miniatures. He taught the fundamentals at the Gor'kii School of Palekh Art, the courses in "Palekh composition" that were based directly on his own training in the tsar's icon-committee school in Palekh from 1902 to 1906. In the 1940s and 1950s, Zinov'ev launched another career as an analyst and propagandist of Palekh art: he was the first "expert" to come from the ranks of the artists themselves. In all these activities, Zinov'ev was inspired by a single goal: to preserve the style of Russian Orthodox icon painting, especially in the face of pressures from his opponents locally and in Moscow who believed that these traditions had no place in Soviet Russian society.

As part of that effort, Zinov'ev by the mid-1950s was devoting much of his time to bringing his views of the Palekh art and style to the more general reading public and to the intelligentsia of Moscow and Leningrad, whose ranks he now believed he had entered. Thus began his odyssey, as he put it in a letter in September 1956, "to sum up my work," by which he meant publishing his thoughts on Palekh. The project consisted of a large body of his own writings composed from the early 1950s until his death in 1979 and contained three elements. First was the assembly in manuscript form of Zinov'ev's "conversations" with beginning Palekh art students. Those conversations covered everything from the history of Palekh (before and after 1917) to the problem of modernity and innovation in Palekh art. The second aspect of his ambitious project involved a detailed description of the technique and style of the lacquer miniature and its organic connection with the Russian icon-painting traditions. It was a kind of how-to production book, complete with a dictionary of specialized terms. Finally, Zinov'ev recorded memories of both his own life before the Russian Revolution and the lives of his cohort. The memoirs were a self-conscious effort to correct what he (and many other Palekhians) felt was the unwarranted denigration of Palekh's prerevolutionary accomplishments by outsiders.[28]

After years of searching for publishers and editors, Zinov'ev finally signed a contract for the project, called simply "The Art of Palekh."[29] With the aid of high-level patrons, including the artist Aleksandr Deineka and the art critic Mikhail Sokol'nikov, the book went to press in 1968 at the publisher Khudozhnik RSFSR. To Zinov'ev's great delight and vindication its ten thousand copies immediately sold out.[30] A second edition followed in 1974 in twenty thousand copies and was also sold out. In the process, Zinov'ev discovered a major ally of prerevolutionary art and mythology: the Soviet consumer.

Perhaps the most striking aspect of Zinov'ev's book is its love-hate relationship with the late imperial era. In Zinov'ev's retelling, this period emerges as both the source of Palekh's problems and the foundation of its cultural renaissance—a clarification, as noted earlier, first approached cautiously in the mid-1950s by some masters. The idea challenged the Soviet convention that culture had declined rapidly and had become decadent following the 1861 emancipation and the rapid development of capitalism. According to the convention, the artistic traditions of Palekh (and elsewhere) thus experienced a decline *(upadok)*, a term actually first applied to Palekh by tsarist elites in the 1880s. Zinov'ev was determined to get the story right and, in the process, correct the public record on Palekh that had been in place since the 1930s. In a letter pitching his manuscript, he noted that the first part of the book would describe "the great masters who brought the traditions of ancient-Russian painting up to the October Revolution and thereby laid down the path and created the firm basis for the flowering of new Soviet Palekh art." He wanted to focus especially on the life and times of the many talented Palekh masters and icon-studio owners with whom he had associated before 1917, whose portrayal until then, he said bluntly, was "inaccurate."[31]

The published book, like the lectures Zinov'ev had been giving for decades to Palekh art students, remained largely true to his project, although he did make compromises. While recounting the supposedly ruthless oppression of masters by the local icon moguls, most of the book's descriptions of prerevolutionary Palekh and its masters actually suggested the opposite. The majority of Palekhians, wrote Zinov'ev, were homeowners and had land to farm. Palekh had a vibrant system of trade and "was famous for being an enterprising village," where one could buy all sorts of things. Contrary to the notion that the icon craft was being increasingly monopolized by greedy capitalists, Zinov'ev noted that prerevolutionary Palekh had a wide range of icon studios and employers. Some, he wrote, "were vicious exploiters and looked upon their business as a source of profit," but others were deeply committed to the art and gave the masters many creative opportunities. "They paid the best of the icon painters well, carefully preserved the ancient traditions, fulfilled orders honestly, and created new types of work." Moreover, masters had the freedom to work in various styles, thus allowing the artists to develop their own artistic voice.[32]

Zinov'ev ended his story about Palekh with a plea to reevaluate the contributions of the late imperial period both to Palekh's art and to Soviet Russian culture. Listing the names of dozens of "humble laborers" from Palekh in the field of religious icon painting at the turn of the century, he said "thanks to them . . . the art of Soviet Palekh was able to be born."[33] Rather than calling his fellow prerevolutionary Palekhians "god-daubers," as was the convention in previous

Soviet treatments of Palekh, he treated them as accomplished national artists.

Sensing that his life was nearing its end, Zinov'ev nevertheless continued to expand his project, the fruits of which were actually realized posthumously. His work on the stylistic traditions of the art of Palekh *(Stilisticheskie traditsii iskusstva Palekha)* was published in 1981. It provided a detailed analysis, with Zinov'ev's own sketches and drawings, of the links between the standard elements of religious Russian icon painting and the Soviet Palekh miniature. The work continued a project that had been initiated by the icon experts of the nineteenth century, the creation of a definitive style manual *(podlinnik)* that would guide artists in the realm of sacred national art. It also publicized the secrets of the trade, the techniques used in making Palekh lacquers, thus completing another critical aspect of the late imperial *podlinnik*, the transformation of traditional Palekh art into a public, national asset.[34]

Meanwhile, Zinov'ev continued writing his memoirs right up until his death in 1979. Some of this work was edited and published in 1987. Adding to the charm of Zinov'ev's work, noted the book's editor, was its conveyance "in a somewhat old-fashioned language," which complemented the increasingly nostalgic and positive treatment of the late imperial period. In his memoirs, Zinov'ev described the paths of each of ten "founders of Soviet Palekh art" as a continuous process of acquiring and mastering the traditions. The process, in Zinov'ev's story, began in the last decades of imperial power, a time that provided the masters with a schooling in icon painting but also instilled in them a desire to achieve fame in secular national art. Rather than opening new vistas, the October Revolution, like the war before it, appears in Zinov'ev's account much like an obstacle in a fairy tale, a challenge to be overcome so that the journey, and the story, can continue. Ever resourceful—and determined to transform themselves into artists as they continued to preserve the ancient traditions—the masters found a new medium and new business in the 1920s. Through their own efforts, they forged their rightful place in Soviet Russian society, though one would be hard pressed to find much of anything Soviet in Zinov'ev's tale. In the end, these stories paid tribute to Palekh itself and the talent and ingenuity of the masters.[35] At the twilight of his life, and of the Soviet Union, the Palekhian Zinov'ev thus wrote a story in which the standard Soviet darkness-to-light paradigm had lost almost all relevance and explanatory power. Far from writing Palekh into the "master narrative" of the October Revolution, Zinov'ev simply wrote his own story—and got it published.

Tellingly, as he struggled to combat failing eyesight and the advanced stages of Parkinson's disease, Zinov'ev painted his last lacquer box in 1974. It was a self-portrait. The eighty-six-year-old artist used the full panoply of religious icon-painting tropes: an inverse perspective, the stylized representation of plants and palaces in the Orthodox Christian tradition, a symbolic approach. He even painted an icon. A large icon of Jesus *(Spas)* hung on a wall in the painted scene, in which the dying Zinov'ev depicted himself on his deathbed.

In the scene, a priest read him his last rites, which he refused to accept. Taunting him, an image of the grim reaper appeared in the background. By the figure of the artist in the scene, Zinov'ev wrote in gold paint: "God does not exist. In the universe there exists matter, which is eternal." Still, one wonders about Zinov'ev's convictions. The message of the box is far from straightforward. The artist seemed to be burdened by a nagging sense of doubt about the problem of God and salvation, which dominated the entire scene. Rather than an image of Lenin, for instance, the central figure in the painting was the figure of Jesus, who seemed to pose problems far more critical than those presented by the plan or the party leadership. As one sociologist of Soviet culture once remarked, "the creation and cessation of life suggest[ed] existential problems that, for the majority of the Soviet population, still require[d] religious answers." As if to second the thought, Zinov'ev hid religious icons in the attic of his house throughout the Soviet era—an ideology and worldview in reserve.[36]

Zinov'ev's life ultimately illustrates defining aspects of Russian cultural development across the revolutionary divide. One was a profound tension between academic experts, who referred to the Palekhians as ignorant and uncultured god-daubers, and the people, whose life and traditions the same experts nonetheless praised and idealized. Starting in the imperial era, Palekh's academician mentors believed the peasant masters must become more educated, more like themselves, yet also demanded that the Palekhians remain true to their national roots. Zinov'ev, responding to this seemingly impossible contradiction dating from the reign of Nicholas II, later became in the Soviet period a People's Artist and helped transform Palekh into a center of traditional Russian art in Soviet culture, eventually becoming an expert himself.

Yet Zinov'ev had a deep feeling of pride in his native Palekh and its peasant roots. If he accepted the tsarist experts' challenge of becoming a state-sanctioned artistic personality, he also rejected much of the intelligentsia's depiction of the Palekhians as ignorant god-daubers. Perhaps more than anything else, it was Zinov'ev's resentment of the experts' patronizing attitudes toward country folk that constituted the essence of his revolutionary identity, even as he strove himself to become an expert and an officially recognized *intelligent*. In this sense, Zinov'ev was thoroughly Soviet, since it was Soviet power, rather than the tsarist system, that officially gave him the status he craved, and that eventually allowed him to challenge the notion that Palekhians had ever been god-daubers in the first place.

Finally, Zinov'ev embodies the contradiction between the idea of the Soviet Union as a cultural tabula rasa, a fundamentally new kind of civilization, and the construction of Soviet culture from the culture of an earlier period. Like Soviet Russian society itself, Zinov'ev was profoundly shaped by both eras. His artistic preferences were first shaped in the late imperial era, and so were his ambitions. As he entered the twilight of his life, Zinov'ev became more and more nostalgic, publicly rehabilitating the late imperial period and its contributions to modern Russian culture. His nostalgic turn was symptomatic of a fundamental change in Soviet Russian culture in the last two decades of Soviet power, namely, its increasing willingness to embrace more and more of the Russian past as part of the "progressive" national legacy. True, the Soviets had always allowed part of the progressive past to be integrated into the new socialist culture. But they drew the line at the last three decades of imperial power, in which the progressive development of capitalism necessarily meant the intense degradation of culture. That line in the late 1960s and 1970s was fading fast, blurred by an increasingly retrospective orientation in Soviet Russian society. As a result, continuity with the prerevolutionary past, rather than a radical break, took precedence in Zinov'ev's story, as it now did more broadly in Soviet Russian society.

The flip side of this wistful vogue was that the "Soviet" half of "Soviet Russian" lost much of its appeal. What did it mean to be Soviet, beyond the fact that one lived and worked in the Soviet Union? By the 1960s and 1970s, Soviet culture had become increasingly cliché-ridden and ritualistic, remote and formalistic. In the words of one Soviet sociologist, Soviet cultural practices were "too uniform, impersonal, overweighted with speeches, and lacking in symbolism." While the cult of Lenin proliferated, so, too, did jokes about communism and Lenin. For many Great Russians, Russian national symbols and traditions, among them the collection and worship of icons, had become far more compelling, and fraught with meaning, than those of a more recent Soviet vintage. For example, by the mid-1980s, fifty million Russians said they were religious believers, thus embracing a worldview still officially condemned by the atheist regime. The results of the 1979 census further mobilized support for Russian national symbols. According to trends clearly noted in the census, birth rates among Great Russians were declining while those of non-Russians, especially the Muslim Central Asians, were on the rise. As a percentage of the Soviet Union's overall population, Great Russians were becoming a national minority. Threatened by the loss of majority status, many Russians redoubled demands for the support and preservation of distinctly Russian national traditions.[37]

Perhaps appropriately, this growing level of comfort and identification with prerevolutionary Russia coincided with the beginning of the end of the Soviet era in Palekh. Zinov'ev, who had come of age under tsarist power, missed this dramatic turn of events in 1989 by a mere decade—in what would have been his 101st year. But in more than one way he had already realized his prerevolutionary ambitions, thanks to the resources and support of Soviet authorities.

A FINAL RESTRUCTURING:
LIVING, DYING, AND LIVING AGAIN ON THE MARKET

For Russian national identity, which was increasingly inseparable from the Soviet system in which it had developed for decades, political and economic collapse came at the moment of seeming national triumph. Indeed, the primary result of Gorbachev's final campaign of revolutionary restructuring (perestroika) was to deprive the nation of its newest and most powerful patron, the Soviet state.

The unraveling of Soviet power in Palekh was amazingly swift. Back in the hamlet, the long-awaited new studio and conference center was nearing completion after more than a decade of continuous construction. It represented the culmination of attempts to transform Palekh into a state-run village academy. In 1989, just as the heating was turned on for the mammoth brick structure, the village experienced an event that locals immediately dubbed "the schism" *(raskol)*, which in turn threatened the legitimacy of Palekh's hard-won synthesis of imperial and Soviet culture. The pretext for the split came in early 1989, when one of the leading artists accompanied an exhibit of Palekh art to the United States and made a shocking discovery: the sale price of his art, as indicated in an English-language catalogue, was magnitudes greater than his wages. In the spirit of glasnost, he took a copy of the price list of Palekh lacquers for American consumers back to the hamlet, showed it to his colleagues, and began complaining loudly and publicly about the theft of his labor. In the spirit of Brezhnevite stagnation, the Palekh production studios, the one and only artistic business in town, fired him.

Under the banner of perestroika, the *raskol'nik* therefore started a new organization, which quickly attracted many artists. The upstarts pitched their new organization as the only rightful heir to the artel that had been founded by seven Palekh masters in December 1924. Mirroring the broader search in the late 1980s for a "NEP alternative," when socialism supposedly had a human face, they proclaimed, "We have thrown off the yoke of the creative dictatorship created by the Generalissimo." The administrators of Palekh, they declared in the spirit of Soviet anti-bureaucratic campaigns, were part of a "heartless bureaucratic machine," an "administrative command system" incapable of reform.[38] "Palekh belongs to no ministries, funds, or art unions! We have had it with bureaucrats. It is time to decide our own fate, the fate of the industry."[39]

Interestingly, many of the rebels were among the most prominent older party members from the postwar period, including those who had struggled for more modern content and style in Palekh art in the mid-1950s. By contrast, those who stayed behind in the old Soviet collective tended to be the masters of the 1960s who had fought for, and won, a decisive return to the traditional style of Palekh's art (which had never really been abandoned). The schism was thus framed in the familiar Palekhian opposition of tradition versus modernity. Neither side, however, claimed to be anti-Soviet. Indeed, just the opposite was true, as both sides continued to appeal to the state for support.[40]

Pecuniary motives and the absence of central authority quickly accelerated the process of division, which Soviet authorities had stymied for seventy years. At first, two new organizations competed for the spoils of the Palekh trade, but soon other artists, taking advantage of the opportunities for small-time private commerce allowed by the economic reforms, formed their own groups. And everyone seemed to be making money. For the first time since the imperial era, masters were legally free to work for themselves. Foreign collectors and traders of lacquers entered directly into negotiations with artists, to whom they promised (and often delivered) princely sums, by Russian standards. The easing of restrictions on travel, and the eagerness of many émigrés from the Soviet Union to cash in on these opportunities, created new distribution and sales outlets for artists. The popularity of Gorbachev in Europe and the United States triggered a boom in Russian exotica. As one *New York Times* correspondent put it in an article on the Moscow shopping scene: "anything handicrafted, especially lacquered boxes . . . is likely to be snapped up if you deliberate too long over your purchase." In the late 1980s, individual Palekh boxes were selling in Soviet foreign-currency shops for one thousand dollars, "and size does not always dictate cost." Some artists began painting religious icons. Some produced classic lacquers of Pushkin fairy tales. Some catered to a curious byproduct of perestroika, the growth of strong demand for socialist realist lacquers as reflections of a dying art form: images of tractors, Lenin, and even Generalissimo Stalin.[41]

In the meantime, the recently completed studio—the showcase of the era of communal labor in the Soviet Russian heartland—closed as soon as it was opened. The single cooperative organization to which it belonged no longer existed. Almost immediately, Palekhians began their own process of privatization, securing bricks from the structure for the many fancy new cottages *(kottedzhi)* that began sprouting up around Palekh like mushrooms after the proverbial rain. Like the ruins of Rome in the Dark Ages, the studio served as building material for the new order. It stands today as a fitting tribute to the Soviet era: a cannibalized skeleton, covered with graffiti and expletives in grammatically incorrect English. Palekhians aptly call it "the Coliseum."[42] On the other side of town, the studio in which the masters had worked since the 1960s—also a large two-story stone structure—is completely abandoned. Its windows are mostly broken, and the weeds and garbage grow high around its edges. In less than a year, the material foundations for communism had been decisively and irreversibly abandoned.

By 1990, the Soviet system of production in Palekh had collapsed. The revolution of October 1917 was overturned, although one would be hard pressed to locate the dramatic events, the storming of so many Bastilles, typically associated with "revolutions." Yeltsin standing atop a Russian tank in Moscow in August 1991 hardly qualified, at least so far as many Palekhians were concerned. If there was a Bastille in Palekh, it was the Coliseum, and rather than being stormed it was simply looted. Like the carcass of the Soviet Union through the 1990s, it was picked over before it even opened for socialist business.

Meanwhile, if the boundaries between imperial and Soviet culture became far more porous in the Brezhnev period, the same can be said of the dividing lines between Soviet and post-Soviet Russian society. One searches in vain for a clear division, a definitive sign that Russia has indeed entered a fundamentally new era. For every sign of a radical break with the Soviet past, there is an equally compelling indication of continuity. Russians still mark celebrations of Palekh's art in Soviet time, and in the same way Putin has reestablished the old music of Stalin's Soviet anthem as the Russian Federation's national hymn. The Russian Federation (aided by funds from the philanthropist free marketer George Soros) thus celebrated Palekh's seventy-fifth anniversary in 1999. The event took as its beginning point the formation of the Artel of Ancient Painting in 1924, rather than the time before 1917 when Palekhians first began painting religious icons.[43] Similarly, the statue to Lenin, erected in 1956 by a prominent Palekh sculptor, still stands directly across from the Exaltation of the Cross Cathedral in Palekh. In the summer of 2001, its future seemed secure, in stark contrast to the fate of the statue it eventually replaced on the very same location, a bust of Tsar Liberator Alexander II, which was unceremoniously tossed into the nearby pond in February 1917. Also secure is the elaborate monument below the hamlet's Exaltation of the Cross Cathedral to the heroic sacrifice of hundreds of Palekhians killed in the Great Patriotic War. Designed by the same Palekhian who had made the statue to Lenin, it sits atop the former site of the village's Aleksandr Nevskii chapel.[44] While that chapel was torn down in the 1930s, the defeat of the Nazis remains an unchallenged achievement of Soviet power. Only the Soviet victory over the Nazis rivals the Soviet Palekh jubilee as a festive occasion in the post-Soviet hamlet.

Attitudes among some artists and art critics have also been very slow to change. With the collapse of the state monopoly over Palekh art in 1989, the old anti-capitalist rhetoric immediately asserted itself, though few stopped to consider the "dirty little secret" that capitalism, even in the Soviet period, had underwritten much of the village academy and its relatively high standard of living. Viewing the *"raskol"* in late 1989, a journalist remarked that "the firebird has been plucked and thrown on the frying pan, roasted by the flames of the dispute." He lamented the dawning of a new age in which the market and its vulgar, corrupting tendencies had finally triumphed over the anti-market mission of Russian national culture. In my interviews with Palekh artists, I was stuck by the extent to which even the most successful ones continue to condemn the "vulgar" influences of the consumer economy upon which they depend. "Fewer artists are really concerned about maintaining the purity of Palekh art," said the disgusted director of the Palekh art museum in 1994. "[And] some just trade this reputation for money."[45]

Curiously, in the aftermath of the collapse of the Soviet Union, one hears little in Palekh about the Stalinist regime's supposed destruction of traditional Russian values, a favorite topic among many artists in the 1960s. If anything, quite the opposite is true. The Soviet Union, according to those who look upon the Soviet era nostalgically, played the role of preserver and protector of Russia's national traditions, which allowed Palekh to flourish and occupy its rightful place on center stage in Russian culture. The Soviet era has thus been recast in a positive role as a defender of Russian national culture. Russia, in their view, is again under siege—this time from the capitalists within, creating a new division of Russia into various and sundry "appanages" and exposing the nation to foreign domination.[46]

True, relative prosperity has helped ease Palekh's transition. Through the 1990s, the artists continued doing what they had been doing very successfully for centuries: producing and selling art. Indeed, few places in Russia were so well equipped to deal with the transition to a market economy. In Palekh, low technology was essential. The Palekhians had a brand name and access to a stable base of customers with foreign currency. They had a long history of contacts with foreign and domestic retailers and a system of production that had always, in fact, been tied to the market. And they had two traditional art forms from which to choose, which is one more than they had during the previous change of regimes: the ancient religious Russian Orthodox icon plus the new "ancient" tradition of the Palekh lacquer created in the 1920s and 1930s.

Creative debates also continue, mirroring debates from the early Soviet period. A small group of serious young artists has broken completely with the notion of Palekh as "folk art." In the mid-1990s, they displayed a new style and content in a series of exhibits called "After the Winter," by which they meant rebirth, referring to the prolonged period of stagnation in Palekh art since the early 1960s. Interestingly, they drew inspiration from the past generation of militant Soviet Palekh artists in the 1930s and 1940s who attempted to break away from their teachers and follow the conventions of socialist realist art. "I would like to think a bit about what is happening in the country and the world," noted one of their leaders, as he condemned the nostalgic and escapist tendencies of Palekh art. The ideological platform of these young artists, like that of their Soviet predecessors, extolled the virtues of "modernity, a secular nature, individuality, relevance, and a freshness of expressed ideas." Like many of the militant Palekh artists/*frontoviki,* they frequently mocked variations of the Palekh folklore classics as "plagiarism" *(plagiat)* and believed the propagation of these classics in the age of the microprocessor should best be left to "the Xerox machine or computer. It takes less time."[47]

Meanwhile, Russian identity seems to be stuck in a kind of indeterminate state between its anti-capitalist past and its post-Soviet bourgeois present. By 1996 the blush was off the private lacquer trade. Foreign collectors and profit seekers had saturated the available market for Palekh art in the West and moved on to other ventures. When the easy money and foreign buyers started coming less frequently to the hamlet, many masters stopped working and lived off their savings, which were then nearly obliterated by the crisis of the ruble in 1998. In the summer of 2001, dozens of new brick homes stood unoccupied by their owners in Palekh. Having endured a number of years without proper heating and winterization, the houses, depending on one's point of view, looked either halfway built or halfway collapsed, much like the new studio-cum-conference center that was closed as soon as it opened. Thus, just as the demise of the new studio represented the collapse of the Soviet dream of a village academy, so too might the half-finished *kottedzhi* of Palekh be seen as the bitter end to a more bourgeois and middle-class longing.

Yet there are also signs of an emerging bourgeois consciousness, as in the Russian Federation more generally. Many masters, and those who trade in lacquers, are completing their houses, buying new cars (sometimes of foreign make), and traveling abroad, where they keep their bank accounts safe from Russian tax inspectors. Money is certainly not as easy to come by for Palekh as it was in the late 1980s and early 1990s, but for those with ambition and drive, savings and creature comforts can be (and are being) accumulated. In addition to icons and boxes on traditional folklore themes, Palekhians are also producing boxes for a new breed of domestic patrons, the "new Russian" mobsters/entrepreneurs. A special store in Moscow caters to their needs, providing, among other things, Palekh boxes featuring images of Mercedes cars, "new Russians" with their naked girlfriends in the sauna, and images from the post-Soviet, cult-hit gangster movie *Brother* and its sequel *Brother 2*. These boxes sell for as much as three thousand dollars each. Such works of art, quipped one artist, "are also part of our history," and they testify to Palekh's amazing ability to adapt its "ancient" traditions to the latest currents in Russian society.[48]

Even many of the older generation have quickly adapted, and one gets the impression that the transition post-1991 was actually facilitated rather than hindered by the Soviet legacy.[49] As in the broader Russian Federation, many of today's new Palekhians were former Komsomol and party leaders locally. In the late Soviet period, they belonged to the union of artists, displayed their boxes at exhibits, and increasingly traveled abroad, where they made friends and potential business contacts, from which they have benefited in the post-Soviet era. They had close relations with retail and wholesale outlets in Moscow and Leningrad that helped give rise to the capitalist retail and wholesale trade business of Moscow and St. Petersburg after 1991.

These former communists have also found a new source of authority and patronage that harkens back to their prerevolutionary identity. By 2001 they had become regular churchgoers. The head of the Palekh branch of the union of artists from the 1970s and 1980s, Aleksei Kochupalov, has built himself a private chapel that stands beside his palatial two-story home. Only Palekh, claimed one prominent Soviet-era artist, had faithfully preserved the traditions of icon painting. That reputation has helped many of the "old-timers," those trained under the Soviets and now growing old in the Putin era, carve out a new identity and livelihood for themselves as painters of religious icons. The old regime's system of elite patronage for religious art has also reemerged. When Mayor Luzhkov helped organize reconstruction of the Kazan Cathedral just off of Red Square, Palekh artists were hired to paint the murals for the new "old" church, which had been blown up in the 1930s. The Palekh artists, with the blessing of the Moscow Patriarch, also have issued a new Bible, complete with nearly 150 illustrations from the hands of the Palekh masters. The patriarch declared the publication, issued in honor of the Soviet defeat of the Nazis, "an event of enormous importance for the culture of the entire Fatherland."[50] Reflecting the new importance of Russian Orthodoxy in national identity, Palekh's two main churches have again become working churches, one in 1989 and the other in 1992. Palekh masters proudly display their newest works of religious art in these churches for public admiration and worship. Their Soviet-era training as lacquer specialists, focused on preserving the techniques if not the content of Russian Orthodox painting, has thus served them well in the post-Soviet era.

Finally, some Palekhians in 2001 were also coming to terms with their pre-revolutionary, capitalist past.[51] In their view, competition and capitalism enriched the artistic traditions of Palekh rather than corrupting and vulgarizing them. This, of course, was a central point in Zinov'ev's Soviet-era account of Palekh. Today, it has provided an alternative, if controversial, identity for many Palekh masters, and for Russians more generally. By the summer of 2001, Palekh had split up into dozens of new businesses and studios, after the model of the prerevolutionary era outlined by Zinov'ev. Some artists, descendants of Palekh's icon moguls, have even recast their operations as direct and legal continuations of pre-1917 businesses. In 1997, for instance, the descendants of the Parilov studio owners from the end of the nineteenth and beginning of the twentieth centuries composed a notarized certificate for their claims. It stated that the present-day Parilovs "are professional artists and inheritors of the more than three-hundred-year-old dynasty of icon-painting Parilovs." The Parilov studio, like its predecessor under Nicholas II, announced that it would be specializing in the local Palekh *"friaz'"* style of religious icon painting. It officially reopened for business in 1996, after nearly eighty years of unanticipated complications.[52] The circle, only partially broken by the Bolshevik interlude, seemed to have finally closed.

EPILOGUE

The Village Academy in Modern Russian History

As the nineteenth century came to a close, Palekh's expert patrons pursued a paradoxical agenda. Although their program identified market culture as a threat to Palekh's traditions, and to Russia's national distinctiveness, these experts demanded that Palekh's traditions be modernized. Just how to do so, however, remained a matter of debate and controversy. The experts' complex agenda of anti-capitalist modernization, made even more confusing by a program of preserving links with a premodern past, brought the state and educated elites directly into the business and culture of Palekh at the beginning of the twentieth century.

The same contradictory agenda continued across the revolutionary divide. The Soviet state, like its predecessor, was hostile to local autonomy and to the supposed "backwardness" and "kulak" tendencies of the peasantry, yet it frequently idealized peasant life as a bastion of national purity untainted by modern capitalist civilization. After the fashion of their tsarist predecessors, Soviet officials called Palekh a "village academy," elaborating a vision of the nation firmly rooted in nineteenth-century populist rather than Marxist ideals. According to this vision, Soviet Russia was to be one part "academy" and one part "village," a synthesis of intellectual and peasant culture that had defined the earlier populist program of the 1870s to "merge with the people" and the later mission of the tsar's icon committee.[1]

Other common features also united cultural practices in the imperial Russian and Soviet periods. Prominent academicians in the imperial era, such as Kondakov, exploited their expertise in an attempt to exercise tutelage over "the people." They had few qualms about allying themselves with a tsarist regime that was openly hostile to democracy and civil society and that fostered a political climate on the eve of the Russian Revolution that was anti-liberal, anti-market, and paternalistic. In this respect the members of the icon committee mentioned in this study were not so different from many intellectuals on the left. As Boris Groys argues, the revolutionary intelligentsia eagerly served the Bolshevik regime and its anti-capitalist policies.[2] In exchange for supporting the state, the intelligentsia anticipated being granted the power to control and define Russian culture, and to defend it from the market. While this project ultimately failed to sever Palekh's dependence on market exchanges, state-sanctioned attempts to control and define culture were remarkable for their duration and intensity.

The story of Palekh also reveals longer-term processes in the development of Russia's national artistic elite, whose life span as a vital social and political force (1840–1991) roughly coincides with the chronology of this study. Whether on the right or left, Russian intellectuals and artists, trained in state-run institutions, looked to some form of organized power to enact various utopian visions of the nation. Indeed, allying with the state to preserve and protect national culture became a fundamental part of their professional identity. The icon experts of the first half of this study, and artists such as Viktor Vasnetsov, belonged to the group of utopians on the right. In the 1840s, they first emerged from the ranks of the nobility. Later, they were joined by individuals from the so-called people of various ranks (raznochintsy). Palekh's artists after 1861 represented a further opening of the Russian artistic elite to those of peasant background— logical enough, given the emancipation of the peasantry. With the help of the tsarist state and conservative Russian nationalist intellectuals, Palekh masters began realizing their dream of becoming national artists. They were encouraged by the tsarist state, which hired Palekhians in 1883 to recreate the murals of the Kremlin Palace of Facets for the coronation of Alexander III. In greater and greater numbers, Palekhians from the 1880s started attending classes in secular painting in Moscow and St. Petersburg, as part of their quest to become members of the Russian official artistic elite and prove that they were not god-daubers. This process of entry into the ranks of Russia's national artists culminated in the Soviet period when many Palekh masters became People's Artists, the highest honor for a Soviet painter. Consequently, when Palekh masters, such as Zinov'ev, examined their conversions into artistic personalities, they dated the beginning of the change well before 1917. The Bolshevik Revolution, in their view, was not the beginning of their transformation into national artists; rather, that process predated and fed into the Bolshevik attempt to create "a new intelligentsia out of the worker and peasant youth."[3]

At the same time, the Palekh masters were extremely grateful for the opportunities provided by Soviet power. The Soviet Union offered Palekh masters status as official artists, something never fully granted by the experts or the regime of the earlier era. Soviet officials invited professional art critics and journalists (the new Soviet experts) to write celebratory books and articles about the village's art. Above all, the Soviet system gave Palekh masters real power to create and define Russian national culture, something that the imperial regime, which was rigidly elitist, could never abide. As a result, the masters developed a strong sense of identification with the Soviet system, despite its unceasing and often incomprehensible demands.

To be sure, it was a kind of Faustian bargain. After 1917, the Palekh masters could no longer publicly paint and worship religious icons, the core of identity for many artists (though not all) in the imperial era. Under the threat of expulsion from the community of privileged artists, they abandoned the previous religious content. The shift to secular themes, given the increasing secularization of Russian society on the eve of the revolution, was perhaps less costly than another fundamental compromise. The Palekh masters came to accept the regime's ideological requirement that no true Soviet artist could allow the market to dictate his or her creativity, an ironic attitude given Palekh's continuing reliance on the market throughout the Soviet era. Rather than acceptance by the market, the Palekh masters learned to validate themselves exclusively through the honors and social status provided by the regime. In doing so, they followed the lead of Russia's Europeanized intelligentsia, right and left, whose statist attitudes and anti-market bigotry melded seamlessly into the new Soviet order, and was eventually absorbed by the Palekhians themselves. It was a remarkable shift in values for the Palekhians when compared with their prerevolutionary past. Business acumen and entrepreneurial skills had been positive attributes of professional identity for the Palekh masters before 1917. After the Russian Revolution, in the face of the continuous denigration of the business skills upon which the masters depended, the masters came to view commercial savvy as a badge of shame rather than honor.

In the post-Soviet era, anti-market values have proved remarkably resilient; they mark perhaps the most significant element of continuity with the Soviet past and, in many respects, with the late imperial era. The collapse of state tutelage, given the endurance of such attitudes, has therefore created a new kind of identity crisis for Palekh, and for Russians more generally. The part of their identity that was linked to the state has collapsed. The masters now stand naked before a market system they had learned to vilify.[4]

An important though unstated subtext in this identity crisis was the acute sense of abandonment felt by Russian artists and intellectuals, who had been allied with the state in the exercise of extraordinary power over Russian culture since before 1917. With the collapse of the Soviet Union and its system of "tutelage" for the arts, the long-standing project of working with the state to control and define culture suffered a grave and irreversible defeat.[5] "The collective [in Palekh] has collapsed," proclaimed one prominent party member and master in 1993, who like many other Palekhians considered himself to be a member of Russia's artistic elite. "Unhealthy competition has begun. Some say this is all quite natural. . . . Maybe. But that does not mean it will always be this way. Everything, good and bad, will pass. That is life. The present chaos will also pass and a normal life will develop again." By normal, the author meant a world where state-controlled organizations established monopolies in all spheres of economic and creative life, and where the "desire to own one's own business" and "make money" had not "destroyed talented artists" and "corrupted the souls of our children."[6]

Today, Palekh masters, like most members of the former Soviet intelligentsia, must find validation for their social status exclusively through the va-
garies of the market. The state no longer employs the art critics who judge
Palekh's work. The state-controlled Union of Artists no longer funds exhibits.
To add insult to injury the few exhibits that display Palekh are mostly financed
by western capitalists such as George Soros. Furthermore, Palekhians must now
solve ideological conflicts and creative debates on their own; the state is no
longer willing to mediate their disputes. The result has been the disintegration
of the hamlet into competing circles of mutually hostile groups, a kind of
Hobbesian natural state. Rather than promoting the development of a vigorous civil society, this situation has resulted in a relentless theft ("privatization") of public assets, coupled with a renewed nostalgia for the Brezhnev era,
which many Palekh masters now see as a golden age of social harmony when
Russian traditions were protected and defended by state authorities. The
dilemma extends far beyond Palekh; it reflects a broader challenge for the legions of professionals (and non-professionals) in Russia, whose status for
decades was derived from official rewards and privileges rather than from the
market. The widespread popularity of President Putin's attacks on Russia's
most successful new entrepreneurs is but one reflection of how deeply ingrained these anti-capitalist attitudes have become.

Back in Palekh, adjusting to the new climate has engendered feelings of be-
wilderment and anger. Palekh may have had a glorious past, as one local journalist put it in 1994, but does "the village academy have a future," especially
at a time when the Russian state has drastically cut back support for all acade-
mies, village or otherwise?[7] The only academy that seems to matter anymore
in Russia is the business school, and perhaps that is not such a bad corrective.
In December 1997, one young Palekh artist, who came of age as an artist under
Gorbachev, offered a bitter pill to his comrades. He said the idea of creating a
new artistic monopoly in Palekh and reviving the "idyllic picture of Palekh
masters sitting behind one table and creating in a unified, creative inspiration" is
gone forever. It has been replaced by the new realities of "commercial success . . .
and the individual creative personality of the artist." There is now no state "art
committee" to judge whether a work would be displayed. "Every author . . .
should know that he is responsible for his own work, and not the brand name
of Palekh, the authority of the older masters, or the creative ideas of 'the
Palekh classics,' which he perhaps mindlessly copies, or, more precisely, beats
like a dead horse."[8] The artist concluded that in the new post-Soviet reality,
Russia must, "like any developing system, remain open for the assimilation of
many directions of world culture." The status of Palekh masters, he added,
would depend exclusively on their ability to negotiate the ever-shifting demands of a new era of globalization and not on their well-honed skills for ex-
tracting patronage and status from cultural bureaucrats in Moscow.[9] In this
context, it is not at all clear that the Palekh masters can retain their much-

coveted status as privileged official artists, or that the village can hold onto its unique role in Russian culture. At best—and this trend already seems to be firmly established—Palekh will become like so many other quaint villages of the modern world: a tourist center providing souvenirs for credit card–carrying visitors in search of a brief respite from the confusing world of commerce, marketing, and cultural homogenization. Perhaps the masters will thrive economically in this environment, but many will not find the sense of state-sanctioned national community that was the hallmark of the Brezhnev era.

It is a trend that offends many Russians, though there seems little they can do about it. At an April 1998 exhibit of Palekh lacquers in a bewildering variety of styles and themes, one Palekh master commented that "it is frightening and in truth terrifying to see . . . works with insulting subjects inspired by the devilish forces of television and other instruments of mass information." The viewer condemned works parodying religious themes and classical Palekh folklore subjects, noting that "this is only a reflection of the monstrous world" above which true artists "must be superior." Another viewer summed up the entire trauma of the post-Soviet experience for many Russians. "My consciousness simply does not accept . . . [these] works." The exhibit, in his view, was definitive proof that a new state monopoly, with "a stern" evaluating committee, had to be re-created in Palekh in order to safeguard the traditions, to ensure the right to be called an artist, and to instill in the younger generation "love" for their profession rather than disrespect and disdain. "I am outraged by the impertinence [of many exhibitors]. Where did [they] come from and who the hell do they think they are?"[10] Perhaps more than any other comment, this question, "who the hell do they think they are?" encapsulates the profound post-Soviet dilemma for Russian artists and intellectuals raised in the Soviet era. These individuals must learn a new set of rules for achieving social status and in the process unlearn a complex system of state control that had become fundamental to their own sense of what it means to be "Russian." Even more than the transition to a market system, learning to accept a less-than-exalted mission, learning to live without state approval (and manipulation), will demand a process of mental "restructuring" every bit as challenging as the one posed for nearly a century by tsarist and Soviet power. Moreover, even if the old Soviet intelligentsia succeeds in this restructuring, its power relative to Russia's new culture will pale in comparison to the earlier era. Abandoned by the state, its role as arbiter of Russian national culture has been usurped, once and for all, by the market. In short, the unique function of the state-sanctioned expert and artist is now an anachronism, and so too is Russia's village academy, one of modern Russia's more curious utopian projects.

NOTES

INTRODUCTION—IN SEARCH OF RUSSIAN NATIONAL IDENTITY

1. Translations from the Russian in this study are provided by the author. Efim Vikhrev, ed., *Paleshane. Zapiski palekhskikh khudozhnikov o ikh zhizni i tvorchestve, napisannye letom 1932 goda i illiustrirovannye imi samimi* (Moscow: Moskovskoe tovarishchestvo pisatelei, 1934), 343–49.

2. Yitzhak M. Brudny, *Reinventing Russia: Russian Nationalism and the Soviet State, 1953–1991* (Cambridge, Mass.: Harvard University Press, 1998).

3. Benedict Anderson, *Imagined Communities: Reflections on the Origin and Spread of Nationalism,* 2nd ed. (New York and London: Verso, 1991), 85.

4. Recent exceptions include Vera Tolz, *Russia* (London: Oxford University Press, 2001); Geoffrey Hosking, *Russia and the Russians: A History* (Cambridge, Mass.: Harvard University Press, 2001).

5. Hans Rogger, *National Consciousness in Eighteenth-Century Russia* (Cambridge, Mass.: Harvard University Press, 1960).

6. These tensions between the particular and universal in Russian national identity were also reflected in the military reform of 1874, which aimed to create a Russian "national" conscript army that would still be open to assimilating non-Russians. See Joshua Sanborn, *Drafting the Russian Nation: Military Conscription, Total War, and Mass Politics, 1905–1925* (DeKalb: Northern Illinois University Press, 2003).

7. On tensions between Marxism and nationalism, see Roman Szporluk, *Communism and Nationalism: Karl Marx versus Friedrich List* (New York: Oxford University Press, 1988).

8. Yuri Slezkine, "The USSR as a Communal Apartment, or How a Socialist State Promoted Ethnic Particularism," *Slavic Review* 53 (Summer 1994): 414–52.

9. Martin Malia, *The Soviet Tragedy: A History of Socialism in Russia, 1917–1991* (New York: Free Press, 1994).

10. RGALI, *f.* 94, *d.* 50, *l.* 9.

11. This was a common pan-European phenomenon. See, for example, J. L. Talmon, *Romanticism and Revolt: Europe, 1815–1848* (New York: Harcourt, Brace & World, 1967).

12. See, for example, Richard S. Wortman, *Scenarios of Power: Myth and Ceremony in Russian Monarchy,* vol. 1, *From Peter the Great to the Death of Nicholas I* (Princeton: Princeton University Press, 1995).

13. On the turn to Muscovite models in the post-emancipation era, see Richard Wortman, *Scenarios of Power: Myth and Ceremony in Russian Monarchy,* vol. 2, *From Alexander II to the Abdication of Nicholas II* (Princeton: Princeton University Press, 2000).

14. See especially Sanborn, *Drafting the Russian Nation.*

15. Stephen Kotkin, *Armageddon Averted: The Soviet Collapse, 1970–2000* (New York: Oxford University Press, 2001).

16. Eileen Boris, *Art and Labor: Ruskin, Morris, and the Craftsman Ideal in America* (Philadelphia: Temple University Press, 1986), xi-xii. See also T. J. Jackson Lears, *No Place of Grace: Antimodernism and the Transformation of American Culture, 1880–1920* (Chicago: University of Chicago Press, 1981), 59–96; and on American populism and the "agrarian myth," see Richard Hofstadter, *The Age of Reform: From Bryan to F. D. R.* (New York: Vintage Books, 1955), 23–82.

17. Wendy Salmond, *Arts and Crafts in Late Imperial Russia: Reviving the Kustar Art Industries, 1870–1917* (New York: Cambridge University Press, 1996); Alison Hilton, *Russian Folk Art* (Bloomington: Indiana University Press, 1995).

18. V. I. Lenin, *Voprosy natsional'noi politiki i proletarskogo internatsionalizma* (Moscow: Politizdat, 1965), 15, 16, cited in Slezkine, "The USSR as a Communal Apartment," 417.

19. Peter Stansky, *Redesigning the World: William Morris, the 1880s, and the Arts and Crafts* (Princeton: Princeton University Press, 1985), 4, 30.

20. Boris, *Art and Labor,* 14.

21. Helene Roberts in *Victorian Periodicals Newsletter* 9 (July, 1970): 6, cited by Stansky, without any article title, in *Redesigning the World,* 21.

22. Salmond, *Arts and Crafts in Late Imperial Russia,* 1.

23. On the conception of romantic anti-capitalism in late imperial Russia, see Katerina Clark, *Petersburg: Crucible of Cultural Revolution* (Cambridge: Harvard University Press, 1995); Steve Smith and Catriona Kelly, "Commercial Culture and Consumerism," in *Constructing Russian Culture in the Age of Revolution: 1881–1940,* ed. Catriona Kelly and David Shepherd (Oxford: Oxford University Press, 1998), 106–56.

24. Boris, *Art and Labor,* 189.

1—OFFICIAL NATIONALITY AND THE RISE OF THE ICON EXPERT

1. *Izograf: Zhurnal ikonografii i drevnikh khudozhestv,* tom 1, vypusk 7 (1884): 38.

2. S. Durylin, "Rannie russkie znakomstva Gete," *Literaturnoe nasledstvo,* nos. 4–6 (1932): 117.

3. The images were an icon of the Virgin Mary and one showing the central calendar feasts. D. F. Kobeko, *O Suzdal'skom ikonopisanii* (St. Petersburg, 1896), 2–3, 5.

4. Kobeko, *O Suzdal'skom ikonopisanii,* 6.

5. Talmon, *Romanticism and Revolt,* 126; Andreas Kappeler, "The Ambiguities of Russification," *Kritika,* no. 2 (Spring 2004): 294.

6. I. L. Kyzlasova, "O starom Palekhe," *Sovetskii khudozhnik,* no. 7 (1979): 34; D. K. Trenev, *Sovremennaia friaz'* (Moscow: Izdanie Deribizova, 1905), 9–10. On the emergence of icon painting as a lay phenomenon, see O. Iu. Tarasov, *Ikona i blagochestie. Ocherki ikonnogo dela v imperatorskoi Rossii* (Moscow: Progress-Kul'tura, 1995), 155–57. Tarasov sees this transformation as reflecting the emergence of "a kind of 'mass culture.'" He suggests that these attempts by the state to control icons reflected, and paralleled, the lay production of icons and the need to replace declining systems of monastic control in the seventeenth century.

7. Wendy Salmond, *Russian Icons at Hillwood* (Washington, D.C.: Hillwood Museum & Gardens, 1998), 74; Vladimir Ivanov, *Russian Icons* (New York: Rizzoli, 1988), 143. See also Wortman, *Scenarios of Power,* vol. 1; Marc Raeff, *The Well-Ordered Police State: Social and Institutional Changes Through Law in the Germanies and Russia, 1600–1800* (New Haven: Yale University Press, 1983); James Cracraft, *The Petrine Revolution in Russian Imagery* (Chicago: University of Chicago Press, 1997); Wendy Salmond, *Traditions in Transi-*

tion: Russian Icons in the Age of the Romanovs (Washington, D.C.: Hillwood Museum & Gardens, 2004), 18; Trenev, *Sovremennaia friaz'*, 11–12.

8. A. S. Lavrov, *Koldovstvo i religiia v Rossii, 1700–1740 gg.* (Moscow: Drevnekhranilishche, 2000), 433–34; "Ikonopistsy," *Zhurnal ministerstva vnutrennykh del*, 1858, chast' 32, otdelenie 3:26–35.

9. William L. Blackwell, *The Beginnings of Russian Industrialization, 1800–1860* (Princeton: Princeton University Press, 1968), 205–9; N. M. Zinov'ev, *Iskusstvo Palekha*, 2nd ed. (Leningrad: Khudozhnik RSFSR, 1974), 22.

10. Tarasov, *Ikona i blagochestie*, 19–21, 24; Salmond, *Russian Icons at Hillwood*, 38; Vera Shevzov, "Miracle-Working Icons, Laity, and Authority in the Russian Orthodox Church, 1861–1917," *Russian Review* 58 (January 1999): 26–48, and *Russian Orthodoxy on the Eve of Revolution* (New York: Oxford University Press, 2004), 244–57.

11. Wayne Dowler, *Dostoevsky, Grigor'ev, and Native Soil Conservatism* (Toronto: University of Toronto Press, 1982), 20; Richard S. Wortman, *Scenarios of Power*, 2:161; David Hoffmann and Yanni Kotsonis, eds., *Russian Modernity: Politics, Knowledge, Practices* (New York: St. Martin's Press, 2000), 3.

12. Edward Thaden, *Conservative Nationalism in Nineteenth-Century Russia* (Seattle: University of Washington Press, 1964), 19; Iu. Bobrov, *Istoriia restavratsii drevnerusskoi zhivopisi* (Leningrad: Khudozhnik RSFSR, 1987), 9–26.

13. G. Vzdornov, *Istoriia otkrytiia i izucheniia russkoi srednevekovoi zhivopisi. XIX vek* (Moscow: Iskusstvo, 1986), 35, 28–46.

14. N. Rubinshtein, *Russkaia istoriografiia* (Moscow: Gospolitizdat, 1941), 217–20; M. V. Nechkina, ed., *Ocherki istorii istoricheskoi nauki v SSSR* (Moscow: Izdatel'stvo Akademii nauk SSSR, 1960), 2:596.

15. Vzdornov, *Istoriia otkrytiia*, 59–70; F. I. Buslaev, *Moi vospominaniia* (Moscow: Tipografiia G. Lissnera i A. Geshel'ia, 1897), 170.

16. F. I. Buslaev, *M. P. Pogodin kak professor* (Moscow: Tipografiia A. Gattsuka, 1876), 7, 13; Nicholas Riasanovsky, *Nicholas I and Official Nationality in Russia, 1825–1855* (Berkeley: University of California Press, 1959), 52–53, 56–57, 102.

17. Vzdornov, *Istoriia otkrytiia*, 47, 51–52, 54–55.

18. Vzdornov, *Istoriia otkrytiia*, 55, 56–57.

19. Vzdornov, *Istoriia otkrytiia*, 57–58.

20. A. Kizevetter', "Zabelin, Ivan Egorovich," *Entsiklopedicheskii slovar' Granat* 20:378–79; A. A. Formozov, *Istorik Moskvy I. E. Zabelin* (Moscow: Moskovskii rabochii, 1984), 52; I. E. Zabelin, *Domashnyi byt russkikh tsarei v XVI i XVII st.*, chast' 1 (Moscow: Tipografiia V. Gracheva, 1862), v–viii.

21. Formozov, *Istorik Moskvy*, 38–40; I. E. Zabelin, "Materialy dlia istorii russkoi ikonopisi," *Vremennik Imperatorskago Moskovskago obshchestva istorii i drevnostei rossiiskikh*, kniga 7 (1850): 1–128.

22. D. A. Rovinskii, *Obozrenie ikonopisi v Rossii do kontsa XVII veka* (St. Petersburg: A. S. Suvorin, 1903), 5, 8, 43–50

23. Rovinskii, *Obozrenie ikonopisi*, 19, 50, 55–56; A. Novitskii, "Pamiati D. A. Rovinskogo," *Russkoe obozrenie* (October 1895): 808; G. Vzdornov, *Istoriia otkrytiia*, 74–75.

24. Talmon, *Romanticism and Revolt*, 24.

25. Buslaev, *Moi vospominaniia*, 128–29, 324; Buslaev, *M. P. Pogodin kak professor*, 12–13; *Pamiati Fedora Ivanovicha Buslaeva* (Moscow: Tipografiia Sytina, 1898), 18, 125–26; Vzdornov, *Istoriia otkrytiia*, 90.

26. Buslaev, *Moi vospominaniia*, 330, 331–48, 356, 348; *Pamiati Fedora Ivanovicha Buslaeva*, 25; S. D. Sheremetev, "Pamiati F. I. Buslaeva i G. D. Filimonova," in *Pamiatniki*

drevnei pis'mennosti i iskusstva, no. 132 (St. Petersburg, 1899): 53; Wortman, *Scenarios of Power,* 2:97–98.

27. F. I. Buslaev, *Sochineniia F. I. Buslaeva,* tom 1, *Sochineniia po arkheologii i istorii iskusstva* (St. Petersburg: Izd. otdeleniia russkago iazyka i slovestnosti Imperatorskoi akademii nauk, 1908), 8–10, 31–32, 41, 257; *Pamiati Fedora Ivanovicha Buslaeva,* 120–22.

28. Wortman, *Scenarios of Power,* 2:440–41; Buslaev, *Sochineniia F. I. Buslaeva,* tom 1:31–32, 149–50, 165, 171–72, 183, 185, 192; *Pamiati Fedora Ivanovicha Buslaeva,* 123.

29. *Pamiati Fedora Ivanovicha Buslaeva,* 122–24; Buslaev, *Sochineniia F. I. Buslaeva,* tom 1:149.

30. *Sochinenniia F. I. Buslaeva,* tom 1:406–7; G. D. Filimonov, "Palekh" [part 2], *Den',* no. 35 (1863): 9–10.

31. Buslaev, *Sochineniia F. I. Buslaeva,* tom 1:408; Filimonov, "Palekh" [part 2]: 9–10.

32. Buslaev, *Sochineniia F. I. Buslaeva,* tom 1:407–8. Count Stroganov's *"podlinnik"* represented the first private attempt to establish a definitive guide for icon painters: *Stroganovskii ikonopisnyi podlinnik (kontsa XVI i nachala XVII stoletii)* (Moscow, 1869).

33. Buslaev, *Sochineniia F. I. Buslaeva,* tom 1:148, 408–10.

34. "Pis'mo ob ikonopisanii," *Khristianskoe chtenie* (March 1857): 204, 207–8; RGIA, *f.* 797, *op.* 33, *otd* 1, *d.* 92, *ll.* 1–4.

35. Cathy Frierson, *Peasant Icons: Representations of Rural People in Late Nineteenth-Century Russia* (New York: Oxford University Press, 1993).

36. By 1879, Bezobrazov's account had inspired a number of notable individuals to visit the three villages. These included Prince V. P. Meshcherskii, the poet N. A. Nekrasov, G. D. Filimonov, L. N. Maikov, D. M. Strukov, V. P. Rybinskii, and A. N. Molchanov. *Vladimirskie gubernskie vedomosti,* December 21, 1879, 2.

37. V. P. Bezobrazov, "Iz putevykh zapisok," *Russkii vestnik* (July 1861): 266, 281–84, 286–87; On the role of peddlers as distributors of literature as well as icons after 1861, see Jeffrey Brooks, *When Russia Learned to Read: Literacy and Popular Literature, 1861–1917* (Princeton: Princeton University Press, 1985), 101–8.

38. I am indebted to Alexander Martin for this point.

39. N. A. Trokhimovskii, "Ofeni," *Russkii vestnik* (June 1866): 565–67, 569, 585, 587, 590; Bezobrazov, "Iz putevykh zapisok," 286–88.

40. Bezobrazov, "Iz putevykh zapisok," 294, 307–8.

41. Bezobrazov, "Iz putevykh zapisok," 294, 298–99, 301.

42. Francis William Wcislo, *Reforming Rural Russia: State, Local Society, and National Politics, 1855–1914* (Princeton: Princeton University Press, 1990). The 1889 institution by the Ministry of Internal Affairs of the Land Captain, with broad power over peasant administration, was also emblematic of this new conservative activism, as was the emergence of Konstantin Pobedonostsev, appointed *ober-prokurer* of the Holy Synod in 1880, and his ambitious program of patriotic and religious education for the peasantry. On Pobedonostsev, see A. Iu. Polunov, *Pod vlast'iu ober-prokurora: Gosudarstvo i tserkkov' v epokhu Aleksandra III* (Moscow: AIRO-XX, 1996).

43. A. Kirpichnikov, "Filimonov, Georgii Dmitrievich," *Entsiklopedicheskii slovar',* vol. 35 (St. Petersburg: Brokgauz-Efron, 1902): 747.

44. Sheremetev, "Pamiati F. I. Buslaeva i G. D. Filimonova," 56.

45. Filimonov, "Palekh" [part 1], *Den',* no. 34:4.

46. Filimonov, "Palekh" [part 2]: 9.

47. Filimonov, "Palekh" [part 1]: 5.

48. Filimonov, "Palekh" [part 1]: 6.

49. Filimonov, "Palekh" [part 2]: 10–11; A. Molchanov, "Po vladimirskoi gubernii," *Novoe vremia,* June 14, 1879, 2–3. The Russian scholar Tarasov believes this divi-

sion of labor emerged in the seventeenth century. Along with the use of fixed models *(podlinniki)* for icon reproduction, Tarasov argues that the separation of tasks in a factory-like manner marked the emergence of distinctly modern cultural and economic practices in the Russian icon industry from at least the seventeenth century. Tarasov, *Ikona i blagochestie,* 179.

50. N. P. Kondakov, *Sovremennoe polozhenie russkoi narodnoi ikonopisi,* Pamiatniki drevnei pis'mennosti i iskusstva, no. 139 (St. Petersburg: Tipografiia I. N. Skorokhodova, 1901), 26–29; Arkhiv Gosudarstvennogo muzeia palekhskogo iskusstva (AGMPI), *f.* Salapin, passim.

51. Though many Europeans considered Russia a backward and reactionary society, others increasingly viewed it as a land of tradition and authenticity, a patriarchal order regulated by native peasant communalism and aristocratic values. August Freiherr von Haxthausen (1792–1866), for instance, came to Russia in the 1840s to study the peasant land commune, which he envisioned as an ancient Slavic institution, embodying patriarchal and conservative values as well as an alternative to modern methods of social and economic organization.

52. The French scholar was E. Viollet-le-Duc. V. I. Butovskii, *Russkoe iskusstvo i mneniia o nem E. Violle-le-diuka, frantsuzskago uchenago arkhitektora i F. I. Buslaeva* (Moscow, 1879), 2:10; G. D. Filimonov, *Samostoiatel'nost' russkago stilia s tochki zreniia sovremennoi kritiki iskusstva na zapade* (Moscow: Katkov, 1879), 9, 6–7.

53. *Vestnik obshchestva drevne-russkago iskusstva pri Moskovskom publichnom muzeie,* nos. 4–5 (1874): 35, 37–40; nos. 1–3 (1874): 7–8, 10, 14, 16; nos. 11–12 (1876): 83–85.

54. Buslaev, *Sochineniia,* tom 1:193; *Vestnik obshchestva drevne-russkago iskusstva,* nos. 1–3 (1874): 12, 15.

55. N. Kolygina, "Prikasaias' k istokam promysla," *Prizyv,* October 21, 1998, 3.

56. Vzdornov, *Istoriia otkrytiia,* 30; Kolygina, "Prikasaias' k istokam promysla," 3; V. Ilarionov, "Ikonopistsy-Suzdal'tsy (Poezdka v ss. Msteru, Kholui, i Palekh)," *Russkoe obozrenie* (April 1895): 743.

57. Molchanov, "Po vladimirskoi gubernii," 2–3; RGIA, *f.* 1331, *op.* 1, *d.* 10, *ll.* 29–30.

58. Wortman, *Scenarios of Power,* 2:192, 196–235.

59. On the role of terrorists in strengthening police surveillance, see Richard Pipes, *Russia Under the Old Regime,* 2nd ed. (New York: Collier Books, 1992), 297–312.

60. Sheremetev, "Pamiati F. I. Buslaeva i G. D. Filimonova," 54.

61. Sheremetev, "Pamiati F. I. Buslaeva i G. D. Filimonova," 56.

62. Wortman, *Scenarios of Power,* 2:224; *Otchety o zasedaniiakh obshchestva liubitelei drevnei pis'mennosti, 1881–1882,* comp. Pavel Tikhanov, Pamiatniki drevnei pis'mennosti i iskusstva, no. 80 (St. Petersburg, 1889): 82; A. Nasibova, *Granovitaia palata moskovskogo kremlia* (Leningrad: Avrora, 1978), 5, 7, 10, 13.

63. *Otchety o zasedaniiakh obshchestva liubitelei drevnei pis'mennosti, 1881–1882,* 82–83.

64. Nasibova, *Granovitaia palata moskovskogo kremlia,* 16.

65. Sheremetev, "Pamiati F. I. Buslaeva i G. D. Filimonova," 57; *Izograf,* tom 1, vypusk 2 (1882): 4–5.

66. RGIA, *f.* 1331, *op.* 1, *d.* 10, *ll.* 9, 11; *Izograf,* tom 1, vypusk 1 (1882): 3. The ecclesiastical press also expressed outrage at the profanation of icon painting by peasant traders and profit motives. Ioann Iakovskii, "O prodazhe ikon pri tserkvakh," *Vladimirskie eparkhial'nye vedomosti,* February 1, 1876, unofficial part, 135–36; and "Neskol'ko slov ob ikonopisi," December 1, 1875, unofficial part, 1153–1156; I. Galabutskii, "Koshchunstvenno-naglie prodelki prodavtsov ikon," *Poltavskie eparkhial'nye vedomosti,* October 15, 1871, unofficial part, 731–39.

67. Molchanov, "Po vladimirskoi gubernii," 2–3.

2—THE COMMERCIALIZATION OF RUSSIAN NATIONAL CULTURE AND ITS MALCONTENTS

1. Sidney Harcave, ed. and trans., *The Memoirs of Count Witte* (New York: M. E. Sharpe, 1990), 328.

2. RGIA, *f.* 721, *op.* 2, *d.* 293, *l.*1. The first scholar to draw attention to the issue of mechanization and icons in late imperial Russia was Robert Nichols, "The Icon and the Machine in Russia's Religious Renaissance, 1900–1909," in *Christianity and the Arts in Russia,* ed. William C. Brumfield and Milos M. Velimirovic (Cambridge: Cambridge University Press, 1991), 131–44.

3. RGIA, *f.* 721, *op.* 2, *d.* 293, *l.* 1.

4. RGIA, *f.* 721, *op.* 2, *d.* 293, *ll.* 2–3.

5. This clash of perspectives, rather than the artistic quality of Palekh's work, represents the focus of the discussion. The present study leaves the question of the quality of Palekh's icon services to art historians, who, in addition, have developed a more nuanced view of Palekh's religious art as a vibrant part of Russian religious and national culture, whatever its aesthetic shortcomings. See, for example, Salmond, *Traditions in Transition,* 21–22, 57, 61, and *Russian Icons at Hillwood,* 79–89; Liudmila Kniazeva, *Ikonopis' Palekha iz sobranii Gosudarstvennogo muzeia palekhskogo iskusstva* (Moscow: Progress, 1994); Vera Torzhkova, *Neizvestnyi Palekh. Ikony* (Moscow: Planeta, 1993).

6. Kondakov, *Sovremennoe polozhenie russkoi narodnoi ikonopisi,* 16.

7. M. A. Tikhomirova, *Nikolai Mikhailovich Zinov'ev. Khudozhnik Palekha* (Leningrad: Khudozhnik RSFSR, 1987), 14.

8. Zinov'ev, *Iskusstvo Palekha,* 18–20.

9. V. D—sov, "Vladimirskie ikonopistsy i Komitet popechitel'stva o russkoi ikonopisi," *Vladimirskie eparkhial'nye vedomosti,* April 15, 1905, unofficial part, 227; *Vysochaishe uchrezhdennago Komiteta popechitel'stva o russkoi ikonopisi i ego zadachi* (St. Petersburg: Komitet popechitel'stva o russkoi ikonopisi, 1907), 5.

10. N. Zinov'ev, "Iz istorii Palekha. Ikonopisnye masterskie is stil'," *Prizyv,* undated newspaper clip in the State Museum of Palekh Art (probably from the late 1960s); Zinov'ev, *Iskusstva Palekha,* 17.

11. D—sov, "Vladimirskie ikonopistsy," 231; ORGRM, *f.* 122, *d.* 19, *l.* 5.

12. For a detailed description of the icon business in the late imperial period, see Tarasov, *Ikona i blagochestie,* 165–81.

13. Kondakov, *Sovremennoe polozhenie russkoi narodnoi ikonopisi,* 29; E. K. Bratchikova, *Palekh. Izbrannye stat'i* (Moscow: Izdatel'skii dom "Parad," 1999), 31; N. N. Bankovskii, ed., *P. D. Korin ob iskusstve. Stat'i. Pis'ma. Vospominaniia o khudozhnike* (Moscow: Sovetskii khudozhnik, 1988), 256, 271.

14. From the 1840s to the 1860s, dozens of Palekh masters cycled through the icon studio of M. S. Peshekhonov in St. Petersburg. The studio copied the style of the murals of St. Isaac's Cathedral in St. Petersburg and Christ the Savior in Moscow, "eclectically combining," as one Russian art critic put it, "the techniques of academism with Byzantine forms." Kniazeva, *Ikonopis' Palekha,* 141; AGMPI, *f.* Sobolevskii, *d.* 1, *ll.* 139–40; Zinov'ev, "Iz istorii Palekha."

15. Aleksandr Zubkov, "Istoriia Arteli drevnei zhivopisi," in Vikhrev, *Paleshane,* 27–29.

16. Brooks, *When Russia Learned to Read,* 58, 334.

17. Bratchikova, *Palekh,* 36–37; V. P. Lapshin, *Khudozhnik Aleksei Mikhailovich Korin, 1865–1923. Sbornik materialov i katalog vystavki proizvedenii* (Moscow: Sovetskii khudozhnik, 1981), 152, 156, 170–71.

18. Zinov'ev, *Iskusstvo Palekha,* 29.

19. Tikhomirova, *Nikolai Mikhailovich Zinov'ev,* 28; Kondakov, *Sovremennoe polozhenie russkoi narodnoi ikonopisi,* 8; Tarasov, *Ikona i blagochestie,* 192.

20. ORGRM, *f.* 122, *d.* 19, *l.* 5; Tikhomirova, *Nikolai Mikhailovich Zinov'ev,* 16; AGMPI, *f.* Salapin, *d.* 1, *l.* 53; OPIGIM, *f.* 276, *op.* 1, *d.* 114, *ll.* 22, 24; *d.* 112, *ll.* 3–4; *f.* 440, *op.* 1, *d.* 82, *ll.* 4–6, 9, 11; *op.* 1, *d.* 186, *l.* 26.

21. N. A. Kriukov, "Prazdnik russkoi ikonopisi," *Sankt-Peterburgskie vedomosti,* April 17, 1901, 2; D. K. Trenev, *Neskol'ko slov o drevnei i sovremennoi russkoi ikonopisi* (Moscow: Izdano pri tserkovno-arkheologicheskom otdele Moskovskago obshchestva liubitelei dukhovnago prosveshcheniia, 1905).

22. Ironically, the supposedly ascetic nature of the ancient Russian icon was based, as icon experts began to discover in the last years of the Old Regime, on a historical fallacy. Ancient icons were originally done in often bright and festive colors. They were darkened by time, smoke from incense, and frequent applications of linseed oil. E. N. Trubetskoi, *Umozrenie v kraskakh. Vopros o smylse zhizni v drevne-russkoi religioznoi zhivopisi* (Moscow: Tipografiia T-va I. D. Sytina, 1916), 13; Trenev, *Sovremennaia friaz',* 5.

23. See Wortman, *Scenarios of Power,* vol. 2.

24. V. Illarionov, "Ikonopistsy-Suzdal'tsy. (Poezdka v ss. Msteru, Kholui, i Palekh) [part 2]," *Russkoe obozrenie* (April 1895): 735.

25. AGMPI, *f.* Salapin, *d.* 1, *l.* 37.

26. "Sviataia Ikona Palekhovskikh ikonopistsev-Belousovykh v Granovitoi Palate," *Vladimirskie eparkhial'nye vedomosti,* May 15, 1884, unofficial part, 328–30.

27. AGMPI, *f.* Salapin, *d.* 1, *l.* 37; Zinov'ev, "Iz istorii Palekha."

28. Zinov'ev, "Iz istorii Palekha"; S. Mineeva, "Palekhskii pocherk. Iz pokoleniia v pokolenie," *Prizyv,* March 2, 2001, 5; "Svedeniia o tserkovnoi stenopisi, ikonakh, i drugikh sviashchennykh predmetakh, ispolniaemykh ikonopistsem L'vom Parilovym," *Vladimirskie eparkhial'nye vedomosti,* April 15, 1897, unofficial part, 262–68.

29. The Palekh artists whose works were represented were M. V. Belousov, I. V. Belousov, I. M. Belousov, L. I. Parilov, I. I. Parilov, V. A. Khokhlov, D. A. Salautin, and K. A. Pershin. "Vladimirskie kustari. Na vystavke v gor. Shue," *Vladimirskie gubernskie vedomosti,* August 17, 1901, 6–9.

30. D. K. Trenev, *Ikonopis' Mstertsev* (Moscow, 1903), 10.

31. Bankovskii, *P. D. Korin ob iskusstve,* 274, 267. Intrigued by peasant icon painters, Nikolai Leskov in the 1860s and 1870s penned his immensely popular stories on peasant craftsmanship, "The Left-Hander" and "The Sealed Angel," whose inspiration was a peasant icon painter he met in St. Petersburg.

32. Lapshin, *Khudozhnik Aleksei Mikhailovich Korin,* 150; AGMPI, *f.* Salapin, *d.* 1, *l.* 50.

33. Chikhachev died under mysterious circumstances in a Vladimir hotel on April 27, 1917 (old style). AGMPI, *f.* Salapin, *d.* 1, *l.* 65.

34. *Kul'turnoe stroitel'stvo v Ivanovskoi oblasti, 1917–1987,* 52; AGMPI, *f.* Salapin, *d.* 1, *l.* 57. For Palekh's restorations in the Vladimir province see: "Vladimirskii Uspenskii sobor i otkrytye v nem freski," *Vladimirskie eparkhial'nye vedomosti,* February 15, 1884, unofficial part, 94–107; "Obnovlenie Vladimirskago Uspenskago Sobora," *Vladimirske eparkhial'nye vedomosti,* unofficial part, November 15, 1884, 683–98; "Obnovlenie i osviashchenie khrama v chest' sv. Proroka Ilii, v gor. Ivanovo-Voznesensk," *Vladimirskie eparkhial'nye vedomosti,* February 1, 1894, unofficial part, 68–72; "Kazanskii sobor v gorode Viaznikakh (Po povodu osviashcheniia ego)," *Vladimirskie eparkhial'nye vedomosti,* October 1, 1894, unofficial part, 459–65.

35. "Obnovlenie Vladimirskago Uspenskago Sobora," *Vladimirskie eparkhial'nye*

vedomosti, November 15, 1884, unofficial part, 686, 691–93, 696, 698.

36. Kondakov, *Sovremennoe polozhenie russkoi narodnoi ikonopisi,* 9; N. Ushakov, "Restavratsiia i osviashchenie Krestovozdvizhenskago khrama v sele Palekha, Viaznikovskago uezda," *Vladimirskie eparkhial'nye vedomosti,* October 4, 1908, unofficial part, 699, and October 11, 1908, unofficial part, 719; Ushakov, "Restavratsiia Krestovozdvizhenskago khrama v sele Palekha, Viaznikovskago uezda," *Trudy Vladimirskoi uchenoi arkhivnoi kommissii,* kn. 10 (1908): 15.

37. Ushakov, "Restavratsiia i osviashchenie Krestovozdvizhenskago khrama v sele Palekha," 723–24. Ushakov, on January 20, 1908, reported on the Palekh restoration to the *gubernator* of the Vladimir guberniia, Ivan Nikolaevich Sazanov. GAVO, *f.* 526, *op.* 1, *d.* 40, *l.* 11.

38. M. P. Solov'ev, "Po povodu restavratsii Novgorodskoi sv. Sofii," *Iskusstvo i khudozhestvennaia promyshlennost',* no. 11 (August 1899): 939–40, 942, 943, 946.

39. Eleonora Paston, "Paradoksy Viktora Vasnetsova," *Nashe nasledie,* 4 (1991): 7; L. I. Iovleva, *Viktor Vasnetsov* (Moscow: Gosudarstvennaia Tret'iakovskaia galereia, 1998), 21.

40. *Memoirs of Count Witte,* 345.

41. RGIA, *f.* 1331, *op.* 1, *d.* 10, *ll.* 4, 6–7, 9–10, 13; GAVO, *f.* 534, *op.* 1, *d.* 3, *l.* 1; *f.* 543, *op.* 1, *d.* 16, *l.* 1; A. Prugavin, "Knigonoshi i ofeni," *Severnii vestnik,* January 1, 1893, 87.

42. Various individuals had attempted to start drawing schools in the three villages since the 1860s, but these efforts were all short-lived and lacked funding. "Korrespondentsiia iz slobody Mstery ob ikonopisanii i knizhnoi torgovle," *Vladimirskie gubernskie vedomosti,* December 21, 1879, 2; I. Golyshev, "O risoval'nykh shkolakh v ikonopisnykh mestnostiakh," *Vladimirskie gubernskie vedomosti,* May 25, 1873, 1–2, and "O risoval'nykh shkolakh dlia uluchsheniia ikonopisaniia v Viaznikovskom uezde," February 20, 1881, 2–3.

43. RGIA, *f.* 1331, *op.* 1, *d.* 10, *l.* 5; GAVO, *f.* 534, *op.* 1, *d.* 3, *l.* 30; V. T. Georgievskii, "Shkola ikonopisaniia v s. Kholue, Vladimirskoi gub.," *Iskusstvo i khudozhestvennaia promyshlennost',* no. 11 (August 1899): 857.

44. The terms *"kul'tura"* and *"kul'turnost'"* entered usage in the 1870s "in connection with the missionary idea of the transmission of education and culture to the backward masses." Catrionia Kelly and David Shepherd, eds., *Russian Cultural Studies: An Introduction* (Oxford: Oxford University Press, 1998), 8.

45. GAVO, *f.* 534, *op.* 1, *d.* 3, *ll.* 19–21, 31; Georgievskii, "Shkola ikonopisaniia v s. Kholue," 851–67.

46. RGIA, *f.* 733, *op.* 171, *d.* 275, *ll.* 18–20. Pobedonostsev's comments are from May 11, 1882.

47. "Kustarnye promysli Vladimirskoi gubernii," *Vestnik Vladimirskago zemstva,* no. 9 (1897): 659.

48. RGIA, *f.* 1331, *op.* 1, *d.* 10, *ll.* 11, 29.

49. RIGA, *f.* 1331, *op.* 1, *d.* 10, *ll.* 11–12.

50. Vzdornov, *Istoriia otkrytiia,* 192.

51. GAVO, *f.* 604, *op.* 1, *d.* 43, *ll.* 3–4.

52. Illarionov, "Ikonopistsy-Suzdal'tsy," *Russkoe obozrenie* (March 1895): 192, 194; POANRF, *f.* 115, *op.* 4, *d.* 98, *ll.* 3, 5.

53. POANRF, *f.* 115, *op.* 4, *d.* 98, *l.* 7.

54. Illarionov, "Ikonopistsy-Suzdal'tsy [part 1]," (March 1895): 183, 193, 211–12; and [part 2] (April 1895): 723. Illarionov was Georgievskii's pseudonym.

55. Illarionov, "Ikonopistsy-Suzdal'tsy" [part 2], 735–36, 744.

56. Illarionov, "Ikonopistsy-Suzdal'tsy" [part 2], 738.

57. Illarionov, "Ikonopistsy-Suzdal'tsy" [part 2], 738–40.

58. Illarionov, "Ikonopistsy-Suzdal'tsy" [part 2], 743–45. One study of cultural history in late Imperial Russia aptly noted that intellectuals "both attempted to provide workers and peasants with the means of thinking independently, and resented it when they did." L. McReynolds and C. Popkin, "The Objective Eye and the Common Good," in *Constructing Russian Culture in the Age of Revolution, 1881–1940*, ed. Catriona Kelly and David Shepherd, 70.

59. Illarionov, "Ikonopistsy-Suzdal'tsy" [part 2], 745.

60. Illarionov, "Ikonopistsy-Suzdal'tsy" [part 2], 741–42, 744.

61. Illarionov, "Ikonopistsy-Suzdal'tsy" [part 1], 215–16; POANRF, *f.* 115, *op.* 4, *d.* 98, *l.* 14.

62. Paston, "Paradoksy Viktora Vasnetsova," 14; Iovleva, *Viktor Vasnetsov,* 18–19.

63. M-e, "Sobor sv. Vladimira v Kieve," *Novoe vremia,* August 30, 1896, 2–3; Solov'ev, "Po povodu restavratsii Novgorodskoi sv. Sofii," 939–40, 942, 943, 946; Paston, "Paradoksy Viktora Vasnetsova," 14; Iovleva, *Viktor Vasnetsov,* 24; M. Pavlovskii, "O nashem ikonopisanii," *Iuzhnyi krai,* June 7, 1901, 3.

64. N. V. Pokrovskii (1848–1917) was an associate of the icon experts Buslaev and Filimonov (Buslaev advised his doctoral dissertation on Byzantine and Russian art). For an overview of his life and work, see A. A. Alekseev, "Nikolai Vasil'evich Pokrovskii—doktor tserkovnoi istorii," in N. V. Pokrovskii, *Ocherki pamiatnikov khristianskogo iskusstva* (St. Petersburg: Liga Plius, 1999), 3–10.

65. ORRNB, *f.* 593, *d.* 212, *ll.* 4–5.

66. GAVO, *f.* 534, *op.* 1, *d.* 3, *l.* 24; ORRNB, *f.* 593, *d.* 212, *l.* 1; POANRF, *f.* 115, *op.* 4, *d.* 98, *ll.* 3, 5.

67. ORRNB, *f.* 593, *d.* 617, *l.* 10.

68. RGIA, *f.* 1088, *op.* 2, *d.* 14, *ll.* 2–3; *Memoirs of Count Witte,* 772 n. 4; RGIA, *f.* 1088, *op.* 2, *d.* 1058, *ll.* 3, 5, 6; Nichols, "The Icon and the Machine," 133, 143 n. 6.

69. I. V. Tunkina, "Materialy k biografii N. P. Kondakova," unpublished article, cited with permission of the author, 3–5; Nichols, "The Icon and the Machine," 133.

70. N. P. Kondakov, "O nauchnykh zadachakh istorii drevne-russkago iskusstva," in *Pamiatniki drevnei pis'mennosti i iskusstva,* no. 132 (St. Petersburg, 1899): 44–47; Tunkina, "Materialy k biografii N. P. Kondakova," 5–7.

71. POANRF, *f.* 115, *op.* 3, *d.* 15, *ll.* 69, 29, 35.

72. The two were on good terms until sometime late in Witte's appointment as premier, when Witte read a perlustrated letter in which Sheremetev described him in "unflattering terms." *Memoirs of Count Witte,* 338, 499n, 520, 679.

73. *Memoirs of Count Witte,* 191, 195–96, 200.

74. *Memoirs of Count Witte,* 772n. 4; POANRF, *f.* 115, *op.* 4, *d.* 485, *l.* 10. The emphasis is in Sheremetev's original letter to Kondakov from October 22, 1899. On police socialism, see Jeremiah Schneiderman, *Sergei Zubatov and Revolutionary Marxism: The Struggle for the Working Class in Tsarist Russia* (Ithaca, N.Y.: Cornell University Press, 1976).

75. POANRF, *f.* 115, *op.* 4, *d.* 98, *l.* 14; *d.* 485, *l.* 13.

76. POANRF, *f.* 115, *op.* 3, *d.* 15, *ll.* 35, 37; N. P. Kondakov, *Vospominaniia i dumy* (Prague: Seminarium Kondakovianum, 1927), 77–78.

77. ORGRM, *f.* KPRI, *d.* 73, *l.* 77; Kondakov, *Vospominaniia i dumy,* 77; POANRF, *f.* 115, *op.* 4, *d.* 98, *l.* 19. Capitalization was in the original letter. On Empress Aleksandra Fedorovna, formerly Princess Alice of Darmstadt, Witte wrote: "Having decided to change her faith, she had to convince herself that Orthodoxy was the only true religion in the world. . . . Given her dull, egotistical character and narrow world view, given the

intoxicating effects of the luxury of the court, it is not odd that she should have completely succumbed to what I call Orthodox paganism, i.e., worship of the former without understanding of the spirit. She succumbed, too, to the conviction that the faith can be propagated by compulsion rather than persuasion and the belief that if you do not bow before me, you are my enemy, against whom I will use my autocratic power because what I wish represents the truth." *Memoirs of Count Witte,* 375.

78. POANRF, *f.* 115, *op.* 4, *d.* 485, *ll.* 2, 8, 17; *op.* 3, *d.* 155, *ll.* 46, 54, 62, 65; N. A. Kriukov, "K voprosu o sviatikh ikonakh," *Sankt-Peterburgskie vedomosti,* April 9, 1900, 2.

79. POANRF, *f.* 115, *op.* 3, *d.* 115, *ll.* 64–66; Kondakov, *Sovremennoe polozhenie russkoi narodnoi ikonopisi,* 7.

80. POANRF, *f.* 115, *op.* 4, *d.* 98, *l.* 19; M. E. Kuz'min, "Neskol'ko soobrazhenii po povodu unichtozhennykh i utselevshikh pamiatnikov stariny v Kievo-pecherskoi Lavre," *Iskusstvo i khudozhestvennaia promyshlennost',* no. 17 (February 1900): 223; Kondakov, *Vospominaniia i dumy,* 77; Kondakov, *Sovremennoe polozhenie russkoi narodnoi ikonopisi,* 20, 26–27, 33.

81. RGIA, *f.* 721, *op.* 2, *d.* 293, *l.* 3; Kondakov, *Sovremennoe polozhenie russkoi narodnoi ikonopisi,* 37–38.

82. Kondakov, *Sovremennoe polozhenie russkoi narodnoi ikonopisi,* 50–56, 62.

83. ORGRM, *f.* 122, letter of Nikolai Mikhailovich Safonov to S. D. Sheremetev, *ll.* 1–3. There was no file number for the file containing the letter.

84. POANRF, *f.* 115, *op.* 4, *d.* 98, *l.* 37; *op.* 3, *d.* 16, *l.* 85; Kondakov, *Vospominaniia i dumy,* 75; ORGRM, *f.* 122, *d.* 145, *l.* 6. On the phenomenon of peasant petitions in late imperial Russia, see Andrew Verner, "Discursive Strategies in the 1905 Revolution: Peasant Petitions from Vladimir Province," *Russian Review* 54 (January 1995): 65–90.

85. ORGRM, *f.* 122, *d.* 24, *ll.* 3–4; POANRF, *f.* 115, *op.* 4, *d.* 537, *l.* 1.

86. POANRF, *f.* 115, *op.* 4, *d.* 485, *ll.* 37–38, 42–43, 47; *op.* 3, *d.* 16, *ll.* 58. 67, 69; *Izvestiia vysochaishe uchrezhdennago komiteta popechitel'stva o russkoi ikonopisi,* vyp. 1 (St. Petersburg, 1902), 29; ORGRM, *f.* KPRI, *d.* 16, *ll.* 8–9.

87. POANRF, *f.* 115, *op.* 3, *d.* 16, *l.* 80.

88. POANRF, *f.* 115, *op.* 4, *d.* 98, *l.* 21.

89. V. Velichko, "Vozrozhdenie ikonopisi," *Svet,* March 29, 1901, 2; Kriukov, "Prazdnik russkoi ikonopisi," 2.

3—PALEKHIANS INTO RUSSIANS, 1901–1918

1. Alain Besancon, *The Forbidden Image: An Intellectual History of Iconoclasm* (Chicago: University of Chicago Press, 2000), 137, 253, 266–75; Velichko, "Vozrozhdenie ikonopisi," 2. For links between arts and crafts, the avant-garde, and neo-realists such as Viktor Vasnetsov, see John Bowlt, *The Silver Age: Russian Art of the Early Twentieth Century and the "World of Art" Group* (Newtonville, Mass.: Oriental Research Partners, 1979). On the avant-garde's interest in the Russian icon, see John Bowlt, "Avant-Garde: Sacred Images in the Work of Goncharova, Malevich, and their Contemporaries," in *Christianity and the Arts in Russia,* ed. William C. Brumfield and Milos M. Velimirovic (Cambridge: Cambridge University Press, 1991), 145–51.

2. Bobrov, *Istoriia restavratsii,* 36–37; Trenev, *Ikonopis' Mstertsev,* 10.

3. Kondakov, *Sovremennoe polozhenie russkoi narodnoi ikonopisi,* 64. For an overview of the committee's program see Nichols, "The Icon and the Machine," 131–44; Tarasov, *Ikona i blagochestie,* 271–89.

4. D—sov, "Vladimirskie ikonopistsy," *Vladimirskie eparkhial'nye vedomosti,* April

15, 1905, unofficial part, 250; Kriukov, "Prazdnik russkoi ikonopisi," 2; Tarasov, *Ikona i blagochestie*, 281; A. N. Kozlov, *Zadachi khudozhnika-ikonopistsa po otnosheniiu k izobrazheniiam sviatikh na ikonakh* (Moscow, 1901); Wortman, *Scenarios of Power*, vol. 2.

5. ORGRM, *f.* KPRI, *d.* 16, *l.* 115; *d.* 15, *ll.* 32–34; *f.* 122, *d.* 19, *l.* 5; *Izvestiia . . . komiteta popechitel'stva o russkoi ikonopisi*, vyp. 1:58, 52.

6. *Tserkovnye vedomosti*, no. 29 (1902): 244–47.

7. ORGRM, *f.* 122, *d.* 73, *l.* 105.

8. Zinov'ev, *Iskusstvo Palekha*, 30–31.

9. *Izvestiia . . . komiteta popechitel'stva o russkoi ikonopisi*, vyp. 2 (St. Petersburg, 1903), 49–50.

10. ORGRM, *f.* KPRI, *d.* 16, *ll.* 8–10.

11. ORGRM, *f.* 122, *d.* 142, *l.* 3; *f.* KPRI, *d.* 66, *l.* 40; *d.* 15, *l.* 56.

12. ORGRM, *f.* KPRI, *d.* 16, *l.* 3; *d.* 16, *l.* 15.*Izvestiia . . . komiteta popechitel'stva o russkoi ikonopisi*, vyp. 1:19, 85.

13. Zinov'ev, *Iskusstvo Palekha*, 31; *Pribavlenie k Tserkovnym vedomostiam*, no. 29 (1902): 978–79.

14. *Izvestiia . . . komiteta popechitel'stva o russkoi ikonopisi*, vyp. 2:51–52, 77–80.

15. *Izvestiia . . . komiteta popechitel'stva o russkoi ikonopisi*, vyp. 2:54.

16. *Izvestiia . . . komiteta popechitel'stva o russkoi ikonopisi*, vyp. 2:55–62.

17. ORGRM, *f.* 122, *d.* 142, *l.* 7; *d.* 52, *l.* 16.

18. *Izvestiia . . . komiteta popechitel'stva o russkoi ikonopisi*, vyp. 1:68–69; *Russkoe narodnoe iskusstvo na vtoroi vserossiiskoi kustarnoi vystavke v Petrograde v 1913 g.* (Petrograd, 1914), 4–5.

19. RGIA, *f.* 797, *op.* 73, *d.* 98, *ll.* 5–8, 22, 9–10, 12, 22.

20. ORGRM, *f.* KPRI, *d.* 10, *l.* 31; *d.* 16, *ll.* 75, 113; POANRF, *f.* 115, *op.* 3, *d.* 16, *l.* 208; *op.* 4, *d.* 17, *l.* 79.

21. RGIA, *f.* 565, *op.* 9, *d.* 31796, *l.* 3; ORGRM, *f.* KPRI, *d.* 16, *l.* 123–124; *f.* 122, *d.* 142, *ll.* 12, 16.

22. ORGRM, *f.* 122, *d.* 73, *ll.* 11, 14.

23. In 1901, six Palekhians agreed to be members of a committee artel. Nonetheless, they stipulated that they would only work on committee orders after completing their other business, which was apparently far more lucrative. ORGRM, *f.* KPRI, *d.* 16, *l.* 6; *Izvestiia . . . komiteta popechitel'stva o russkoi ikonopisi*, vyp. 2:24.

24. ORGRM, *f.* KPRI, *d.* 16, *ll.* 23, 126–27; *d.* 101, *ll.* 48, 58–59; *d.* 123, *l.* 63; Zinov'ev, *Iskusstvo Palekha*, 31, 33.

25. ORGRM, *f.* KPRI, *d.* 52, *ll.* 16, 28–29, 37.

26. POANRF, *f.* 115, *op.* 4, *d.* 17, *l.* 80.

27. The comment was made by Minister of Internal Affairs Plehve regarding the political benefits of war with Japan.

28. *Memoirs of Count Witte*, 386.

29. ORRNB, *f.* 757, *d.* 37, *l.* 6; ORGRM, *f.* 122, *d.* 145, *ll.* 51, 54.

30. ORGRM, *f.* 122, *d.* 145, *ll.* 26, 28, 29–30; *d.* 118, *ll.* 19–20; *d.* 118, *ll.* 19–20.

31. Zinov'ev, *Iskusstvo Palekha*, 32.

32. ORGRM, *f.* KPRI, *d.* 52, *ll.* 14–15; Zinov'ev, *Iskusstvo Palekha*, 31–32.

33. ORGRM, *f.* KPRI, *d.* 52, *l.* 15.

34. ORGRM, *f.* KPRI, *d.* 52, *ll.* 33, 45, 66.

35. ORGRM, *f.* KPRI, *d.* 10, *ll.* 91–91, 94–96, 127–29. On peasant activism in the Vladimir province as expressed through the submission of petitions, see Verner, "Discursive Strategies in the 1905 Revolution," 65–90.

36. POANRF, *f.* 115, *op.* 4, *d.* 429, *ll.* 45–46. Trenev's letter, though undated, was probably from late 1906 or early 1907.

37. ORRNB, *f.* 757, *d.* 37, *ll.* 37, 43.

38. ORRNB, *f.* 757, *d.* 38, *ll.* 2, 10.

39. O. Subbotina, "Aleksandr Ivanovich Zubkov," *Prizyv,* September 29, 1990, 2; G. I. Gorbunov, ed., *Palekh* (Ivanovo: Ivanovskoe knizhnoe izdatel'stvo, 1954), 54; Tikhomirova, *Nikolai Mikhailovich Zinov'ev,* 124, 129.

40. POANRF, *f.* 115, *op.* 3, *d.* 152, *ll.* 12, 17.

41. RGIA, *f.* 1278, *op.* 2, *d.* 208, *l.* 149; *f.* 565, *op.* 9, *d.* 31796, *l.* 4.

42. D. K. Trenev, *O russkoi ikonopisi po povodu voprosa o nei v gosudarstvennoi dume* (Moscow, 1910), 25–28.

43. POANRF, *f.* 115, *op.* 3, *d.* 17, *l.* 858; *op.* 4, *d.* 485, *l.* 83.

44. Thus while industrial managers depended on the science of labor analysis and "Taylorism" to control and "deskill" labor, the *podlinnik* relied on archaeology to command the labor of icon painters. On the "deskilling" of labor, see Harry Braverman, *Labor and Monopoly Capital: The Degradation of Work in the Twentieth Century* (New York: Monthly Review Press, 1974).

45. For a different interpretation of the committee's *podlinnik* project, see Tarasov, *Ikona i blagochestie,* 261–71.

46. *Izvestiia . . . komiteta popechitel'stva o russkoi ikonopisi,* vyp. 2:43–45; ORGRM, *f.* KPRI, *d.* 4, *ll.* 10–11; *d.* 144, *l.* 6; "Ikonopisanie na Rusi," *Peterburgskii listok,* March 28, 1901, 2; Trenev, *Ikonopis' Mstertsev,* 8–9; *Izvestiia . . . komiteta popechitel'stva o russkoi ikonopisi,* vyp. 2:46–48.

47. *Izvestiia . . . komiteta popechitel'stva o russkoi ikonopisi,* vyp. 1:88; "Deiatel'nost' Komiteta popechitel'stva o russkoi ikonopisi," *Tserkovnye vedomosti,* 7 July 1903, 882; Iv. L-skii, "Khudozhestvennye novosti," *Moskovskie vedomosti,* January 26, 1905, 5.

48. N. P. Kondakov, *Litsevoi ikonopisnyi podlinnik,* tom 1, *Ikonografiia Iisusa Khrista* (St. Petersburg: R. Golike i A. Vil'borg, 1905), 40–41, 57–59, 62–64; A. Ia., "Znachenie i kharakter starinnykh rukovodstv po ikonografii," *Pravitel'stvennyi vestnik,* January 29, 1906, 2–3; N. P. Kondakov, "Ikonografiia bogomateri," in *Ikonopisnyi sbornik,* vyp. 4 (St. Petersburg, 1910), 4–5.

49. Tarasov, *Ikona i blagochestie,* 270; RGIA, f. 797, op. 73, d. 98, l. 38; *Izvestiia . . . komiteta popechitel'stva o russkoi ikonopisi,* vyp. 2:25–27; ORGRM, *f.* 122, *d.* 73, *ll.* 14–15, 22, 31, 41–42; RGIA, *f.* 797. *op.* 73, *d.* 98, *l.* 30. On eliminating restrictions on Old Believers, see the *Memoirs of Count Witte,* 411–13; Shevzov, *Russian Orthodoxy on the Eve of Revolution,* 12–13.

50. POANRF, *f.* 115, *op.* 4, d. 485, *l.* 85.

51. ORGRM, *f.* KPRI, *d.* 73, *ll.* 1, 28, 79, 81, 99; *d.* 79, *ll.* 18, 51; *d.* 85, *l.* 42; RGIA, *f.* 797, *op.* 73, *d.* 98, *ll.* 29–30.

52. ORGRM, *f.* KPRI, *d.* 67, *l.* 62; *d.* 79, *ll.* 51, 59, 74, 79. The state organ *Pravitel'stvennyi vestnik* attempted to compensate for this lack of attention in a glowing review: A. Ia., "Znachenie i kharakter starinnykh rukovodstv po ikonografii," 2–3.

53. ORGRM, *f.* KPRI, *d.* 154, *l.* 30.

54. RGIA, *f.* 565, *op.* 9, *d.* 31796, *l.* 6; ORRNB, *f.* 757, *d.* 37, *l.* 17; ORGRM, *f.* KPRI, *d.* 71, *l.* 91; POANRF, *f.* 115, *op.* 3, *d.* 16, *ll.* 159–72; V. P. Riabushinskii, "N. P. Kondakov i Russkaia ikona," in *Obshchestvo "Ikona" v Parizhe,* ed. G. I. Vzdornov (Moscow-Paris: Progress-Traditsiia, 2002), 2:171.

55. The letter is unfortunately not dated but probably coincides with Platonov's dramatic rise in academic bureaucratic circles in 1911 and 1912. In 1912, for instance, he

was offered but turned down the position of minister of enlightenment. V. S. Brachev, *Delo istorikov, 1929–1931 gg.*, 2nd ed. (St. Petersburg: Nestor, 1998), 29.

56. ORRNB, *f.* 585, *d.* 964, *ll.* 1–6. Platonov's critique of the previous experts was added to those of a new generation of experts. See, for example, N. Shchekotov, "Ikonopis' kak iskusstvo: po povodu sobraniia ikon I. S. Ostroukhova i S. P. Riabushinskago," *Russkaia ikona*, sb. 2 (1914): 115–42.

57. *Izvestiia . . . komiteta popechitel'stva o russkoi ikonopisi*, vyp. 3 (Petrograd, 1916), 39–40, 62.

58. M. N., "Russkie sviatye," *Novoe vremia*, August 29, 1913, 4.

59. K. Romanov, "Pis'ma v redaktsiiu," *Novoe vremia*, September 18, 1913, 6.

60. ORGRM, *f.* KPRI, *d.* 231, *l.* 2, 14.

61. ORGRM, *f.* KPRI, *d.* 79, *l.* 222.

62. RGIA, *f.* 797, *op.* 86, *d.* 151, *ll.* 1–8; *f.* 1088, *op.* 2, *d.* 22, *ll.* 3, 5; ORRNB, *f.* 757, *d.* 37, *l.* 26; Trenev, *O russkoi ikonopisi*, 8–16; Trenev, *Sovremennaia friaz'*, 4; "Drevnerusskaia ikonopis' v staroobriadskikh khramakh," *Svetil'nik*, nos. 9–12 (1915): 116, 118.

63. POANRF, *f.* 115, *op.* 4, *d.* 98, *ll.* 82, 93; ORGRM, *f.* KPRI, *d.* 262, *l.* 7; *Izvestiia . . . komiteta popechitel'stva o russkoi ikonopisi*, vyp. 3:28; POANRF, *f.* 115, *op.* 4, *d.* 98, *ll.* 99, 103; Bobrov, *Istoriia restavratsii*, 43. On Sheremetev's reorientation of the committee around Romanov, Druzhinin, and Platonov and his engineering of Georgievskii's dismissal, see ORRNB, *f.* 585, *d.* 4621, *ll.* 14, 15, 19, 22; *d.* 964, *ll.* 1–6. Interestingly, while Platonov and Sheremetev were plotting Georgievskii's demise as the committee's chief operating officer, Georgievskii and Platonov conducted a warm correspondence. ORRNB, *f.* 585, *d.* 2624, *ll.* 24–25.

64. ORGRM, *f.* KPRI, *d.* 123, *ll.* 63–66, 70, 76.

65. Viktor Nikol'skii, *Istoriia russkogo iskusstva: Zhivopis', arkhitektura, skul'ptura, dekorativnoe iskusstvo* (Berlin: Grzhebina Verlag, 1923), 99, 101, 133; Shchekotov, "Ikonopis' kak iskusstvo," 115, 126, 128, 130.

66. *Izvestiia . . . komiteta popechitel'stva o russkoi ikonopisi*, vyp. 3:76; ORGRM, *f.* KPRI, *d.* 231, *ll.* 2.

67. *Izvestiia...komiteta popechitel'stva o russkoi ikonopisi*, vyp. 3:24, 42, 80–83, 104, 106–8.

68. Bakanov (1870–1936) had worked in the Safonov studio as one of its leading masters, performing numerous restorations, often under academician artists, since 1888. After returning from the Russo-Japanese war on an English steamboat via Shanghai and Odessa (he fought two years in the Far East and had earlier served in the army in the 1880s), Bakanov settled again in Palekh, where he directed restoration of Palekh's central cathedral. Tikhomirova, *Nikolai Mikahailovich Zinov'ev*, 123, 124; AGMPI, *f.* Salapin, *l.* 32.

69. ORGRM, *f.* KPRI, *d.* 216, *l.* 17; *d.* 231, *ll.* 17, 22; *d.* 247, *l.* 6.

70. Hubertus F. Jahn, *Patriotic Culture in Russia during World War I* (Ithaca, N.Y.: Cornell University Press, 1995), 171, 173, 174; Sanborn, *Drafting the Russian Nation*, 69–70; Vera Shevzov, "Icons, Miracles, and the Ecclesial Identity in Late Imperial Russian Orthodoxy," *Church History* 69 (September 2000): 621. See Shevzov, 610–31, for the growing rift between popular forms of worship and the church hierarchy's vision of the faith.

71. ORRNB, *f.* 585, *d.* 4626, *l.* 7.

72. Leonid Matsulevich, "K istorii russkoi nauki ob iskusstve (otvet N. Shchekotovu)," *Russkaia ikona*, sb. 2, (1914): 143–49. On the lively market for fake ancient icons in turn-of-the-century Russia, see Trenev, *Ikonopis' Mstertsev*, 8–9; Bobrov, *Istoriia restavratsii*, 44–45.

73. ORRNB, *f.* 585, *d.* 4626, *l.* 28; RGIA, *f.* 1276, *op.* 14, *d.* 547, *ll.* 1–6.

74. When the Bolsheviks requisitioned Sheremetev's personal belongings in February

1918, Sheremetev wrote to Platonov that Lunacharskii was present. Lunacharskii, he wrote, "was very respectful toward me in the business of requisition. What an aesthete!" ORRNB, *f.* 585, *d.* 4627, *l.* 4.

75. ORRNB, *f.* 585, *d.* 4627, *ll.* 5, 24. The committee received a new charter from the Provisional Government on October 20, 1917 (already after the Bolshevik takeover), according to which it was placed under the Ministry of Enlightenment and renamed "The Committee of Russian Icon Painting." RGIA, *f.* 733, *op.* 156, *d.* 281, *l.* 31; *op.* 188, *d.* 4, *ll.* 30–43.

76. Georgievskii's last hurrah as an icon expert was with the posthumous publication of a manuscript written in 1917 on the monuments of Russian antiquity in the Suzdal museum. Trotsky's wife helped Georgievskii's daughter publish the manuscript in 1927. V. Georgievskii, *Pamiatniki starinnogo russkogo iskusstva Suzdal'skogo muzeia* (Moscow: Glav. upr. nauch. uchrezhdeniiami, 1927).

77. ORGRM, *f.* KPRI, *d.* 270, *ll.* 55–57, 59–60, 77; *d.* 286, *l.* 1. Among the committee's members in late 1918 were A. E. Presniakov, S. A. Zhebelev, N. Ia. Marr, A. A. Vasil'ev, I. A. Orbeli, M. D. Priselkov, G. F. Tsereteli, D. V. Ainalov, P. L. Gusev, N. V. Malitskii, and B. V. Farmakovskii. Part of the unpublished manuscript for volume 2 of the *podlinnik* is in ORGRM, *f.* KPRI, *d.* 294. Many icon experts who fled Russia regrouped in 1927 in Paris and formed an "icon society" that both studied and painted icons for émigré communities. See Vzdornov, *Obshchestvo "Ikona" v Parizhe*.

78. Yanni Kotsonis, *Making Peasants Backward: Agricultural Cooperatives and the Agrarian Question in Russia, 1861–1914* (New York: St. Martin's Press, 1999).

4—THE LAST SHALL BE THE FIRST

1. V. Kochupalov, "Stranitsy letopisi," *Pryzyv*, November 5, 1994, 2; Vikhrev, *Paleshane*, 35; N. Voitinskaia, "Palekhovtsy," *Nizhegorodskaia iarmarka*, September 1, 1926, 2; Anatolii Bakushinskii, *Iskusstvo Palekha* (Moscow-Leningrad: Academia, 1934), 117, 205–6.

2. RGALI, *f.* 2322, *op.* 1, *d.* 77, *l.* 14; GAVO, *f.* R-662, *op.* 1, *d.* 2, *ll.* 6, 45, 81; *d.* 2a, *ll.* 5, 7, 19; *f.* R-515, *op.* 1, *d.* 166, *l.* 22; RGALI, *f.* 94, *d.* 65, *l.* 6.

3. RGALI, *f.* 94, *d.* 65, *ll.* 9–11; Ia. Tugendkhol'd, "Kustar' i revoliutsiia," *Izvestiia*, October 2, 1924, 7; "Kustarnoe iskusstvo na Parizhskoi vystavke," *Izvestiia*, February 15, 1925, 5; "SSSR na Parizhskoi vystavke," *Izvestiia*, February 10, 1925, 6; ORGRM, *f.* KPRI, *d.* 146, *l.* 25; *d.* 79, *l.* 221; Liudmila Pirogova, *Palekh: Istoriia i sovremennost'* (Moscow: Izdatel'stvo "Iskusstvo," 1994), 181.

4. Attuned to broader cultural currents, Golikov also filled orders for the firm Fabergé before 1917 (a detail he left out of his Soviet-era autobiography, along with his educational experience). RGASPI, *f.* 142, *op.* 1, *d.* 547, *ll.* 19–21.

5. Since the beginning of the nineteenth century, Fedoskino, just south of Moscow, had produced a variety of papier-mâché boxes for perfume, soaps, snuff, candies, and the like. Unlike the Palekhians, the Fedoskinites were not connected with religious traditions. They painted in a realistic manner, producing copies of Russian realist painters from the nineteenth century, troikas, Russian landscapes, Russian barons on a hunting trip with their Russian wolfhounds, peasants drinking tea from a samovar, and so forth. For a history of Fedoskino, see Galina Ialovenko, *Russkie khudozhestvennye laki* (Moscow: Vsesoiuznoe kooperativnoe izdatel'stvo, 1959), 7–10, 16–26.

6. *Eksport kustarno-khudozhestvennykh izdelii i kovrov* (January 1931): 12; Vitalii Timofeevich Kotov, *Khudozhnik Ivan Golikov* (Iaroslavl': Verkhne-Volzhskoe knizhnoe izdatel'stvo, 1973), 20; Vikhrev, *Paleshane*, 86–89; Viktor Poltoratskii, "Zhivye rodniki," *Nash sovremennik*, no. 2 (1970): 103.

7. The German Dürer (1471–1528) produced accurate and delicate drawings characterized by profuse and literate detail.

8. Vikhrev, *Paleshane,* 83.

9. Kotov, *Khudozhnik Ivan Golikov,* 21–25; A. N. Reinson-Pravdin, *Ivan Ivanovich Golikov* (Moscow: Sovetskii khudozhnik, 1956), 9–10, 13.

10. Bakushinskii, *Iskusstvo Palekha* (1934 ed.), 207–9; Vikhrev, *Paleshane,* 225.

11. ORGTG, *f.* 15, *d.* 730, *ll.* 1–3; John Bowlt, *Russian Art, 1875–1975: A Collection of Essays* (New York: MSS Information Corp., 1976), 21; V. M. Vasilenko, "Teoretik, kritik, vydaiushchiisia pedagog," in A. V. Bakushinskii, *Issledovaniia i stat'i,* comp. I. A. Liberfort (Moscow: Sovetskii khudozhnik, 1981), 7.

12. ORGTG, *f.* 15, *d.* 730, *l.* 3; *d.* 722, *l.* 1; *d.* 725, *l.* 1; *d.* 734, *l.* 1; *d.* 750, *l.* 1.

13. ORGTG, *f.* 15, *d.* 174, *ll.* 1–4; Bakushinskii, "Sovremennost' i khudozhestvennaia kul'tura," in his *Issledovaniia i stat'i,* 49. Spengler, in the words of one scholar, "declared Russia to be 'organically' different from the Occident, now in full decay; because of Russia's 'young' yet 'Byzantine' essence she possessed the inner strength to cast off the desiccating 'civilization' imported from the Western 'megalopolis' and return to true 'culture.'" Martin Malia, *Russia under Western Eyes: From the Bronze Horseman to the Lenin Mausoleum* (Cambridge, Mass.: Harvard University Press, 1999), 350. Spengler's book had tremendous success in Europe and Soviet Russia. The first volume was translated into Russian in 1923 and sold ten thousand copies, a record for book sales at the time. Mikhail Agursky, *The Third Rome: National Bolshevism in the USSR* (Boulder: Westview Press, 1987), 229.

14. ORGTG, *f.* 15, *d.* 230, *ll.* 4, 6, 13–14; *d.* 864, *ll.* 11–14; *d.* 368, *l.* 1.

15. Ia. Tugendkhol'd, "'Russkoe' i 'sovetskoe' iskusstvo v Parizhe," *Izvestiia,* October 6, 1925, 6.

16. A. V. Lunacharskii, "Sovetskoe gosudarstvo i iskusstvo," *Izvestiia,* January 29, February 5, and February 19, 1922, reprinted in his *Ob iskusstve,* tom 2, *Russkoe sovetskoe iskusstvo* (Moscow: Iskusstvo, 1982), 116.

17. A. V. Lunacharskii, "Eshche k voprosu o kul'ture," *Izvestiia,* November 3, 1922, reprinted in A. E. Gorpenko, *Iz istorii sovetskoi esteticheskoi mysli, 1917–1932. Sbornik materialov* (Moscow: Iskusstvo, 1980), 71; reprint of Lunacharskii speech in Petrograd, October 10, 1918, in his *Ob iskusstve,* 58–59, 57. In late 1918, Lunacharskii defended the icon painters of the Vladimir-Suzdal region. See "Lozhka protivoiadiia," *Iskusstvo kommuna,* December 29, 1918, reprinted in his *Ob iskusstve,* 67–68.

18. Ia. Tugendkhol'd, "Promyslovaia kooperatsiia i khudozhestvennaia promyshlennost'," *Vserossiiskaia vystavka khudozhestvennoi promyshlennosti,* no. 2 (1923): 23.

19. RGAE, *f.* 480, *op.* 7, *d.* 98, *l.* 5; Ia. Tugendkhol'd, "Itogi khudozhestv.-promyshl. vystavki," *Izvestiia,* May 11, 1923, 6; Ia. Tugendkhol'd, "Iskusstvo i sel'skokhoziaistvennaia vystavka," *Izvestiia,* April 7, 1923, 5.

20. RGAE, *f.* 480, *op.* 7, *d.* 103, *l.* 100; A. V. Bakushinskii, "Palekhskie laki," *Iskusstvo,* no. 2 (1925): 205; RGAE, *f.* 480, *op.* 7, *d.* 98, *ll.* 8, 16, 28, 31–34, 41; *d.* 101, *l.* 202; L. Sosnovskii, "Kustarnyi otdel vystavki," *Vestnik promyslovoi kooperatsii,* nos. 3–4 (1923): 28–30; GARF, *f.* A-5449, *op.* 1, *d.* 3053, *l.* 10.

21. Kameneva was doubly connected as the sister of Trotsky and the wife of Politburo member Lev Kamenev.

22. RGALI, *f.* 94, *d.* 65, *l.* 2; Vikhrev, *Paleshane,* 37. Smitten with Russian exotica, Italy eliminated most import duties on Russian arts and crafts in its trade agreement with the Soviet government in 1924. Ia. Tugendkhol'd, "Sovetskoe iskusstvo i vystavka v Venetsii," *Izvestiia,* March 29, 1924, 6.

23. Kotov, *Khudozhnik Ivan Golikov*, 31–33; Reinson-Pravdin, *Ivan Ivanovich Golikov*, 20; Vikhrev, *Paleshane*, 242; Tugendkhol'd, "Kustar' i revoliutsiia," 7; "V obshchestve sodeistviia razvitiiu khudozh.-promyshlennoi kul'tury," *Izvestiia*, November 21, 1925, 7.

24. France's diplomatic recognition of the Soviet Union in 1924 triggered the invitation to participate in the exhibit. For Soviet coverage in *Izvestiia* of the Paris exhibit, see Ia. Tugendkhol'd's reports: "Mezhdunarodnaia vystavka v Parizhe v 1925 g. i my" (September 7, 1924), 5; "K uchastiiu SSSR na mezhdunarodnoi vystavke v Parizhe" (November 23, 1924), 5; "Eshche o predstoiashchem vystuplenii SSSR na Parizhskoi vystavke" (December 25, 1924), 3; "SSSR na Parizhskoi vystavke" (February 10, 1925), 6; "Kustarnoe iskusstvo na Parizhskoi vystavke" (February 15, 1925), 5; "Podgotovka k Parizhskoi vystavke" (February 4, 1925), 6; "K vozrozhdeniiu kustarno-khudozhestvennoi promyshlennosti" (February 17, 1925); and "SSSR na Parizhskoi mezhdunarodnoi vystavke" (April 8, 1925), 7.

25. Bakushinskii, "Palekhskie laki," 210.

26. A. V. Bakushinskii, "Palekhskie mastera," *Krasnaia niva*, no. 4 (1926): 10–11; N. Bartram, "Novoe v kustarnom dele," *Krasnaia niva*, no. 12 (1925): 285.

27. Ia. Tugendkhol'd, "Stil' 1925 goda (mezhdunarodnaia vystavka v Parizhe)," *Pechat' i revoliutsiia*, kn. 7, 1925: 54, 66; and Tugendkhol'd's reports in *Izvestiia*: "K bor'be za kachestvo khudozhestvennoi promyshlennosti" (November 19, 1925), 6; "K itogam Parizhskoi vystavki" (September 29, 1925), 5; "K izucheniiu iskusstva narodnostei SSSR" (July 1, 1926), 5.

28. GAIO, *f.* 2977, *op.* 1, *d.* 4, *ll.* 2, 3, 5; *f.* 372, *op.* 1, *d.* 15, *l.* 4; "Slovo k molodym: N. Zinov'ev, narodnyi khudozhnik RSFSR, laureat gosud. premii imeni Repina," *Prizyv*, August 24, 1974, 2; RGALI, *f.* 94, *d.* 279, *l.* 15.

29. GAIO, *f.* 2977, *op.* 1, *d.* 3, *ll.* 38–42; *d.* 7, *ll.* 34–42; Vikhrev, *Paleshane*, 100.

30. GAIO, *f.* 2977, *op.* 1, *d.* 5, *ll.* 1–13 contains records of the Paris shipment.

31. Reinson-Pravdin, *Ivan Ivanovich Golikov*, 120.

32. Sigmund Birkenmayer, *Nikolaj Nekrasov: His Life and Poetic Art* (The Hague, Paris: Mouton, 1968), 117.

33. GAIO, *f.* 2877, *op.* 1, *d.* 7, *l.* 12a.

34. GAIO, *f.* 2977, *op.* 1, *d.* 7, *l.* 12a.

35. GAIO, *f.* 2977, *op.* 1, *d.* 7, *ll.* 34–42; *d.* 3, *ll.* 38–42.

36. GAIO, *f.* 2977, *op.* 1, *d.* 7, *ll.* 79–86; *d.* 16, *ll.* 4, 21; Efim Vikhrev, "Palekh, selo-akademiia," *Nashi dostizheniia*, nos. 5–6 (1935): 20–21.

37. For a long list of the enemies in Bolshevik demonology during the civil war, see Victoria Bonnell, *Iconography of Power: Soviet Political Posters under Lenin and Stalin* (Berkeley: University of California Press, 1997), 191.

38. N. M. Zinov'ev, *Stilisticheskie traditsii iskusstva Palekha* (Leningrad: Khudozhnik RSFSR, 1981), 122.

39. In late 1925, a 22-by-22-centimeter Palekh lacquer cost 40 rubles, hardly small change for a Soviet factory worker making just 58 rubles a month. Roger A. Clarke and Dubravko J. I. Matko, *Soviet Economic Facts, 1917–1981* (New York: St. Martin's Press, 1983), 39.

40. GAIO, *f.* 2977, *op.* 1, *d.* 10, *l.* 38; *d.* 8, *ll.* 1–32.

41. GAIO, *f.* 2977, *op.* 1, *d.* 14, *ll.* 63, 65; *d.* 10, *l.* 22; RGALI, *f.* 94, *d.* 276, *l.* 8; *f.* 2322, *op.* 1, *d.* 44, *ll.* 39–40.

42. GAIO, *f.* 2977, *op.* 1, *d.* 10, *l.* 22; *d.* 14, *ll.* 27, 32, 38, 49.

43. GAIO, *f.* 2977, *op.* 1, *d.* 14, *ll.* 37, 40–41, 45–47, 56–58; *d.* 16, *l.* 22.

44. GAIO, *f.* 2977, *op.* 1, *d.* 10a, *l.* 39; *d.* 14, *ll.* 68–69; A. V. Lunacharskii, "Itogi vystavki gosudarstvennykh zakazov k desiatiletiiu oktiabria," *Izvestiia*, February 16, 1928, reprinted in his *Ob iskusstve*, 226.

45. In 1928, Yan Rudzutak, People's Commissar for Transport and a Politburo member, ordered a box portraying a Red Army soldier in the village. Rudzutak had apparently seen a similar box in the home of another senior Bolshevik in Moscow. Gostorg (the State Import-Export Trade Bureau) also relayed an emergency order for two desk-sets, like the one for Rykov, for unnamed powerful political figures. In December of 1927, another one of Lenin's former deputies, A. D. Tsuriupa, requested a desk-set on a revolutionary theme. Bonch-Bruevich, Lenin's former secretary and an expert on sectarians, preferred a Russian folk theme over revolutionary subject matter, ordering four boxes based on the tale "Ivan Tsarevich" in 1928. GAIO, *f.* 2977, *op.* 1, *d.* 16, *ll.* 10, 24; *d.* 21, *l.* 6.

46. The desk-set contained Golikov's signature *Battle* scene (renamed *Reds versus Whites*), the Third International, a worker demonstration, and three emblems: those of the Soviet Union, the RSFSR, and the city of Moscow (St. George slaying the dragon). Reinson-Pravdin, *Ivan Ivanovich Golikov,* 122.

47. RGALI, *f.* 94, *d.* 119, *l.* 2. Before 1917, Gorky covered Russian arts and crafts at the Nizhnii Novgorod fairs. As a youngster, he also worked in an icon shop run by Palekhians in Nizhnii Novgorod, an experience described in the second volume of his 1913 autobiography *My Apprenticeship* and subsequently reprinted in a collection of Palekh autobiographies, in which he was designated an honorary Palekhian. Efim Vikhrev, *Palekh: 1927–1932. Vtoraia kompozitsiia* (Moscow, 1938), 177–91, 406–7.

48. Interview with Nikolai Ivanovich Golikov (b. 1924), May 4, 2000, Palekh.

49. Khalatov promised 8,000 rubles for the Palekhians, as did Stepanov-Skvortsov. Uritskii pledged 1,000 rubles, and Gostorg chipped in another 1,000—all to be put toward a new art studio. Reinson-Pravdin, *Ivan Ivanovich Golikov,* 122; GAIO, *f.* 2977, *op.* 1, *d.* 16, *l.* 66.

50. Gorky cancelled his planned trip to Palekh, unaware that the road from Shuia to Palekh, even under the best of circumstances, was often impassable except by horse. He did, however, meet Palekh patrons in Moscow and at his country residence on three later occasions. GAIO, *f.* 2977, op. 1, *d.* 10, *l.* 37; *d.* 16, *ll.* 56, 64, 69, 75.

51. G. Belaia, *Don Kikhoty dvadtsatykh godov: "Pereval" i sud'ba ego idei* (Moscow: Sovetskii pisatel', 1989), 7.

52. A. Lezhnev, "Vmesto prologa," *Rovesniki,* no. 7 (1930): 20. On Lezhnev, see G. A. Belaia, "Kritika v kontekste estetiki (o deiatel'nosti i tvorchestve A. Lezhneva)," in A. Lezhnev, *O literature. Stat'i* (Moscow: Sovetskii pisatel', 1987), 3–38.

53. N. Zarudin, ed., *Pereval'tsy. Antologiia. Sodruzhestvo pisatelei revoliutsii "pereval"* (Moscow: Federatsiia, 1930), 14, 17.

54. A. K. Voronskii, *Iskusstvo i zhizn'. Sbornik statei* (Moscow: Krug, 1924), cited in Belaia, *Don Kikhoty,* 37; *Protiv Burzhuaznogo liberalizma v khudozhestvennoi literature. Diskussiia o "Perevale" (aprel' 1930)* (Moscow: Kommunisticheskaia akademiia, 1931), 100.

55. Iu. Melent'ev, ed., "Khudozhnik, soratnik khudozhnikov," in Efim Vikhrev, *Rodniki* (Moscow: Sovetskaia Rossiia, 1984), 4, 30.

56. P. Kuprianovskii, "Efim Fedorovich Vikhrev," in E. F. Vikhrev, *Izbrannye proizvedeniia* (Ivanovo: Ivanovskoe knizhnoe izd-vo, 1961), 5; G. F. Gorbunov, *Dmitrii Furmanov. Efimovo schast'e* (Iaroslavl': Verkhne-Volzshskoe khnizhnoe izdatel'stvo, 1971), 190–91. On the Vikhrev family, see V. Biakovskii, "Vikhrevy," *Prizyv,* November 29, 1994, 2.

57. "[Balmont's] poetry is extravagant in its oscillation between the demonic and the earthly, in its historical and geographical grasp of world events. A yearning for the infinite, pride in the great mission of the poet, and the cult of individualism are frequent themes of his poetry, which always . . . reflected the spirit of symbolist expression he created to oppose realistic and rational trends." *Dictionary of Russian Literature since 1917,*

ed. Wolfgang Kasack and Maria Carlson, trans. Jane T. Hedges (New York: Columbia University Press, 1988), 36.

58. Kuprianovskii, "Efim Fedorovich Vikhrev," 8, 10.

59. Kuprianovskii, "Efim Fedorovich Vikhrev," 10.

60. He cultivated a number of contacts in the literary world: Mikhail Prishvin, Artem Vesyelii, Sergei Esenin, N. Aseev, A. Zharov, A. Bezymenskii, and A. Chapygin. Kuprianovskii, "Efim Fedorovich Vikhrev," 12; Gorbunov, *Dmitrii Furmanov*, 218–21; Vikhrev, *Paleshane*, 122.

61. Gorbunov, *Dmitrii Furmanov*, 222–23.

62. For discussions of the origin of the myth of "The Left-Hander," see B. Bukhshtab, "Ob istochnikakh 'Levshi' N. S. Leskova," *Russkaia literatura*, no. 1 (1964): 49–64.

63. E. Vikhrev, "Iz roda v rod," *Rabochii krai*, 25 December 1926, 3.

64. RGALI, *f.* 94, *d.* 61, *l.* 23.

65. RGALI, *f.* 94, *d.* 59, *l.* 70; *d.* 70, *l.* 16; *f.* 1884, *op.* 1, *d.* 13, *l.* 6.

66. Gorbunov, *Dmitrii Furmanov*, 226, 234, 237.

67. Efim Vikhrev, *Palekh* (Iaroslavl': Verkhne-Volzhskoe knizhnoe izdatel'stvo, 1974), 167; RGALI, *f.* 94, *d.* 51, *ll.* 56, 65.

68. RGALI, *f.* 94, *d.* 20, *l.* 17.

69. RGALI, *f.* 94, *d.* 119, *l.* 2; *d.* 10, *l.* 21.

70. The nature writer M. Prishvin on a number of occasions invited Vikhrev to Zagorsk to discuss the Palekh project. Gorbunov, *Dmitrii Furmanov*, 240–44.

71. *Perepiska A. N. Tolstogo v dvukh tomakh*, tom 2 (Moscow: Khudozhestvennaia literatura, 1989), 110. A common thread among some of Palekh's patrons in the late 1920s and early 1930s was sympathy for the Change of Signs movement that identified the Bolshevik Revolution with the resurrection of a strong Russian state. According to Agursky, the *perevalets* Voronskii found much of value in the writings of the *smenovekhovtsy*. Agursky, *The Third Rome*, 259.

72. Gorbunov, *Dmitrii Furmanov*, 245–46; RGALI, *f.* 94, *d.* 217, *l.* 26–27; *d.* 119, *ll.* 3–6.

73. B. N., "Vystavka dekorativnykh iskusstv v Montse-Milane," *Krasnaia Niva*, no. 38 (1927): 11; D. Arkin, "Na vystavke Sovetskogo iskusstva v Tokio," *Krasnaia niva*, no. 29 (1927): 18; "Pervaia pokazatel'naia vystavka Sovetskogo soiuza v N'iu Iuorke," *Russkii golos*, February 5, 1928, 1; "Progulka po vystavka SSSR," *Russkii golos*, February 9, 1928, 2; "Gromadnyi uspekh Sovetskoi vystavki," *Russkii golos*, February 15, 1928, 1; pages (unnumbered) in *Soviet Russian Art and Handicraft Exposition: Grand Central Palace, New York, February 1929* (New York, 1929); "Viewing the Art of Russian Peasants," *New York Times*, February 17, 1929, 88.

74. *New Republic*, February 20, 1929, 18–19.

75. GAIO, *f.* 2977, *op.* 1, *d.* 13, *ll.* 1, 3; *d.* 16, *l.* 34; Ia. Ganetskii, "Palekhskie khudozhniki," *Izvestiia*, May 20, 1928, 5.

76. Ia. Tugendkhol'd, "Nasha khudozhestvennaia zhizn' budet uregulirovana," *Pravda*, July 19, 1928, 6, and "O gosudarstvennykh zakazakh," *Izvestiia*, August 10, 1928, 6.

77. GARF, *f,* 5449, *op.* 1, *d.* 1204, *l.* 2; *Eksport kustarno-khudozhestvennykh izdelii i kovrov* (September–November, 1930): 1; (March–May, 1931): 2; (August–September, 1931): 5; GARF, *f.* 5449, *op.* 1, *d.* 1453, *l.* 18; *d.* 1232, *ll.* 2–3; *d.* 1240, *ll.* 20, 70–72; *d.* 1239, *l.* 9.

78. ORGTG, *f.* 15, *d.* 599, *ll.* 1–5, 10–14.

79. Vikhrev, *Paleshane*, 52; GAIO, *f.* 2977, *op.* 1, *d.* 40; V. Koval'skii, "Proletarskuiu tematiku v kustarno-khudozhestvennye promysli," *Eksport kustarno-khudozhestvennykh izdelii i kovrov*, no. 1 (1932): 3.

80. GAIO, *f.* 2977, *op.* 1, *d.* 36, *l.* 11. The *krestnyi khod* is a traditional procession in which participants carry icons and crosses, usually around the cathedral.

81. ORGTG, *f.* 15, *d.* 2663, *ll.* 1, 7.

82. ORGTG, *f.* 15, *d.* 2663, *l.* 1.

83. ORGTG, *f.* 15, *d.* 2663, *l.* 5.

84. ORGTG, *f.* 15, *d.* 2663, *ll.* 2–3.

85. A. Vinner, "Preobrazovanie Palekhskikh masterskikh," *Literatura i iskusstvo,* nos. 7–8 (1931): 93–101.

86. GAIO, *f.* 2977, *op.* 1, *d.* 26, *l.* 38; RGALI, *f.* 94, *d.* 70, *l.* 63; *d.* 50, *ll.* 3, 9, 22.

87. GAIO, *f.* 2977, *op.* 1, *d.* 26, *l.* 52; *d.* 20, *ll.* 43, 46, 49.

88. GAIO, *f,* 2977, *op.* 1, *d.* 26, *ll.* 39, 45; RGALI, *f.* 94, *d.* 70, *ll.* 63–64; *d.* 119, *l.* 6; *d.* 142, *ll.* 4–5.

89. GAIO, *f.* 94, *d.* 127, *ll.* 192–94.

90. GAIO, *f.* 94, *d.* 127, *l.* 98; *d.* 142, *l.* 45; *d.* 80, *l.* 3; Ida Treat, "With the Peasant Painters of Palek," *Asia,* no. 6 (1934): 337.

91. RGALI, *f.* 94, *d.* 142, *l.* 19; Dmitrii Semenovskii, *Selo Palekh i ego khudozhniki* (Moscow, 1932); Anatolii Bakushinskii, *Iskusstvo Palekha* (Moscow: Vses. kooperativnoe ob"edinennoe izd-vo, 1932); Bakushinskii, *Iskusstvo Palekha* (1934 ed.). For references to the extensive coverage of Palekh in the Soviet press, see the very useful bibliography compiled in honor of Palekh's fiftieth year of Sovietization: Z. Korchagina, *Iskusstvo Sovetskogo Palekha: Bibliograficheskii ukazatel' literatury* (Ivanovo: Ivan. obl. nauchnaia biblioteka, 1976).

92. Efim Vikhrev, "Palekh. Ocherki," *Novyi mir,* no. 3 (1929): 224; Vikhrev, *Paleshane,* 43, 46–48, 52, 150–51, 155, 236.

93. Robert Conquest, *Stalin: Breaker of Nations* (New York: Viking, 1991).

94. Melent'ev, "Khudozhnik, soratnik khudozhnikov," 30, 19; Vikhrev, "Palekh: Ocherki," 218, 204.

95. E. Vikhrev, "Palekh," *Nashi dostizheniia,* no. 9 (1930): 49, 50.

96. Vikhrev, "Palekh: Ocherki," 221, 224; Vikhrev, "Palekh," 53; Vikhrev, "Palekh, selo-akademiia," 28; N. Zarudin, "Sledy na zemle," *Nashi dostizheniia,* nos. 5–6 (1935): 76.

97. RGALI, *f.* 94, *d.* 276, *l.* 4; Gorbunov, *Dmitrii Furmanov,* 262; Vikhrev, "Palekh, selo-akademiia," 26. The émigré smenovekhovets Yurii Potekhin regarded Blok "as a genius who could discern the invisible Christ under the Revolutionary banner." Agursky, *The Third Rome,* 249.

98. Vikhrev, "Palekh, selo-akademiia," 39. Vikhrev's vision, incidentally, reflected the view among many advocates of the Change of Signs movement, for whom "the Russian Revolution was a popular mutiny in the style of Stepan Razin (1630–1671) and Pugatchev." Agursky, *The Third Rome,* 248.

99. Vikhrev, *Paleshane,* 12, and "Palekh, selo-akademiia," 23–24, 28, 30; interview with Golikov in Palekh.

100. RGALI, *f.* 94, *d.* 127, *l.* 32.

101. Ivan Bakanov, "Moi kompozitsii," in *Paleshane,* ed. Vikhrev, 122; B. Pil'niak, "Rozhdenie prekrasnogo," *Novyi mir,* no. 10 (1934): 37, 40.

102. N. Zarudin, "Sledy na zemle," 60; Vikhrev, "Palekh, selo-akademiia," 38, and "Palekh," 51. Vikhrev complained that members of the executive committee of the Ivanovo Soviet wanted to change Palekh's enchantingly ambiguous name. Officials from Ivanovo, "wanted to paint Palekh with the textile industry brush. Frothing at the mouth . . . they said Palekh has the name of some 'Palitskikh' princes, that they wanted to give it a revolutionary name that fits in, so to speak, with the character of our *guberniia.* And so they recommended rechristening it as the village of Nogino." Vikhrev, "Palekh: Ocherki," 212.

103. RGALI, *f.* 94, *d.* 59, *l.* 70.

104. RGALI, *f.* 94, *d.* 59, *l.* 70; *d.* 51, *l.* 20.

105. Nikolai Golikov, the son of Ivan Golikov and a celebrated artist in his own right, is sure Vikhrev was poisoned (and also his father in 1937) by the NKVD. He is less clear on a motive, except to point out that most of the brigade of writers who joined Vikhrev in late 1934 (Zarudin, Kataev, Pil'nyak, and Boris Guber) were arrested and shot in the Great Terror, along with the chairman of the Palekh artel' Aleksandr Zubkov, their host. He claims the NKVD prevented an autopsy from being performed on Vikhrev—to cover up the crime—and had the assassins arrested and shot. Interview with Golikov.

106. Zarudin, "Sledy na zemle," 78. The metro opened in May 1935.

107. For an excellent examination of the proletarian culture strain in early Soviet culture, see Rolf Hellebust, *Flesh to Metal: Soviet Literature and the Alchemy of Revolution* (Ithaca, N.Y.: Cornell University Press, 2003).

108. D. Semenovskii, "Paleshane," *Rabochii krai,* August 7, 1933, 4; Vikhrev, "Iz roda v rod," 3.

109. A. Nekrasov, "Russiche Lackmalerei," *Slavische Rundschau,* Jahrgang 3 (1931): 163–69; A. Bakuschinsky, "Die Russichen Ikonenmalerei," *Osteuropa* (October 1929): 10–23; Efim Vihriov, "Palekh," *Bifur* 7 (1930): 84–99.

110. Regine Robin notes that although officials were unable to define the exact nature of socialist realism in the 1930s, they broadly agreed that socialist art, paradoxically, should be both realistic and romantic. Regine Robin, *Socialist Realism: An Impossible Aesthetic,* trans. Catherine Porter (Stanford: Stanford University Press, 1992), 14. John Bowlt notes that late imperial interest in the primitive and the reaction against positivism and realism continued through the 1930s. Bowlt also sees the Soviet tension between romanticism and realism as continuing a prerevolutionary dynamic in Russian culture. Bowlt, *Russian Art, 1875–1975,* 161, 173. For a discussion of the complex roots and multiple realistic and romantic manifestations of socialist realism, see Thomas Lahusen and Evgeny Dobrenko, eds., "Socialist Realism Without Shores," *South Atlantic Quarterly,* 94, no. 3 (Summer 1995).

111. See, for example, Katerina Clark, "The City Versus the Countryside in Soviet Peasant Literature of the Twenties: A Duel of Utopias," in *Bolshevik Culture: Experiment and Order in the Russian Revolution,* ed. Abbot Gleason, Peter Kenez, and Richard Stites (Bloomington: Indiana University Press, 1985), 175–90.

112. J. L. Talmon, *The Origins of Totalitarian Democracy* (London: Secker & Warburg, 1955), 6–7, 244; Malia, *Russia under Western Eyes,* 257, 260, 281, 285–86, 314, 329, 342.

113. Terry Martin, "An Affirmative Action Empire: The Soviet Union as the Highest Form of Imperialism," in *A State of Nations: Empire and Nation-Making in the Age of Lenin and Stalin,* ed. Ronald Grigor Suny and Terry Martin (New York: Oxford University Press, 2001), 71–75, 78, 80–81; Slezkine, "The USSR as a Communal Apartment," 418–19, 424–26, 433–35, 442–44.

114. For this argument, see, for example, David Brandenberger, *National Bolshevism: Stalinist Mass Culture and the Formation of Modern Russian National Identity, 1931–1956* (Cambridge: Harvard University Press, 2002).

5—PALEKH IN THE AGE OF TERROR, 1933–1941

1. The uncensored nature of Palekh's art stands in stark contrast to other areas of Soviet iconography such as poster imagery. See Bonnell, *Iconography of Power,* 6, 11–12. In contrast, a recent article highlights the role of chaos and contingency in the production of Stalinist iconography: Susan Reid, "Socialist Realism in the Stalinist Terror: The 'Industry of

Socialism´ Art Exhibition, 1935–1941," *Russian Review* 60 (April 2001): 153–84.

2. GAIO, *f.* 2977, *op.* 1, *d.* 46, *ll.* 2, 5–8, 8–13.

3. GAIO, *f.* 2977, *op.* 1, *d.* 46, *ll.* 15–20, 28–31; ORGTG, *f.* 15, *d.* 138, *ll.* 6–7.

4. GAIO, *f.* 2977, *op.* 1, *d.* 46, *ll.* 34–37, 39–42; E. Zhuravleva and V. Chepelev, *Brigada khudozhnikov,* nos. 4–5 (1932): 39–40, 41–42; Vinner, "Preobrazovanie Palekhskikh masterskikh," 95.

5. GAIO, *f.* 2977, *op.* 1, *d.* 46, *ll.* 42, 55–56.

6. ORGTG, *f.* 15, *d.* 285, *l.* 2; RGALI, *f.* 94, *d.* 141, *l.* 19.

7. GAIO, *f.* 2977, *op.* 1, *d.* 42, *ll.* 24, 26, 28, 87, 90; *f.* 372, *op.* 1, *d.* 6, *l.* 6; RGALI, *f.* 94, *op.* 1, *d.* 207, *ll.* 11, 13–14, 17.

8. Karen Petrone, *Life Has Become More Joyous, Comrades: Celebrations in the Time of Stalin* (Bloomington: Indiana University Press, 2000).

9. The celebration of Palekh's jubilee on March 14 was broadcast live across the Soviet Union. A film was also made of the events for inclusion in newsreel clips. Vitalii Kotov, "Mif o sele-akademii," *Prizyv,* September 9, 1995, 2; Vikhrev, *Paleshane;* "Velikii prazdnik Sovetskogo iskusstva. S torzhestvennogo zasedaniia posviashchennogo desiatiletiiu palekhskoi arteli," *Rabochii krai,* March 14, 1935, 1; "Nezabyvalyii den'. Ot nashikh spetsial'nykh korrespondentov," *Rabochii krai,* March 15, 1935, 1; L. Gordeeva, "Khudozhnik Palekha Aristarkh Dydykin (1874–1954)," *Prizyv,* April 6, 1989, 2; Ivan Kataev, "Nebyvalyi prazdnik," *Pravda,* March 15, 1935, 4.

10. GAIO, *f.* 2969, *op.* 1, *d.* 20, *ll.* 11, 26; RGALI, *f.* 2322, *op.* 1, *d.* 77, *ll.* 38–39.

11. Hayden White, *Metahistory: The Historical Imagination in Nineteenth-Century Europe* (Baltimore: Johns Hopkins University Press, 1973), 9.

12. RGALI, *f.* 94, *d.* 141, *l.* 19.

13. GAIO, *f.* 2969, *op.* 1, *d.* 15, *l.* 8; *d.* 28, *l.* 32; RGALI, *f.* 2322, *op.* 1, *d.* 293, *l.* 8.

14. *Prizyv,* January 15, 1994, 2; RGALI, *f.* 2322, *op.* 1, "Predislovie"; *op.* 1, *d.* 52, *ll.* 1–4, 27; Kotov, "Mif o sele akademii," 2; Aleksandr Vikhrev, "Pochetnoe zvanie Palekha," *Prizyv,* December 5, 1995, 2; V. V. Pavlov, "German Vasil'evich Zhidkov v Palekhe," in *Muzei narodnogo iskusstva i khudozhestvennye promysly. Sbornik trudov NIIKhP,* vyp. 5 (Moscow: Nauchno-issledovatel'skii institut khudozhestvennoi promyshlennosti, 1972), 101–2; PAIO, *f.* 676, *op.* 1, *d.* 21, *l.* 116.

15. "Velikii prazdnik Sovetskogo iskusstva," *Rabochii krai,* March 14, 1935, 1; S. Dinamov, "Ob iskusstve Palekha," *Sovetskoe iskusstvo,* April 17, 1935, 1. For a similar point of view, see S. Fin, "Molodoi Palekh," *Komsomol'skaia pravda,* April 3, 1935, 2.

16. Vl. Kostin, "Iskusstvo Palekha," *Sovetskoe iskusstvo,* October 23, 1934, 3; RGALI, *f.* 613, *op.* 3, *d.* 28, *ll.* 15–16; *op.* 1, *d.* 5858, *ll.* 10, 12, 13; *d.* 5857, *ll.* 18, 35, 37–38, 40.

17. GAIO, *f.* 2977, *op.* 1, *d.* 47, *ll.* 1–2.

18. Soviet planners in the 1930s did harbor delusions of total planning for the consumption and distribution of some basic consumer goods, but these plans were complete failures. See Elena Osokina, *Za fasadom "Stalinskogo izobiliia": Raspredelenie i rynok v snabzhenii naseleniia v gody industrializatsii, 1927–1941* (Moscow: ROSSPEN, 1998), 44–45.

19. Interview with Golikov; GAIO, *f.* 2977, *op.* 2, *d.* 2, *l.* 14, 21.

20. RGAE, *f.* 4433, *op.* 1, *d.* 136, *ll.* 3–4.

21. For the consistently anti-trade orientation of Soviet authorities in the 1930s, and its disastrous consequences for Soviet consumers and traders alike, see Osokina, *Za fasadom "Stalinskogo izobiliia."* For a very different interpretation of the role of trade in official Stalinist values, which my study does not support, see Amy Randall, "'Revolutionary Bolshevik Work': Stakhanovism in Retail Trade," *Russian Review* 59 (July 2000): 425–41.

22. RGAE, *f.* 413, *op.* 13, *d.* 1972, *l.* 70; *f.* 8345, *op.* 1, *d.* 145, *ll.* 9–11.

23. RGAE, *f.* 8345, *op.* 1, *d.* 135, *l.* 95; *d.* 138, *ll.* 50, 63, 66–67; GAIO, *f.* 2977, *op.* 1, *d.* 52, *l.* 33; RGAE, *f.* 8345, *op.* 1, *d.* 145, *l.* 2.

24. RGAE, *f.* 8345, *op.* 1, *d.* 145, *l.* 9.

25. Aleksandr Zubkov, "Istoriia Arteli drevnei zhivopisi," in Vikhrev, *Paleshane,* 23–25; GAIO, *f.* 2977, *op.* 1, *d.* 13, *l.* 1; *d.* 10, *l.* 13; Vikhrev, *Paleshane,* 29–33; RGALI, *f.* 94, *d.* 297, *l.* 1.

26. GAIO, *f.* 2875, *op.* 3, *d.* 245, *l.* 3; Treat, "With the Peasant Painters of Palek," 336–37.

27. It is curious that the article was only brought to Zubkov's attention at this time. Even more curious, no such article for this date (or any other dates in the 1930s) appeared in any English-language newspaper (that I can find) called *The Sunday Times.*

28. GAIO, *f.* 2977, *op.* 1, *d.* 52, *ll.* 61–63.

29. GAIO, *f.* 2977, *op.* 1, *d.* 52, *ll.* 33–34, 75; RGALI, *f.* 2322, *op.* 1, *d.* 360, *l.* 69a.

30. G. V. Zhidkov, *Pushkin v iskusstve Palekha* (Moscow: Gos. izd-vo izo-brazitel'nykh iskusstv, 1937), 21–25; E. Vikhrev, "Pushkin i Gor'kii v iskusstve Palekha," *Novyi mir,* kn. 9 (1933): 236; RGALI, *f.* 94, *d.* 142, *l.* 5.

31. Vikhrev, "Pushkin i Gor'kii v iskusstve Palekha," 234–43, and "Pushkin—Palekh," *Nashi dostizheniia,* nos. 5–6 (1935): 19–22; Zhidkov, *Pushkin v iskusstve Palekha,* 15–17, 26, 159; D. Semenovskii, "Pushkin i narodnye khudozhniki oblasti," *Ivanovskaia oblast',* kn. 3–4 (November 1936): 104–9, and "Vystavka narodnogo tvorchestva," *Ivanovskaia oblast',* kn. 2 (February 1937): 99–111; GAIO, *f.* 2969, *op.* 1, *d.* 20, *l.* 11.

32. RGALI, *f.* 2322, *op.* 1, *d.* 52, *l.* 37b; Zhidkov, *Pushkin v iskusstve Palekha,* 13, 158. In 1937, Academia published the following titles by A. S. Pushkin: *Skazka o zolotom petushke,* illustrated by I. Vakurov, *Skazka o mertvoi Tsarevne i o semi bogatyriakh,* illustrated by O. Bakanov, *Skazka o pope i o rabotnike ego Balde,* illustrated by D. Butorin, *Skazka o rybake i rybke,* illustrated by I. Zubkov, *Skazka o Tsare Saltane, syne ego, slavnom i moguchem bogatyre kniaze Gvidone Saltanoviche, i prekrasnoi tsarevnoe-Lebedi,* illustrated by I. Golikov, *Skazki,* 7th ed., ed. A. Slonimskii with illustrations by various members of the Palekh artel'. The next year the Palekhians also illustrated a collection of Russian epic tales: *Bylini stariny* (Moscow, 1938). In 1939, the Palekhians illustrated: *Zazhglas' zolotaia zaria. Skazki i legendy* (Moscow: Academia, 1939); M. S. Kriukova, *Zaria-solnyshko. Skazanie* (Moscow-Leningrad: Academia, 1939); V. Porudominskii, "Chudo, sozdannoe revoliutsiei," *V mire knig,* no. 12 (1974): 77; Zhidkov, *Pushkin v iskusstve Palekha,* 158.

33. *Ivanovskii gorodskoi dvorets pionerov i shkol'nikov* (Ivanovo, 1989), 3; RGALI, *f.* 2322, *op.* 1, *d.* 62, *ll.* 1–2.

34. GAIO, *f.* 2969, *op.* 1, *d.* 48, *ll.* 1–7, 77, 85, 109, 143, 191; V. Kemenov, "Vystavka narodnogo tvorchestva," *Pravda,* January 13, 1937, 6; V. Kemenov, "Sokrovishcha russkogo narodnogo iskusstva," *Pravda,* March 17, 1937, 4; Natalia Sokolova, "Palekh, Mstera, Kholui. Vystavka narodnogo tvorchestva v Ivanovo," *Sovetskoe iskusstvo,* January 17, 1937, 2.

35. Sh. Niurenberg, "Pushkin i Paleshane," *Pravda,* October 14, 1936, 3.

36. GAIO, *f.* 2977, *op.* 1, *d.* 70, *ll.* 1, 7; *d.* 57, *l.* 2; *d.* 58, *ll.* 3, 12–13; *f.* R-2969, *d.* 49, *ll.* 6–7; ORGTG, *f.* 15, *d.* 590. *l.* 1; PAIO, *f.* 676, *op.* 1, *d.* 30, *l.* 22.

37. RGALI, *f.* 2322, *d.* 55, *l.* 4; GAIO, *f.* 2977, *op.* 1, *d.* 57, *ll.* 17–18, 20, 22; L. Fedder, "Podniatie Sovetskim Palekhom," *Rabochii krai,* January 21, 1937, 3.

38. GAIO, *f.* 2977, *op.* 1, *d.* 62, *ll.* 17, 33, 35; *d.* 59, *l.* 34.

39. Ganetskii, a Pole born in Warsaw, was posthumously rehabilitated after Stalin's death. For a biographical sketch, see R. A. Ermolaeva, "Iakov Stanislavovich Ganetskii" (k

85-letiiu so dnia rozhdeniia), *Voprosy istorii KPSS* (March 1964): 96–100.

40. GAIO, *f.* 2977, *op.* 1, *d.* 65, *ll.* 35–36, 42, 82.

41. PAIO, *f.* 676, *d.* 16, *ll.* 1, 11; *f.* 1070, *dd.* 1–4; Stephen Kotkin, *Magnetic Mountain: Stalinism as a Civilization* (Berkeley: University of California Press, 1995), 353; "Biografiia K. K. Evmenenko," *Tribuna Palekha,* November 26, 1950.

42. RGALI, *f.* 2322, *op.* 1, *d.* 123, *ll.* 134, 21–22; PAIO, *f.* 676, *d.* 23, *ll.* 15–16, 19; interview with Golikov.

43. PAIO, *f.* 676, *d.* 23, *ll.* 73, 79–80; *d.* 21, *l.* 116. Zhidkov was transferred to a curator's position at the Tret'iakov in Moscow in March 1938. The transfer not only allowed him to return to Moscow but freed him from the growing political storm in Palekh. From Moscow, Zhidkov continued to be an effective patron for Palekh until his death from a heart attack in 1953.

44. PAIO, *f.* 1070, *d.* 4, *ll.* 1–4; *f.* 676, *d.* 21, *ll.* 84, 207–9.

45. GAIO, *f.* 2977, *op.* 1, *d.* 61, *l.* 2. The church was converted into a warehouse, its icons removed, and its murals whitewashed. I. Elkhovikov, "Tiazhelye vremena," *Prizyv,* September 26, 1995, 2; "Pamiat' ob o. Ioanne Rozhdestvenskom," *Prizyv,* June 12, 1993, 3.

46. PAIO, *f.* 676, *d.* 23, *ll.* 103–5; *d.* 30, *ll.* 21–22, 180.

47. PAIO, *f.* 676, *d.* 30, *ll.* 100–2; GAIO, *f.* 2969, *op.* 1, *d.* 141, *l.* 26.

48. The material above is from an article about Zubkov's arrest by a reporter who was given permission to see Zubkov's NKVD file: Viktor Sokolov, "Sniav tiazhkii obet molchaniia . . . Delo No. 9734: Istoriia tragicheskoi gibeli predsedatelia palekhskoi 'Arteli drevnei zhivopisi' A. I. Zubkova," *Tribuna Palekha,* December 4, 1990, 3–6. The FSB, the KGB's successor, denied my request for access to Zubkov's case file.

49. GAIO, *f.* 2969, *op.* 1, *d.* 15, *ll.* 14–17; *d.* 91, *l.* 30.

50. For the appropriation of Nevskii as a symbol of a unified state, see Mikhail Heller and Aleksandr Nekrich, *Utopia in Power: The History of the Soviet Union from 1917 to the Present,* trans. Phyllis B. Carlos (New York: Summit Books, 1986), 296–98. Saint Nevskii's purge suggests the danger of applying the concept of a "Great Retreat" to Stalinist society.

51. PAIO, *f.* 1070, *d.* 5, *ll.* 5–6; *d.* 6, *l.* 6; *f.* 676, *d.* 38, *ll.* 20–21.

52. Interview with Mikhail Subbotin, May 6, 2000, Palekh.

53. GAIO, *f.* 2977, *op.* 1, *d.* 80, *l.* 1; RGALI, *f.* 2075, *op.* 7, *d.* 241, *ll.* 13–16.

54. "Slovo k molodym," 2.

55. GAIO, *f.* 2977, *op.* 1, *d.* 70, *ll.* 4–7, 14; RGALI, *f.* 2322, *op.* 1, *d.* 205, *ll.* 3–4, 7, 9–10.

56. GAIO, *f.* 2977, *op.* 1, *d.* 72, *l.* 20; *d.* 70, *ll.* 1–3. The following analysis is based on a comparison of the thematic plan for the 1939 exhibit (*f.* 2977, *op.* 1, *d.* 74, *ll.* 1–6) with the actual exhibit items as described in *Iskusstvo Palekha* (Moscow: Vsekokhudozhnik, 1939), 9–27.

57. GAIO, *f.* 2977, *op.* 1, *d.* 70, *ll.* 1–3; "Soviet Exposition Wins Great Praise," *New York Times,* August 2, 1939, 2; "New Editions, Fine and Otherwise," *New York Times,* August 13, 1939, BR9.

58. GAIO, *f.* 2977, *op.* 1, *d.* 74, *ll.* 8, 14.

59. PAIO, *f.* 676, *d.* 38, *l.* 319; GAIO, *f.* 2977, *op.* 1, *d.* 78, *l.* 3.

60. GAIO, *f.* 2977, *op.* 1, *d.* 74, *ll.* 31–43.

61. PAIO, *f.* 676, *d.* 38, *l.* 319; GAIO, *f.* 2977, *op.* 1, *d.* 78, *l.* 3; N. Blokhin, "Puti razvitiia palekhskogo iskusstva," *Rabochii krai,* November 28, 1939, 3; A. Romm, "Na rasput'i," *Sovetskoe iskusstvo,* December 14, 1939, 3; "Lacquer Art Shown in Soviet Exhibition: Many Artists Link Folklore to Modern War Instruments," *New York Times,* November 26, 1939, 42; M. P. Sokol'nikov, "Introduction," in *Iskusstvo Palekha* (Moscow, 1939),

4–6, 7–8; PAIO, *f.* 676, *d.* 49, *ll.* 70–71; GAIO, *f.* 2977, *op.* 1, *d.* 78, *l.* 3.

62. GAIO, *f.* 2977, *op.* 1, *d.* 71, *ll.* 17, 30; *d.* 76, *ll.* 9, 51–54.

63. PAIO, *f.* 676, *d.* 50, *ll.* 3–19.

64. GAIO, *f.* 2977, *op.* 1, *d.* 67, *ll.* 130, 127, 137; PAIO, *f.* 676, *d.* 72, *l.* 76.

65. Amir Weiner, *Making Sense of War: The Second World War and the Fate of the Bolshevik Revolution* (Princeton: Princeton University Press, 2001), 68.

6—SAVED BY THE WAR!

1. PAIO, *f.* 676, *d.* 72, *l.* 78.

2. Cited from NKVD reports on Korin published in V. I. Tereshkina, "' . . . Eto ne ukhodiashchaia Rus', a Rus' sushchestvuiushchaia . . . unichtozhit' ee nel'zia'. (P. D. Korin v doneseniiakh upravlenii NKVD—NKGB SSSR. 1941–1945 gg.)," *Otechestvennye arkhivy,* no. 2 (2000): 79; GMPI, *f.* Sobolevskii, *l.* 268.

3. GAIO, *f.* 2977, *op.* 1, *d.* 67, *l.* 124.

4. The ballet exceeded available resources and was temporarily shelved—indefinitely, as it turned out. Preparations for the ballet were also reported in the September 11, 1942, edition of *Vecherniaia Moskva.* GAIO, *f.* 372, *op.* 2, *d.* 1, *l.* 1; G. N. Dobrovol'skaia, *Baletmeister Leonid Iakobson* (Leningrad: Iskusstvo, 1968), 29; PAIO, *f.* 676, *d.* 62, *l.* 20; *d.* 72, *ll.* 76, 79–80; "War's Story Told in Russian Ballet," *New York Times,* February 4, 1943, 20.

5. GAIO, *f.* 2977, *op.* 1, *d.* 67, *ll.* 122–24; PAIO, *f.* 676, *d.* 86, *l.* 244; *d.* 62, *ll.* 19–20; RGALI, *f.* 2322, *op.* 1, *d.* 174, *l.* 10.

6. RGALI, *f.* 2322, *d.* 174, *l.* 9; N. Bariutin, "Rabota Palekhskogo muzeia v dni otechestvennoi voiny," *Tribuna Palekha,* August 19, 1943, 2.

7. N. Bariutin, "Tvorcheskii put' narodnogo khudozhnika," *Tribuna Palekha,* November 25, 1943, 2; PAIO, *f.* 1070, *d.* 7, *l.* 31; *f.* 676, *d.* 72, *l.* 80.

8. GAIO, *f.* 2969, *op.* 1, *d.* 103, *l.* 3; M. Shoshin, "Palekh v dni voiny," *Rabochii krai,* January 18, 1943, 2.

9. GAIO, *f.* 2969, *op.*1, *d.* 90, *ll.* 2–3, 14, 18, 21, 27, 38; *d.* 95, *l.* 7; *f.* 372, *op.* 1, *d.* 29, *l.* 5; RGALI, *f.* 2322, *d.* 174, *l.* 7; PAIO, *f.* 676, *d.* 72, *l.* 78.

10. GAIO, *f.* 2977, *op.* 1, *d.* 91, *l.* 3; PAIO, *f.* 676, *d.* 72, *l.* 21; GAIO, *f.* 2969, *op.* 1, *d.* 103, *l.* 10; *f.* 372, *d.* 33, *op.* 2, *l.* 7; *f.* 2875, *op.* 3, *d.* 376, *l.* 1.

11. GAIO, *f.* 2977, *op.* 1, *d.* 86, *ll.* 46, 117, 120; PAIO, *f.* 676, *d.* 143, *l.* 30; N. N. Ivanova, "Izdeliia narodnykh khudozhestvennykh promyslov na mezhdunarodnykh vystavkakh," in *Sbornik trudov,* vyp. 3, of the Nauchno-issledovatel'skii institut khudozhestvennoi promyshlennosti (Moscow: Legkaia industriia, 1966), 5, 9–10.

12. This policy of preservation was explicitly extended to the preservation of Russian Orthodox churches. Alexander Werth, *Russia at War, 1941–1945* (New York: Avon Books, 1964), 406.

13. Authorities shut down the journal *Sovetskoe kraevedenie* in the mid-1930s and arrested its leading representatives as apologists for the old regime who hid "under the flag of preserving monuments of antiquity," according to an article in the journal in 1932, which was quoted in L. Klein, *Fenomen Sovetskoi arkheologii* (St. Petersburg: FARN, 1993), 20; Bobrov, *Istoriia restavratsii,* 71; Vzdornov, *Obshchestvo "Ikona" v Parizhe,* 1:21.

14. On the sale of Russian cultural artifacts from 1928–1938, see "The Trade: Russian Art and Western Money, 1928–1938" and "Selling the Romanov Treasure," in Robert C. Williams, *Russia Imagined: Art, Culture, and National Identity, 1840–1995* (New York: P. Lang, 1997), 215–49.

15. Igor' Grabar', *O drevnerusskom iskusstve. Issledovaniia, restavratsiia, i okhrana pamiatnikov* (Moscow: Sovetskii khudozhnik, 1966), 10 n. 15, 23; Werth, *Russia at War, 1941–1945*, 402–10.

16. Tereshkina, "Eto ne ukhodiashchaia Rus'," 72.

17. Tereshkina, "Eto ne ukhodiashchaia Rus'," 73, 85.

18. Tereshkina, "Eto ne ukhodiashchaia Rus'," 73; see previous chapter for the 1939 icon purge following the purge of Zubkov, chairman of the cooperative.

19. Tereshkina, "Eto ne ukhodiashchaia Rus'," 92.

20. N. Kolygina, "Ne v spore rozhdaetsia iskusstvo," *Prizyv*, April 25, 1995, 1; RGALI, *f*. 2075, *op*. 7, *d*. 334, *ll*. 6, 8; GAIO, *f*. 2969, *op*. 1, *d*. 109, *l*. 3; PAIO, *f*. 1070, *d*. 7, *l*. 34.

21. K. Pomerantsev, "Okhraniaite pamiatniki narodnogo tvorchestva," *Tribuna Palekha*, June 25, 1943, 2; Tereshkina, "Eto ne ukhodiashchaia Rus'," 89; Bariutin, "Rabota Palekhskogo muzeia," 2.

22. GAIO, *f*. 2969, *op*. 1, *d*. 99, *ll*. 6–7, 12; *d*. 108, *ll*. 17–19; *d*. 116, *ll*. 6, 20, 23, 90, 95–96; *d*. 125, *ll*. 201–2.

23. GAIO, *f*. 2969, *op*. 1, *d*. 108, *ll*. 28, 34, 37; PAIO, *f*. 676, *d*. 86, *l*. 244.

24. GAIO, *f*. 2977, *op*. 1, *d*. 91, *l*. 28; *d*. 99, *ll*. 16, 34–35; *d*. 67, *l*. 122; PAIO, *f*. 676, *d*. 111, *ll*. 99–100, 120; E. Miliutina, "V dome osnovatelia palekhskogo iskusstva," *Prizyv*, April 25, 1995, 2.

25. N. Bushkova, "On obladal udivitel'no zorkim glazom," *Prizyv*, July 2, 1994, 3; A. Lapenko, "Palekhskii samorodok," *Prizyv*, December 4, 1993, 2.

26. Bushkova, "On obladal udivitel'no zorkim glazom," 3; Lapenko, "Palekhskii samorodok," 2.

27. GAIO, *f*. 372, *op*. 1, *d*. 33, *l*. 2; N. Zinov'ev, "Tvorchestvo P. D. Bazhenova," *Tribuna Palekha*, May 1, 1945, 2; interview with Anna Aleksandrovna Kotukhina, January 15, 2000, Palekh.

28. GAIO, *f*. 372, *op*. 1, *d*. 29, *l*. 14; *f*. 2977, *op*. 1, *d*. 94, *ll*. 89–91.

29. GAIO, *f*. 2976, *op*. 2, *d*. 2, *ll*. 2, 5; PAIO, *f*. 676, *d*. 96, *l*. 110; RGALI, *f*. 2075, *op*. 5, *d*. 51, *ll*. 45, 47, 49, 54–59.

30. The first four women entered the Palekh art school in 1930. V. A. Guliaev, "Palekhskii artel' drevnei zhivopisi v 1920-e gody (po arkhivnym materialam Ivanovskoi oblasti)," in *Sbornik trudov*, vyp. 6, of the Nauchno-issledovatel'lskii institut khudozhestvennoi promyshlennosti (Moscow, 1972), 35; RGALI, *f*. 2322, *d*. 175, *ll*. 1–2; GMPI, *f*. Sobolevskii, *l*. 249.

31. Pirogova, *Palekh. Istoriia i sovremennost'*, 183–84, 189; L. Mel'nikova, "Zhivaia istoriia palekhskogo iskusstva," *Prizyv*, June 10, 1995, 2; G. Zhidkov, "Laki," *Iskusstvo*, no. 2 (March–April 1947): 34, 35; RGALI, *f*. 2322, *op*. 1, *d*. 110, *l*. 1, 18.

32. RGALI, *f*. 2075, *op*. 5, *d*. 51, *ll*. 10, 54.

33. A. Kotukhina, "Khudozhniki Palekha v dni voiny," *Tribuna Palekha*, May 5, 1942, 2; V. Kotov, "Zhivoe iskusstvo. K iubileiu narodnogo khudozhnika SSSR Anny Aleksandrovny Kotukhinoi," *Prizyv*, June 6, 1995, 2.

34. Interview with Kotukhina.

35. Kotov, "Zhivoe iskusstvo," 2.

36. Kotukhina also did the cover art for the March 1943 issue of *Krasnoarmeets* and the October 1943 issue of *Krasnoflotets*. N. Bariutin, "Molodye khudozhniki Palekha," *Komsomol'skaia pravda*, March 4, 1944, 4.

37. Interview with Kotukhina; L. Mel'nikova, "Zhivaia istoriia palekhskogo iskusstva," *Prizyv*, June 10, 1995, 2; Kotov, "Zhivoe iskusstvo," 2.

38. The term came from the journal *Sovetskoe iskusstvo* in February 1945. In the art of the Palekh master Aristarkh Dydykin, it noted, "one can easily detect the features of

authentic nationality *(narodnost')*. They emerge from the ancient Novgorod images." Interestingly, the article linked "authentic nationality" to Novgorod, with its supposedly democratic traditions, rather than to Muscovy, its successor and vanquisher. "Vystavka rabot masterov Palekha," *Sovetskoe iskusstvo,* February 13, 1945, 3.

39. Shoshin, "Palekh v dni voiny," 2; GAIO, *f.* 1010, *op.* 1, *d.* 201, *ll.* 1–7.

40. PAIO, *f.* 1070, *d.* 7, *l.* 27; Marc Garcelon, "The Shadow of the Leviathan: Public and Private in Communist and Post-Communist Society," in *Public and Private in Thought and Practice: Perspectives on a Grand Dichotomy,* ed. Jeff Weintraub and Krishan Kumar (Chicago: University of Chicago Press, 1997), 303–32.

41. GAIO, *f.* 2969, *op.* 1, *d.* 71, *ll.* 93–94.

42. ORGTG, *f.* 15, *d.* 231, *l.* 2; Natalia Sokolova, "Palekh, Mstera, Kholui: Vystavka narodnogo tvorchestva v Ivanovo," *Sovetskoe iskusstvo,* January 17, 1937, 2; RGALI, *f.* 2322, *op.* 1, *d.* 77, *ll.* 23, 46.

43. Treat, "With the Peasant Painters of Palek," 335.

44. N. Bariutin, "Mastera stil'nogo portreta," *Rabochii krai,* April 26, 1944, 3.

45. PAIO, *f.* 1070, *d.* 7, *l.* 25; GAIO, *f.* 2977, *op.* 1, *d.* 137, *l.* 46. Bariutin first discussed Butorin's use of traditional religious icon-painting techniques to paint the image of Stalin in "Dmitrii Nikolaevich Butorin," *Tribuna Palekha,* October 14, 1943, 2. Five months later, an article on Palekh portraiture noted (in an asterisk) that the portions of its article exploring Palekh's attempt to paint Stalin using the techniques of ancient Russian icon painting were to have been included in the earlier article but had been edited out. ("Mastera stil'nogo portreta," 2.) The later article also reflected the draft in Bariutin's personal archive. (RGALI, *f.* 2283, *op.* 1, *d.* 8, *l.* 27.) Though Bariutin did not elaborate, anyone reading the later article in March 1944 would have understood that a fundamental shift in attitude toward the Palekh style and *vozhd'* iconography had occurred. The later article, which included the more detailed discussion, was also reprinted in the Ivanovo oblast' newspaper *Rabochii krai,* April 26, 1944, 3. *Literatura i iskusstvo,* however, refused to publish the piece, saying simply that it was "too general, not for a specialist audience." GAIO, *f.* 2969, *op.* 1, *d.* 107, *l.* 14.

46. By January 1, Butorin had changed the name of his box on Stalin from *The Organizer of Victories* to *The Generalissimo of Victories.* N. Bariutin, "Khudozhniki patrioty," *Rabochii krai,* January 12, 1946, 3.

47. RGALI, *f.* 2283, *op.* 1, *d.* 8, *l.* 27.

48. "Novaia rabota paleshan," *Komsomol'skaia pravda,* July 27, 1946, 3.

49. GAIO, *f.* 2977, *op.* 2, *d.* 45, *l.* 3.

50. Interview with Kotukhina.

51. GAIO, *f.* 2977, *op.* 1, *d.* 91, *ll.* 2–3; *[Vos'maia] 8-ia oblastnaia khudozhestvennaia vystavka. Katalog* (Ivanovo, 1945–1946), 14–16. Historical figures (Minin and Pozharskii, Donskoi, Nevskii) and folklore *(bogatyri,* the golden cockerel, the snow-maiden, the firebird) dominated Palekh's contribution.

52. GAIO, *f.* 2977, *op.* 1, *d.* 86, *l.* 42; *d.* 91, *ll.* 2–3; *d.* 96, *ll.* 46–49; *d.* 99, *ll.* 8, 11; *d.* 105, *ll.* 19–20, 58–62.

53. GAIO, *f.* 2977, *op.* 1, *d.* 89, *ll.* 33–36; *d.* 86, *l.* 6; *f.* 2969, *op.* 1, *d.* 103, *l.* 3.

54. PAIO, *f.* 1070, *d.* 7, *ll.* 19, 34–35; *f.* 676, *d.* 94, *ll.* 28–29; *d.* 96, *l.* 110; GAIO, *f.* 2977, *op.* 1, *d.* 99, *ll.* 8, 11, 33.

55. GAIO, *f.* 2977, *op.* 1, *d.* 89, *l.* 2.

56. GAIO, *f.* 2977, *op.* 1, *d.* 91, *ll.* 7, 10, 12, 17, 18, 19; PAIO, *f.* 1070, *d.* 7, *ll.* 35, 36.

57. On the confusion this policy caused in the Ukraine, see Weiner, *Making Sense of War,* 310–12.

58. Weiner, *Making Sense of War,* 310; Dimitry Pospielovsky, *The Orthodox Church in the History of Russia* (Crestwood, N.Y.: St. Vladimir's Seminary Press, 1998), 286; T. A. Chumachenko, *Gosudarstvo, pravoslavnaia tserkov', veruiushchie, 1941–1961gg.* (Moscow: AIRO-XX, 1999), 69, 71, 228, 231.

59. GAIO, *f.* 2953, *op.* 1, *d.* 269, *ll.* 1, 4–5, 11–14.

60. PAIO, *f.* 1070, *d.* 9, *l.* 7.

61. RGALI, *f.* 2283, *op.* 1, *d.* 15, *ll.* 7–8, 21–22.

62. Tereshkina, "Eto ne ukhodiashchaia Rus'," 82.

63. Weiner refers to the phenomenon of "hierarchical heroism," in which "the various nations of the Soviet Union were ranked in a pyramid-like order based on their alleged contributions to the war effort." Weiner, *Making Sense of War,* 208.

7—THE CULTURAL TRANSFORMATION CONTINUES, 1947–1958

1. GAIO, *f.* 2977, *op.* 2, *d.* 39, *l.* 1.

2. PAIO, *f.* 1070, *d.* 23, *l.* 25.

3. GAIO, *f.* 2977, *op.* 1, *d.* 99, *l.* 34.

4. William O. McCagg, *Stalin Embattled, 1943–1948* (Detroit: Wayne State University Press, 1978); Werner G. Hahn, *Postwar Soviet Politics: The Fall of Zhdanov and the Defeat of Moderation, 1946–1953* (Ithaca, N.Y.: Cornell University Press, 1982). For an intriguing discussion of the Zhdanov/Beria conflict, see David Brandenberger, "Stalin, the Leningrad Affair, and the Limits of Postwar Russocentrism," *Russian Review* 63 (April 2004): 241–55.

5. RGASPI, *f.* 17, *op.* 132, *d.* 245, *ll.* 11, 98–102, 127–30; John Dunlop, *The Faces of Contemporary Russian Nationalism* (Princeton: Princeton University Press, 1983), 83.

6. RGALI, *f.* 2283, *op.* 1, *d.* 98, *l.* 2, 4–6; *d.* 220, *l.* 1; Kotov, "Zhivoe iskusstvo," 2.

7. Speech of V. T. Kotov, "Sovremennoe iskusstvo i traditsiia," September 39, 1998, Palekh. From a tape recording in the private archive of Mikhail Larionov; RGALI, *f.* 2322, *op.* 1, *d.* 110, *ll.* 13–14, 16–18, 22, 25; GARF, *f.* A-396, *op.* 1, *d.* 325, *ll.* 5–8, 149–52, 160–63, 222, 244–46; "Vozhrozhdennyi Palekh," *Rabochii krai,* October 15, 1947.

8. RGASPI, *f.* 17, *op.* 125, *d.* 569, *ll.* 197–98, 204; RGALI, *f.* 2075, *op.* 5, *d.* 51, *l.* 35.

9. GAIO, *f.* 2977, *op.* 1, *d.* 99; *d.* 129, *l.* 59; RGASPI, *f.* 17, *op.* 132, *d.* 245, *l.* 138; GAIO, *f.* 2977, *op.* 2, *d.* 6, passim; *d.* 9, *l.* 9; *d.* 10, *ll.* 5–6; *d.* 17, *ll.* 7–10; *d.* 18, *ll.* 1, 19; V. Kotov, "Khudozhniki obsuzhdaiut raboty," *Tribuna Palekha,* February 9, 1956, 2.

10. Among the twenty-eight "creative works" for 1948 were *Liberation of the Village, Stalin Raising a Toast to the Russian People,* numerous portraits of Stalin (in a strictly realistic style), *The Union of Indestructible Republics, A Call for Competition, The Pilot, The Taking of Berlin, Parachutists, On the Road to Berlin, Attacking the Enemy,* and *Partisans.* At the same time, many fairy-tale and Russian folklore themes were also represented as "creative works," including the repertoire of Pushkin fairy tales. By the mid-1950s, folkloric themes and fairy tales again eclipsed modern socialist themes in the cooperative's "creative works," just as such subject matter dominated *"massovka."* GAIO, *f.* 2977, *op.* 1, *d.* 129, *ll.* 9–10; GAIO, *f.* 2977, *op.* 3, *d.* 14, *ll.* 7–9.

11. GAIO, *f.* 2977, *op.* 1, *d.* 107, *ll.* 5, 69–70, 108–9.

12. Party rules on censorship in the Stalin era contributed to this situation. Although a party report on censorship of artistic production in August 1951 explicitly excluded arts and crafts industries from formal censorship, the folk art items themselves were, of course, still subject to review by the art committees of the artistic collectives and the overseeing bodies in Moscow. It is unclear why the party excluded such a large

category of artistic production from the systems of censorship applied to more conventional easel art. Perhaps it was another reflection of the regime's own inability to grapple with the ideological significance of folk art. RGASPI, *f.* 17, *op.* 133, *d.* 374, *l.* 36; *f.* 17, *op.* 133, *d.* 335, *ll.* 87–88, 91.

13. N. P. Zimarina, ed., *Russkii rubl'. Dva veka istorii, XIX–XX vv.* (Moscow: "Progress-Akademiia," 1994), 250–51.

14. GAIO, *f.* 2977, *op.* 1, *d.* 109, *l.* 28; *d.* 123, *l.* 29; *d.* 117, *l.* 44; Zimarina, *Russkii rubl'*, 250; RGASPI, *f.* 17, *op.* 125, *d.* 572, *ll.* 75–76, 83.

15. GAIO, *f.* 2977, *op.* 1, *d.* 110, *l.* 60; *d.* 117, *ll.* 20–21.

16. GAIO, *f.* 2977, *op.* 1, *d.* 107, *ll.* 74–75.

17. GAIO, *f.* 2977, *op.* 1, *d.* 132, *ll.* 25–26, 32.

18. PAIO, *f.* 676, *d.* 170, *l.* 68; GAIO, *f.* 2977, *op.* 1, *d.* 123, *ll,* 42–43, 66; *f.* 372, *op.* 1, *d.* 6, *l.* 22.

19. GARF, *f.* A-643, *op.* 1, *d.* 351, *ll.* 5–6, 10–11, 38, 41–42, 49–57, 60–61, 67–68, 82.

20. GMPI, visitor comment books (*knigi otzyvov,* hereafter *kn. ot.*) for a traveling exhibit of Palekh art in Iaroslavl', June 1949, *l.* 7; *kn. ot.* for traveling exhibit in the city of Molotov, July 1949, *ll.* 2, 5-7, 10, 13, 16, 21; *kn. ot.,* July 1947 *l.* 31; *kn. ot.,* March 1948, traveling exhibit in Shuia, *l.* 12.

21. PAIO, *f.* 676, *d.* 196, *ll.* 193–94; GAIO, *f.* 2977, *op.* 1, *d.* 133, *ll.* 8–9; G. Gorbunov, "Palekhskim khudozhnikam nuzhna pomoshch'," *Rabochii krai,* December 14, 1948, 3.

22. RGASPI, *f.* 17, *op.* 132, *d.* 245, *ll.* 153–54.

23. N. Sobolevskii, "Vystavka 'Pushkin v proizvedeniakh narodnykh masterov RS-FSR'," *Sovetskaia etnografiia,* no. 4 (1949): 196–99; B. S. Pushkarev, *Kommunisticheskii rezhim i narodnoe soprotivlenie v Rossii, 1917–1991,* 2nd ed. (Moscow: "Posev," 1998), 27.

24. Works included: Stalin in the center of an oval lacquer, surrounded by an inner circle of Politburo members and an outer circle of various nationalities; Stalin overseeing a military parade on Red Square; Stalin toasting the Russian people and their victory over the Nazis; Stalin the great teacher of adolescent youth; Stalin as wartime leader. D. Semenovskii, "Obraz velikogo vozhdia v tvorchestve paleshan," *Rabochii krai,* December 21, 1949, 3.

25. A. Isaichev, "Paleshane—v dar vozhdiu," *Rabochii krai,* December 18, 1949, 3; L. Aleksandrov, "Khudozhniki Palekha—k velikoi date," *Tribuna Palekha,* December 15, 1949, 2; GAIO, *f.* 2977, *op.* 1, *d.* 138, *l.* 2.

26. Interviews in Palekh with Golikov, May 15, 2000; Aleksei Dmitrievich Kochupalov, July 15, 2001; Vadim Grigor'evich Zotov, August 31, 2001; Irina Vadimovna Livanova, August 31, 2001; K. Bokarev, "A chto budet zavtra?" *Prizyv,* July 1, 1993, 1–2; M. A. Nekrasova, *Iskusstvo Palekha* (Moscow: Sovetskii khudozhnik, 1966), and *Narodnoe iskusstvo kak chast' kul'tury. Teoriia i praktika* (Moscow: Izobrazitel'noe iskusstvo, 1983).

27. RGALI, *f.* 2075, *op.* 7, *d.* 291, *ll.* 10, 13–17, 51–52, 132–33, 146, 154–56, 194; GAIO, *f.* 2977, *op.* 2, *d.* 10, *l.* 6; PAIO, *f.* 1070, *d.* 19, *ll.* 30, 32; *d.* 17, *l.* 12; *d.* 19, *l.* 30.

28. GAIO, *f.* 2977, *op.* 1, *d.* 133, *ll.* 30–31; *f.* 2976, *op.* 2, *d.* 5, 12; GMPI, *f.* Sobolevskii, unpublished autobiography of I. V. Markichev, *l.* 277; GAIO, *f.* 2977, *op.* 1, *d.* 133, *l.* 4.

29. V. Kotov, "Zashchita diplomnykh rabot vypusknikami khudozh. uchilishcha," *Tribuna Palekha,* July 8, 1954, 2; PAIO, *f.* 2487, *d.* 9, *l.* 16; K. Bokarev, "Vremia vse rasstavit na svoi mesta, no luchshe, esli my sdelaem eto sami," *Prizyv,* May 12, 1999, 3; "Novye raboty khudozhnikov-frontovikov," *Tribuna Palekha,* May 13, 1949, 2.

30. Gorbunov, *Palekh,* 88–89.

31. GAIO, *f.* 2976, *op.* 2, *d.* 5, *l.* 2; Gorbunov, *Palekh,* 95–97; K. V'iugin, ed., *Sovetskaia tema v iskusstve Palekha* (Shuia, 1960), 19; A. Kovalev, "Volnuiushchaia tema," *Prizyv,* May 7, 1970, 2; GMPI, *f.* Sobolevskii, *ll.* 231, 233–34, 236–37.

32. V. Dudorov, "Tvorcheskie uspekhi khudozhnikov," *Tribuna Palekha,* November 7, 1953, 2.

33. RGALI, *f.* 2075, *op.* 7, *d.* 425, *ll.* 27–28.

34. GAIO, *f.* 2977, *op.* 1, *d.* 140, *ll.* 144–47, 148.

35. GAIO, *f.* 2977, *op.* 2, *d.* 9, *ll.* 53–58.

36. S. Iurov, "Samobytnoe iskusstvo," *Leninets,* August 1, 1954, 3.

37. Vitalii Kotov, "Vzgliad skvoz' gody," *Prizyv,* April 3, 1998, 3.

38. PAIO, *f.* 2487, *op.* 1, *d.* 9, *ll.* 3–4, 7, 15–18, 25, 30–35, 37–38, 46; GAIO, *f.* 2976, *op.* 2, *d.* 12, *l.* 4; N. Sobolevskii, "Khudozhestvennye laki," *Iskusstvo,* no. 3 (1952): 69; GAIO, *f.* 2977, *op.* 2, *d.* 10, *ll.* 1–4.

39. Solov'ev was relieved temporarily from his position (for the second time for drunkenness!) and given an official party censure. PAIO, *f.* 676, *d.* 276, *ll.* 21–22; RGALI, *f.* 2075, *op.* 7, *d.* 291, *l.* 154; S. Iurov, "Samobytnoe iskusstvo," *Leninets,* August 1, 1954, 3.

40. RGALI, *f.* 2907, *op.* 1, *d.* 46, *l.* 25.

41. RGALI, *f.* 2283, *op.* 1, *d.* 97, *l.* 1; "Pamiatnik V. I., Leninu v Palekhe," *Rabochii krai,* August 30, 1956, 1; G. Gorbunov, "Torzhestva v Palekhe," *Rabochii krai,* August 26, 1956, 3.

42. There had been earlier versions of such a bureau (1926–1927, 1936–1937), but they were short-lived. Immediately after the war, a new attempt to create such a bureau was made but failed due to Stalin's resistance. See Terry Martin, *The Affirmative-Action Empire: Nations and Nationalism in the Soviet Union* (Ithaca, N.Y.: Cornell University Press, 2001), 394–401, 414; Brandenberger, "Stalin, the Leningrad Affair, and the Limits of Postwar Russocentrism," 248–53.

43. *Iskusstvo Palekha v muzeiakh RSFSR. Katalog,* 3, 50–51, 17–46, 55–56, 14; GAIO, *f.* 372, *op.* 1, *d.* 15, *l.* 6; *d.* 32, *ll.* 7, 10, 13; V. Kotov, "Rastet interes k Palekhskomu iskusstvu," *Tribuna Palekha,* June 17, 1956; P. Solonin, "Uspekhi peredvizhnoi vystavki palekhskogo iskusstva," *Rabochii krai,* June 29, 1956, 4.

44. Gorbunov, *Palekh.* The art critic Sobolevskii also collected materials for another collection of Palekh autobiographies, which for reasons that are unclear, was not published. It is contained in the State Museum of Palekh Art archive (*fond* Sobolevskii).

45. Gorbunov, *Palekh,* 63.

46. GAIO, *f.* 2977, *op.* 3, *d.* 14, *ll.* 7, 9, 20, 30, 38, 39, 45; *d.* 15, *ll.* 7, 28; *d.* 16, *ll.* 1, 10.

47. GAIO, *f.* 2976, *op.* 2, *d.* 20, *l.* 58; V'iugin, *Sovetskaia tema,* 13, 18, 37. The box of Stalin was a portrait from 1951 by the artist N. A. Pravdin. In May 2000 the director of the State Museum of Palekh Art proudly informed me that the Palekh museum, unlike many of its counterparts, did not destroy its collection of works depicting Stalin after the "secret speech."

48. Kotov's idea was not far-fetched. As noted in chapter 2, many young Palekh masters circa 1900 were profoundly influenced by the so-called Wanderers and the neorealist Viktor Vasnetsov.

49. V. Kotov, "Iskusstvo Sovetskogo Palekha," *Kommuna,* September 22, 1954, 3; V'iugin, *Sovetskaia tema,* 6–10.

50. Opposing interpretations of the life and work of Ivan Golikov followed a similarly selective interpretation of his oeuvre. One group of art critics chose the works with modern content as the essence of his creative legacy, while others completely ignored those works and focused only on the works that adhered to a supposedly authentic

ancient Russian style and rural imagery. For Golikov the bard of Soviet modernity, see Reinson-Pravdin, *Ivan Ivanovich Golikov.* For Golikov the preserver of the ancient traditions, see M. Nekrasova, "Khudozhnik-Poet," *Dekorativnoe iskusstvo SSSR,* no. 8 (1958): 33–38.

51. Khrushchev's speech to the Twentieth Party Congress, quoted in Bohdan Nahaylo and Victor Swoboda, *Soviet Disunion: A History of the Nationalities Problem in the USSR* (New York: Free Press, 1990), 118.

52. Nahaylo and Swoboda, *Soviet Disunion,* 120.

53. GAIO, *f.* 2977, *op.* 2, *d.* 38, *l.* 29; *d.* 20, *ll.* 3–6; GMPI, *f.* Sobolevskii, *l.* 241.

8—TRIUMPH, COLLAPSE, AND REGENERATION, 1958–2001

1. Andrei Amalrik, *Will the Soviet Union Survive until 1984?* (New York: Harper & Row, 1970), 39. On the alliance between intelligentsia nationalists and party elites, see also Brudny, *Reinventing Russia.*

2. K. Aimermakher, ed., *Ideologicheskie komissii TsK KPSS, 1958–1964. Dokumenty* (ROSSPEN: Moscow, 1998), 7, 12, 326, 328.

3. On empty rituals and the lack of the population's identification with public Soviet culture, see Christel Lane, *The Rites of Rulers: Ritual in Industrial Society—The Soviet Case* (London: Cambridge University Press, 1981), 240–41, 249; Vladimir Shlapentokh, *Public and Private Life of the Soviet People: Changing Values in Post-Stalin Russia* (New York: Oxford University Press, 1989), 12–15.

4. V. Kotov, "Est' li budushchee u sela-akademii?" *Prizyv,* January 5, 1995, 2; K. Aimermakher, "Partiinoe upravlenie kul'turoi i formy ee samoorganizatsii (1953–1964/67)," in his *Ideologicheskie komissii TsK KPSS, 1958–1964,* 7, 12; Tereshkina, "Eto ne ukhodhiashchaia Rus'," 75.

5. "Problemy sovremennogo Palekha: Kruglyi stol," *Dekorativnoe iskusstvo SSSR,* no. 12 (1974): 10; Nikolai Radichev, "Gnezdo zhar-ptitsy," *Sovetskaia kul'tura,* November 19, 1974; V. Mazur in "Nuzhen li nimb Iude?" *Prizyv,* April 15, 1997, 3.

6. Frank Ninkovich, "Culture, Power, and Civilization: The Place of Culture in the Study of International Relations," in *On Cultural Ground: Essays in International History,* ed. Robert David Johnson (Chicago: Imprint Publications, 1994), 12; N. N. Ivanova, "Izdeliia narodnykh khudozhestvennykh promyslov na mezhdunarodnykh vystavkakh," *Sbornik trudov,* vyp. 3, of the Nauchno-issledovatel'skii institut khudozhestvennoi promyshlennosti (Moscow: Legkaia industriia, 1966), 6–7, 9; Kotov, "Est' li budushchee u sela-akademii?"; GMPI, *kn. ot.* 1962–1964, *l.* 117. Palekh in 1960 was exhibited, among other places, in East Germany, Iraq, Italy, Romania, Ethiopia, Hungary, Norway, Poland, China, Afghanistan, Austria, Syria, Bulgaria, Yugoslavia, Tunisia, Indonesia, Turkey, and Czechoslovakia. In 1963, Palekh produced lacquer boxes for sixty-three international exhibits in countries including East Germany, Australia, Hungary, Poland, Syria, Canada, Turkey, Afghanistan, Czechoslovakia, Yugoslavia, Austria, Greece, Italy, Finland, Tunisia, Pakistan, Mali, and Burma. GAIO, *f.* 2977, *op.* 3, *d.* 74, *l.* 1; *d.* 42, *l.* 20; *op.* 4, *d.* 17, *l.* 72; PAIO, *f.* 676, *d.* 346, *ll.* 105.

7. GAIO, *f.* 2977, *op.* 3, *d.* 94, *ll.* 52, 57, 60; *d.* 96, *l.* 25; *d.* 99, *ll.* 49, 51, 16; Nekrasova, "Ot miniatiura k stenopisi"; GARF, *f.* A-10004, *op.* 1, *d.* 3, *l.* 2; *d.* 7, *ll.* 8–9, 11; *d.* 10, *l.* 1; *d.* 11, *ll.* 33, 35, 60, 200, 202, 225; *d.* 21, *ll.* 48, 50; interview with Aleksei Gennad'evich Smirnov, July 14, 2001, Palekh; GAIO, *f.* 2977, *op.* 3, *d.* 99, *ll.* 15, 83–84; GMPI, *kn. ot.* 1960–1962, *l.* 43.

8. RGANI, *f.* 5, *op.* 37, *d.* 98, *ll.* 52–62; GAIO, *f.* 372, *op.* 1, *d.* 11, *l.* 1.

9. Priscilla Johnson and Leopold Labedz, eds., *Khrushchev and the Arts: The Politics*

of Soviet Culture, 1962–1964 (Cambridge, Mass.: M.I.T. Press, 1965), 32, 106, 174; "Sergei Khruschev Repays Gift of Butterflies with Box of Them," *New York Times,* January 21, 1960, 33; "Russia Offers Art for London Sale," *New York Times,* May 6, 1963, 31.

10. PAIO, *f. 676, d. 379, ll.* 169–73. The Palekh party archive in the post-Stalin era is full of lurid stories about the drunken escapades and dalliances of leading Palekh artists.

11. Iu. Birev, "Vecherom," *Tribuna Palekha,* March 26, 1961, 3; PAIO, *f. 676, d. 379, ll.* 169–73.

12. "V nikh russkii dukh, v nikh Rus'iu pakhnet," *Rabochi krai,* January 28, 1964, 4.

13. V. Kotov, "Palekhskii gerb. Kakim emu byt'?" *Prizyv,* January 29, 1991, 2–3; GAIO, *f.* 2977, *op.* 4, *d.* 34, *l.* 87; GARF, *f.* 501, *op.* 1, *d.* 5019, *l.* 2.

14. Interview with Kochupalov.

15. M. Nekrasova, "Vtoroe rozhdenie," *Prizyv,* February 3, 1994, 2–3; Viktor Golov, "Palekh: Upadok ili vozrozhdenie?" *Prizyv,* July 4, 1995, 2; Nekrasova, "Poetika Palekha," *Sovetskaia kul'tura,* December 8, 1964, 3, and "Predmet i miniatiura," *Dekorativnoe iskusstvo SSSR,* no. 2 (1959): 17–20.

16. Dunlop, *Faces of Contemporary Russian Nationalism,* 67–68; unpublished paper by the Palekhian Valerii Iuskov, May 31, 1997, in the private archive of Mikhail Larionov; Vzdornov, *Obshchestvo "Ikona" v Parizhe,* 1:22.

17. Dunlop, *Faces of Contemporary Russian Nationalism,* 64–66, 72–75, and *The New Russian Nationalism* (New York, Praeger, 1985), 2–3, 10–14.

18. P. Korin, "Palekhu 40 let," *Dekorativnoe iskusstvo SSSR,* no. 12 (1964): 1; "Ulitsa Palekhskaia v Moskve," *Prizyv,* February 16, 1988, 4; Pavel Solonin, *Zdravstvyui, Palekh! Liricheskie etiudy o masterakh russkikh lakov iz malen'kogo poselka sredinnoi Rossii* (Iaroslavl': Verkhne-Volzhskoe knizhnoe izdatel'stvo, 1974), 157–58; Iu. Rudnitskaia, review of Aleksandr Navozov, *Palekhskoe chudo. Rasskazy o khudozhnikakh* (Iaroslavl': Verkhne-Volzhskoe knizhnoe izdatel'stvo, 1970) in *Don,* no. 2 (1972): 185, 187; G. Sukharev, "Odno iz chudes . . .," *Volga,* no. 7 (1971): 172; Iurii Melent'ev, "Bylinnost' i ogon' sovremennosti," *Ogonek,* no. 50 (1974): 8.

19. Radichev, "Gnezdo zhar-ptitsy," 5; "Art Form Evolves From Icon-Painting," *New York Times,* June 24, 1973, 4; *Rabochii krai,* December 13, 1974, 2; "Radio Schedule," *New York Times,* March 14, 1975, 79.

20. V. Babkin, "Iskusstvennye 'rody,'" *Prizyv,* March 17, 1994, 2.

21. Interview with the Palekh master Boris Kukuliev, May 30, 2000, Palekh; Radichev, "Gnezdo zhar-ptitsy," 5.

22. Interview with Valerii Konstantinovich Bokarev, August 4, 2001, Palekh.

23. "Slovo k molodym," 2; Shlapentokh, *Public and Private Life of the Soviet People,* 13; V. Garov, "Plakha dlia Palekha," *Trud,* October 7, 1989, 2; A. Kovalev, "S vysokimi pokazateliami," *Prizyv,* February 2, 1988, 1; "Consumer Guide to Moscow," *New York Times,* February 21, 1982, XX17; "Tblisi, the Volga and Siberia, Too," *New York Times,* March 20, 1983, 492; "Personal Beauty," *New York Times,* August 4, 1977, 50. For examples of display ads, see the following editions of the *New York Times,* September 19, 1979, A20; October 30, 1977, 14; January 12, 1974, 8; November 9, 1980, 66.

24. Aleksandr Navozov, *Palekhskoe chudo* (Moscow: Sovetskaia Rossiia, 1976), 133. In 1984 his house was converted into a museum.

25. O. Zhurikhina, "Smysl zhizni—tvorchestvo," *Prizyv,* May 4, 1988, 2–3; GAIO, *f.* 372, *op.* 1, *d.* 1, *l.* 1.

26. A. Navozov, "On byl chelovekoliubtsem," *Prizyv,* May 24, 1988, 2.

27. Tikhomirova, *Nikolai Mikhailovich Zinov'ev,* 108.

28. RGALI, *f.* 2283, *d.* 80, *l.* 5; GAIO, *f.* 372, *op.* 2, *d.* 9, *l.* 4; Zinov'ev, *Iskusstvo Palekha*, 5, 15.

29. GAIO, *f.* 372, *op.* 2, *d.* 9, *l.* 7.

30. GAIO, *f.* 372, *op.* 2, *d.* 9, *l.* 7; *d.* 10, *l.* 1; *d.* 13, *l.* 12.

31. O. S. Popova, "Narodnoe dekorativnoe-prikladnoe iskusstvo," *Sovetskaia etnografiia*, no. 5 (1957): 108; V. Kotov, "Muzei Palekhskogo iskusstva," *Tribuna Palekha*, November 11, 1954, 2, and "Odno iz chudes revoliutsii," *Nauka i religiia*, no. 1 (1961): 26–30; Nik. Kruzhkov, "Paleshane," *Ogonek*, no. 6 (1965): 24; GAIO, *f.* 2875, *op.* 3, *d.* 9, *l.* 1; *f.* 372, *op.* 2, *d.* 9, *ll.* 4, 9.

32. Zinov'ev, *Iskusstvo Palekha*, 16–17, 27.

33. GAIO, *f.* 372, *op.* 1, *d.* 18, *ll.* 17–18, 19a; *d.* 29, *l.* 6.

34. Zinov'ev, *Stilisticheskie traditsii iskusstva Palekha*. Interestingly, though many Palekhians applauded publication of the work, some also were afraid that anyone with artistic talent might pick up Zinov'ev's style manual and use it as a guide for making "imitation" Palekh lacquers. Interview with Kotukhina, January 15, 2000, Palekh.

35. Tikhomirova, *Khudozhnik Palekha*, 110–46.

36. A. Kotukhina, "Uchitel' i drug," *Prizyv*, May 19, 1988, 3; Tikhomirova, *Khudozhnik Palekha*, 49–50; Lane, *Rites of Rulers*, 247.

37. Lane, *Rites of Rulers*, 240; Nahaylo and Swoboda, *Soviet Disunion*, 362–63.

38. K. Kochetov, "Vmesto ili vmeste?" *Prizyv*, March 30, 1989, 2.

39. V. Garov, "Plakha dlia Palekha," 2.

40. V. Zotov, "Ne o forme, no o soderzhanii," *Prizyv*, May 18, 1991, 3–4; V. Kotov, "V ego iskusstve est' dusha," *Prizyv*, December 3, 1991, 1–2, and "Kak zazhech' putevodnuiu zvezdu," *Prizyv*, November 25, 1989, 2.

41. Evgenii Zhiriakov, "A mozhet byt', vmeste?" *Prizyv*, July 21, 1992, 2; Golov, "Palekh: Upadok ili vozrozhdenie?" 2; A. Korneva, "V edinstve dukhovnykh i tvorcheskikh tselei," *Prizyv*, November 10, 1994, 2; Garov, "Plakha dlia Palekha," 2; "Soviet-Run Stores For Souvenirs," *New York Times*, May 22, 1988, 22; "Where Tourists Rummage in Communism's Attic," *New York Times*, September 21, 1991, A4.

42. V. Mazurin, "Ne ubit' by Zhar-ptitsu," *Prizyv*, April 3, 1997, 3.

43. In February 1998, the Soros Fund met in Palekh to discuss its ambitious plans for funding Palekh's art and cultural institutions. Tape of meeting with the Soros Fund, February 21, 1998, from the private archive of Mikhail Larionov.

44. O. Zhurikhina, "Ivany, ne pomniashchie rodstva," *Prizyv*, November 6, 1991, 2; "Iz istorii," *Prizyv*, July 31, 1993, 3. Appropriating the Soviet victory over the Nazis and the glory of the Red Army, President Putin has also reinstated the red star as the Russian military's emblem and ordered that the name Volgograd be removed from the Tomb of the Unknown Soldier and replaced with the city's previous name, Stalingrad.

45. Garov, "Plakha dlia Palekha," 2; "For Icon Artists, Freedom Brings Iconoclasm," *New York Times*, April 28, 1994, A3.

46. Iurii Melent'ev, "Vernost' traditsii—fundament edinstva," *Prizyv*, December 20, 1994, 2.

47. Elena Leonova, "Traditsionnyi avangardist Mikhail Larionov," *Khronometr-Ivanovo*, March 10, 1999, 10; V. Kotov, "Novyi stil' i tvorchestvo," *Prizyv*, February 2, 2001, 4; M. Larionov, "Snova 'Posle zimy,'" *Prizyv*, December 3, 1997, 3; I. Korshunova, "Posle zimy," *Chastnik*, April 29, 1998, 1.

48. "Olden Arts Mock the Newly Rich (and Their Toys)," *New York Times*, May 6, 1998, A4; "Kak lakovyi 'mers' naekhal na palekh," *Komsomol'skaia pravda*, September 13, 2001, downloaded from the newspaper's online archive.

49. Golov, "Palekh: Upadok ili vozrozhdenie?" 2.

50. V. Kotov, "Tserkov' sviatogo proroka Il'i v Palekhe," *Prizyv,* February 22, 1992, 3; Iu. Golikov, "O narodnom," *Prizyv,* February 27, 1996, 2; V. Volotko, "S blagosloveniem Patriarkha," *Prizyv,* December 5, 1995, 2; Golov, "Palekh: Upadok ili vozrozhdenie?" 2; "Muzei, masterskaia, khram . . .," *Prizyv,* November 24, 1994, 2; Nina Filinkovskaia, "Mastera," *Prizyv,* April 22, 1998, 3; Voice of Russia broadcast of June 22, 2004.

51. See, for example, O. Subbotina, "Palekh ikonopisnyi. Rasskazyvaet Dmitrii Ivanovich Salapin . . .," *Prizyv,* February 22, 1992, 3–4; "Iz tetradi D. I. Salapina," *Prizyv,* February 22, 1992, 5.

52. Vladimir Mazurin, "Ne ubit' by Zhar-ptitsu" and "Nuzhen li nimb Iude?" *Prizyv,* April 15, 1997, 3.

EPILOGUE—THE VILLAGE ACADEMY IN MODERN RUSSIAN HISTORY

1. Martin Malia, "What is the Intelligentsia?," in *The Russian Intelligentsia,* ed. Richard Pipes (New York: Columbia University Press, 1961), 16.

2. Boris Groys, *The Total Art of Stalinism: Avant-Garde, Aesthetic Dictatorship, and Beyond,* trans. Charles Rougle (Princeton: Princeton University Press, 1992).

3. Igal Halfin, *From Darkness to Light: Class, Consciousness, and Salvation in Revolutionary Russia* (Pittsburgh: University of Pittsburgh Press, 2000), 203.

4. V. Kotov, "Tak chto zhe my vytvoriaem?" *Prizyv,* June 27, 1992, 2, "Est' li budushchee u sela-akademii?" 2, "Mif o sele-akademii," 2, and "Narodnoe li iskusstvo 'Palekh'," *Prizyv,* December 23, 1995, 2.

5. V. Kotov, "Predvaritel'nye soobrazheniia ob organizatsii obucheniia masterstvu palekhskogo iskusstva pri kooperative," unpublished 1992 document from the private archive of Mikhail Larionov.

6. Ol'ga Kondrat'eva, "Spaset li promysel Rossiiu?" *Prizyv,* September 10, 1992, 2; Bokarev, "A chto budet zavtra?"

7. Kotov, "Est' li budushchee u sela-akademii?" 2.

8. Larionov, "Snova 'Posle zimy,'" 3.

9. Elena Leonova, "Traditsionnyi avangardist Mikhail Larionov," *Khronometr-Ivanovo,* March 10, 1999, 10; press release for the exhibit "Palekh-Palekh," February 23, 2000, Ivanovo State Museum of Art.

10. Unnumbered page in visitor comment books from 1998 and 1999 for the exhibit "Posle Zimy." Private archive of Mikhail Larionov.

SELECTED BIBLIOGRAPHY

ARCHIVES

Rossiiskii gosudarstvennyi arkhiv literatury i iskusstva (RGALI), Moscow:
Fond 94, the personal archive of Efim Fedorovich Vikhrev (1901–1935)
Fond 2075, Komitet po delam iskusstv (Committee for Art Affairs)
Fond 2283, the personal archive of Nikolai Nikolaevich Bariutin (1889–1960)
Fond 2322, the personal archive of German Vasil'evich Zhidkov (1903–1953)
Fond 2907, archive of Vsekokhudozhnik (All-Russian Cooperative Association of Artists)
Fond 2940, Union of Artists of the Russian Federation

Otdel rukopisei Gosudarstvennoi Tret'iakovskoi galerei (ORGTG), Moscow:
Fond 15, the personal archive of Anatolii Vasil'evich Bakushinskii (1883–1938)

Otdel rukopisei Gosudarstvennogo russkogo muzeia (ORGRM), St. Petersburg:
Fond Komiteta popechitel'stva o russkoi ikonopisi (Committee for the Tutelage of Russian Icon Painting)
Fond 122, the personal archive of Vasilii Timofeevich Georgievskii (1861–1923)

Peterburgskoe otdelenie Akademii nauk rossiiskoi federatsii (POANRF), St. Petersburg:
Fond 115, the personal archive of Nikodim Pavlovich Kondakov (1844–1925)

Rossiiskii gosudarstvennyi istoricheskii arkhiv (RGIA), St. Petersburg:
Fond 398, files from the Ministry of State Properties
Fond 797, 796, files from the Holy Synod
Fond 1088, the personal archive of Count Sergei Dmitrievich Sheremetev (1844–1918)
Fond 1331, files from the Commission for the Study of Craft Industries in Russia

Gosudarstvennyi arkhiv rossiiskoi federatsii (GARF), Moscow:
Fond A-501, archive of the Ministry of Culture of the Russian Federation
Fond A-643, archive of the Scientific Research Institute of Artistic Industries (1932–1980)
Fond A-5449, archive of the All-Russia Union of Industrial Cooperation
Fond A-10004, archive of the Administration of Foreign Tourism

Rossiiskii gosudarstvennyi arkhiv sotsial'no-politicheskoi istorii (RGASPI), Moscow:
Fond 17, records of the party's Central Committee
Fond 142, personal archive of Anatolii Vasil'evich Lunacharskii

Rossiiskii gosudarstvennyi arhkiv ekonomiki (RGAE), Moscow:
  Fond 413, the Ministry of External Trade of the USSR
  Fond 635, the All-Union Chamber of Commerce
  Fond 5339, the All-Union Committee of Industrial Cooperation
  Fond 8345, the All-Union Association for the Export of Arts and Crafts and
    Carpets

Gosudarstvennyi arkhiv ivanovskoi oblasti (GAIO), Ivanovo:
  Fond R-372, the personal archive of Nikolai Mikhailovich Zinov'ev (1888–1979)
  Fond R-2969, files from the State Museum of Palekh Art (1934–1991)
  Fond R-2976, files from the State School of Palekh Art (1934–1991)
  Fond R-2977, files from the Palekh Cooperative of Ancient Russian Painting
    (1925–1991)

Gosudarstvennyi arkhiv vladimirskoi oblasti (GAVO), Vladimir:
  Fond 526, Vladimir Provincial Archival Commission
  Fond 534, Aleksandr Nevskii Brotherhood
  Fond 604, Ivan Aleksandrovich Golyshev
  Fond 662, Mstera Artistic Artel of Artists and Embroiderers

Partiinyi arkhiv ivanovskoi oblasti (PAIO), Ivanovo:
  Fond 676, files from the Palekh party organization (1935–1991)
  Fond 1070, files from the party organization of the Palekh Cooperative of Ancient
    Russian Painting (1935–1991)
  Fond 2487, files from the party organization of the State School of Palekh Art
    (1935–1991)

Otdel pis'mennykh istochnikov Gosudarstvennogo istoricheskogo muzeia (OPIGIM),
  Moscow:
  Fond 440, Diaries of Ivan Egorovich Zabelin

Otdel rukopisei Rossiiskoi natsional'noi biblioteki (ORRNB), St. Petersburg:
  Fond 585, the personal archive of Sergei Fedorovich Platonov (1860–1933)
  Fond 593, the personal archive of Nikolai Vasil'evich Pokrovskii (1848–1917)
  Fond 757, the personal archive of Nikolai Vladimirovich Sultanov (1850–1908)

Arkhiv Gosudarstvennogo muzeia palekhskogo iskusstva (AGMPI), Palekh:
  Fond Sobolevskii
  Knigi otzyvov (Museum Comment Books)

Private Archive of Mikhail Larionov (Palekh)

EXHIBIT CATALOGUES/CONFERENCE PROCEEDINGS
(ARRANGED BY DATE)

Russkoe narodnoe iskusstvo na vtoroi vserossiiskoi kustarnoi vystavke v Petrograde v 1913 godu.
  Petrograd, 1914.
Vserossiiskaia vystavka khudozhestvennoi promyshlennosti. Moscow, 1923, no. 2 [i.e., second
  exhibit].

Vystavka khudozhestvennykh proizvedenii k desiateletnemu iubileiu Oktiabr'skoi revoliutsii. Katalog. Moscow, 1928.

Soviet Russian Art and Handicraft Exposition. Grand Central Palace, New York, February 1929.

Palekhskie miniatiury. Katalog rabot vystavki Palekhskoi arteli drevnei zhivopisi. Leningrad, 1930.

Katalog vystavki "Iskusstvo Palekha". Moscow, 1932.

Russkie khudozhestvennye laki. Moscow, 1933.

Khudozhestvennaia vystavka "15 let RKKA". Moscow, 1933.

Vystavka kartin "Khudozhniki IPO za 16 let". Ivanovo, 1933.

Ivanovskaia promyshlennaia oblast' v izobrazitel'nom iskusstve. Katalog 2–oi oblastnoi khudozhestvennoi vystavki. Ivanovo, 1935.

A. S. Pushkin v Gosudarstvennoi Tret'iakovskoi galeree. Katalog. Moscow, 1936.

Katalog vystavki narodnogo tvorchestva v zalakh Gosudarstvennoi Tret'iakovskoi gallerei. Moscow, 1937.

3-ia [Tret'ia] oblastnaia khudozhestvennaia vystavka. Katalog. Ivanovo, 1937.

Iskusstvo Palekha. Katolog. Moscow, 1939.

Vsesoiuznaia khudozhestvennaia vystavka "Industriia sotsializma". Moscow, 1939.

4-ia [Chetvertaia] oblastnaia khudozhestvennaia vystavka. Katalog. Ivanovo, 1940.

8-ia [Vos'maia] oblastnaia khudozhestvennaia vystavka. Katalog. Ivanovo, 1945–46.

IX [Deviataia] oblastnaia khudozhestvennaia vystavka. Katalog. Ivanovo, 1947.

12-ia [Dvenadtsataia] oblastnaia khudozhestvennaia vystavka. Katalog. Ivanovo, 1952.

13-ia [Trinadtsataia] oblastnaia vystavka proizvedenii khudozhnikov Ivanovskoi oblasti. Ivanovo, 1953.

30 [Tridtsat'] let iskusstva sovetskogo Palekha. Katalog vystavki. Moscow, 1955.

Vystavka proizvedenii khudozhnikov Ivanovskoi oblasti. Katalog. Ivanovo, 1956.

16-ia [Shestnadtsataia] Ivanovskaia oblastnaia khudozhestvennaia vystavka. Katalog. Ivanovo, 1957.

Iskusstvo sovetskogo Palekha. Shuia, 1957.

Iskusstvo Palekha v muzeiakh RSFSR. Katalog. Moscow, 1958.

Sovetskaia tema v iskusstve Palekha. Shuia, 1960.

Respublikanskaia vystavka dekorativno-prikladnogo iskusstva. Katalog. Moscow-Leningrad, 1964.

2-ia [Vtoraia] respublikanskaia vystavka "Sovetskaia Rossiia." Katalog. Moscow, 1965.

40 [Sorok] let iskusstva sovetskogo Palekha. Katalog vystavki. Moscow, 1965.

3-ia [Tret'ia] respublikanskaia khudozhestvennaia vystavka "Sovetskaia Rossiia." Katalog. Moscow, 1968.

Katalog vystavki. Palekh na poroge tret'ego tysiacheletiia. K 75–letnemu iubileiu palekhskoi lakovoi miniatury. Moscow, 1999.

Palekh—Palekh. Katalog vystavki. Ivanovo, 2000.

JOURNALS AND NEWSPAPERS, PRE-1917

Bibliograficheskaia letopis'. St. Petersburg.

Den'. Moscow.

Ikonopisnyi sbornik. St. Petersburg.

Iskusstvo i khudozhestvennaia promyshlennost'. St. Petersburg.

Izograf: Zhurnal ikonografii i drevnikh iskusstv. St. Petersburg.

Izvestiia imperatorskago russkago arkheologicheskago obshchestva. St. Petersburg.

Izvestiia vysochaishe uchrezhdennago komiteta popechitel'stva o russkoi ikonopisi. St. Petersburg.
Khristianskoe chtenie. St. Petersburg.
Mir iskusstva. St. Petersburg.
Moskovskie vedomosti.
Novoe vremia. Moscow.
Novosti i birzhevaia gazeta. St. Petersburg.
Otechestvennye zapiski. Moscow.
Pamiatniki drevnei pis'mennosti. St. Petersburg.
Peterburgskii listok.
Pravitel'stvennyi vestnik. St. Petersburg.
Russkaia ikona. St. Petersburg
Russkii vestnik. Moscow.
Russkoe obozrenie. St. Petersburg.
Russkoe slovo. Moscow.
Sankt-Peterburgskie vedomosti.
Svetil'nik. Moscow
Trudy Vladimirskoi uchenoi arkhivnoi kommissii. Vladimir.
Tserkovnye vedomosti. St. Petersburg.
Vestnik arkheologii i istorii. St. Petersburg.
Vestnik obshchestva drevne-russkago iskusstva pri Moskovskom publichnom muzeie. Moscow.
Vladimirskie eparkhial'nye vedomosti. Vladimir.
Vladimirskie gubernskie vedomosti. Vladimir.
Zhurnal ministerstva vnutrennykh del. St. Petersburg.

JOURNALS AND NEWSPAPERS, POST-1917

Bloknot agitatora. Ivanovo.
Dekorativnoe iskusstvo SSSR. Moscow.
Eksport kustarno-khudozhestvennykh izdelii i kovrov. Moscow.
Iskusstvo. Moscow.
Ivanovskii al'manakh. Ivanovo.
Izvestiia. Moscow.
Khudozhnik. Moscow.
Kniga i revoliutsiia: Zhurnal politiki, kul'tury, kritiki, i bibliografii. Moscow.
Knizhnoe obozrenie. Moscow.
Komsomol'skaia pravda. Moscow.
Kustarnyi biulleten'. Moscow.
Legkaia industriia. Moscow.
Literatura i zhizn'. Moscow.
Literaturnaia gazeta. Moscow.
Molodaia gvardiia. Moscow.
Narodnoe tvorchestvo. Moscow.
Nashi dostizheniia. Moscow.
Nauka i religiia. Moscow.
Nizhegorodskaia iarmarka. Nizhnii Novgorod.
Nizhegorodskaia kommuna. Nizhnii Novogorod.
Novyi mir. Moscow.
Ogonek. Moscow.
Plamia. Ivanovo.
Pravda. Moscow.

Prizyv. Palekh.
Rabochii krai. Ivanovo.
Sovetskaia etnografiia. Moscow.
Sovetskaia Rossiia. Moscow.
Sovetskaia torgovlia. Moscow.
Sovetskoe iskusstvo. Moscow.
Teatr. Moscow.
Tribuna Palekha. Palekh.
Trud. Moscow.
Vecherniaia Moskva. Moscow.
Vestnik promyslovoi kooperatsii. Moscow.

BOOKS AND ESSAYS

Agursky, Mikhail. *The Third Rome: National Bolshevism in the USSR.* Boulder, Colo.: Westview Press, 1987.

Amalrik, Andrei. *Will the Soviet Union Survive until 1984?* New York: Harper & Row, 1970.

Anderson, Benedict. *Imagined Communities.* 2nd ed. New York: Verso, 1991.

Bakushinskii, A. V. *Muzeino-esteticheskie ekskursii.* Moscow, 1919.

———. "Palekhskie laki." *Iskusstvo,* no. 2 (1925): 200–212.

———. *Iskusstvo Palekha.* Moscow: Vserossiskii kooperativnyi soiuz khudozhnikov, 1932.

———. *Iskusstvo Palekha.* Moscow-Leningrad: Academia, 1934.

———. *Issledovaniia i stat'i.* Comp. I. A. Liberfort. Moscow: Sovetskii khudozhnik, 1981.

Belaia, G. *Don Kikhoty dvadtsatykh godov: "Pereval" i sud'ba ego idei.* Moscow: Sovetskii pisatel', 1989.

Bezobrazov, V. T. "Iz putevykh zapisok." *Russkii vestnik* (July 1861): 265–308.

Boguslavskaia, I. Ia., ed. *Narodnoe iskusstvo. Issledovaniia i materialy. Sbornik statei k 100-letiiu Gosudarstvennogo russkogo muzeia.* St. Petersburg: Gosudarstvennyi russkii muzei, 1995.

Bonnell, Victoria. *Iconography of Power: Soviet Political Posters under Lenin and Stalin.* Berkeley: University of California Press, 1997.

Boris, Eileen. *Art and Labor: Ruskin, Morris, and the Craftsman Ideal in America.* Philadelphia: Temple University Press, 1986.

Bowlt, John E. *Russian Art, 1875–1975: A Collection of Essays.* New York: MSS Information Corp., 1976.

Boym, Svetlana. *Common Places: Mythologies of Everyday Life in Russia.* Cambridge, Mass.: Harvard University Press, 1994.

Brandenberger, David. *National Bolshevism: Stalinist Mass Culture and the Formation of Modern Russian National Identity, 1931–1956.* Cambridge, Mass.: Harvard University Press, 2002.

Bratchikova, E. K. *Palekh. Izbrannye stat'i.* Moscow: Izdatel'skii dom "Parad," 1999.

Brudny, Yitzhak. *Reinventing Russia: Russian Nationalism and the Soviet State, 1953–1991.* Cambridge, Mass.: Harvard University Press, 1998.

Brumfield, William C., and Milos M. Velimirovic, eds. *Christianity and the Arts in Russia.* Cambridge: Cambridge University Press, 1991.

Buslaev, F. I. *M. P. Pogodin kak professor.* Moscow: Tipografiia A. Gattsuka, 1876.

———. *Moi vospominaniia.* Moscow: Tipografiia G. Lissnera i A. Geshel'ia, 1897.

———. *Pamiati Fedora Ivanovicha Buslaeva.* Moscow: Tipografiia Sytina, 1898.

———. *Sochineniia F. I. Buslaeva.* 3 vols. St.Petersburg-Leningrad: Izdatel'stvo Akademii nauk SSSR, 1908–1930.

———. *O russkoi ikone. Obshchie poniatiia o russkoi ikonopisi*. Moscow: Mezhdunarodnyi pravoslavnyi fond "Blagovest," 1997.

Cherkasova, N. V. *Narodnye khudozhestvennye promysli. Teoriia i praktika. Sbornik nauch-nykh trudov k 50-letiiu Nauchno-issledovatel'skogo instituta khudozhestvennoi promyshlennosti*. Moscow: Nauchno-issledovatel'skii institut khudozhestvennoi promyshlennosti, 1982.

Chumachenko, T. A. *Gosudarstvo, pravoslavnaia tserkov', veruiushchie, 1941–1961 gg.* Moscow: AIRO-XX, 1999.

Clark, Katerina. *Petersburg: Crucible of Cultural Revolution*. Cambridge, Mass.: Harvard University Press, 1995.

Conquest, Robert. *Stalin: Breaker of Nations*. New York: Viking, 1991.

Cracraft, James. *The Petrine Revolution in Russian Imagery*. Chicago: University of Chicago Press, 1997.

Denisov, V. "Palekhovskie mastera i sovremennost'." *Sovetskoe iskusstvo*, no. 7 (1927): 37–48.

Dobrenko, E., and T. Lahusen, eds. *Socialist Realism without Shores*. Durham, N.C.: Duke University Press, 1997.

Dunham, Vera. *In Stalin's Time: Middleclass Values in Soviet Fiction*. Durham, N.C.: Duke University Press, 1990.

Dunlop, John. *The Faces of Contemporary Russian Nationalism*. Princeton: Princeton University Press, 1983.

———. *The New Russian Nationalism*. New York, Praeger, 1985.

Egorov, V. L., ed. *Zabelinskie nauchnye chteniia*. Trudy Gosudarstvennogo istoricheskogo muzeia. Moscow: Gosudarstvennyi istoricheskii muzei, 1993–1998.

Filimonov, G. D. *Simon Ushakov i sovremennaia emu epokha russkoi ikonopisi*. Moscow: Universitetskaia tipografiia, 1873.

Formozov, A. A. *Istorik Moskvy I. E. Zabelin*. Moscow: Moskovskii rabochii, 1984.

Frierson, Cathy. *Peasant Icons: Representations of Rural People in Late Nineteenth-Century Russia*. New York: Oxford University Press, 1993.

Gellner, Ernest. *Nations and Nationalism*. Ithaca, N.Y.: Cornell University Press, 1983.

Georgievskii, V. T. *Pamiatniki starinnogo russkogo iskusstva suzdal'skogo muzeia*. Moscow: Glavnauka, 1927.

Gleason, A., P. Kenez, and R. Stites, eds. *Bolshevik Culture: Experiment and Order in the Russian Revolution*. Bloomington: Indiana University Press, 1985.

Golitsyn, F. S. *Neobkhodimyi dlia Rossii stroi truda*. St. Petersburg: [s. n.], 1912.

———. *Kustarnoe delo v Rossii v sviazi s umstvenno-dukhovnym razvitiem russkago naroda*. St. Petersburg: Tipografiia V. F. Kirshbauma, 1904–1913.

Gorbunov, G. I. *Dmitrii Furmanov. Efimovo schast'e*. Iaroslavl': Verkhne-volzhskoe knizhnoe izdatel'stvo, 1971.

———, ed. *Palekh*. Ivanovo: Ivanovskoe knizhnoe izdatel'stvo, 1954.

Grabar', I. E. *Kooperatsiia i iskusstvo*. Moscow: Tipografiia N. A. Sazanovoi, 1919.

———. *Pis'ma, 1917–1941*. Moscow: Nauka, 1977.

Groys, Boris. *The Total Art of Stalinism: Avant-Garde, Aesthetic Dictatorship, and Beyond*. Translated by Charles Rougle. Princeton: Princeton University Press, 1992.

Guliaev, V. A. *Russkie khudozhestvennye promysly 1920-kh godov*. Leningrad: Khudozhnik RSFSR, 1985.

Gushchin, A. S. *Palekhovskie miniatiury*. Leningrad: Gosudarstvennyi istoricheskii muzei, 1930.

Halfin, Igal. *From Darkness to Light: Class, Consciousness, and Salvation in Revolutionary Russia*. Pittsburgh: University of Pittsburgh Press, 2000.

Hellbeck, Jochen. "Fashioning the Stalinist Soul: The Diary of Stepan Podlubnyi." *Jahrbucher für Geshichte Osteuropas* 44 (1996): 344–73.

Hilton, Alison. *Russian Folk Art.* Bloomington: Indiana University Press, 1995.

Hirsch, Francine. "The Soviet Union as a Work in Progress: Ethnographers and the Category Nationality in the 1926, 1937, and 1939 Censuses." *Slavic Review* 56, no. 2 (1997): 415–50.

Hobsbawm, E. J. *Nations and Nationalism since 1780: Programme, Myth, Reality.* New York: Cambridge University Press, 1990.

Holquist, Peter. "Information Is the Alpha and Omega of Our Work: Bolshevik Surveillance in Its Pan-European Context." *Journal of Modern History* 69 (September 1997): 415–50.

Hosking, Geoffrey. *Russia and the Russians: A History.* Cambridge, Mass.: Harvard University Press, 2001.

Ialovenko, G. V. *Russkie khudozhestvennye laki.* Moscow: Vsesoiuznoe kooperativnoe izdatel'stvo, 1959.

Ianovskii, A. D., ed. *I. E. Zabelin: 170 let so dnia rozhdeniia. Materialy nauchnykh chtenii GIM, 29–31 Oktiabria 1990 goda.* Moscow: Gosudarstvennyi ordena Lenina istoricheskii muzei, 1992.

"Ikonopistsy." *Zhurnal ministerstva vnutrennykh del,* 1858, chast' 32, otdelenie 3:26–35.

Ivanova, T. G., ed. *Russkaia folkloristika v biograficheskikh ocherkakh.* St. Petersburg: D. Bulanin, 1993.

Jahn, H. *Patriotic Culture in Russia during World War I.* Ithaca, N.Y.: Cornell University Press, 1995.

Johnson, Priscilla, and Leopold Labedz, eds. *Khrushchev and the Arts: The Politics of Soviet Culture, 1962–1964.* Cambridge, Mass.: M.I.T. Press, 1965.

Kalugin, V. I. *Pole slavy.* Moscow: Molodaia gvardiia, 1981.

Kappeler, Andreas. "The Ambiguities of Russification." *Kritika,* no. 2 (Spring 2004): 291–97.

Kharkhordin, Oleg. *The Collective and the Individual in Russia: A Study of Practices.* Berkeley: University of California Press, 1999.

Kniazeva, L. *Ikonopis' Palekha iz sobranii Gosudarstvennogo muzeia palekhskogo iskusstva.* Moscow: Progress, 1994.

Kobeko, D. F. *O Suzdal'skom ikonopisanii.* St. Petersburg, 1896.

Kondakov, N. P. "O nauchnykh zadachakh istorii drevne-russkago iskusstva." In the series Pamiatniki drevnei pis'mennosti i iskusstva, no. 132. St. Petersburg: Tipografiia I. N. Skorokhodova, 1899.

———. *Sovremennoe polozhenie russkoi narodnoi ikonopisi.* Pamiatniki drevnei pis'mennosti i iskusstva, no. 139. St. Petersburg: Tipografiia I. N. Skorokhodova, 1901.

———. *Ikonografiia Gospoda Boga i Spasa nashego Iisusa Khrista. Istoricheskii i ikonograficheskii ocherk, sochinenie akademika N. Kondakova.* Izdanie Vysochaishe uchrezhdennago Komiteta popechitel'stva o russkoi ikonopisi. St. Petersburg: Tovarishchestvo R. Golike i A. Vil'borg, 1905.

———. "Ikonografiia Bogomateri." In *Ikonopisnyi sbornik,* vyp. 4. St. Petersburg, 1910.

———. *Vospominaniia i dumy.* Prague: Seminarium Kondakovianum, 1927.

———. *The Russian Icon.* Prague: Seminarium Kondakovianum, 1928–1933.

Korchagina, Z. *Iskusstvo Sovetskogo Palekha: Bibliograficheskii ukazatel'.* Ivanovo: Ivan. Obl. Nauch. B-ka, 1976.

Kotkin, Stephen. *Magnetic Mountain: Stalinism as a Civilization.* Berkeley: University of California Press, 1995.

———. *Armageddon Averted: The Soviet Collapse, 1970–2000.* New York: Oxford University Press, 2001.

Kotov, V. T. *Golikov, Ivan Ivanovich. Khudozhnik revoliutsionnogo vikhria.* Shuia, 1959.

———. *Iskusstvo Palekha. Putevoditel'.* Moscow: Izdatel'stvo literatury na inostrannykh iazykakh, 1960.

———. *Khudozhnik Ivan Golikov.* Iaroslavl': Verkhne-volzhskoe knizhnoe izdatel'stvo, 1973.

———. *Palekh. The State Museum of Palekh Art.* Moscow: Izobrazitel'noe iskusstvo, 1981.

Kotsonis, Yanni. *Making Peasants Backward: Agricultural Cooperatives and the Agrarian Question in Russia, 1861–1914.* New York: St. Martin's Press, 1999.

Kratkoe opisanie ikon sobraniia P. M. Tret'iakova. Moscow: Sinodal'naia tipografiia, 1905.

Kyzlasova, I. L. *Istoriia izucheniia vizantiiskogo i drevnerusskogo iskusstva v Rossii. F. I. Buslaev, N. P. Kondakov. Metody, idei, teorii.* Moscow: Izdatel'stvo Moskovskogo universiteta, 1985.

Lahusen, Thomas. *How Life Writes the Book: Real Socialism and Socialist Realism in Stalin's Russia.* Ithaca, N.Y.: Cornell University Press, 1997.

Lane, Christel. *The Rites of Rulers: Ritual in Industrial Society—The Soviet Case.* London: Cambridge University Press, 1981.

Lavrov, A. S. *Koldovstvo i religiia v Rossii, 1700–1740 gg.* Moscow: Drevnekhranilishche, 2000.

Lazarev, V. N. *Nikodim Pavlovich Kondakov.* Moscow: Izdatel'stvo avtora, 1925.

Lears, T. J. Jackson. *No Place of Grace: Antimodernism and the Transformation of American Culture, 1880–1920.* Chicago: University of Chicago Press, 1981.

Leskov, N. S. *N. S. Leskov o literature i iskusstve.* Leningrad: Izdatel'stvo Leningradskogo universiteta, 1984.

Likhachev, N. P. *Istoricheskoe znachenie italo-grecheskoi ikonopisi.* St. Petersburg: Izdatel'stvo Imperatorskago russkago arkheologicheskago obshchestva, 1911.

Malia, Martin. *The Soviet Tragedy: A History of Socialism in Russia, 1917–1991.* New York: Free Press, 1994.

———. *Russia under Western Eyes: From the Bronze Horseman to the Lenin Mausoleum.* Cambridge, Mass.: Belknap Press of Harvard University Press, 1999.

Martin, T. *The Affirmative-Action Empire: Nations and Nationalism in the Soviet Union, 1923–1939.* Ithaca, N.Y.: Cornell University Press, 2001.

Meyendorff, J. *Rome, Constantinople, Moscow: Historical and Theological Studies.* Crestwood, N.Y.: St. Vladimir's Seminary Press, 1996.

Nahaylo, Bohdan, and Victor Swoboda. *Soviet Disunion: A History of the Nationalities Problem in the USSR.* New York: Free Press, 1990.

Nekrasova, M. A. *Iskusstvo Palekha.* Moscow: Sovetskii khudozhnik, 1966.

———. *Palekhskoe iskusstvo. Palekh Miniature Painting.* Leningrad: Khudozhnik RSFSR, 1978.

———. *Narodnoe iskusstvo kak chast' kul'tury. Teoriia i praktika.* Moscow: Izobrazitel'noe iskusstvo, 1983.

———. *Iskusstvo drevnei traditsii. Palekh.* Moscow: Sovetskii khudozhnik, 1984.

———, comp. *Russian Lacquer Miniature Art: The Inna Kaufman Gallery.* Zwolle, The Netherlands: Waanders Printers, 2000.

Nichols, Robert L. "The Icon and the Machine in Russia's Religious Renaissance, 1900–1909." In *Christianity and the Arts in Russia,* edited by William C. Brumfield and Milos M. Velimirovic, 131–44. Cambridge: Cambridge University Press, 1991.

Nilsson, Nils Ake, ed. *Art, Society, Revolution: Russia, 1917–1921.* Stockholm: Almqvist & Wiksell International, 1979.

Oreshkin, D. "Palekh v Bor'be za stil'." *Narodnoe tvorchestvo,* no. 3 (1938): 9–13.

Osokina, Elena. *Za fasadom "Stalinskogo izobiliia." Raspredelenie i rynok v snabzhenii naseleniia v gody industrializatsii, 1927–1941.* Moscow: ROSSPEN, 1998.

Ouspensky, L., and V. Lossky. *The Meaning of Icons.* Translated by G. Palmer and E. Kadloubovsky. Crestwood, N.Y.: St. Vladimir's Seminary Press, 1989.

Owen, T. *Russian Corporate Capitalism from Peter the Great to Perestroika.* New York: Oxford University Press, 1995.

Pil'niak, B. "Rozhdenie prekrasnogo." *Novyi mir,* no. 10 (1934): 37–43.

———. *Sozrevanie plodov.* Moscow: Khudozhestvennaia literatura, 1936.

Pirogova, L. *Palekh. Istoriia i sovremennost'.* Moscow: Izdatel'stvo "Iskusstvo," 1994.

———. *Lakovaia miniatiura Palekh.* Moscow: "Interbuk-biznes," 2001.

Podobedova, O. I. *Igor' Emmanuilovich Grabar'. Zhizn' i tvorcheskaia deiatel'nost'.* Moscow: Sovetskii khudozhnik, 1964.

Pokrovskii, N. V. *Litsevoi podlinnik i ego znacheniia dlia sovremennago tserkovnago iskusstva.* Pamiatniki drevnei pis'mennosti i iskusstva, no. 134. St. Petersburg: O.L.D.P., 1899.

———. *Ocherki pamiatnikov khristianskoi ikonografii.* 2d ed. St. Petersburg: Tipografiia A. P. Lopukhina, 1900.

Polunov, A. Iu. *Pod vlast'iu ober-prokurora: Gosudarstvo i tserkov' v epokhu Aleksandra III.* Moscow: AIRO-XX, 1996.

Raeff, Marc. *The Well-Ordered Police State: Social and Institutional Changes through Law in the Germanies and Russia, 1600–1800.* New Haven: Yale University Press, 1983.

Reinson-Pravdin, A. N. *Ivan Ivanovich Golikov.* Moscow: Sovetskii khudozhnik, 1956.

Rogger, Hans. *National Consciousness in Eighteenth-Century Russia.* Cambridge, Mass.: Harvard University Press, 1960.

Rovinskii, D. A. *Istoriia russkikh shkhol ikonopisanii do kontsa XVII veka.* St. Petersburg: Tip. II-go otdeleniia sobstvennoi E.I.V. kantseliarii, 1856.

———. *Materialy dlia russkoi ikonografii.* St. Petersburg: Ekspeditsiia Zagotovleniia Gosudarstvennykh Bumag, 1884–1891.

———. *Obozrenie ikonopisi v Rossii do kontsa XVII veka.* St. Petersburg: A. S. Suvorin, 1903.

Salmond, Wendy. *Arts and Crafts in Late Imperial Russia: Reviving the Kustar Art Industries, 1870–1917.* New York: Cambridge University Press, 1996.

———. *Russian Icons at Hillwood.* Washington, D.C.: Hillwood Museum & Gardens, 1998.

———. *Traditions in Transition: Russian Icons in the Age of the Romanovs.* Washington, D.C.: Hillwood Museum & Gardens, 2004.

Sanborn, Joshua. *Drafting the Russian Nation: Military Conscription, Total War, and Mass Politics, 1905–1925.* DeKalb: Northern Illinois University Press, 2003.

Semenovskii, D. M. *Selo Palekh i ego khudozhniki.* Moscow: Vsesoiuznoe kooperativnoe ob"edninennoe izdatel'stvo, 1932.

———. *Izbrannye proizvedeniia.* Moscow: Khudozhestvennaia literature, 1976.

Shevzov, Vera. "Miracle-Working Icons, Laity, and Authority in the Russian Orthodox Church, 1861–1917." *Russian Review* 58 (January 1999): 26–48.

———. *Russian Orthodoxy on the Eve of the Revolution.* New York: Oxford University Press, 2004.

Shlapentokh, Vladimir. *Public and Private Life of the Soviet People: Changing Values in Post-Stalin Russia.* New York: Oxford University Press, 1989.

Slezkine, Yuri. *Arctic Mirrors: Russia and the Small Peoples of the North.* Ithaca, N.Y.: Cornell University Press, 1994.

———. "The USSR as a Communal Apartment, or How a Socialist State Promoted Ethnic Particularism." *Slavic Review* 53 (Summer 1994): 414–52.

Smith, Steve, and Catriona Kelly. "Commercial Culture and Consumerism." In *Constructing Russian Culture in the Age of Revolution, 1881–1940*, edited by Catriona Kelly and David Shepherd, 106–56. Oxford: Oxford University Press, 1998.

Sokol'nikov, M. "Ivan Golikov i ego rabota nad slovom o polku igoreve." *Iskusstvo*, nos. 7–8 (1938): 31–48.

Stansky, Peter. *Redesigning the World: William Morris, the 1880s, and the Arts and Crafts*. Princeton: Princeton University Press, 1985.

Surin, A., and A. Gladuniuk, eds. *Poeziia Palekha. Kniga stikhov*. Ivanovo: Ivanovskaia gazeta, 1997.

Szporluk, Roman. *Communism and Nationalism: Karl Marx versus Friedrich List*. New York: Oxford University Press, 1988.

Talmon, J. L. *The Origins of Totalitarian Democracy*. London: Secker & Warburg, 1955.

———. *Romanticism and Revolt: Europe, 1815–1848*. New York: Harcourt, Brace & World, 1967.

Tarasov, O. Iu. *Ikona i blagochestie. Ocherki ikonnogo dela v imperatorskoi Rossii*. Moscow: Progess-Kul'tura, 1995.

Taubman, William. *Khrushchev: The Man and His Era*. New York: Norton, 2003.

Tikhomirova, M. A. *Nikolai Mikhailovich Zinov'ev. Khudozhnik Palekha*. Leningrad: Khudozhnik RSFSR, 1987.

Tolz, Vera. *Russia*. London: Oxford University Press, 2001.

Torzhkova, V. *Neizvestnyi Palekh. Ikony*. Moscow: Planeta, 1993.

Trenev, D. K. *Russkaia ikonopis' i ee zhelaemoe razvitie*. Moscow: Izdano pri Tserkovno-arkheologicheskom otdele Moskovskago obshchestva liubitelei dukhovnago prosveshcheniia, 1902.

———. *Neskol'ko slov o drevnei i sovremennoi russkoi ikonopisi*. Moscow: Izdano pri Tserkovno-arkheologicheskom otdele Moskovskago obshchestva liubitelei dukhovnago prosveshcheniia, 1905.

———. *Sovremennaia friaz'*. Moscow: Izdanie Deribizova, 1905.

———. *Sokhranenie pamiatnikov drevne-russkoi ikonopisi*. St. Petersburg: Tovarishchestvo R. Golike i A. Vil'borg, 1907.

———. *O russkoi ikonopisi po povodu voprosa o nei v gosudarstvennom dume*. Moscow: I. M. Mashistov, 1910.

Trotsky, Leon. *The Revolution Betrayed: What Is the Soviet Union and Where Is It Going?* Translated by Max Eastman. 10th printing. New York: Pioneer Publishers, 1996.

Trubetskoi, E. N. *Umozrenie v kraskakh. Vopros o smysle zhizni v drevne-russkoi religioznoi zhivopisi*. Moscow: Tipografiia Tovarishchestva I. D. Sytina, 1916.

Tugendkhol'd, I. A. *Iz istorii zapadnoevropeiskogo, russkogo, i sovetskogo iskusstva. Izbrannye stat'i i ocherki*. Moscow: Sovetskii khudozhnik, 1987.

Uspenskii, B. *The Semiotics of the Russian Icon*. Lisse, Belgium: Peter de Ridder Press, 1976.

Vainshtein, O. L. *Istoriia sovetskoi medievistiki*. Leningrad: Nauka, Leningradskoe otdelenie, 1968.

Vasnetsov, V. M. *Viktor Mikhailovich Vasnetsov. Mir khudozhnika. Pis'ma, dnevniki, vospominaniia, suzhdeniia sovremennikov*. Moscow: "Iskusstvo," 1987.

Vikhrev, E. F. "Palekh. Ocherki." *Novyi mir*, no. 3 (1929): 203–25.

———. "Palekh." *Nashi dostizheniia*, no. 9 (1930): 49–61.

———. *Palekh*. Moscow: "Nedra," 1930.

———. "Pushkin i Gor'kii v iskusstve Palekha." *Novyi mir*, no. 9 (1933): 234–43.

———. "Palekh, selo-akademiia." *Nashi dostizheniia*, nos. 5–6 (1935): 9–49.

———. *Palekh, 1927–1932. Vtoraia kompozitsiia*. Moscow: Khudozhestvennaia literatura, 1938.

———. *Izbrannye proizvedeniia.* Ivanovo: Ivanovskoe knizhnoe izdatel'stvo, 1961.

———. *Palekh.* Iaroslavl': Verkhne-volzhskoe knizhnoe izdatel'stvo, 1974.

———. *Rodniki.* Moscow: Sovetskaia Rossiia, 1984.

———. *Tainstvennoe svoistvo.* Ivanovo: Ivanovskii gosudarstvennyi khim-tekhnologich-eskii institut, 2001.

———, ed. *Paleshane. Zapiski palekhskikh khudozhnikov o ikh zhizni i tvorchestve, napissan-nye letom 1932 goda.* Moscow: Moskovskoe tovarishchestvo pisatelei, 1934.

Vinner, A. "Preobrazovanie palekhskikh masterskikh." *Literatura i iskusstvo,* nos. 7–8 (1931): 93–101.

Vzdornov, G. I. *Istoriia otkrytiia i izucheniia russkoi srednevekovoi zhivopisi. XIX vek.* Moscow: Iskusstvo, 1986.

———. *Obshchestvo "Ikona" v Parizhe.* 2 vols. Moscow-Paris: Progress-Traditsiia, 2002.

Walicki, Andrzej. *The Slavophile Controversy: History of a Conservative Utopia in Nineteenth-Century Russian Thought.* Translated by Hilda Andrews-Rusiecka. Oxford: Claren-don Press, 1975.

———. *Marxism and the Leap to the Kingdom of Freedom: The Rise and Fall of the Communist Utopia.* Stanford: Stanford University Press, 1995.

Wcislo, Francis William. *Reforming Rural Russia: State, Local Society, and National Politics, 1855–1914.* Princeton: Princeton University Press, 1990.

Weiner, A. *Making Sense of War: The Second World War and the Fate of the Bolshevik Revolu-tion.* Princeton: Princeton University Press, 2001.

Werth, Alexander. *Russia at War.* New York: Avon, 1964.

Witte, S. U. *The Memoirs of Count Witte.* Translated and edited by Sidney Harcave. Ar-monk, N.Y.: M. E. Sharpe, 1990.

Wortman, Richard. *Scenarios of Power: Myth and Ceremony in the Russian Monarchy.* Vol. 1. *From Peter the Great to the Death of Nicholas I.* Vol. 2. *From Alexander II to the Abdica-tion of Nicholas II.* Princeton: Princeton University Press, 1995, 2000.

Zabelin, I. E. "Materialy dlia istorii russkoi ikonopisi." *Vremennik Imperatorskago Moskovskago obshchestva istorii i drevnostei rossisskikkh,* kniga 7 (1850): 1–128.

———. *Domashnyi byt russkikh tsarei v XVI i XVII st.,* chast' 1. Moscow: Tipografiia V. Gracheva, 1862.

Zarudin, N. "Sledy na zemle." *Nashi dostizheniia,* nos. 5–6 (1935): 47–76.

———, ed. *Pereval'tsy. Antologiia. Sodruzhestvo pisatelei revoliutsii "pereval".* Moscow: Feder-atsiia, 1930.

Zhidkov, G. V. *Pushkin v iskusstve Palekha.* Moscow: Izdatel'stvo izobrazitel'nykh iskusstv, 1937.

———. "Palekhskie rospisi v Leningradskom dvortse pionerov." *Arkhitektura SSSR,* no. 4 (1937): 14–20.

Zinov'ev, N. M. *Iskusstvo Palekha.* Leningrad: Khudozhnik RSFSR, 1969.

———. *Iskusstvo Palekha.* 2nd ed. Leningrad: Khudozhnik RSFSR, 1974.

———. *Stilisticheskie traditsii iskusstva Palekha.* Leningrad: Khudozhnik RSFSR, 1981.

Zubkova, Elena. *Poslevoennoe sovetskoe obshchestvo. Politika i povsednevnost', 1945–1953.* Moscow: ROSSPEN, 2000.

INDEX

*Italicized page numbers indicate illustrations
and photographs.*

25, 28, 34, 53, 56, 77, 81–82; among
icon traders, 30, 43; in Mstera, 30;
Sergei Witte's view of, 56; in Kondakov's *podlinnik*, 73, 74; lifting of restrictions on, 74, 82; as model for
Palekh, 78, 82;
Orthodoxy and Russian identity: before
1917, 5–6, 9–10, 11, 15, 18–19, 21–28,
31–35, 37–38, 39–40, 43–44, 46–50,
51–56, 60, 61–62, 65–67, 72–76, 79,
81–82; in Soviet period, 105, 115, 128,
140, 142, 146, 150, 152, 154–56, 162,
163, 166–67, 183, 184, 188, 191–92,
194–95, 196, 205; post-Soviet, 205

Palekh masters: as "god-daubers," 38, 40,
47–48, 49, 51, 62, 64, 82, 84, 113, 118,
125, 126, 129–31, 148, 178, 182, 191,
193, 195, 204; as kulaks, 40, 56, 57, 58,
63, 65, 107, 116, 128; as banners of
Russian peasant "elementalness," 106,
119–20, 122; as peasant rebels, 106,
122, 227n98; as lovers of irony, 111,
122; as holy fools, 119–20, 122
Parilov, Lev: and marketing of religious
icons, 45
Parilov, M. P.: and profiteering from icon
committee, 68
Parilov, N. M.: and complaint about evaluation of *The Golden Cockerel,* 178
Parilov, Pavel: and complaint about financial pressures, 129
Patriarch Nikon, 19
People's autocracy, 35
Perestroika: impact of, on Palekh and
Russian identity, 13, 197–98
Pereval, 109–10, 112, 120, 121, 226n71
Pershin, I. A.: and complaint about obligatory government loans, 147
Peter the Great: westernization policies
of, 6, 9, 28; and view of Russian icons,
19, 20; and Palace of Facets, 37; image
of, linked to Stalin, 162; and Palekh's
restoration of his "Monplaisir" lac-
quer cabinet, 181
Peter's Summer Palace: restoration of,
154
Petitions of Palekh artists to tsar, 58–59,
64, 70

Piatakov, Georgii: as patron of Palekh,
117
Pil'niak, Boris: as patron of Palekh, 108,
120, 136, 138, 139, 140, 142; and
journalistic representation of Palekh,
120
Platonov, Sergei: and role in icon committee, 75–76, 77, 79, 80; rise of, in
academic circles, 220n55
Pobedonostsev, Konstantin: and opposition to icon schools, 49–50; and resistance to icon committee, 67; politics of, 212n42
Podlinniki (icon style manuals): importance of, to icon experts, 23–24, 25,
28, 31, 53, 54, 80–81; Palekh's icon
studios as collectors of, 32, 52; Kondakov's creation of, 72–77; Zinov'ev's
Soviet version of, 194
Pogodin, Mikhail: as pioneer in study
of Russian culture and history,
22–24
Pokrovskii, N. V.: and interest in *podlinniki*, 54; background of, 217n64
Police socialism, 56, 217n74
Populism, 7–8, 122, 203
Pravdin, A. N.: and critique of Palekh,
173
Preservation: under Nicholas I, 21–22;
during WWII, 153–56, 232nn12–14;
in Brezhnev era, 185, 188–89
"Privilege of backwardness," 9, 21, 104
Proletarian culture: and populism, 6; and
Palekh art in relation to socialism, 8,
11, 86, 103, 108, 109, 112, 114–16,
123; in Soviet culture generally,
228n107
Purges: of Palekh patrons, 138, 140;
impact of, on Palekh, 139–40,
142–43; of Palekh cooperative chairman, 140–43; of religious icons in
Palekh, 141–42, 154; memory of, in
Palekh, 149
Pushkin and Palekh: 105, 107, 125, 130,
136–37, 145–46, 151, 152, 174, 186,
187, 191, 230n32
Putin, Vladimir: and restoration of Soviet
symbols, 199, 240n44; and popularity
of attacks on oligarchs, 206